VITAL STATISTICS
of
NORTH HAMPTON
NEW HAMPSHIRE

1742–1942

William Haslet Jones

HERITAGE BOOKS
2014

HERITAGE BOOKS

AN IMPRINT OF HERITAGE BOOKS, INC.

Books, CDs, and more—Worldwide

For our listing of thousands of titles see our website
at
www.HeritageBooks.com

Published 2014 by
HERITAGE BOOKS, INC.
Publishing Division
5810 Ruatan Street
Berwyn Heights, Md. 20740

International Standard Book Numbers
Paperbound: 978-0-7884-1395-7
Clothbound: 978-0-7884-8988-4

TABLE OF CONTENTS

INTRODUCTION

North Hampton, N.H. is one of a number of N.H. Towns for which the Vital Statistics have never been compiled and published. This book satisfies that need. Birth, death and marriage records were collected from all known sources. These records came primarily from old Town Books, church records, cemetery records and from Annual reports.

The Town of Horth Hampton was initially a part of the Town of Hampton. It was first separated on 17 Nov. 1738 for parochial purposes. It was called North Hill parish. On 26 Nov. 1742 North Hill parish was incorporated as the new toen of North Hampton.

The APPENDIX contains lists of town officers, historical documents, Revolutionary War serice names, the 1776 Association Test names and Warning-Out records of interest.

William Haslet Jones

MAP OF NORTH HAMPTON

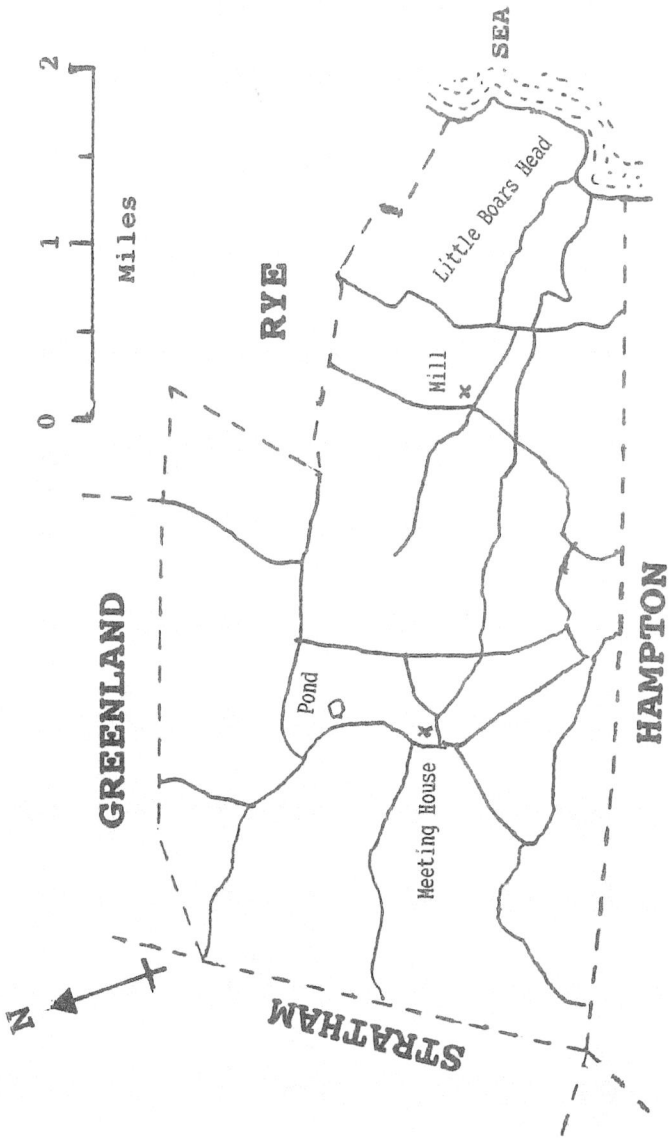

ABBREVIATIONS

ae	-	aged
b.	-	born
c.	-	circa (about)
ch.	-	children
d.	-	died
div.	-	divorced
d/o	-	daughter of
d.s.p.		died single person
d.y.	-	died young
Int.	-	Marriage Intentions.
md.	-	married
m.1,	-	1st marriage
m.2,	-	2nd marriage, etc
s/o	-	son of
unmd	-	unmarried
w/o	-	wife of
wid.	-	widow/widower

SOURCE CODES

[AR]	Annual Town Report 1890 - 1943
[Arch]	NH Archive Records.
[CEM]	Cemetery Records
[CH]	Curch Records
[TR]	Town Records
[VS}	Vital Statistics, Concord, NH

NORTH HAMPTON, N.H.

BIRTHS

1742 - 1942

ALLEN:
Dorothy May, d/o Howard & Florence, 1st child born. 13 May 1932. [AR]
Shirley Jeannette, d/o Allison & Laura (Booker), 1st child, born 10 Sep.
   1935. [AR]

AJEMIAN:
Hagop, s/o Ajem & Araxie (Bedrosian) 2d child, born 14 Feb. 1928. [AR]

AKMAKJIAN:
Audrey Joyce, d/o Elliot & Mary (Sahagian) 2d child, born 15 May 1937. [AR]

AUSTIN:
Son of Thomas M. & Martha Wilson, 1st child, born 1 Dec. 1896. [TR][AR]

AYERS:
John born 11 Sep. 1790. [CH]

BACHELDER: See Batchelder

BANALL:
Annie Lewis, d/o John L. & Marie (Lewis), 4th child, b. 15 July 1892. [TR]

BARNARD:
Moses, s/o Samuel & Elizabeth bp 20 Oct. 1744. [CH]

BARROWS:
Frederick Andrew, s/o John Otis & Clara L.F. born 5 Nov. 1865. [CH]

BARTLETT:
Dau. of Cyrus R. & Josephine E. (Moulton) 1st child, born 8 Oct. 1903. [AR]

BARTON:
Charles Chancy, s/o George W. & Gertrude N. Sabell, 1st child, born 9 Feb.
   1891. [TR]
Charles W., s/o Charles L. & Bessie E. Sabell born 4 July 1890. [TR][AR]
Dau. of Charles S. & Bessie C. Sabell, 2d child, born 1 June 1888. [TR]
Ethel Jenness, d/o James William & Eliza Perkins (Jenness) born 23 Sep. 1890.
   [TR]
Ethel, d/o James W. Eliza (Jenness) b. 29 Sep. 1894. [TR]
Son of James W. & Eliza P. Jenness, 3d child, born 21 Mar. 1889. [TR]
Son of George E. & Gertrude N. Saball born 9 Feb. 1891. [AR]

BARROLL:
Anne Lewis, d/o John L. & Maria Lewis, 4th child, born 15 July 1892. [TR]

BARWELL:
Dau. of Glen L. & Maria Stocker Lewis, 1st child, born 19 July 1886. [TR]
Son of John Leeds & Maria H. Lewis, 2d child, born 8 June 1888. [TR]

BATCHELDER:

Abigail d/o John born 3 Oct. 1802. [CH]
Abigail Dalton, d/o John born 19 May 1782. [CH]
Abraham, s/o Samuel Jr. born 2 Sep. 1750. [CH]
Alfred Johnson, s/o Josiah born 30 Apr. 1815. [CH]
Ann Sherburne, d/o John born Apr. 1791. [CH]
Anna Towle, twin, d/o Josiah & Molly born 16 July 1820. [CH]
Arthur, s/o Mark & Sophia born 25 Aug. 1839. [CH]
Bethiah, d/o Henry born 24 Sep. 1747. [CH]
Benjamin, s/o Peter born 10 July 1765. [CH]
Betsy, d/o Josiah & Abigail born 13 Nov. 1785. [CH]
Betsy, d/o Nathaniel born 7 Sep. 1800. [CH]
Caroline Chesley, d/o Thos. Ira & Ellen (McDonald), 3d child, born 16 May 1885. [TR]
Child of Thomas, 2d child, born 7 Aug. 1883. [TR]
Comfort, d/o Josiah born 10 Oct. 1775. [CH]
Dau. of Arthur, 1st child, born 4 Oct. 1868. [TR]
Dau. of Charles & Martha 3d child born 25 May 1875. [TR]
Dau. of Arthur F., 3d child, born 27 Jan. 1877. [TR]
Dau. of Charles & Martha born 31 Dec. 1879. [TR]
Dau. of Thomas J. & Lillian, 4th child, born 27 Nov. 1886. [TR]
Dau. of Charles L. & Jessie F. (Butler) 3d child, born 27 Mar. 1913. [AR]
Dau. of George D. & Frankie M. (Tuttle) 2d child, born 4 June 1913. [AR]
Dau. of Charles L. & Jessie F. (Butler) 4th child, born 17 Apr. 1915. [AR]
David William, s/o Richard A. & Marion E. (Dyer), 3d child, born 27 July 1943. [AR]
Davis, s/o Davis born 28 Aug. 1768. [CH]
Deborah, d/o Benjamin born 6 Nov. 1757. [CH]
Deborah, d/o Stephen born 3 Dec. 1752. [CH]
Elinor, d/o Stephen born 31 Mar. 1765. [CH]
Elizabeth, d/o Henry born 8 July 1744. [CH]
Elizabeth, d/o James & Mehitable b. 29 Aug. & bp 8 Sep. 1771. [TR][CH]
Elizabeth, d/o John born 8 July 1798. [CH]
Elizabeth Abigail, d/o Mark & Sophia born 30 Mar. 1828. [CH]
Ella Eliza, d/o Nathaniel & Mary J. born 1 May 1853. [CH]
Frederick Augustus, s/o Josiah & Molly born 6 Aug. 1809. [CH]
George Edwin, s/o G.D. & Frankie (Tuttle) 5th child, born 26 Oct. 1921. [AR]
Hannah, d/o Stephen Jr. born 1 Mar. 1748. [CH]
Henry, s/o Davis born 20 July 1755. [CH]
Henry Lyford, s/o Mark & Sophia born 25 Apr. 1847. [CH]
James, s/o John born 27 June 1795. [CH]
James, s/o Stephen born 15 Aug. 1762. [CH]
James Albert, s/o James L. & Viola (Redden) 1st child, born 25 Jan. 1918, at Portsmouth. [AR]
Jane, d/o Stephen born 3 Nov. 1751. [CH]
Jane, d/o Stephen born 17 Aug. 1755. [CH]
Jeremiah, s/o John born 21 Sep. 1800. [CH]

BATCHELDER Cont:
Jeremiah, s/o Mark & Sophia born 1 July 1827. [CH]
John, s/o Henry born 16 May 1755. [CH]
John, s/o Davis born 5 Jan. 1757. [CH]
John, s/o James & Mehitable b. 6 Oct. & bp 20 Nov. 1757. [TR][CH]
John, s/o Josiah born 20 June 1773. [CH]
John, s/o Nathaniel born 1 Oct. 1786. [CH]
John, s/o Samuel Jr. born 17 Apr. 1768. [CH]
John Taylor, s/o Josiah & Molly born 10 Mar. 1826. [CH]
Jonathan Jenness adult bapt. 1 Apr. 1832. [CH]
Jonathan Towle, twin s/o Josiah & Milly born 16 July 1820. [CH]
Jonathan, s/o Nathaniel & Elizabeth born 19 Sep. 1802. [CH]
Josiah, s/o John born 17 July 1806. [CH]
Josiah, s/o Josiah born 30 June 1776. [CH]
Judith, d/o Davis born 17 Feb. 1765. [CH]
Levi, s/o John born 19 July 1795. [CH]
Levi, s/o Abigail, wid. of John born 17 Aug. 1823. [CH]
Mark, s/o John born 6 July 1800. [CH]
Mary, d/o John born 5 June 1786. [CH]
Mary, d/o John born 17 Aug. 1805. [CH]
Mary Charlotte, d/o Charles L. & Jessie (Butler) 5th child, born 4 Jan. 1919.
    [AR]
Mary Dearborn, d/o Josiah born 3 May 1812. [CH]
Mary Laura, d/o Thomas & Saddie (McDonald) born 27 Nov. 1888. [TR]
Minerva, d/o Nathaniel & Eliza born 31 Aug. 1823. [CH]
Mira Ward, d/o Mark & Sophia born 12 July 1841. [CH]
Molly, d/o Davis born 19 Oct. 1780. [CH]
Molly, d/o Stephen of Deerfield born 11 July 1780. [CH]
Nathaniel, s/o Josiah born 20 Apr. 1783. [CH]
Nathaniel, s/o Josiah & Molly born 6 Dec. 1807. [CH]
Nathaniel, s/o Samuel Jr. born 29 June 1755. [CH]
Nathaniel Frank, s/o Nathaniel & Mary J. born 22 July 1857. [CH]
Olive Brown, d/o Mark & Sophia born 15 Jan. 1837. [CH]
Orlando, s/o Jona. C. & Mary Ann born 17 Feb. 1817. [TR]
Patience, d/o Henry born 30 Nov. 1755. [CH]
Patty, d/o John born 17 June 1798. [CH]
Phebe, d/o Stephen born 19 June 1757. [CH]
Polly, d/o Josiah born 1 Oct. 1797. [CH]
Richard Alden, s/o George D. & Frankie (Tuttle) 4th child, born 13 Apr. 1919.
    [AR]
Sally, d/o John born 11 Oct. 1789. [CH]
Sally, d/o John born 19 July 1795. [CH]
Sally, d/o Mark & Sophia born 2 May 1830. [CH]
Samuel, s/o Henry & Mary born 23 Aug. 1741. [CH]
Samuel, s/o Samuel Jr. born 3 June 1753, [CH]
Samuel, s/o Samuel Jr. born 18 Sep. 1757. [CH]
Samuel, s/o Samuel born 15 Oct. 1780. [CH]

BATCHELDER Cont.
Samuel Knowles, s/o John born 9 Apr. 1797. [CH]
Samuel Leavitt, s/o Josiah & Molly born 16 July 1820. [CH]
Sarah, d/o Dea. born 7 Jan. 1760. [CH]
Sarah, d/o James & Mehitable b. 29 May & bp 1 June 1760. [TR][CH]
Sarah, d/o Samuel Jr. born 7 July 1771. [CH]
Sarah, d/o Nathaniel & Eliza born 30 May 1784. [CH]
Sarah born Oct. 1796. [CH]
Simon, s/o Davis born 12 Mar. 1758. [CH]
Simon, s/o John born 12 Apr. 1806. [CH]
Son of Nathaniel & Elizabeth born 7 Dec. 1783. [CH]
Son of Ozam & Ella Bean born 5 Apr. 1879. [TR]
Son of Orren & Ella Brown, 2d child, born 6 Jan. 1883. [TR]
Son of Albert & Abbie Mary (Lamprey), 3d child, born 28 Feb. 1884. [TR]
Son of Alponzo & Ethel L., 1st child, born 20 July 1887. [TR]
Son of George A. & Ethel M. (Locke) 3d child, born 30 Jan. 1901. [AR]
Son of Richard A. & Marion E. (Dyer) 2d child born 1 Feb. 1941. [AR]
Sophia Ann, d/o Mark & Sophia born 6 July 1834. [CH]
Stephen, s/o Stephen born 17 Feb. 1760. [CH]

BEEDE:
Milton Douglas, s/o Joseph W. & Eleanor G. (Hadlock) 2d child, born 14 Dec.
   1941. [AR]

BERRY:
Burr Cummings, s/o John W. & Valorie (Brown) born 13 Mar. 1880. [TR]
Clarence M. Walter, s/o Haven S. & Mabel J. born 15 Oct. 1890. [TR]
Dau. stillborn of Edward H. & Addie (Fogg) born 23 Oct. 1884. [TR]
Dau. of Haven S. & Mabel Dow, 2d child, born 17 Sep. 1892. [TR][AR]
Dau. of Frank E. & Ethel M. (Brock), 1st child, born 27 Jan. 1894. [TR][AR]
Dau. of John W. & Emma (Locke) 2d child, born 28 May 1901. [AR]
Mabel Phoebe, d/o Fred W. & Esther (Moulton), 2d child, born 27 Oct. 1885.
   [TR]
Shaun G., s/o Joseph & Alberta (Frisbee), 1st child, born 16 Mar. 1939. [AR]
Son of John & Emma Lock, 1st child, born 2 July 1889. [TR]
Son of Frank P. & Ethel May Burk, 2d child, born 14 June 1896. [TR][AR]
Son of Frank L. & Gertrude E. (Robinson) 1st child, born 19 Sep. 1905. [AR]

BLAKE:
John, s/o S____ born 30 July 1795. [CH]

BLOCK:
Dau. of Carl R. & Lila A. (Dearborn) 1st child born 12 June 1906. [AR]
Dau. of Carl R. & Lila A. (Dearborn) 2d child born 8 Oct. 1907. [AR]

BOISVERT:
Barbara Ann, d/o Robert F. & Barbara R. (Wentworth) 1st child, born 25 Apr.
   1941. [AR]

BOLLING:
Son of John M., 4th child born 25 Oct. 1876. [TR]

BOOKER:
Dau. of Asa A. & Emma Brown 2d child, born 19 Dec. 1910. [AR]
Mary Virginia, d/o Asa A. & Emma (Brown) 5th child, born 10 Oct. 1918. [AR]
Richard Ivan, s/o Ivan R. & Beatrice C. (Hormel) 1st child, born 16 July
   1943. [AR]

BORDEN:
Dau. of Louis L. & Jeanne (McConnelong) 2d child, born 13 Aug. 1907. [AR]

BOTHWELL:
Stillborn son of James & Anne (Campbell) 2d child, born 30 Dec. 1922. [AR]

BOUNVEY:
Dau. of Miss Ida born 25 Aug. 1878. [TR]

BOWLEY:
Joseph Alex., s/o Alex. & Alice (Irving) 5th child, born 14 Nov. 1929. [AR]
Josephine Ellen, d/o Alex. & Alice (Irving) 6th child, born 7 Jan. 1931. [AR]
Margaret Annie, d/o Alex. L. & Alice (Irving) 7th child, born 28 Jan. 1932.
   [AR]
Son of Eben H. & Sarah B. (Kelly), 2d child, born 4 June 1893. [TR][AR]

BOYNSTON:
Dau. of George & Abba, 1st child, born 31 Jan. 1877.]TR]
Dau. of George A. & Abbie L., 3d child, born 20 Aug. 1882. [TR]
Son of George A. & Abbie born 30 May 1887. [TR]

BRADSTREET:
Charles Moses, s/o Moses & Sarah L. of Rowley, Mass. born 29 Nov. 1863. [CH]

BREED:
Dau. of William 2d child born 14 Apr. 1875. [TR]

BREWSTER:
Elizabeth Ann, d/o Paul E. & Barbara (Barton) born 29 Oct. 1929. [AR]
William Ralph, s/o Paul E. & Barbara (Barton) 1st child, born 31 May 1937.
   [AR]

BRIAR:
Abigail, d/o Thomas born 1 Sep. 1745. [CH]

BROWN:
Abigail Lock, d/o Stephen born 10 Sep. 1797. [CH]
Abigail Osgood, d/o Davis Jr. & Abigail born 1 July 1823. [CH]

BROWN Cont.
Adeline, d/o John Jr. & Mary born 11 July 1816. [TR][CH]
Augusta Ann, d/o Jeremiah & Elizabeth born 29 Nov. 1840. [CH]
Barbara Ann, d/o Evan D. & Edith (Polton) 1st child, born 14 May 1932. [AR]
Barbara Jean, d/o Harry & Sadie M. (Brooks) 3d child, born 15 Oct. 1938. [AR]
Batchelder, s/o Benjamin born 6 Dec. 1761. [CH]
Benjamin, s/o Benjamin born 1 Aug. 1771. [CH]
Benjamin, s/o Jeremiah born 25 sep. 1808. [CH]
Benjamin, s/o Stephen & Mary born 17 June 1804. [CH]
Bessie A., d/o Fred A. & Lizzie A. (Knowles) born 8 Feb. 1891. [AR]
Carol Jean, d/o Abbott & Eleanor (Lane) 1st child, born 30 Nov. 1931. [AR]
Caroline Ann, d/o Edward A. & Maude (Gillette) 1st child, born 15 Nov. 1943.
   [AR]
Daniel, s/o John born 10 Sep. 1780. [CH]
Daniel, s/o Stephen born 5 May 1799. [CH8 Feb. 1891. [AR]
Daniel Herbert, s/o Herbert T. & Vira M. (Nesbitt) 1st born 14 Aug. 1943.
   [AR]
Dau. of Albert & Polly, 1st child, born 8 June 1877. [TR]
Dau. of Otis & Emma, 5th child, born 25 Jan. 1878. [TR]
Dau. of Emmons T. & Annie M. Palmer, 2d child, born 2 June 1882. [TR]
Dau. of Frank & Clara Bell (Marden), 1st child, born 5 Mar. 1884. [TR]
Dau. of John H. Hattie (Henderson) born 11 June 1891. [AR]
Dau. stillborn of Frace O. & Alice C. Snow, 1st child, born 21 Nov. 1892.
   [TR][AR]
Dau. of Fred A. & Lizzie A. (Knowles) born
Dau. of Fred A. & Lizzie A. Knowles, 3d child, born 15 July 1894. [TR][AR]
Dau. of Arthur W. & Maud M. (Carr) 1st child, born 13 May 1911. [AR]
Dau. of Frank P. & Eva M. (Horne) 1st child, born 1 Aug. 1912. [AR]
Dau. of Arthur W. & Maud (Carr) 2d child, born 5 Dec. 1912. [AR]
David, s/o Jacob born 30 Nov. 1777. [CH]
David, s/o John born 22 Apr. 1792. [CH]
David Page, s/o Benjamin born 17 May 1779. [CH]
Deborah, d/o Stephen born 18 Feb. 1756, [CH]
Dolly, d/o Nathan & Mary born 20 Mar. 1804. [CH]
Dorothy, d/o Benjamin born 3 Sep. 1775. [CH]
Dorothy, d/o Stephen & Mary born 31 July 1808. [CH]
Elias, s/o Ephraim & Rachel born 17 Jan. 1744. [CH1]
Elijah, s/o David Jr. & Abigail born 8 Sep. 1821. [CH]
Elijah, s/o John born 22 Dec. 1782. [CH]
Elisha, s/o John born 10 July 1785, [CH]
Eliza, d/o John Jr. & Mary born 16 July 1798. [TR]
Elizabeth, d/o Benjamin born 27 Nov. 1768, [CH]
Elizabeth, d/o Jacob born 11 Oct. 1767. [CH]
Elizabeth, d/o John & Mary born 17 Nov. 1800. [CH]
Florinda, d/o David & Abigail born 27 July 1817. [CH]
Hannah, d/o John born Nov. 1793. [CH]
Hannah Jenness, d/o Nathan & Mary born 31 July 1808. [CH]

BROWN Cont.

Hannah Mary, d/o David Jr. & Abigail born 4 May 1828. [CH]

Ira, s/o Simon born Oct. 1795. [CH]

Ira Nelson, s/o Emmons t. & Annie M. (Palmer), 3d child, born 18 Nov. 1885. [TR]

Jenness, s/o John Jr. & Mary (Polly), born 12 Feb. 1808. [TR][CH]

Jenness Wardell, s/o Jenness & Lydia of Newburyport, Mass. born 30 June 1861. [CH]

Jeremiah, s/o Jeremiah born 25 Sep. 1808. [CH]

Jeremiah, s/o John Jr. & Mary born 18 Sep. 1810. [TR][CH]

Jerusha, d/o Stephen born 30 Sep. 1818. [CH]

John, s/o John born 29 Jan. 1775. [CH]

John, s/o Simon & Marey b. 7 Sep. & bp 17 Sep. 1775. [TR][CH]

John, s/o Betty born 17 Dec. 1797. [CH]

John Trueworthy, s/o John Jr. & Polly born 15 Feb. 1818. [CH]

Jonathan, s/o Stephen born 5 Oct. 1751. [CH]

Jonathan, s/o Joseph born 31 Dec. 1780. [CH]

Joseph, s/o Nathan & Molly born 1 Sep. 1811. [CH]

Joseph, s/o Stephen born 11 Aug. 1816. [CH]

Joseph Jenness, s/o Nathan born 4 July 1816. [CH]

Josiah Philbrick, s/o Mr. born 8 July 1798. [CH]

Leonard, s/o John Jr. & Mary born 17 Apr. 1806. [TR][CH]

Martha Marston, d/o Nathan Jr. & Clarissa born 14 Nov. 1844. [CH]

Mary, d/o Samuel & Mary born 6 Apr. 1744. [CH1]

Mary, d/o Simon & Mary b. 5 Nov. & bp 6 Nov. 1768. [TR][CH]

Mary, adult ? bp 11 Sep. 1790. [CH]

Mary, d/o John Jr. & Mary born 25 June 1800. [TR][CH]

Mary, w/o Stacey bp 5 June 1808. [CH]

Mary Ellen, d/o Jenness & Lydia born 13 Apr. 1845. [CH]

Mary Webster, d/o David Jr. & Abigail born 6 Oct. 1816. [CH]

Moody, s/o Jeremy & Elisabeth born 20 Dec. 1739. [TR]

Moses, s/o Ephraim & Rachel born 23 Dec. 1745. [CH1]

Nancy, d/o Stephen born 5 May 1811. [CH]

Nathan, s/o Nathan born 12 June 1814. [CH]

Nathan Godfrey, s/o John born 18 July 1775. [CH]

Patty Dow, d/o Nathan & Mary born 14 Feb. 1802. [CH]

Pauline Katherine, d/o Haydon M. & Margaret (Nesbitt) 2d child, born 15 Jan. 1938. [AR]

Sally, d/o Jacob born 29 Jan. 1780. [CH]

Sarah, d/o Benjamin & Abigail born 30 Aug. 1745. [CH1]

Sarah, d/o Benjamin born 20 June 1773. [CH]

Sarah, d/o Simon & Marey b. 30 Nov. & bp 5 Dec. 1773. [TR][CH]

Simon, s/o Simon & Mary b. 14 Aug. & bp 30 Nov. 1766. [TR][CH]

Simon, s/o John Jr. & Mary born 27 Aug. 1804. [TR]

Simon, s/o John & Polly born 2 June 1805. [CH]

Son of Oliver & Polly born 20 May 1878. [TR]

Son of Alvin A. & Polly born 1 May 1880. [TR]

BROWN Cont.
Son of Commery & Annie Palmer born 14 Aug. 1880. [TR]
Son of John H. & Harriet M. born 11 Oct. 1880. [TR]
Son of John H. & Hattie Henderson, 7th child, born 22 Sep. 1889. [TR]
Son of Fred A. & Lizzie A. Knowles, 2d child, born 20 July 1892. [TR]
Son of Fred A. & Lizzie A. (Knowles) born 20 Jan. 1897. [AR]
Son of Arthur A. & Anne (Edwards) 1st child, born 6 Mar. 1903. [AR]
Son of Arthur A. & Anne (Edwards) 3d child, born 22 Apr. 1907. [AR]
Son of Arthur W. & Annie (Edwards) 4th child, born 19 Jan. 1910. [AR]
Son of Samuel & Elizabeth W. (Gilpatrick) 2d child, born 2 Dec. 1913. [AR]
Stacey, s/o Benjamin born 4 Aug. 1782. [CH]
Stephen, s/o Benjamin born 15 Apr. 1770. [CH]
Stephen, s/o Stephen & Mary born 8 June 1806. [CH]
Valeria, d/o Nathan Jr. & Clarissa born 16 Sep. 1838. [CH]

BROWSTER:
Elizabeth Ann, d/o Paul E. & Barbara (Barton) 2d child, born 29 Oct. 1939.
[AR]

BUNKER:
Dau. of James & Carrie (Page) born 5 Nov. 1880. [TR]
Son of James & Carrie born 7 Dec. 1878. [TR]

BURNETT:
Barbara D., d/o Joseph D. & Mildred L. (Messer) 3d child, born 15 Apr. 1943.
[AR]
Harold Whitney, s/o Joseph D. & Mildred L. (Messer) 2d child, born 24 Sep.
1941. [AR]
Joseph Daire Jr., s/o Joseph D. & Mildred (Messer) 1st child, born 18 Mar.
1940. [AR]

BURNHAM:
Joseph Harold, s/o Carl H. & Margaret F. (Durgin) 1st child born 23 Feb.
1943. [AR]

CAMMETT:
Son of Fred A. & Anna M. (Colbath) 3d child, born 13 May 1897. [AR]

CARGILL:
Dau. of Thomas & Susan (Duncan), 1st child, born 10 June 1890. [TR]

CARLSON:
Helen Marie, d/o John O. & Edith M. (Johnson) 4th child, born 29 Jan. 1921.
[AR]

CARTER:
Charles William Jr., s/o Charles Wm. & Todd B. (Nesbitt) 1st child, born 18
    July 1930. [AR]
Daniel, s/o Daniel & Hannah born 23 Aug. 1744. [CH1]
Dau. of Harry E. & Nellie L. (Marston) 1st child, born 18 Aug. 1907. [AR]
Dau. of Harry E. & Nellie M. (Marston) 3d child, born 27 July 1913. [AR]
Dorothy Lois, d/o Harry E. & Nellie (Marston) 4th child, born 15 Oct. 1918.
    [AR]
Dudley Einer, s/o Charles W. & Todd (Nesbitt) 2d child, born 23 Nov. 1932.
    [AR]
Ephraim, s/o Ephraim & Abigail born 23 May 1744. [CH1]
Harlan Edward, s/o Harry E. & Nellie L. (Marston) 5th child, born 7 July
    1926. [AR]
John Leslie, s/o C. William & Todd B. (Nesbitt) 4th child, born 2 Apr. 1941.
    [AR]
Joseph Edmund, s/o G. Wesley & Elecnora (Zarnowski) 1st child, born 6 Sep.
    1939. [AR]
Martha Lee, d/o Charles Wm. & Todd B. (Nesbitt) 3d child, born 21 Oct. 1937.
    [AR]
Mary, d/o Thomas & Mary born 2 July 1745. [CH1]
Son of George G. & Martha D. (Page) 1st child, born 4 Oct. 1905. [AR]
Son of George G. & Martha E. (Page) 4th child, born 14 Nov. 1911. [AR]

CASEY:
Patricia Ann, d/o Patrick & Josephine (Chevalier) 1st child, born 9 Mar.
    1935. [AR]

CHANDER:
Dau. of Wilfred & Elizabeth (Philbrick) born 15 Jan. 1881. [TR]
Son of Willfred & Elizabeth (Philbrick), 2d child born 1 Oct. 1882. [TR]

CHAPMAN:
Abigail, d/o Penuel & Sarah born 19 Aug. 1753. [TR]
Abigail, d/o Penuel born 8 Sep. 1755. [CH]
Abigail, d/o Samuel & Abigail b. 21 May & bp 27 May 1759. [TR][CH]
Abigail, d/o Samuel born 16 June 1799. [CH]
Althen Sarah, d/o Samuel & Sarah of Boston, Mass. born 24 Mar. 1861. [CH]
Benjamin, s/o Samuel born 31 Oct. 1796. [CH]
Benjamin James, s/o Benjamin born 16 Aug. 1834. [CH]
Dolly, d/o Job born 30 Oct. 1743. [CH]
Dolly, d/o Samuel & Abigail b. 30 Apr. & bp 5 May 1754. [TR][CH]
Elizabeth Jenness, d/o Samuel Jr. & Patty born 23 May 1824. [CH]
Hannah, d/o Job & Rachel born 1739. [CH]
Hannah, d/o James & Abigail born 17 June 1804. [CH]
Hannah, d/o Samuel & Abigail b. 23 May & bp 6 June 1768. [TR][CH]
Hannah Augusta, d/o Joseph Edward & Hannah born 25 July 1852. [CH]
James, s/o Samuel & Abigail born 15 June 1761. [TR]

CHAPMAN Cont.

James. s/o Benjamin & Hannah born 19 Aug. 1821. [CH]
James, s/o James & Abigail born 24 Sep. 1805. [CH]
John, s/o Samuel born 21 Nov. 1802. [CH]
John, s/o John & Leocada born 6 June 1834.]CH]
Joseph Edward, s/o Benjamin & Hannah born 21 May 1826. [CH]
Juliana, d/o Samuel & Mercy born 30 June 1805. [CH]
Lauranda, d/o Samuel born 25 June 1809. [CH]
Leander, s/o Benjamin & Hannah born 14 Jan. 1838. [CH]
Leander, s/o Leonard W. & Elizabeth J. born 3 Dec. 1848. [CH]
Leonard Willey, s/o Benjamin & Hannah born 15 June 1823. [CH]
Lucretia, twin d/o John & Leocada born 2 Sep. 1839. [CH]
Martha Ann, twin d/o John & Leocada born 2 Sep. 1839. [CH]
Mary, d/o Penuel & Sarah born 23 May 1748. [TR][CH]
Mary, d/o Samuel & Abigail b. 4 Oct. & bp 5 Oct 1751. [TR][CH]
Mary, d/o Benjamin & Hannah born 25 Aug. 1820. [CH]
Mary, d/o Samuel Jr. & Patty W. born 3 Sep. 1820. [CH]
Molly, d/o Samuel born 18 Jan. 1795. [CH]
Phebe, d/o Panuel & Sarah b. 19 Jan. & bp 10 Mar. 1745. [TR][CH]
Rachel, d/o Job & Rachel born 27 Jan. 1742. [CH]
Rebecca Sarah, d/o Benjamin & Hannah born 1 Aug. 1830. [CH]
Rosamond Brown, d/o John & Leocada born 21 Aug. 1836. [CH]
Rosamond Martha, d/o John & Leocada born 19 Mar. 1843. [CH]
Ruth, d/o Penuel & Sarah b. 12 Apr. & bp 27 Apr. 1746. [TR][CH]
Ruth, d/o Samuel & Abigail b. 23 Sep. 1764. [TR][CH]
Samuel, s/o Samuel & Abigail born 14 Dec. 1750. [TR]
Samuel, s/o Penuel & Sarah b. 11 Jan. & born 18 Jan. 1756. [TR][CH]
Samuel, s/o Samuel born 19 Dec. 1756. [CH]
Samuel, s/o Samuel Jr. born 30 Sep. 1792. [CH]
Samuel, s/o John & Sarah born 29 July 1827. [CH]
Sarah, d/o Penuel & Sarah born 18 Nov. 1750. [TR][CH]
Sarah Frances, d/o Job & Leocada born 22 Jan. 1832. [CH]
Simon Leavitt, s/o Benjamin & Hannah born 29 May 1836. [CH]
Thomas Hobbs, s/o John & Sarah born 29 May 1825. [CH]

CHEVALIER:

Dau. of Louis & Grace L. (Morse) 4th child, born 9 Feb. 1908. [TR]
Dau. of Lewis A. & Grace (Morse) 5th child, born 25 Oct. 1911. [AR]
Kendall Wilfred, s/o Raymond M. & Gladys M. (Hobbs) 4th child, born 8 Oct.
   1937. [AR]
Nancy Lou, d/o Raymond & Gladys (Hobbs) 5th child, born 21 Feb. 1939. [AR]
Son of Louis A. & Grace L. (Morse) 1st child, born 30 May 1903. [AR]
Son of Lewis A. & Grace L. (Morse) 2d child, born 29 Apr. 1904. [AR]

CHICK:

Dau. of Everett E. & Annie E. (Blake) 7th child, born 9 July 1906. [AR]
Son of Everett E. & Annie A. (Blake) 4th child, born 25 Mar. 1904. [AR]

CHRISTOPHER:
Son of Joseph P. & Nellie G. (Ellis) 1st child, born 28 Sep. 1941. [AR]

CLARK:
Dau., twins, of Albion C. & Ida M. Cammentt born 25 May 1895. [AR]
Dau. of Albion S. & Ola M. Cammett, 2d child, born 25 May 1896. [TR]
Son of Walter H. & Garda C. (Edstrom), 1st child, born 2 Apr. 1905. [AR]
Thomas Peabody, s/o Mayhew born 3 Jan. 1779. [CH]

CLIFFORD:
Abraham, s/o David born 6 Jan. 1745. [CH]
Child of David born 25 June 1746. [CH]

COCHRAN:
William Peregine, s/o John & Sarah of Great Island born 17 Sep. 1775. [CH]

COLCORD:
Anna, d/o Isreal bp Sep. 1792. [CH]
Comford, d/o Isreal bp Sep. 1792. [CH]
Gideon, s/o Isreal bp Sep. 1792. [CH]

COLE;
Donald Sanderson, s/o Richard I. & Mildred (Sanderson) 3d child, born 4
   Sep. 1932. [AR]

COLLINS:
Benjamin, s/o Ephraim & Abigail born 9 Aug. 1745. [CH1]
Moses, s/o Richard & Anna born 5 Nov. 1744. [CH1]

CORLISS:
Annie Mildred, d/o Martin J. & Annie M. (Dalton) 3d child, born 19 Jan. 1922.
   [AR]
John Dalton, s/o Martin & Annie (Dalton) 2d child, born 4 Oct. 1919. [AR]
Martin Clarence, s/o Martin J. & Annie M. (Dalton) 1st child, born 18 June
   1918. [AR]

CORMIER:
Richard Joseph, s/o Joseph W. & Violet M. (Manson) 2d child, born 13 Sep.
   1937. [AR]

COTTON:
Anna d/o Thomas Jr. born 1 Apr. 1781. [CH]
Jonathan, s/o John born 1 Mar. 1778. [CH]
Jonathan, s/o Morris & Huldah born 8 Apr. & bp 4 July 1802. [TR][CH]
Levi, s/o Thomas born 22 Mar. 1769. [CH]
Morris, s/o Thomas & Abigail born 11 May 1777. [CH]
Morris, s/o Thomas & Abigail born 1 June 1828. [CH]

COTTON Cont.
Sarah, d/o John born 9 Nov. 1783. [CH]
Sarah Abigail, d/o Jonathan & Abigail born 5 Dec. 1830. [CH]
Thomas, s/o Thomas born 25 May 1783. [CH]
Thomas, s/o Morris & Huldah born 31 July & bp 3 Oct. 1803. [TR][CH]

COULTER:
Dau. of George L. & Alice M. (Arnold) 3d child, born 19 June 1906. [AR]

CRAIG:
Peter David, s/o George A. & Roberts (Taylor) 1st child, born 6 Jan. 1939. [AR]
Son of George A. & Mary (Stockman) 2d child, born 21 Sep. 1914. [AR]
Son of George A. & Mary (Stockman) born 31 Oct. 1915. [AR]

CRIMBAL:
Charles, s/o Charles born 25 June 1751. [CH]
Mary, d/o Charles born 18 May 1755. [CH]

CUMMINGS:
George William Jr., s/o George W. & Rachel (Bernard) 2d child, born 19 July 1932. [AR]
Joan Mary, d/o George W. & Rachel (Bernard) 1st child, born 5 Apr. 1930. [AR]

CURRIER:
Anne, d/o Phillip & Ruth born 27 Aug. 1744. [CH1]
Dorothy, d/o Henry & Elizabeth born 17 Aug. 1745. [CH1]
James, s/o Richard & Sarah born 1 July 1744. [CH1]
Samuel, s/o Samuel & Hannah born 16 Oct. 1744. [CH1]
Son of Gilbert T. & Annie E. (Locke) 2d child, born 24 Sep. 1916. [AR]
Thomas, s/o Capt. Jonathan & Judith born 14 Mar. 1745. [CH1]

CUTTS:
Sarah Gertrude, d/o Robert & Lena B. (Wiggin) 2d child, born 17 Oct. 1938. [AR]

DALTON:
Alice Marjorie, d/o Eben H. & Celia A. (Warner) born 22 Feb. 1885. [TR]
Benjamin Brown, s/o Tristram & Dolly born 14 Jan. 1800. [TR]
Betty, d/o Samuel born 31 Dec. 1763. [CH]
Carl Hugh, s/o Harrison & Eunice (Brown) 1st child, born 24 Oct. 1935. [AR]
Charles C., s/o Ebenezer & Celia A. (Warner) born 7 Nov. 1872. [TR]
Dau. of Leavitt born 17 Apr. 1873. [TR]
Dau. of Charles C. & Jennie (Weare) 1st child, born 20 Jan. 1897. [AR]
Dolly Brown, d/o Tristram born 10 May 1810. [CH]
Dorothy, d/o Tristram & Huldah born 1 Oct. 1809. [TR]
Ebenezer Marden, s/o Timothy & Elesebeth b. 3 Oct. & bp 16 Oct. 1768. [TR][CH]

DALTON Cont.

Elizabeth, d/o Michael born June 1791. [CH]

Esther, d/o Timothy & Elesebeth b. 9 July & bp 2 Aug. 1772. [TR][CH]

Esther, d/o Ebenezer M. & Love born 16 June 1805. [CH]

Eva Marie, d/o Harrison E. & Celia A. born 19 Feb. 1865. [TR]

John, s/o Timothy & Elesebeth b. 23 May & bp 27 May 1771. [TR][CH]

Lydia, d/o Tristram & Huldah born 6 Feb. 1813. [TR]

Marjorie Mae, d/o Harrison & Eunice (Brown) 2d child, born 6 Aug. 1937. [AR]

Maria, d/o Ebenezer M. & Love born 2 May 1802. [CH]

Marey, d/o Timothy & Elesebeth born 1 July 1766. [TR]

Mary, w/o Benjamin bp 11 Feb. 1753. [CH]

Michael, s/o Timothy born 20 Nov. 1743. [CH]

Michael, s/o Timothy & Elesebeth b. 14 Aug. & bp 11 Nov. 1764. [TR][CH]

Molly, d/o Samuel born 19 Apr. 1761. [CH]

Morris Cotton, s/o Tristram & Huldah born 28 Sep. 1805 & bp 8 June 1806.
 [TR][CH]

Philemon, twin s/o Samuel born 16 Apr. 1769. [CH]

Rufus, s/o Ebenezer M. & Love born 17 July 1806. [CH]

Samuel, twin s/o Samuel born 16 Apr. 1769. [CH]

Samuel, s/o Samuel born 1 Aug. 1771. [CH]

Samuel Rufus, s/o Ranison E. & Celia A. born 13 Jan. 1868. [TR]

Sarah, d/o Samuel & Sarah born 16 Nov. 1756. [CH]

Son of Irving & Emma (Jenness) born 20 Sep. 1879. [TR]

Son of James W. & Emma (Jenness), 4th child, born 21 Mar. 1889. [TR]

Son of Charles C. & Jennie (Weare) 2d child, born 22 Oct. 1909. [AR]

Thomas, s/o Ebenezer born 27 Dec. 1797. [CH]

Timothy, s/o Timothy & Elesebeth b. 18 Nov. 1776 & bp Feb. 1777. [TR][CH]

Tristram, s/o Timothy & Elesebeth b. __ Feb. & bp 20 Feb. 1774. [TR][CH]

DAVIES:

Ann, d/o Reginald H. & Gladys B. (Keene) 1st child, born 7 Feb. 1934. [AR]

DAVIS:

Molly Griffin, adopted by Samuel Davis, b. 31 July 1785. [CH]

Son of Chester A. & Elizabeth M. (Philbrick) 1st child, born 17 Feb. 1910.
 [AR]

DEARBORN:

Agigail, d/o Jeremiah & Sarah born 4 Apr. 1743. [TR][CH]

Abigail, d/o Jeremy Jr. & Mary born 18 Feb. 1750. [TR][CH]

Abigail, d/o John & Abigail b. 5 Jan. & bp 6 Jan. 1771. [TR][CH]

Abner, s/o John & Abigail b. 23 Aug. & bp 28 Aug. 1763. [TR][CH]

Abraham Drake, s/o Freese born 24 Oct. 1802. [CH]

Alexander, s/o Rhodolphus & Betsey born 12 Feb. 1816. [TR][CH]

Almira, d/o Trueworthy Gove born 14 May 1797. [CH]

Andrew, s/o Ebenezer & Anna born 17 Dec. 1803. [TR]

Andrew, s/o Ebenezer born 10 Mar. 1811. [CH]

DEARBORN Cont.

Angelia, d/o David & Sarah born 4 Aug. 1839. [CH]
Anna, d/o Jeremiah & Sarah b. 30 July & bp 25 Aug. 1745. [TR][CH]
Anna, d/o Reuben Gove born 21 Aug. 1748. [CH]
Anna, d/o Levi born 25 Mar. 1759. [CH]
Anna, d/o Levi born 17 Oct. 1762. [CH]
Anna, d/o Reuben Gove Jr. & Elisabeth b. 27 Mar. & bp 29 May 1774. [TR][CH]
Asahel, s/o Josiah born 10 Jan. 1762. [CH]
Belinda, d/o Ebenezer born 10 Mar. 1811. [CH]
Benjamin, s/o Simon & Sarah born 13 Feb. 1745. [TR]
Benjamin, s/o Levi born 20 May 1753. [CH]
Benjamin, s/o Levi born 27 May 1770. [CH]
Benjamin, s/o Reuben born 22 Sep. 1751. [CH]
Benjamin, s/o Mrs. Ruth born 22 June 1755. [CH]
Benjamin, s/o Simon born 16 Feb. 1746. [CH]
Betsey, w/o R. born 27 Mar. 1786. [TR]
Betsy, d/o Joseph born 30 June 1792. [CH]
Brainerd, s/o David & Sarah born 15 May 1842. [CH]
Calvin Luther, s/o Nathan & Lydia born 19 Oct. 1838. [CH]
Caroline, d/o Nathan & Lydia born 19 Oct. 1838. [CH]
Curtis, s/o Reuben born 15 Nov. 1760. [CH]
Daniel, s/o Reuben Gove born 15 July 1750. [CH]
David, s/o Samuel & Hannah born 20 Mar. 1793. [TR][CH]
David, s/o Dea. Nathaniel & Lucy born 7 Nov. 1813. [CH]
David Marston, s/o Ebenezer born 10 Mar. 1811. [CH]
David Nudd, s/o Nathan & Lydia born 17 Aug. 1823. [CH]
Dau. of Simon born 11 Sep. 1790. [CH]
Deborah, d/o Simon & Sarah born 13 Feb. 1744/5. [TR][CH]
Dolly Garland, d/o Dea. Nathaniel & Lucy born 19 July 1812. [CH]
Dudley, changed to Henry, s/o Simon born 17 Feb. 1751. [CH]
Edmund Batchelder, s/o Samuel 3d born 11 Oct. 1807. [CH]
Edwin, s/o Nathan & Lydia born 19 Oct. 1838. [CH]
Eliphalet, s/o Simon & Sarah born 6 Sep. 1740. [TR][CH]
Elizabeth, d/o Jeremiah born 19 Nov. 1752. [CH]
Elizabeth, d/o Levi born 14 Sep. 1760. [CH]
Elizabeth, twin d/o Reuben Gove Jr. born 26 Sep. 1784. [CH]
Elizabeth, d/o Mr. of Effingham bp Sep. 1792. [CH]
Emily Ann, d/o Nathan & Lydia born 17 Aug. 1823. [CH]
Fanny, d/o John & Bethiel b. 18 July & bp 18 Aug. 1776 [TR][CH]
Fanny Neal, d/o Daniel & Anna b. Apr. 1775 & bp 14 Dec. 1777. [TR][CH]
Francis Page, s/o Reuben Jr. bp 6 June 1779. [CH]
George Odell, s/o Nathan & Lydia bp 17 Aug. 1823. [CH]
Hannah, d/o Phineas bp 30 Nov. 1777. [CH]
Hannah, d/o Mr. of Effingham bp Sep. 1792. [CH]
Hannah, d/o Ebenezer of Deerfield bp 6 Feb. 1814. [CH]
Hannah Page, d/o Nathan & Lydia bp 19 Aug. 1823. [CH]
Harriet, d/o Joseph bp 14 July 1799. [CH]

DEARBORN Cont.

Henry, was Dudley, s/o Simon bp 17 Feb. 1751. [CH]
Henry, s/o Simon b. 12 July & bp 19 July 1795. [TR][CH]
Henry R., s/o Rhodolphus & Betsey born 29 Jan. 1814. [TR][CH]
Henry Washington, s/o Swon & Mary bp 12 Aug. 1801. [CH]
Horatio, s/o John bp 6 July 1798. [CH]
Ira, s/o Ebenezer & Anna born 17 Dec. 1801. [TR]
Ira, s/o Ebenezer bp 10 Mar. 1811. [CH]
Isabella, d/o David & Sarah bp 4 Aug. 1839. [CH]
Jarmiah, s/o Samuel & Hannah born 19 Sep. 1787. [TR]
Jeremiah, s/o Jeremiah & Mary born 31 May 1766. [TR]
Jeremiah, s/o Simeon bp 7 Dec. 1817. [CH]
Jesse, s/o Dea. Nathaniel & Dolly bp 8 Mar. 1807. [CH]
John, s/o Simon & Sarah born 3 Oct. 1738. [TR]
John, s/o Simen bp 5 Oct. 1760. [CH]
John, s/o John & Abigail b. & bp 17 Oct. 1761. [TR][CH]
John, s/o Simon & Mary born 23 Nov. 1787, [TR]
John, s/o John & Sarah bp July 1789. [CH]
John, s/o Phineas, b. betw. Oct. 1795 & Apr. 1796. [CH]
John, s/o Ebenezer & Anna born 13 Oct. 1806. [TR]
John, s/o Ebenezer bp 10 Mar. 1811. [CH]
John, s/o Dea. Nathaniel & Lucy bp 21 July 1811. [CH]
John, s/o Rhodolphus & Betsey born 2 Jan. & bp 30 July 1812. [TR][CH]
John Haven, s/o Levi Jr. bp 25 May 1783. [CH]
John Shepard, s/o Joseph bp 31 July 1774. [CH]
Jonathan, s/o Reuben Gove Jr. bp 29 June 1783 [CH]
Jonathan, s/o Joseph & Betsy born 22 Feb. 1790. [TR]
Jonathan, s/o Joseph of Ossipee bp Nov. 1800. [CH]
Jonathan, s/o Samuel bp 13 Sep. 1812. [CH]
Jonathan French, s/o Nathaniel & Dolly bp 9 May 1802. [CH]
Joseph, s/o Reuben Gove bp 28 Dec. 1746. [CH]
Joseph, s/o Reuben Gove bp 13 Apr. 1755. [CH]
Joseph, s/o John & Abigail b. 17 May & bp 5 June 1768. [TR][CH]
Joseph, s/o Reuben Gove Jr. & Elisabeth b. 19 July & bp 1 Aug. 1772. [TR][CH]
Joseph Ruuel, s/o Joseph & Betsy, born 31 Dec. 1796 at)ssipee, age about 5
    yrs bp 27 Dec. 1801. [TR] Grandson of Capt. John. [CH]
Josiah, s/o Freese bp 5 July 1807. [CH]
Lawrence, s/o Dea. Nathaniel & Lucy bp 15 Dec. 1828. [CH]
Leocada, d/o John & Bethiah b. 28 Mar. & bp 11 Apr. 1784. [TR][CH]
Leocada, d/o Rhodolphus & Betsey born 24 Dec. 1808 or 1809 [CH]
Levi, s/o Simon & Sarah born 23 Feb. 1747. [TR]
Levi, s/o Levi bp 2 July 1757, [CH]
Levi, s/o Simon bp 28 Feb. 1748. [CH]
Levi, s/o Reuben Jr. bp 19 Mar. 1769. [CH]
Levi, s/o Levi Jr. bp 5 June 1785. [CH]
Lucinda, d/o Simon & Mary born 5 May 1790. [TR][CH]

DEARBORN Cont.
Lucy, d/o Reuben bp 10 Feb. 1754. [CH]
Lucy Parker, d/o Dea. Nathaniel & Lucy bp 18 Feb. 1754. [CH]
Lydia, d/o Simeon bp 7 Dec. 1817. [CH]
Lydia Smith, twin d/o Nathan & Lydia bp 19 Oct. 1838. [CH]
Lyman, s/o Ebenezer of Deerfield bp 6 Feb. 1814. [CH]
Margaret Tilton, d/o Rhodolphus & Betsey born 8 Sep. 1818. [TR]
Martha, d/o Reuben Jr. bp 5 June 1786. [CH]
Mary, d/o Jeremy & Sarah b. 23 Mar. & bp 23 Mar. 1740. [TR][CH]
Mary, d/o Henry bp 10 Aug. 1746. [CH]
Mary, d/o Jeremiah & Mary b. 16 May & bp 21 May 1758. [TR][CH]
Mary, d/o Simon & Mary born 28 Dec. 1805. [TR][CH]
Mary Abbie, twin d/o Nathan & Lydia bp 19 Oct. 1838. [CH]
Mary Marston, d/o Samuel Jr. & Lydia bp 28 May 1820. [CH]
Melinda, d/o Ebenezer & Anna born 30 Apr. 1805. [TR]
Miriam, d/o Reuben G. bp 21 Mar. 1762. [CH]
Molly, d/o Phineas bp 10 Sep. 1780. [CH]
Morris, s/o Mr. of Effingham bp Sep. 1792. [CH]
Nancy, d/o Ebenezer bp 10 Mar. 1811. [CH]
Nancy Knowles ae 3, d/o Simon & Polly bp 18 Aug. 1833. [CH]
Nathan Philbrick, s/o Samuel & Hannah b. 6 Mar. 1789 & bp 9 May 1783.
   [TR][CH]
Nathaniel, s/o Samuel & Hannah b. 28 Aug. 1777 & bp 1 May 1778. [TR][CH]
Nathaniel, s/o Nathan & Lydia bp 22 May 1825. [CH]
Olive, d/o Jeremy Jr. & Mary b. 19 Feb. & bp 15 May 1748. [TR][CH]
Olive, d/o Joseph bp 30 June 1792. [CH]
Olive, d/o Joseph & Betsy, b. 3 Feb. 1792 at Ossipee, bp 27 Dec. 1801.
   Granddau. of Capt. John. [TR][CH]
Oliver, s/o Joseph bp 30 June 1792. [CH]
Oliver, s/o Simeon bp 3 Jan. 1805. [CH]
Oliver, s/o Simeon bp 7 Dec. 1817. [CH]
Peter Tilton, s/o Rhodolphus & Betsey born 5 Feb. 1810. [TR][CH]
Phebe, d/o Reuben Gove bp 17 June 1759. [CH]
Phineas, s/o Phineas bp 30 Nov. 1777. [CH]
Polly, d/o Benjamin bp 29 Apr. 1792. [CH]
Polly, d/o Joseph bp 30 June 1792. [CH]
Rachel, d/o Reuben Gove & Elisabeth b. 25 Feb. & bp 9 June 1776. [TR][CH]
Rachel, d/o John & Bethiel born 30 June ___. [TR]
Rachel Smith ae 6, d/o Simon & Polly bp 18 Aug. 1833. [CH]
Rebecca, d/o Mr. of Effingham bp Sep. 1792. [CH]
Reuben, s/o Josiah bp 23 July 1769. [CH]
Reuben, twin s/o Reuben Gove Jr. bp 26 Sep. 1784. [CH]
Reuben Gove, s/o Reuben Gove bp 29 Apr. 1753. [CH]
Rhodolphus, twin s/o John & Bethiah born 28 Mar. & bp 11 Apr. 1784. [TR][CH]
Richard Clark, s/o Phineas bp 1 June 1783. [CH]
Richard Greenlief, s/o Samuel 3d bp 4 June 1809. [CH]
Richard Greenlief, s/o Samuel bp 15 Sep. 1812. [CH]

DEARBORN Cont.

Ruth, d/o Simon & Sarah bp 6 Sep. 1741. [CH]
Ruth Leavitt, d/o Samuel Jr. bp no date given. [CH]
Sally, d/o John bp Oct. 1786. [CH]
Sally, s/o John Jr. bp 1 Oct. 1786. [CH]
Sally, d/o Joseph bp 30 June 1792. [CH]
Sally, d/o Freeze bp 3 Aug. 1800. [CH]
Sally Smith, d/o Nathan & Lydia bp 17 Aug. 1823. [CH]
Samuel, s/o Jeremiah & Mary b. 20 Nov. 1754. [TR] bp 24 Nov. 1754. [CH]
Samuel, s/o Reuben bp 3 Oct. 1756. [CH]
Samuel, s/o Samuel & Hannah b. 29 June 1781. [TR][CH]
Samuel, s/o Mr. of Effingham bp Sep. 1792. [CH]
Samuel, s/o Nathaniel & Dolly bp 21 July 1805. [CH]
Samuel Harris, s/o Samuel Jr. & Lydia bp 10 July 1831. [CH]
Sarah, d/o Jeremiah & Sarah born 27 May 1728. [TR]
Sarah, d/o Jeremiah & Sarah born 11 July 1738. [TR]
Sarah, d/o Levi bp 7 Sep. 1750. [CH]
Sarah, d/o Reuben Gove bp 8 May 1757. [CH]
Sarah, d/o Simon bp 16 Sep. 1759. [CH]
Sarah, d/o Jeremiah & Mary b. 24 July & bp 28 July 1760. [TR][CH]
Sarah, d/o John & Abigail b. 18 Dec. 1772 & bp 3 Jan. 1773. [TR][CH]
Sarah, d/o Daniel & Anne born 21 Aug. 1778. [TR]
Sarah, d/o Reuben Gove bp 12 Nov. 1780. [CH]
Sarah, d/o Samuel& Hannah b. 20 Jan. & bp 29 Jan. 1786. [TR][CH]
Sarah, d/o Benjamin bp 10 Sep. 1797. [CH]
Sarah, w/o David bp 5 May 1839. [CH]
Sarah Ann, d/o Nathaniel & Dolly bp 27 Nov. 1803. [CH]
Sherburn, s/o Henry & Margaret b. 2 Sep. & bp 9 Sep. 1744. [TR][CH]
Simeon, s/o Simeon bp 11 July 1756, [CH]
Simeon, s/o Reuben Jr. bp 6 Nov. 1768. [CH]
Simeon, s/o Reuben Jr. bp 27 July 1778. [CH]
Simeon, s/o Samuel & Hannah b. 21 Mar. & bp 2 May 1779. [TR][CH]
Simon, s/o John & Abigail born 28 Apr. 1766. [TR]
Simon, s/o Simon bp 30 Nov. 1750. [CH]
Simon, s/o Rueben Gove & Elisabeth born 8 June 1778. [TR]
Susan Leavitt, d/o Samuel Jr. & Lydia bp 25 July 1824. [CH]
Thomas Ward, s/o John Jr. & Salley born 22 Nov. 1815. [TR]
True Worthy Goer, s/o Daniel & Anna b. June 1772 & bp 14 Dec. 1777. [TR][CH]

DIMMOCK:
Son of Henry & Alice (Franklin) 1st child, born 17 Oct. 1902. [AR]

DINAN:
Son of William & Sarah J. (Marston) born 1 Mar. 1880. [TR]

DINMERY:
Son of William & Sarah Jane born 1 Oct. 1878. [TR]

DONNELL:
Son of Jennie O. 1st child, born 19 May 1913. [AR]

DOE: See Dow
Ebenezer, s/o John bp Sep. 1792. [CH]
Elizabeth, d/o John bp Sep. 1792. [CH]
Mary, d/o John bp Sep. 1792. [CH]
Nancy, d/o John bp Sep. 1792. [CH]
Stephen, s/o John bp Sep. 1792. [CH]
Susanna, d/o John bp Sep. 1792. [CH]

DOW:
Abrahm Browne, s/o Daniel & Rachel b. 30 Aug. & bp 6 Dec. 1767. [TR][CH]
Bruce Gordon, s/o Gordon S. & Edith G. (Golter) 1st child, born 7 Mar. 1935. [AR]
Cattie M., d/o George C. & Fannie N. born 22 June 1874. [TR]
Child of Simon bp 15 Nov. 1798. [CH]
Cynthia Jean, d/o Gordon S. & Edith G. (Golter) 2d child, born 22 June 1936. [AR]
Danel, s/o Simon & Love born 13 July 1791. [TR]
Daniel, s/o Simon bp 27 Sep. 1795. [CH]
David Marston, s/o Daniel & Lucinda bp 7 Sep. 1823. [CH]
Dau. of Samuel A. & Emma, 2d child, born 30 Oct. 1875. [TR]
Dau. of Samuel & Emma born 24 Mar. 1878. [TR]
Dau. of Abram C. & Addie F. (Tuttle) 1st child, born 27 Apr. 1906. [AR]
Dau. of Abram C. & Addied F. (Tuttle) 2d child, born 1 May 1907. [AR]
Elesebeth, d/o Simon & Love born 7 Apr. 1789. [TR]
Elisabeth, d/o David & Rachel born 23 July 1753. [TR]
Elizabeth, d/o Daniel bp 1 Feb. 1756. [CH]
Elizabeth, d/o Simon bp 27 Sep. 1795. [CH]
Elmara, d/o Daniel & Lucinda bp 12 June 1825. [CH]
George, s/o Abraham B. & Love born 16 Mar. & bp 20 July 1817. [TR][CH]
James, s/o Simon bp 1 Oct. 1756. [CH]
Josephine Plummer, d/o Benjamin & Sarah A. bp 14 June 1868. [CH]
Margaretta, d/o Abraham B. & Love born 4 Oct. & bp 18 Nov. 1811. [TR][CH]
Mariam, d/o Simon & Love born 21 May & bp 27 Sep. 1795. [TR][CH]
Miriam, d/o Daniel bp 1 Feb. 1756. [CH]
Miriam, d/o Daniel & Rachel b. 21 Mar. & bp 16 May 1762. [TR][CH]
Nellie H., d/o George & Fannie N. born 29 Mar. 1876. [TR]
Rachel, d/o Daniel & Rachel b. 7 Sep.1756 & bp 12 June 1757. [TR][CH]
Rachel, d/o Simon & Love born 3 Nov. & bp 12 Aug. 1801. [TR][CH]
Sarah, d/o Nathan & Mary born 5 Mar. 1744. [CH1]
Simon, s/o Daniel & Rachel b. 7 June & bp 26 Aug. 1759. [TR][CH]
Simon, s/o Abraham B. & Love born 17 Mar. & bp 16 Aug. 1807. [TR][CH]
Son of Samuel A. & Emma Marston, 6th child, born 8 Apr. 1886. [TR]
Son of Fred L. & Gertrude E. (Robinson) 1st child, born 24 Sep. 1905. [AR]

DOWNING:

Dau. of Jonas & Anna (Mysen) 1st child, born 7 Apr. 1912. [AR]

DRAKE:

Abigail, d/o Abram & Abigail born 20 Sep. 1740. [TR]
Abigail, d/o Abraham & Abigail b. 23 Dec. 1761 & bp 3 Jan. 1762. [TR][CH]
Abigail, d/o Weare & Anna b. 8 Dec. & bp 25 Dec. 1763. [TR][CH]
Abigail, d/o Wear & Anna born 8 Dec. 1769. [TR]
Abigail, d/o Abraham Jr. bp 15 Oct. 1780. [CH]
Abigail, d/o Samuel & Mehitabel bp 22 May 1825. [CH]
Abraham, s/o Abraham & Abigail b. 3 Feb. & bp 17 Feb. 1745. [TR][CH]
Abraham, s/o Jonathan b. 10 Mar. & bp 15 Apr. 1786. [TR][CH]
Abraham, s/o Francis & Mary bp 13 Oct. 1816. [CH]
Betsey, d/o Nathaniel & Betsey bp 8 Jan. 1786. [CH]
Child of Wear & Anna born 10 Feb. 1763. [TR]
Child of Justin E. & Ethyline (Tobey) born 10 May 1899. [AR]
Clara Bryant, d/o Nathaniel & Ann S. bp 31 Aug. 1854. [CH]
Clifford L., s/o Frank A. & Sarah Hodsdon born 30 Mar. 1876. [TR]
Cora Pierce, d/o Nathaniel & Anna S. bp 18 June 1853. [CH]
Data, d/o Abraham & Abigail born 7 Jan. 1764. [TR]
Data, d/o Jonathan b. 25 Apr. & bp 22 Apr. 1792. [TR][CH]
Dau. of Justin E. & Ethylen (Tobey) 5th child, born 8 Oct. 1902. [AR]
Dau. of Clifford S. & Ruth (Jones) 1st child, born 11 June 1912. [AR]
Delia Brown, d/o Nathaniel & Molly bp 6 Dec. 1801. Grandfather is William
   Godfrey. [CH]
Elizabeth, d/o Abraham bp 19 July 1752. [CH]
Elizabeth, d/o Abram & Abigail born 15 July 1753. [TR]
Elizabeth, d/o Weare & Anna b. 11 July & bp 18 Aug. 1765. [TR][CH]
Elizabeth, d/o Nathaniel & Mary bp 12 Aug. 1801. [CH]
Elizabeth Jenness, d/o Francis & Mary bp 15 Feb. 1818. [CH]
Elmer Ellsworth, s/o Joshua P. & Sarah bp 30 Aug. 1851. [CH]
Emily, d/o Nathaniel & Betsey bp 31 Aug. 1806. [CH]
Emily Augusta, d/o Samuel & Mehitabel bp 2 May 1840. [CH]
Ester Pickering, d/o Justin E. & Ethel Tobay born 10 Apr. 1894. [TR]
Fabin, s/o Samuel & Mehitabel bp 18 July 1819. [CH]
Francis, s/o Abram & Mary bp 6 Nov. 1785/ [CH]
Francis Robinson, s/o Nathaniel & Anna bp 8 Jan. 1850. [CH]
Freeman, s/o Samuel & Mehitabel bp 6 Nov. 1835. [CH]
Hannah, d/o Jonathan & Sarah b. 16 Sep. 1783 & bp 30 June 1784. [TR][CH]
Harmon Edwards, s/o Joshua P. & Sarah D.L. bp 2 July 1852. [CH]
Jeremiah, s/o Abraham bp 29 Sep. 1754. [CH]
John, s/o Abraham bp 30 June 1751. [CH]
John, s/o Weare & Anna b. 6 Nov. & bp 13 Nov. 1768. [TR][CH]
Jonathan, s/o Abraham & Abigail b. 15 Jan. & bp 12 Feb. 1758. [TR][CH]
Jonathan, s/o Jonathan born 18 May 1779. [TR]
Joseph, s/o Weare bp 11 Oct. 1761. [CH]
Joseph, s/o Weare & Anna b. 15 Oct. & bp 2 Nov. 1766. [TR][CH]

DOW Cont.

Joshua Pickering, s/o Samuel & Mehitabel bp 2 Jan. 1823. [CH]

Julianna Fabyans, d/o Joshua P. & Sarah bp 21 June 1865. [CH]

Justin Edward, s/o Joshua P. & Sarah bp 2 May 1856. [CH]

Lottie R., d/o Joshua P. & Sarah L. born 4 Apr. 1868. [TR]

Marion L., d/o Jonathan E. & Ethylan Tobay, 4th child, born 1 May 1899. [TR]

Martha Adaline, d/o Joshua P. & Sarah bp 30 July 1854. [CH]

Mary, d/o Abram & Abigail born 8 Nov. 1743. [TR]

Mary, d/o Weare & Anna b. 6 Aug. & bp 12 Aug. 1770. [TR][CH]

Mary Elizabeth, d/o Samuel bp 5 Feb. 1832. [CH]

Mary Jenness, d/o Francis & Mary bp 30 Apr. 1822. [CH]

Mary Joyce, d/o Joshua F. & Helen V. (Brown) 1st child, born 2 May 1930. [AR]

Mercy, d/o Abraham & Abigail b. 9 July & bp 8 July 1746. [TR][CH]

Mercy, d/o Abraham bp 2 Aug. 1747. [CH]

Mercy, d/o Abraham Jr. bp 14 May 1769. [CH]

Nathaniel, s/o Abraham & Abigail b. 5 Feb. & bp 10 Feb. 1760. [TR][CH]

Mathaniel, s/o Francis bp 4 June 1815. [CH]

Nathaniel, s/o Francis & Mary bp 2 Oct. 1825. [CH]

Nathaniel, s/o Nathaniel bp 13 Aug. 1797. [CH]

Nima, d/o Frank R. & Sarah C. (Hodsdon) born 16 Apr. 1881. [TR]

Olive Ann, d/o Samuel & Mehitabel bp 16 Apr. 1828. [CH]

Samuel, s/o Samuel bp 3 Sep. 1749. [CH]

Samuel, s/o Nathaniel bp 5 May 1793. [CH]

Samuel Fabyan, s/o Samuel J. & Mary bp 9 Apr. 1843. [CH]

Samuel Jenness, s/o Samuel & Mehitabel bp 1 June 1823. [CH]

Sarah, d/o Nathaniel bp 7 Oct. 1744. [CH]

Sarah, d/o Abram & Abigail b. 24 Mar. & bp 29 Mar. 1756. [TR][CH]

Sarah, d/o Jonathan b. 25 July 1789. & bp 11 Sep. 1790. [TR][CH]

Sarah Abigail, d/o Francis & Mary bp 5 Oct. 1828. [CH]

Son stillborn of Justin E. & Ethlyn (Tobey), 2d child, born 4 June 1896.
    [TR][AR]

Son of Justin E. & Ethlyn (Tobey) 3d child, born 24 Jan. 1898. [AR]

Son of Clifford S. & Delania T. (Ayers) 1st child, born 18 Oct. 1902. [AR]

Son of Clifford S. & Delania T. (Ayers) 2d child, born 20 Sep. 1904. [AR]

Theodate, d/o Abraham bp before Apr. 1764. [CH]

Theodate, d/o Abraham Jr. bp 14 June 1772. [CH]

Walter Leavitt, s/o Samuel J. & Mary bp 26 July 1846. [CH]

DREW:

Child of Willie P. & Ada B. (Tarlton) born 8 <ar. 1899. [AR]

Dau. of Fred A. & Ella M. (Tarlton), 1st child, born 22 Aug. 1893. [TR][AR]

Dau. of Fred A. & Ella M. (Tarlton) 2d child, born 7 Nov. 1901. [AR]

Leon Stephen, s/o Willie Paul & Ada Bryant Tarlton born 7 Apr. 1887. [TR]

Son of Willie F. & Ada B. (Tarlton) born 26 Aug. 1891. [AR]

DROWNE:
Dau. of L.A. & Ethel M. (Clark) 1st child, born 7 Apr. 1901. [AR]
Dau. of Archie & Ethel M. (Clark) 2d child, born 26 Nov. 1902. [AR]
Dau. of Archie & Ethel M. (Clark) 3d child, born 21 Mar. 1904. [AR]

DRYSDALE:
Dau. of William & Margaret E. (Cannon) 2d child, born 27 May 1903. [AR]
Dau. of William & Margaret I. (Cannon) 3d child, born 9 Nov. 1906. [AR]
Margaret Isabella, d/o William & Margaret (Cannon) 5th child, born 10 July 1918. [AR]
Son of William & Margaret (Cannon) 4th child, born 12 Sep. 1909. [AR]

EASTMAN:
Jeremiah, s/o Jeremiah & Deborah born 27 Nov. 1745. [CH1]

EATON:
Mary an adult bp 7 Dec. 1817. [CH]

ELKINS:
John Henry, s/o Henry & Miriam bp 4 July 1841. [CH]
Lydia Ann, d/o Henry & Miriam bp 19 Oct. 1838. [CH]
Mary Colby, d/o Henry & Miriam bp 19 Oct. 1838. [CH]
Sarah Ellen, d/o Henry & Miriam bp 5 July 1844. [CH]

EVANS:
Child of David H. & Cornelia C. (Draper) born 9 Apr. 1899. [AR]
Dau. of David H. & Cornelia C. (Draper) 2d child, born 19 Mar. 1905. [AR]

FARRELL:
Dau. of Hiram & Nellie L. Jenness 3d child, born 21 Jan. 1901. [AR]

FARRER:
John, s/o Jonathan & Rebecca (French) born 10 Feb. 1818. [TR]

FENWICK:
Dau. of blank & Hattie Marston, 3rd child, born 17 July 1883. [TR]

FITTS:
Ephraim, s/o Richard & Sarah born 10 May 1745. [CH1]

FLANDERS:
Mary, d/o John & Hannah born & died 4 July 1745. [CH1]
Miriam, d/o Josiah & Mehitabel born 22 Aug. 1745. [CH1]
Onesiphorus, twin s/o Samuel & Mary born 5 Sep. 1745. [CH1]
Samuel, twin s/o Samuel & Mary born 5 Sep. 1745. [CH1]

FOGG:

Abigail, d/o Abner Jr. bp 2 July 1769. [CH]

Abigail, d/o Samuel bp 30 Sep. 1770. [CH]

Abigail, d/o Jeremiah bp 10 May 1810. [CH]

Abner, s/o Seth bp 6 June 1779. [CH]

Abner, s/o Jeremiah bp 10 May 1810. [CH]

Amy May, d/o Clarence L. & Phebe G. (Storer) 1st child, born 5 Aug. 1918. [AR]

Andrew Jackson, s/o David & Eliza bp 31 May 1829. [CH]

Bethiah, d/o Samuel bp 27 Feb. 1774. [CH]

Daniel, s/o Samuel bp 27 Mar. 1768. [CH]

Daniel, s/o Seth bp 2 Dec. 1770. [CH]

Daniel Storer, s/o Clarence L. & Phebe G. (Storer) 5th child, born 1 May 1926. [AR]

Dau. of Emory & Ida (Norton) born 24 Aug. 1875. [TR]

Dau. of Emory & Lula (Norton) born 25 Dec. 1880. [TR]

Dau. of Levi W. & Mary E. (Tarlton) born 8 Dec. 1892. [TR][AR]

David, s/o David & Eliza bp 12 May 1848. [CH]

David Wendell, s/o Clarence & Phebe G. (Storer), 6th child born 22 Feb. 1928. [AR]

Eliza Ann, d/o David & Eliza bp 15 May 18e1. [CH]

Emery Dalton, s/o Roy E. & Maude (Dalton) 3d child, born 4 June 1922. [AR]

Fanny, d/o Dr. John & Sally b. 7 Nov. 1803 & bp 8 July 1804. [TR][CH]

Florence Lillian, d/o Clarence L. & Phebe G. (Storer) 4th child, born 9 May 1922. [AR]

Forrest S., s/o Levi W. & Mary Ellen (Tarlton) born 28 Jan. 1877. [TR]

Harriet, d/o David & Eliza bp 1 July 1842. [CH]

James, s/o Seth bp 28 Feb. 1773. [CH]

Jeremiah William, s/o Dr. John & Sally b. 9 Oct. 1806 & bp 20 Sep. 1807. [TR][CH]

Jeremiah William, s/o John & Sarah born 14 Dec. 1813, bp 15 May 1814. [TR][CH]

John s/o Dearborn bp 11 Mar. 1792. [CH]

John, s/o John bp 3 Sep. 1797. [CH]

John, s/o John & Sarah born 7 Aug. 1799. [TR]

John Leslie, s/o Clarence L. & Phebe G. (Storer) 6th child born 22 Feb. 1928. [AR]

Levi Woodbury, s/o David & Eliza bp 5 Sep. 1845. [CH]

Mary, d/o John b. 14 Feb. & bp 1794. [TR][CH]

Mary, d/o John Jr. & Ruth born 6 May 1797. [TR]

Mary, d/o Seth bp 10 July 1863. [CH]

Mary Abby, d/o David & Eliza bp 17 May 1835. [CH]

Mary Elizabeth, d/o John & Sarah born 17 Jan. 1812, bp 15 May 1814. [TR][CH]

Nancy, d/o Dearborn bp 24 Jan. 1790. [CH]

Newhall, s/o Jeremiah & Sally b. 15 May 1786 & bp 3 Oct. 1789. [TR][CH]

Orice, d/o David & Eliza bp Oct. 1839. [CH]

Phebe Louise, d/o Clarence L. & Phebe G. (Storer) 2d child, born 7 May 1920. [AR]

FOGG Cont.

Phyllis Barbara, d/o Clarence L. & Phebe G. (Storer) 3d child, born 23 May 1921. [AR]
Ray Emery, s/o Emery & Ida C. Norton born 20 Dec. 1893. [TR]
Richard, s/o Abner Jr. bp 12 Apr. 1772. [CH]
Richard, s/o Jeremiah bp 18 Aug. 1799. [CH]
Rhoda Jane, d/o David & Eliza bp 28 May 1837. [CH]
Roy Emery, s/o Emery & Ida L. (Norton) born 20 Dec. 1893. [AR]
Samuel, s/o Thomas & Marey bprn 8 Sep. 1767. [TR]
Samuel, s/o Samuel bp 9 Nov. 1777. [CH]
Samuel, s/o Dearborn bp 5 Jan. 1794. [CH]
Samuel Dearborn, s/o David & Eliza bp 19 May 1833. [CH]
Samuel Robie, s/o Abner bp 3 Apr. 1743. [CH]
Sarah, d/o Seth bp 16 Sep. 1764. [CH]
Seth, s/o Seth & Mary bp 2 Nov. 1766. [CH]
Simon, s/o Seth bp 7 Jan. 1776. [CH]
Son of Dudley & Mary J., 1st child, born 25 Jan. 1877. [TR]
Son of Emery & Lula Norton, 4th child, born 1 Jan. 1887. [TR]
William Cutter, s/o Dr. John & Sally b. 30 Apr. & bp 20 June 1805. [TR][CH]
William Godfrey, s/o Seth bp 17 June 1782. [CH]

FOSS:

Eunice Wells, w/o Clark bp 8 July 1823. [CH]
Jeremiah, s/o Wid Eunice bp 2 Oct. 1825. [CH]
John Hobbs, s/o Wid Eunice bp 2 Oct. 1825. [CH]
William Eaton, s/o Wid. Eunice bp 2 Oct. 1825. [CH]

FOWLER:

Child of William P. & Susan F. (Smith) born 5 Aug. 1900. [AR]
Dau. of Nathan & Gertrude M. (Stout) 3d child, born 12 Aug. 1901. [AR]
Dau. of William P. & Susan F. (Smith) 2d child, born 12 June 1902. [AR]
Dorothy, d/o William P. & Ellen (Sprague) 2d child, born 14 Aug. 1929. [AR]
Mary, d/p Abner & Sarah born 11 Mar. 1744. [CH1]
Richard, s/o William P. & Ellen (Sprague) 3d child, born 1 June 1931. [AR]
Susan, d/o William P. & Ruth H. (Miller) 1st child, born 9 Oct. 1943. [AR]
William P., s/o William P. & Susan F. (Smith) born 5 Aug. 1900. [TR]

FRENCH:

Abigail, twin d/o Joseph & Hannah born 3 Jan. 1745. [CH1]
Abigail, d/o Rev. Jonathan & Rebecca bp 5 Aug. 1810. [CH]
Anna Dore, d/o John F. & Lemira bp 19 Oct. 1856. [CH]
Arthur Sperry, s/o Ebenezer S. & Harriert H. bp 26 Nov. 1854. [CH]
Charles Henry Hayden, s/o Samuel F. & Ann R. bp 31 Apr. 1841. [CH]
Daniel, s/o Daniel & Sarah born 16 Dec. 1745. [CH1]
Damiris, twin d/o Joseph & Hannah born 3 Jan. 1745. [CH1]
Ebenezer, s/o Ebenezer & Elizabeth born 13 July 1745. [CH1]
Ebenezer Sperry, s/o Rev. Jona. & Rebecca born 9 Jan. 1823. [TR][CH]

FRENCH Cont.

Elijah, s/o Nathaniel & Anne born 26 Aug. 1745. [CH1]
Elisabeth Dorcus, d/o Rev. Jonathan & Rebecca born 26 Jan. 1829. [TR][CH]
Elizabeth Fabyan, d/o Samuel F. & Ann Ringe bp 26 Jan. 1837. [CH]
Ellen Lemira, d/o John F. & Kemira bp 17 Nov. 1844. [CH]
Frank Newell, s/o E. Sperry & Harriet H. bp 23 Dec. 1860. [CH]
Hannah, d/o Samuel & Mary born 22 Dec. 1745. [CH1]
Harriet, d/o E. Sperry & Harriet H. bp 26 Nov. 1868. [CH]
James, s/o Rev. Jonathan & Rebecca bp 2 Apr. 1815. [CH]
John Farrer, s/o Jonathan & Rebecca born 10 Feb. 1818. [TR][CH]
John Leavitt, s/o John F. & Lemira bp 2 Mar. 1849. [CH]
Jonathan, s/o Rev. Jonathan & Rebecca born 13 Dec. 1805. [CH][TR]
Lester David 3d, s/o Lester D. & Lena (Stern) 4th child, born 30 Dec. 1943.
    [AR]
Lucy Ann, d/o Rev. Jona. & Rebecca born 5 Sep. & bp 11 Sep. 1825. [TR][CH]
Mary Holyoke, d/o Rev. Jonathan & Rebecca bp 29 Nov. 1812. [CH]
Mary Robinson, d/o E. Sperry & Harriet H. bp 29 Apr. 1859. [CH]
Oliver Simon, s/o John F. & Lemira bp 3 July 1851. [CH]
Rebecca Mercy, d/o Rev. Jona. & Rebecca b. 2 Feb. & bp 8 Feb. 1807. [TR][CH]
Samuel Farrer, s/o Rev. Jonathan & Rebecca born 11 Jan. & bp 15 Jan. 1809.
    [TR][CH]
Sarah, d/o Rev. Jona. & Rebecca born 25 May & bp 28 May 1820. [TR][CH]

FROST:

Dau. of George E. & Marie G. born 18 Dec. 1891. [AR]
Sadie Ola, d/o George F. & Eva E. (Storer) 3d child, born 18 Nov. 1921. [AR]

FULLER:

Son of Alvan T. & Viola (Davenport) 1st child, born 14 July 1911. [AR]

GARGILL:

Dau. of Thomas & Susan (Duncan) born 10 June 1890. [AR]

GARLAND:

Anna, d/o Joseph bp 6 July 1777. [CH]
Bessie Frances, d/o George L. & Isadore (Page) born 21 Dec. 1874. [TR]
Child of Charles L.A. & Alice Jones born 27 Oct. 1899. [AR]
Comfort, d/o Joseph bp 16 Apr. 1763. [CH]
Daniel Page, s/o Page & Fredora A. (Tebbetts) 1st child, born 20 Dec. 1938.
    [AR]
Dau. of George Leavitt & Isadore (Page) born 5 Mar. 1876. [TR]
Georgette, d/o George & Isadore (Page) born 30 Nov. 1877. [TR]
Hannah, d/o Joseph bp 11 Sep. 1768. [CH]
James, s/o Joseph bp 21 June 1761. [CH]
Mercy, d/o Joseph bp 11 July 1773. [CH]
Olive, d/o Joseph bp 3 June 1759. [CH]
Rachel, d/o Joseph bp 21 June 1761. [CH]

GARLAND Cont.

Samuel P., s/o George L. & Isadore (Page) born 19 July 1881. [TR]
Sarah, d/o Joseph bp 29 Dec. 1771. [CH]
Son of Charles L.A. & Alice (Jones) 2d child, born 1 Aug. 1901. [AR]
Son of Harold R. & Alice S. (Downing) 2d child, born 18 Aug. 1910. [AR]
Urjulia Howe bp 6 Aug. 1837. [CH]

GILMAN:

Ann Marguerite, d/o Clifton I. & Viola M. (Jones) 2d child, born 12 Mar.
    1936. [AR]
Barbara Elaine, d/o Clifton I. & Viola M. (Jones) 1st child, born 4 Nov.
    1934. [AR]
Elizabeth Audrey, d/o Clifton I & Viola M. (Jones) 3d child, born 3 Apr.
    1938. (AR]

GILPATRICK:

Dau. of William M. & Alice (Kersham) 1st child, born 30 July 1905. [AR]
Dau. of William M. & Alice (Kersham) 2d child, born 6 Sep. 1907. [AR]
Dau. of William M. & Alice (Kersham) 3d child, born 14 Aug. 1909. [AR]

GODFREY/GODFREE:

Abiel, d/o John bp 17 July 1763. [CH]
Abigail, d/o John Jr. & Abigail b. 6 Nov. 1744 & bp 6 Jan. 1745. [TR][CH]
Abram, s/o James & Patience born 25 May 1746. [TR]
Anne, d/o James & Patience b. 17 Apr. & bp 22 Apr. 1744. [TR][CH]
Charles, s/o Dearborn & Sarah bp 12 Aug. 1823. [CH]
Deborah, d/o John Jr. & Abigail b. 12 Apr. & bp 20 Apr. 1746. [TR][CH]
Eliza Jane, d/o James & Mary Ann bp 25 Aug. 1839. [CH]
Elizabeth Anne, d/o James & Mary Ann bp 16 Apr. 1841. [CH]
Emeline, d/o Dearborn & Sarah bp 17 Aug. 1823. [CH]
Henry, s/o Moses bp 9 Mar. 1760. [CH]
James, s/o Moses bp 26 Mar. 1758. [CH]
James, s/o William & Anna b. 27 Mar. & bp 1 Apr. 1770. [TR][CH]
James, s/o Jeremiah, dead bp 25 Oct. 1807. [CH]
James. s/o Dearborn & Sarah bp 17 Aug. 1823. [CH]
Jeremiah, s/o William & Anna born 8 Apr. 1766. [TR]
Jeremiah, s/o Jeremiah bp 12 Aug. 1798. [CH]
Jeremiah, s/o Dearborn & Sarah bp 17 Aug. 1823. [CH]
John, s/o John Jr. bp 24 Mar. 1751. [CH]
John, s/o John bp 14 Dec. 1760. [CH]
Jonathan, s/o Moses bp 8 Aug. 1773. [CH]
Jonathan, s/o Patience bp 9 Nov. 1783. [CH]
Joseph, twin s/o William & Anne b. 10 May & bp 12 May 1776. [TR][CH]
Lydia, d/o John bp 29 Apr. 1753. [CH]
Mary, d/o James & Patience b. _6 Jqn. & bp 31 Jan. 1742. [TR][CH]
Mary, d/o John bp 16 Oct. 1756. [CH]
Mary, twin d/o William & Anne b. 10 May & bp 12 May 1776. [TR][CH]

GODFREY Cont.
Mary Ann, d/o Joseph & Sally bp 6 Feb. 1803. [CH]
Mehitabel, d/o John Jr. & Abigail b. 2 Sep. & bp 6 Sep. 1747. [TR][CH]
Molly, d/o Patience bp 9 Nov. 1783. [CH]
Patience, d/o James &Patience b. 19 Feb. & bp 5 Feb. 1748/9. [TR][CH]
Patience, d/o William & Anna b. 20 Jan. & bp 24 Jan. 1768. [TR][CH]
Priscilla, d/o Joseph & Sally bp 26 May 1805. [CH]
Sarah, d/o John bp 15 Aug. 1756. [CH]
Sarah, d/o William & __ b. 5 Oct. & bp 10 Oct. 1773. [TR][CH]
Simon, s/o Moses bp 11 Oct. 1761. [CH]
Simon, s/o Isaac bp 1 Aug. 1784. [CH]
William, s/o James bp 1 Jan. 1746. [CH]

GOODWIN:
Dau. of Joseph & Grace B. (Runford) 2d child, born 12 Dec. 1915. [AR]
Dau. of Joseph & Grace (Runford) 2d child, born 20 Nov. 1916. [AR]
Son of Danial E. & Ruth B. (Cousens) 1st child, born 19 Oct. 1910. [AR]

GOOKIN:
Anne, d/o Rev. Nathaniel & Love b. 3 Aug. & bp 9 Aug. 1752. [TR][CH]
Daniel, s/o Rev. Nathaniel & Love b. 2 Mar. & bp 7 Mar. 1756. [TR][CH]
Dorothy, d/o Rev. Nath. & Love Wingate born 11 Sep. 1749. [TR][CH]
Elizabeth, d/o Rev. Nathaniel & Anna (Fitch) born 13 Dec. 1743. [TR][CH]
Elizabeth, twin d/o Rev. Nath. & Love Wingate born 22 Apr. 1754. [TR][CH]
Elizabeth (twin), d/o Daniel & Abigail b. 23 July & bp Oct. 1795. [TR][CH]
Hannah, twin d/o Rev. Nath. & Love Wingate born 22 Apr. 1754. [TR][CH].
Harriet (twin), d/o Daniel & Abigail b. 23 July & bp Oct. 1795. [TR][CH]
John Wingate, s/o Rev. Nathaniel & Anna (Fitch) born 31 July 1745. [CH]
John Wingate, s/o Daniel & Abigail born 27 June 1788. [TR]
Margaret, d/o Rev. Nathaniel & Anne born 31 July 1843. [TR]
Martha, d/o Rev. Nathaniel & Love (Wingate) born 20 Mar. 1758. [TR][CH]
Mary, d/o Rev. Nathaniel & Love (Wingate) born 12 Dec. 1750. [TR][CH]
Nathaniel, s/o Rev. Nathaniel & Anna (Fitch) born 10 Jan. 1747. [TR][CH]
Sarah, d/o Rev. Nathaniel & Love (Wingate) born 12 Jan. 1760. [TR][CH]
Sarah, d/o Daniel & Abigail b. 3 Dec. 1792 & bp 22 Mar. 1793. [TR][CH]

GOSS:
Son of Walter W. & Fannie B. (Knowles) 1st child, born 24 Jan. 1901. [AR]

GRANT:
Eleanor Frances, d/o Harold I. & Lilla (Hartford) 3d child, born 22 Aug.
    1943. [AR]
Son of Fred A. & Sarah A. Leavitt, 1st child, born 30 Apr. 1889. [TR]

GRANWILL:
Fanny, d/o Joseph bp Sep. 1792. [CH]
Lydia, d/o Joseph bp Sep. 1792. [CH]
Mary, d/o Joseph bp Sep. 1792. [CH]
Sally, d/o Joseph bp Sep. 1792. [CH]
Stephen, s/o Joseph bp Sep. 1792. [CH]
Thomas, s/o Joseph bp Sep. 1792. [CH]

GREEN:
Son of Otis W. & Mabel P. (Berry) 1st child, born 18 Nov. 1903. [AR]

GRIFFIN:
Jacob, s/o Jonathan & Deborah born 26 Jan. 1744. [CH1]
Jonathan, s/o Jonathan & Deborah born 1 Oct. 1745. [CH1]
Molly, adopted d/o Samuel Davis bp 31 July 1785.

HACKETT:
Marilyn Jane, d/o Lawrence C. & Carrie (Hopkins) 1st child, born 3 Aug.
    1939. [AR]

HAINES:
Benjamin, s/o Thomas bp 24 Feb. 1765. [CH]
Deborah, d/o Thomas & Deborah b[17 Jan. 1768. [CH]
James, s/o Wid. Deborah bp 24 Dec. 1773. [CH]
Joshua, s/o Simon bp 16 Feb. 1783. [CH]
Lillian French, d/o Thomas & Mary (French) born 13 Apr. 1876. [TR]
Lucy, d/o Wid. Lucy bp 8 Dec. 1782. [CH]
Mary, d/o Thomas bp 4 Mar. 1753. [CH]
Mary, d/o Thomas Jr. bp 29 Feb. 1756. [CH]
Phebe Piper, d/o Simon bp 1 Aug. 1784. [CH]
Rachel, d/o Thomas Jr. bp 16 Sep. 1750. [CH]
Roy Edward, s/o Edward W. & Gertrude N. (Sabell) born 11 Apr. 1891. [TR][AR]
Sarah, d/o Thomas bp 5 Dec. 1762. [CH]
Simon, s/o Thomas bp 9 Apr. 1758. [CH]
Son of Edward W. & Gertrude a. (norton) born 11 Apr. 1891. [AR]
Thomas, s/o Thomas bp 1 June 1760. [CH]

HARDY/HARDAY:
Abigail, d/o Samuel & Elizabeth b. 12 Apr. & bp 23 Apr. 1773. [TR][CH]
Anna, d/o Samuel & Elizabeth b. 8 Dec. & bp 16 Dec. 1771. [TR][CH]
Hannah, d/o Samuel & Elizabeth b. 8 Mar. 1768. [TR][CH]
Samuel, s/o Samuel & Elizabeth b. 31 Mar. & bp 28 Apr. 1776. [TR][CH]

HARVEY:
Dau. of Frank J. & Mary D. (Marston), 1st child, born 1 Nov. 1883. [TR]
Dau. of Frank J. & Mary J., 2d child, born 2 Apr. 1886. [TR]
Son of Frank J. & Mary L. (Marston), 3d child, born 6 Apr. 1888. [TR]

HAYDEN:
Ralph Jr., s/o Ralph & Mary (Hanlon) 1st child, born 3 Sep. 1932. [AR]

HEATH:
Son of George W. & Lily A. (Bunn) 1st child, born 20 July 1901. [AR]
Son of George W. & Lily A. (Bunn), 2d child born 9 Feb. 1904. [AR]

HEDDEN:
Son of Kenneth H. & Ethel M. (Carle__) 3d child, born 11 Aug. 1914. [AR]

HENDRY:
Dau. of Clinton C. & Emily C. born 17 Mar. 1886. [TR]
Robert Walter, s/o Clinton E. & Hazel (Gannett) 1st child, born 11 Aug. 1940.
[AR]

HIDER:
Franklin Delano, s/o Martin B. & Mary (Williams) 3d child, born 20 June 1922.
[AR]

HILL:
Child of Lewis D. & Ina H. (Parshley) born 19 Mar. 1900. [AR]

HOBBS:
Abiah, d/o Jonathan bp Sep. 1792. [CH]
Abigail, d/o Joseph bp 17 Mar. 1754. [CH]
Abigail, d/o Deacon bp 1 Mar. 1778. [CH]
Abigail, d/o John bp 25 Mar. 1793. [CH]
Abigail Cotton, d/o Thomas & Abigail of Candia bp 25 Sep. 1808. [CH]
Abraham Drake, s/o Oliver & Sarah bp 22 May 1836. [CH]
Ada, d/o John B. & Ella F. (Jenness) born 18 Apr. 1871. [TR]
Anna, d/o Nathaniel bp 3 July 1785. [CH]
Benjamin, s/o Benjamin & Mercy bp 27 July 1740. [CH]
Benjamin, s/o Nathaniel & Anna bp 25 Jan. 1767. [CH]
Benjamin, s/o David bp 1800. [CH]
Benjamin, s/o Jonathan bp 12 Feb. 1800. [CH]
Beth Towne, d/o James F. & Helen (Spear) 3d child, born 5 Jan. 1929. [AR]
Bethiah, d/o Benjamin bp 17 Feb. 1765. [CH]
Betty, d/o benjamin bp 21 Nov. 1762. [CH]
Charlotte, d/o Love bp 22 Mar. 1793. [CH]
Child of Webster D. & Bessie G. (Garland) born 26 Jan. 1899. [AR]
Daniel Sanborn, s/o Jonathan bp 12 Feb. 1800. [CH]
Date, d/o Lt. Jonathan & Mary bp 5 Aug. 1810. [CH]
Date, d/o Thomas J. & Abigail bp 19 Sep. 1808. [CH]
Dau. of James & Elizabeth N. Towne, 2d child, born 28 Dec. 1883. [TR]
Dau. of Joseph O. & Anna F. (French), 3rd child, born 25 Dec. 1888. [TR]
David, s/o Benjamin bp 12 Feb. 1758. [CH]
David, s/o Benjamin bp 6 July 1760. [CH]

HOBBS Cont.

Deborah Batchelder, d/o Benjamin bp 14 July 1751. [CH]

Eliot Alden, s/o James Jr. & Helen (Spear) 1st child, born 7 May 1922. [AR]

Eliza Sarah, d/o Joseph Stacey & Mary bp 2 Nov. 1849. [CH]

Elizabeth Ann, d/o Jonathan 3d & Mary H, bp 8 Dec. 1839. [CH]

Elizabeth Buxton, d/o Thomas & Fanny bp 4 May 1855. [CH]

Elizabeth Cotton, d/o Morris Jr. & Abigail bp 6 June 1802. [CH]

Emily, d/o Jonathan 3d & Mary H. bp 30 Jan. 1842. [CH]

Emma Merdora, d/o Thomas & Fanny bp 29 Apr. 1853. [CH]

Esther, d/o Nathaniel bp 21 May 1769. [CH]

Fanny, d/o Jonathan Jr. & Fanny born 23 Nov. 1810, bp 3 May 1812. [TR][CH]

Fanny Dearborn, d/o Jonathan Jr. & Fanny bp 19 Sep. 1802. [CH]

Frances Abby, d/o Thomas & Fanny bp 20 Feb. 1836. [CH]

Francis Drake, s/o Jonathan & Mary H. bp 29 June 1845. [CH]

Frederic Abbott, s/o Jonathan 3d & Mary H. bp 5 Sep. 1855. [CH]

Hannah, d/o Joseph bp 28 Aug. 1768. [CH]

Hannah, d/o Samuel of Parsonfield bp Sep. 1792. [CH]

Hannah, d/o John bp 25 Mar. 1795. [CH]

Harriet Ann, d/o Oliver & Sarah bp 4 Sep. 1846. [CH]

Harriet Newell, d/o Jonathan & Fanny bp 23 Apr. 1820. [CH]

Henry, s/o John & Lucinda bp 16 July 1820. [CH]

Hezekiah, s/o Caleb Jr. & Anne born 22 May 1744. [CH1]

Horatio, s/o Horatio D. & Emeline bp 27 Oct. 1844. [CH]

Horatio Dearborn, s/o Jonathan Jr. & Fanny born 20 Apr. & bp 3 May 1812. [TR][CH]

Huldah, d/o Morris & Sarah born 26 Feb. 1753. [TR]

James Fabyan, s/o Jonathan 3d & Mary H. bp 24 Sep. 1843. [CH]

James Frances, s/o James F. & Elizabeth Harvey (Towne) born 22 May 1890. [TR]

Joanna, d/o Paul W. & Dorothy (Tarr) 1st child, born 4 Apr. 1932. [AR]

John, s/o Simon bp 1 May 1768. [CH]

John, s/o Joseph bp 28 Nov. 1768. [CH]

John, s/o Thomas bp 12 June 1785. [CH]

John, s/o Josiah bp 15 Mar. 1786. [CH]

John, s/o Josiah & Mary (Wedgwood) born 22 Dec. 1788. [TR]

John Alden, s/o Jonathan 3d & Mary H.F. bp 4 July 1852. [CH]

John Dow, s/o John bp 4 Aug. 1799. [CH]

John Leavitt, s/o Morris Jr. & Abigail bp 10 sep. 1809. [CH]

John Oliver, s/o Ray O. & Gertrude (Carter) 2d child, born 14 Sep. 1922. [AR]

John Sherburne, s/o Thomas of Candia bp 24 Sep. 1815. [CH]

John Sherburne, s/o John & Lucinda bp 23 Mar. 1817. [CH]

John William Fogg, twin s/o Jonathan Jr. & Fanny born 3 Jan. & bp 3 Sep. 1815. [TR][CH]

Jonathan, s/o Jonathan bp 13 Oct. 1754. [CH]

Jonathan, s/o Morris bp 27 Aug. 1769. [CH]

Jonathan, s/o Nathaniel bp 12 Jan. 1772. [CH]

Jonathan, s/o Thomas bp 20 June 1773. [CH]

Jonathan, s/o Dea. Benjamin bp 20 May 1770. [CH]

HOBBS Cont.

Jonathan, s/o Jonathan & Date bp 22 Sep. 1805. [CH]
Jonathan French, s/o Oliver & Sarah bp 15 Jan. 1832. [CH]
Joseph, s/o Dea. Benjamin bp 2 Aug. 1772. [CH]
Joseph bp 18 May 1777. [CH]
Joseph Stacey, s/o Oliver & Sarah bp 22 Apr. 1827. [CH]
Josiah, d/o Joseph bp 13 Jan. 1760. [CH]
Josiah Wilton, s/o Benjamin & Nabby bp 10 Sep. 1797. [CH]
Leavitt, s/o Thomas & Fanny bp 23 June 1833. [CH]
Lemira, d/o Joseph G. & Annie F. (French) born 25 May 1888. [TR]
Leocade, d/o Jonathan Jr. born 23 May 1804. [TR]
Lewis French, s/o Jonathan 3d & Mary H.F. bp 20 Dec. 1835. [CH]
Love, d/o Thomas bp 6 Dec. 1772. [CH]
Lucinda, d/o John & Lucinda bp 25 Sep. 1814. [CH]
Lucy, d/o Jonathan bp 15 Oct. 1752. [CH]
Lucy, d/o Nathaniel bp 16 Dec. 1764. [CH]
Lydia, d/o Samuel of Parsonsfield bp Sep. 1792. [CH]
Margaret, living with Benjamin Hobbs bp 20 Aug. 1758. [CH]
Mary, d/o Benjamin & Marey b. 7 June & bp 17 June 1744. [TR][CH]
Mary, d/o Morris & Mary born 29 Feb. 1755. [TR]
Mary, d/o Benjamin Jr. bp 23 Nov. 1781. [CH]
Mary, d/o Thomas bp 13 Apr. 1783. [CH]
Mary, d/o thomas of Candia bp 23 Sep. 1810. [CH]
Mary, d/o John & Lucinda bp 15 Apr. 1832. [CH]
Mary Elizabeth, d/o Raymond D. & Gertrude (Carter) 1st child, born 30 May 1919. [AR]
Mary Ellen, d/o Oliver & Sarah bp 1 July 1841. [CH]
Mary Fogg, d/o Jonathan Jr. & Fanny born 27 Nov. 1794. [TR]
Mary French, d/o Jonathan 3d & Mary H.F. bp 18 July 1847. [CH]
Mary Jane. d/o Thomas & Fanny bp 14 Jan. 1838. [CH]
Molly, d/o Morris, bp 31 Jan. 1779. [CH]
Molly, d/o Josiah bp Jan. 1792. [CH]
Molly Dow, d/o Dea. Benjamin bp 25 June 1775. [CH]
Morris, s/o Morris & Mary born 1 Apr. 1747. [TR]
Morris, s/o Morris bp 6 Jan. 1771. [CH]
Morris, s/o Morris bp 18 Aug. 1776. [CH]
Morris, s/o Morris bp 4 Aug. 1799. [CH]
Morris, s/o Morris & Abigail bp 2 July 1815. [CH]
Nathaniel, s/o Benjamin & Mercy bp 27 June 1742. [CH]
Nathaniel, s/o Nathaniel bp 20 Mar. 1774. [CH]
Nancy Cotton, d/o Morris Jr. & Abigail bp 2 June 1805. [CH]
Olive, d/o David & Charlotte of Parsonsfield bp 17 June 1804. [CH]
Oliver, s/o Jonathan & Date bp 26 Sep. 1802. [CH]
Oliver, s/o Abraham & Ruby A. born 31 Mar. 1868. [TR]
Paul Kendall, s/o Paul W. & Dorothy (Tarr) 2d child, born 13 June 1934. [AR]
Polly, d/o Samuel of Parsonsfield bp Sep. 1792. [CH]
Polly, d/o Jonathan, bp 30 Sep. 1795. [CH]

HOBBS Cont.

Polly Fogg, d/o Jonathan bp 4 Aug. 1799. [CH]
Raymond A., s/o Octavia , 1st child, born 23 Aug. 1894. [TR]
Rebecca Abby, d/o Jonathan 3d & Mary Holyoke (French) bp 4 May 1834. [CH]
Reuben, s/o Nathaniel bp 2 June 1782. [CH]
Samuel, s/o Joseph bp 11 July 1756. [CH]
Samuel. s/o Josiah of Parsonsfield bp Sep. 1792. [CH]
Samuel, s/o Samuel of Parsonsfield bp Sep. 1792. [CH]
Samuel Dearborn, s/o Nathaniel bp 12 Sep. 1779. [CH]
Samuel Farrar, s/o Jonathan 3d & Mary Holyoke (French) bp 19 May 1850. [CH]
Sarah, d/o Jonathan bp 28 Oct. 1750. [CH]
Sarah, d/o Thomas bp 17 Sep. 1775. [CH]
Sarah, d/o Jonathan Jr. & Fanny born 18 July & bp 2 Aug. 1806. [TR][CH]
Sarah Adelaide, d/o Thomas & Fanny bp 25 Feb. 1844. [CH]
Sarah Ann, d/o John Jr. & Lucinda bp 30 July 1809. [CH]
Sarah Leavitt, d/o Thomas Jr. & Abigail bp 12 Feb. 1804. [CH]
Sarah Theodate, d/o Jonathan 3d & Mary H.F. bp 3 Dec. 1837. [CH]
Simon, s/o Simon bp 1 Sep. 1765. [CH]
Simon, s/o Simon & Abigail bp 30 Nov. 1766. [CH]
Simon Leavitt, s/o Thomas of Candia bp 19 Sep. 1813. [CH]
Son of Abraham D. & Ruby (Meers) born 30 May 1874. [TR]
Son of James F. & Elizabeth H. (Towne) born 26 Jan. 1879. [TR]
Son of Joseph & Unice (French?). 2d child, born 27 May 1887. [TR]
Son of Albert & Susan (Berry), 2d child born 20 Aug. 1888. [TR]
Son of Webster D. & Bessie T. (Garland), 1st child, born 22 July 1894.
    [TR][AR]
Son of Oliver S. & Mary E. (Smith) 1st child, born 20 Aug. 1894. [AR]
Son of Joseph O. & Annie W. (Hoyt) 1st child, born 2 June 1907. [AR]
Thersea Dearborn, d/o Horatio & Emeline bp 10 Oct. 1841. [CH]
Thomas, s/o Morris & Mary born 8 Jan. 1749. [TR]
Thomas, s/o Thomas bp 24 Sep. 1778. [CH]
Thomas, s/o Thomas & Abigail of Candia bp 6 June 1806. [CH]
Thomas, s/o John & Lucinda bp 16 Nov. 1823. [CH]
Thomas Albert, s/o Thomas Jr. & Fanny bp 5 Mar. 1847. [CH]
Tommy, s/o Lt. Jonathan bp before July 1800. [CH]
William John Cutter, twin s/o Jonathan Jr. & Fanny born 3 Jan. & bp 3 Sep.
    1815. [TR][CH]
Willis Farrar, s/o Jonathan 3d & Mary H. (French) bp 5 May 1854. [CH]
Woodbury, s/o Horatio D. & Emeline bp 1 Jan. 1837. [CH]

HOBSON:

Child of Arthur L. & Alice C. (Gale) born 23 Aug. 1900. [AR]

HODGDON:

Dau. of William & Emily (Hunt), 1st child, born 29 Nov. 1886. [TR]
Dau. of John William & Emily (Hunt), 1st child, born 2 May 1889. [TR]
Dau. of J. William & Emily A. (Hunt), 4th child, born 24 Dec. 1892. [TR][AR]

HODGDON Cont.
Phyllis, d/o William J. & Emily A. (Hunt), 5th child, born 18 Jan. 1894.
[TR][AR]
Son of William & Emily (Hunt), 3rd child, born 25 Apr. 1888. [TR]

HOOK:
Henry W., s/o John W. & Nina born 20 May 1876. [TR]

HOYT:
Dorothy, d/o Ezekiel & Rebeckah born 10 June 1744. [CH1]

HUTCHINS:
Dau. of Percy C. & Sarah C. born 3 Oct. 1868. [TR]
Lena, d/o Benjamin & Sarah C. born 29 June 1866. [TR]
Leslie Victor Jr., s/o Leslie V. & Phyllis C. (Thompson) 2d child, born 20
Aug. 1936. [AR]

ILSLEY:
Anna Silloway an adult bp 1 Apr. 1832. [CH]

INGALLS:
Mary, d/o Samuel bp 11 Oct. 1741. [CH]

INGLIS:
Harold L., s/o Ralph W. & Elsie R. (VanHorne) 6th child, born 18 Oct. 1943.
[AR]

JAMES:
Samuel, s/o John bp 8 Mar. 1747. [CH]

JAQUES:
Son of William H. & Mary A. (Genever) 2d child, born 4 July 1901. [AR]

JELMBERG:
Fred David, s/o Frederick A. & Margaret A. (Kelly), 1st child born 9 Mar.
1941. [AR]

JENNESS:
Abigail, d/o Jeremiah & Molly bp 20 Jan. 1805. [CH]
Charles Wallace, s/o Edwin & Mary bp 3 Jan. 1847. [CH]
Chester Philbrick, s/o Orrin & Lydia born 23 Sep. 1893. [TR]
Dau. of Alonzo & Martha, 2d child, born 6 Jan. 1878. [TR]
Dau. of Alonzo & Martha (Brown), 4th child, born 24 May 1883. [TR]
Dau. of Frank W. & Mary (Jewell) 2d child, born 27 Nov. 1904. [AR]
George Edwin, s/o Edwin & Mary bp 10 Sep. 1858. [CH]
George Warren, s/o Benjamin & Dolly bp 24 July 1846. [CH]
George William, s/o Samuel A. & Martha (Brown) born 9 Nov. 1875. [TR]

JENNESS Cont.

Harriet, d/o Jeremiah & Mary bp 6 June 1802. [CH]
John, s/o Thomas bp 5 Aug. 1754. [CH]
Martha Elizabeth, d/o Edwin & Mary bp 3 Nov. 1848. [CH]
Mary Ann, d/o Jeremiah bp before July 1800. [CH]
Mary Elizabeth, d/o Charles & Eliza born 4 May 1877. [TR]
Mercy, d/o Isaac bp 27 Aug. 1781. [CH]
Molly, d/o Samuel bp 18 Jan. 1778. [CH]
Roswell French, s/o Edwin & Mary bp 3 July 1851. [CH]
Samuel ALonzo, s/o Edwin & Mary bp 16 July 1843. [CH]
Sarah Martha, d/o Benjamin & Dolly bp 29 May 1842. [CH]
Son of Alonzo & Martha (Brown) born 7 June 1880. [TR]
Son of Frank W. & Mary S. (Jewell) 1st child, born 18 Aug. 1901. [AR]

JEWELL:

Anna, d/o Daniel bp 16 Oct. 1768. [CH]
Asa, s/o Daniel bp 30 Mar. 1783. [CH]
Charlotte, d/o Daniel bp 26 Sep. 1784. [CH]
Daniel, s/o David bp 10 June 1744. [CH]
Daniel, bp 17 May 1778. [CH]
David, s /o David bp 25 Dec. 1742. [CH]
David, s/o Daniel & Sarah bp 2 Aug. 1767. [CH]
Elizabeth, d/o David bp 28 Aug. 1750. [CH]
Elizabeth, d/o D____ bp 22 Sep. 1765. [CH]
Jacob. s/o David bp 9 June 1754. [CH]
Joseph, s/o David & Elizabeth bp 23 Aug. 1741. [CH]
Lydia, d/o David bp 23 Nov. 1746. [CH]
Lydia, d/o Daniel bp 9 Dec. 1770. [CH]
Mary, d/o David bp 9 May 1756. [CH]
Sarah, d/o David bp 9 Aug. 1752. [CH]
Sarah, d/o Daniel bp 31 Jan. 1773. [CH]
Stillborn of Bloomer & Abbie M. born 23 Dec. 1875. [TR]
Susanna, d/o David bp 21 Aug. 1748. [CH]
Thomas, s/o David bp 26 Aug. 1759. [CH]

JOHNSON:

Benjamin, s/o Benjamin bp 9 July 1758. [CH]
Hannah, d/o Benjamin bp 31 Dec. 1769. [CH]
John, s/o Benjamin bp 9 July 1758. [CH]
Leonard, s/o Caleb of Exeter bp 27 Oct. 1800. [CH]
Mary, d/o Benjamin bp 25 Nov. 1753. [CH]
Philip. s/o Philip bp 17 Nov. 1751. [CH]
Rachel, d/o Benjamin bp 21 Nov. 1756. [CH]
Sarah, d/o Banjamin bp 10 Mar. 1755. [CH]
Simeon, s/o Benjamin bp 31 Jan. 1762. [CH]

JOLMBERG:
Fred David, s/o Frederick A. & Margaret A. (Kelly) 1st child, born 9 Mar.
1941. [AR]

KALLUM/KELLUM:
Son of John & Mary (Keating) 1st child, born 28 June 1902. [AR]
Son of John & Mary (Keating) 2d child, born 12 Aug. 1905. [AR]

KELLEY:
Abigail, d/o Samuel bp 9 aug. 1761. [CH]

KENNISON:
Sarah, d/o Josiah bp 31 Mar. 1765. [CH]

KEOUS:
Abigail, d/o William bp 5 July 1795. [CH]

KNOWLES:
Betsy, d/o Samuel bp 18 Jan. 1795. [CH]
Brandon Kenneth, s/o Leon M. & Marion (Drake) 3d child, born 11 June 1917.
[AR]
Child of Herbert S. & Edith B. (Rand) born 13 June 1900. [AR]
Clark Woodbury, d/o Levi Woodbury & Estella (Corson) born 19 Aug. 1877. [TR]
Dau. of Levi W. & Emma E. (Courson) born 6 Feb. 1895. [AR]
David, s/o David & Deborah born 23 Aug. 1751. [TR]
David Arthur, s/o Stanley J. & Marion E. (Smith) 4th child, born 25 Mar.
1941. [AR]
Deborah, d/o David & Deborah b. 15 Aug. & bp 4 Oct. 1767. [TR][CH]
Earl Henry, s/o Woodbury & Emma E. (Corson), 8th child, born 14 Nov. 1896.
[TR]
Ella, d/o Samuel J. & Sarah A. born 11 Sep. 1871. [TR]
Ethel Estella, d/o Levi & Emma Estella (Corson) born 14 Feb. 1883. [TR]
Everett, s/o Edward Ev & Cora Ella (Page) born 3 Sep. 1881. [TR]
Ezekial, s/o David & Deborah b. 16 Apr. & bp 23 Apr. 1758. [TR][CH]
Fannie Belle, d/o Edward & Corasella born 6 Feb. 1877. [TR]
Forrest Everett Jr., s/o Forrest E. & Mildred J. (Ewen) 1st child, born 28
Sep. 1938. [AR]
George H., s/o Charles S. & Emily Grace, 1st child, born 4 May 1884. [TR]
Hannah, d/o David & Deborah b. 3 Oct. & bp 15 Nov. 1760. [TR][CH]
Hannah Brown, d/o Simon & Nancy bp 1 June 1823. [CH]
Herbert S., s/o George W. & L. Almira born 9 Oct. 1866. [TR]
Jonathan, ae 2½, s/o Simon & Nancy bp 7 Jan. 1827. [CH]
Joseph, s/o Jonathan bp 14 Oct. 1750. [CH]
Joseph, s/o Jonathan bp 15 Mar. 1757. [CH]
Josiah, s/o Samuel bp 9 Oct. 1796. [CH]
Josiah James, s/o Simon & Nancy bp 20 Nov. 1831. [CH]
Julia Granby, d/o Simon & Nancy bp 27 Dec. 1842. [CH]

KNOWLES Cont.

Lottie Blanche, d/o Levi W. & Cu___va born 11 Aug. 1887. [TR]
Marland D., s/o Herbert B. & Edith B. (Rand), 1st child, born 13 June 1900.
[TR]
Martha Ann, twin d/o Simon & Nancy bp 20 Nov. 1831. [CH]
Mary, d/o Simon & Nancy bp 1 June 1823. [CH]
Minnie Pearl, d/o Levi W. & Emma E. (Courson) born 27 July 1884. [TR]
Nathan, s/o David & Deborah b. 9 Mar. 1779. [TR] bp 11 Mar. 1770. [CH]
Robert Ellsworth, s/o Leon M. & Marion (Drake) 4th child, born 12 May 1919.
[AR]
Ruth Mary, d/o Woodbury & Emma B. (Courson), 7th child, born 6 Mar. 1895.
[AR]
Samuel, s/o Jonathan bp 22 Oct. 1752. [CH]
Samuel. s/o David & Debrah b. 14 May & bp 10 July 1763. [TR][CH]
Samuel, s/o Jonathan Jr. & Marey b. 24 Jan. & bp 2 Feb. 1772. [TR][CH]
Samuel, s/o Simon & Nancy bp 1 June 1823, [CH]
Sarah Abigail, twin d/o Simon & Nancy bp 20 Nov. 1831. [CH]
Simeon, s/o David & Deborah b. 29 Dec. 1754 & bp 9 Feb. 1755. [TR][CH]
Simon, s/o Jonathan bp 22 June 1748. [CH]
Simon, s/o Samuel bp 17 June 1798. [CH]
Son of Dumas J. & Lamarisa?, 1st child, born 15 June 1884. [TR]
Son of Harvey & Almira (Philbrick), 2d child, born 16 July 1886.]TR]
Son of S. Jewell & Sarah A., 4th child, born 15 Dec. 1889. [TR]
Son of Levi W. & Emma G. (Corson), 6th child, born 10 Apr. 1893. [TR][AR]
Son of Levi W. & Emma L. (Corson) 8th child, born 14 Nov. 1896. [AR]
Stanley Wayne, s/o Stanley & Marion (Smith) 1st child, born 10 Sep. 1935.
[AR]

KYSER:

George Justin, s/o Harvey J. & Esther (Drake) 3d child, born 1 Apr. 1922.
[AR]

LAFLAME:

Dau. of Homer G. & Albina (Martineau) 2d child, born 3 Jan. 1932. [AR]

LAMPREY:

Abigail, d/o John bp 23 Apr. 1780. [CH]
Abigail Dearborn, twin d/o Benjamin bp 13 Jan. 1773. [CH]
Anna, d/o Benjamin bp 20 Nov. 1774. [CH]
Austin, s/o David & Clara (Nudd), 1st child, born 28 Nov. 1867. [TR]
Beaty, d/o Benjamin & Abigail born 3 Aug. 1768. [TR] (see Betty)
Benjamin, s/o Benjamin & Abigail b. 28 June & bp 15 July 1762. [TR][CH]
Benning, s/o Mr. of Rye bp 18 Jan. 1795. [CH]
Betty, d/o Benjamin bp 7 Aug. 1768. [CH]
Betty, d/o Simon bp 9 Apr. 1775. [CH]
Charles Austin, s/o Morris & Gertrude (Dow) 1st child, born 20 Sep. 1935.
[AR]

LAMPREY Cont.
Daniel, s/o Benjamin bp 4 Feb. 1759. [CH]
Dau. of Edwin M. & Mary G. (Brown) born 2 Feb. 1873. [TR]
Dau. of Oliver born 11 June 1873. [TR]
Dau. of Edwin M. & Mary S. (Brown) born _____. [TR]
Dau. of Austin & Josephine (Drake) 1st child, born 2 Feb. 1909. [AR]
Dau. of Ernest B. & Anna W. (Severnce) 1st child, born 17 July 1911. [AR]
Elizabeth, d/o Morris Jr. bp 7 Aug. 1768. [CH]
Hannah, d/o Benjamin & Abigail b. 4 May & bp 13 June 1755.]TR][CH]
Hannah, d/o Simon bp 2 Aug. 1772. [CH]
Helen May, d/o Edwin M. & Mary E. born 11 May 1869. [TR]
James, s/o Simon bp 19 Aug. 1770. [CH]
Jesse, s/o Abigail bp 8 Sep. 1754. [CH]
John, twin s/o Benjamin bp 13 Jan. 1773. [CH]
John, s/o John bp 25 June 1775. [CH]
Josephine Ann, d/o D. Morris & Gertrude (Dow) 3d child, born 22 Aug. 1940.
    [AR]
Levi, s/o Benjamin Jr. bp 22 July 1750. [CH]
Levi, s/o Benjamin Jr. & Abigail born 2 July 1752. [TR][CH]
Lucy, d/o Simon bp 22 Mar. 1761. [CH]
Lucy, d/o Simon bp 30 Jan. 1763. [CH]
Molly, d/o Simon bp 18 Oct. 1767. [CH]
Molly, d/o John bp 3 Apr. 1774. [CH]
Morris, s/o Jone bp 16 Aug. 1778. [CH]
Samuel, s/o John bp 14 May 1755. [CH]
Sarah, d/o Benjamin & Abigail b. 3 July & bp 18 Aug. 1754. [TR][CH]
Sarah, d/o Simon bp 2 Dec. 1759. [CH]
Simon, s/o Benjamin bp 12 Aug. 1754. [CH]
Simon, s/o Simon bp 30 June 1755. [CH]
Simon Dearborn, s/o Benjamin & Abigail bp 29 July 1767. [CH]
Son of David & Clara (Nudd) born 10 Dec. 1875. [TR]
Son of Uri A. & Addie J. (Palmer), 6th child, born 22 July 1886. [TR]
Son of Austin & Josephine (Drake) 2d child, born 26 May 1910. [AR]
Son of Harold I. & Josephine (Severence) 1st child, born 2 Feb. 1911. [AR]

LANE:
Charles N. bpt. 2 July 1899. [TR]
Charles Nelson, s/o Uri Abbot (22) & Addia (Palmer) (17) born 28 Nov. 1878.
    [TR]
Dau. of Lewis A.K. & Ida (Tarlton), 3d child, born 22 Dec. 1888. [TR]
Dau. of George W. & Mae E. (Batchelder), 1st child, born 13 Apr. 1896. [TR]
Elizabeth, d/o Simon bp 6 Oct. 1776. [CH]
John, s/o Capt. Thomas bp 27 May 1786. [CH]
Lydia, d/o Simon bp 11 Apr. 1779. [CH]
Marion, d/o Lewis N.H. & Ida Belle (Tarlton), 3d child, born 1 June 1887.
    [TR]
Nelson P., s/o Charles N. (30) & Lillian (Chapman)(26) born 28 June 1878.
    [TR]

LANE Cont.
Ruth, d/o Simon bp 27 Oct. 1771. [CH]
Sarah, d/o Simon bp 11 Jan. 1761. [CH]
Simon, s/o Simon bp 15 Sep. 1765. [CH]
Son of Lewis A.K. & Ida (Tarlton), 1st child, born 19 Feb. 1886. [TR]
Son of Uri A. & Addie J. (Palmer), 6th child born 22 July 1886. [TR]

LANG:
Hannah, d/o John of Effingham bp 16 Feb. 1812. [CH]

LEAVITT:
Abby Elizabeth, d/o James r. & Elizabeth bp 24 Nov. 1850. [CH]
Abigail, d/o Thomas & Mary born 3 Mar. 1781. [TR]
Abigail, d/o Simon bp 8 Apr. 1781. [CH]
Abigail, d/o Thomas bp 28 Apr. 1782. [CH]
Abigail, d/o Jeremiah bp Sep. 1792. [CH]
Abigail gd/o Capt. Benjamin bp 7 Dec. 1817. [CH]
Abigail, d/o Simon 3d bp 1 June 1823. [CH]
Abihal, d/o Moses & Elesebeth born 12 Apr. 1766. [TR]
Abraham, s/o Simon bp 20 feb. 1780. [CH]
Abraham, s/o Abraham & Sarah bp 19 Oct. 1838. [CH]
Alfred Johnson, s/o Samuel Fogg & Anna bp 2 Jan. 1803. [CH]
Anna, d/o Benjamin & Ruth b. 1 Mar. & bp 7 Mar. 1773. [TR][CH]
Anna, d/o Moses & Elesebeth born 14 May 1782 & bp 3 Oct. 1784. [TR][CH]
Anna Sanborn, d/o Carr & Lydia b. 3 Mar. 1798 & bp before July 1798. [TR][CH]
Benjamin, s/o John & Abiel born 27 Aug. 1737. [TR]
Benjamin, ae 13, s/o Capt. Benjamin bp 7 Dec. 1817. [CH]
Benning, s/o Ebenezer bp 1794. [CH]
Betty, d/o Moses & Elesebeth b. 21 Apr. & bp 28 Apr. 1776. [TR][CH]
Carr, s/o John & Abiel b. 2 July & bp 7 July 1751. [TR][CH]
Carr, s/o Banjamin & Ruth b. 26 June & bp 28 June 1778. [TR][CH]
Child of Moses bp 18 July 1743. [CH]
Clarecy, d/o Thomas & Mary born 31 Mar. 1788. [TR]
Daisy Elida, d/o Toppan & Lucinda (Marston) born 20 July 1876. [TR]
Daniel, gs/o Dea. Benjamin (Hobbs) bp 2 Oct. 1785. [CH]
Daniel, s/o Luther & Miriam bp 3 Sep. 1820. [CH]
Dau. of Horace A. & Margaret born 14 Mar. 1873. [TR]
David MacClure, s/o Moses & Elesebeth b. 18 June & bp 22 June 1777. [TR][CH]
Dearborn, s/o Thomas & Marey b. 30 Jan. & bp 31 Jan. 1779. [TR][CH]
Deborah, d/o John & Abiel b. 30 Feb. & bp 25 Mar. 1749. [TR][CH]
Dorothy Abby, d/o James B.? & Elizabeth bp 16 July 1843. [CH]
Dorothy Adeline, d/o Simon & Juliana bp 5 Nov. 1841. [CH]
Dorothy Frances, d/o James R. & Elizabeth bp 31 Dec. 1852. [CH]
Ebenrzer, s/o Benjamin & Ruth b. 25 Sep. 1769. [TR][CH]
Ebenezer, s/o Moses & Elesebeth b. 28 Nov. & bp 2 Dec. 1770. [TR][CH]
Ebenezer, s/o Benjamin & Ruth b. 2 Mar. & bp 10 Mar. 1771. [TR][CH]
Elbridge Augustus, s/o Philip & Dolly bp 17 Aug. 1823. [CH]

LEAVITT Cont.
Elizabeth, d/o John & Elizabeth b. 2 May 1765. [TR][CH]
Elizabeth, d/o John of Leavittstown bp Sep, 1792. [Ch]
Elizabeth Abby, d/o Thomas Cotton & Mary bp 7 Sep. 1834. [CH]
Elizabeth Waterbury, d/o Capt. Simon & Elizabeth bp 24 Feb. 1850. [CH]
Ellsworth Marston, s/o George H. & Clara H. (Rock) 3d child, born 25 Mar. 1920. [AR]
George, s/o George & Elizabeth (Batchelder), 1st child, born 22 Aug. 1869. [TR]
Hannah, d/o Abraham & Sarah bp 24 Nov. 1816. [CH]
Horace, s/o Thomas Cotton & Mary bp 25 Nov. 1837. [CH]
Isabella, d/o Simon & Juliana bp 24 Feb. 1839. [CH]
James Addison, s/o James R. & Juliana bp 18 Nov. 1838. [CH]
[first child bapt. at new meeting house]
James Cornelius, s/o James R. & Elizabeth bp 2 July 1837. [CH]
James Freeman, s/o Orin B. & Mary O. (Drake) born 28 Nov. 1890. [TR]
James Rundlet, s/o Philip & Dolly bp 17 Aug. 1823. [CH]
Jeremiah, s/o John & Abiel b. 12 June & bp 22 June 1755. [TR][CH]
Jeremy, s/o Jeremiah bp Sep. 1792. [CH]
John, s/o John & Abial b. 7 Oct. & bp 18 Oct. 1740. [TR][CH]
John, s/o John Jr. bp 21 Aug. 1763. [CH]
John, s/o Benjamin & Ruth b. 15 May & bp 20 May 1765. [TR][CH]
John, s/o John Jr. & Elizabeth b. 23 Dec. & bp 27 Dec. 1767. [TR][CH]
John, s/o Carr bp 1 Nov. 1778. [CH]
John, s/o Simon bp 19 Jan. 1783. [CH]
John, s/o Thomas & Mary born 26 Mar. 1785. [TR]
John born 26 Mar. 1786. [TR]
John, s/o Jeremiah bp Sep. 1792. [CH]
John an adult bp 7 Dec. 1817. [CH]
John, s/o Elizabeth, wid of John bp 30 Apr. 1822. [CH]
John, s/o Abraham & Sarah bp 19 Oct. 1838. [CH]
John Tilton, s/o Simon & Elizabeth bp 4 Nov. 1853. [CH]
Joseph Stacey, s/o Thomas & Marey b. 2 Mar. & bp 3 Mar. 1771. [TR][CH]
Julia Mianda, d/o Simon 3d & Juliana bp 2 May 1830. [CH]
Laura Jane, d/o Simon & Juliana bp 21 aug. 1836. [CH]
Lavinia, twin d/o Abraham & Sarah bp 24 Nov. 1816. [CH]
Louisa, twin d/o Abraham & Sarah bp 24 Nov. 1816. [CH]
Luamira, d/o Simon 3d & Dolley born 30 Mar. 1823. [TR]
Luther, s/o Benjamin bp 19 May 1799. [CH]
Lyman, s/o Thomas Cotton & Mary bp 9 Apr. 1832. [CH]
Martha Ann, twin d/o James R. & Elizabeth M. bp 4 Dec. 1854. [CH]
Martha Ann Chapman, d/o Simon 3d & Juliana bp 16 Sep. 1827. [CH]
Mary, d/o Sarah bp 31 May 1742. [CH]
Mary, d/o Moses & Sarah b. 4 July & bp 15 July 1744. [TR][CH]
Mary, d/o Moses & Sarah born 5 July 1745. [TR]
Mary, d/o John & Abiel b. 9 Feb. & bp 16 Mar. 1747. [TR][CH]

LEAVITT Cont.

Mary, d/o Moses & Elesebeth b. 2 Mar. 1763 & bp 18 Nov. 1764. [TR][CH]
Mary, d/o Thomas bp 19 Jan. 1770. [CH]
Maey, d/o Thomas & Marey born 26 Apr. & bp 29 Apr. 1776. [TR][CH]
Mary, d/o Carr bp 25 Oct. 1777. [CH]
Mary, d/o John bp 1 Nov. 1778. [CH]
Mary, wid. of James Stacey Leavitt bp 7 June 1818. [CH]
Miriam Dow, d/o Philip & Dolly bp 17 Aug. 1823. [CH]
Molly, gd/o Dea. Benjamin Hobbs bp 2 Oct. 1785. [CH]
Morris, s/o John Jr. bp 20 May 1770. [CH]
Moses, s/o John & Abiel b. 1 Nov. & bp 7 Nov. 1742. [TR][CH]
Moses, s/o Moses & Elesebeth b. 14 Mar. & bp 23 Apr. 1769. [TR][CH]
Moses, s/o John & Elisabeth born 18 May 1770. [TR]
Nathaniel Drake, s/o Elizabeth, wid of John bp 30 Apr. 1822. [CH]
Lever, s/o Joseph & Mary born 21 Dec. 1792. [TR]
Olive Row, d/o Philip & Dolly bp 17 Aug. 1823. [CH]
Orrin Benjamin, s/o James & Elizabeth bp 25 Nov. 1848. [CH]
Paul Chase, twin s/o Norman & Frances (Chase) 2d child, born 1 June 1935.
    [AR]
Payson, s/o Thomas Cotton & Mary bp 11 Apr. 1841. [CH]
Philip, s/o Benjamin Jr. bp Apr. 1791. [CH]
Priscilla Elizabeth, twin d/o Norman & Frances (Chase) 2d child, born 1 June
    1935. [AR]
Raelene Addison, d/o Orin B. & Mary C. Drake born 18 Sep. 1895. [TR][AR]
Rebecca French, d/o Simon & Juliana bp 2 Sep. 1832. [CH]
Rebecca French, d/o Simon & Juliana bp 2 Feb. 1834. [CH]
Richard James, s/o Harold E. & Barbara S. (Horton) 1st child, born 12 June
    1943. [AR]
Rufus, s/o Abraham & Sarah bp 24 Nov. 1816. [CH]
Ruth, d/o Moses & Elesebeth b. 15 July & bp 20 July 1773. [TR][CH]
Sally, d/o Capt. Thomas & Mary b. 12 Feb. & bp 11 Mar. 1792. [TR][CH]
Sally, d/o John & Minerva bp 12 Aug. 1801. [CH]
Samuel Fogg, s/o Thomas & Mary bp 20 Dec. 1767. [CH]
Sarah, d/o Benjamin & Ruth b. 5 Oct. & bp 17 Oct. 1763. [TR][CH]
Sarah, d/o Moses & Elesebeth b. _ Jan. & bp 5 Oct. 1784. [TR][CH]
Sarah, d/o Abraham & Sarah bp 24 Nov. 1816. [CH]
Sarah Abby, d/o Wid. Dolly bp 25 Aug. 1839. [CH]
Sarah Althea, d/o James R. & Elizabeth M. bp 11 Oct. 1857. [CH]
Sarah Drake, d/o Simon 3d & Juliana bp 29 May 1825. [CH]
Sarah Elizabeth, d/o Elizabeth, wid of John bp 30 Apr. 1822. [CH]
Simon, s/o John & Abiel b. 4 June & bp 10 June 1753. [TR][CH]
Simon, s/o John Jr. & Elizabeth b. 27 Dec. & bp 29 Dec. 1771. [TR][CH]
Simon, s/o Elizabeth, wid of John bp 30 Apr. 1822. [CH]
Simon Howard, s/o Simon & Juliana bp 11 Oct. 1846. [CH]
Son of Hart & Mary, 5th child, born 13 June 1874. [TR]
Son of Horace & Mary C. (Dow) born 7 July 1879. [TR]
Son of Orrin B. & Mary D. (Drake) born 28 Nov. 1890. [AR]

LEAVITT Cont.
Son of Horace & Mary E. (Dow) 1st child, born 2 June 1892. [TR][AR]
Son of Fred C. & Fannie P. (Marston) 1st child, born 31 Mar. 1905. [AR]
Tappan, ae 2 s/o Tappan dead bp 13 Sep. 1820. [CH]
Thomas, s/o John & Abiel b. 15 Oct. & bp 21 Oct. 1744. [TR][CH]
Thomas, s/o Thomas & Marey b. 26 Sep. & bp 10 Oct. 1773. [TR][CH]
Thomas, s/o Elizabeth, wid of John bp 30 Apr. 1822. [CH]
Tommy, s/o Samuel Fogg born 7 Mar. 1794. [TR][CH]

LEVEQUE:
Joseph Raymond, s/o Joseph & Leona (Trudeau) 4th child, born 30 July 1919.
   [AR]

LEWIS:
Alfred Bedlow, s/o James & Adelaide C. of Derby, Ct. bp 8 May 1852. [CH]
Anna, d/o John L. BBarroll & Maria (Lewis) born 15 July 1892. [AR]
Dau. of Charles E. & Fannie M. (Brown) born 9 July 1891. [AR]
Son of Edwin & Fanny (Brown), 3d child, born 4 Dec. 1886. [TR]

LIBBY:
Reuben, s/o Reuben bp 4 Aug. 1765. [CH]

LOCKE:
Albert Everett, s/o Morris & Mary E. bp 12 May 1861. [CH]
Almira, d/o Samuel & Mary bp 15 July 1838. [CH]
Ashton Colin, twin s/o James & Edith (Cogswell) born 8 Dec. 1870. [TR]
Cora Belle, twin d/o James & Edith (Cogswell) born 8 Dec. 1870. [TR]
Dau. of Morris H. born 22 Jan. 1873. [TR]
Dau. of Albert E. & Susie A. (Berry) born 29 Aug. 1883. [TR]
Dau. of Walter C. & Elvira G. (Marden), 3d child, born 25 Dec. 1888. [TR]
Dau. of Walter E. & Elvira C. (Marden), 4th child, born 2 Jan. 1892. [TR][AR]
Dau. of Albert F. & Susan A. (Berry), 3d child, born 5 Nov. 1893. [TR][AR]
Dau. of Walter E. & Elvira (Marden), 1st child born 13 Feb. or 15 Mar. 1894.
   [TR][AR]
Dau. of Robert E. & Mary A. (Roberts) born 31 Mar. 1895. [AR]
Ellen Sarah, d/o Morris & Mary E. bp 25 June 1865. [CH]
Emma Elizabeth, d/o Morris & Mary F. bp 8 Sep. 1867. [CH]
John, s/o Samuel & Mary bp 13 Sep. 1826. [CH]
Morris, s/o Samuel & Mary bp 30 Nov. 1828. [CH]
Percy Walton, s/o Walton & Elvira (Marden), 2d child, born 3 July 1882. [TR]
Samuel, s/o Samuel & Mary bp 20 Oct. 1833. [CH]
Sarah Ann, d/o Samuel & Mary bp 29 May 1831. [CH]
Son of Warren & **blank** (Heath), 1st child, born 22 Nov. 1886. [TR]
Son of Albert & Susan (Berry), 2d child, born 20 Aug. 1888. [TR]
Son of Charles W. & Mary L. (Paige), 1st child, born 27 Dec. 1892. [TR][AR]
Warren Ellsworth, s/o Morris & Mary E. bp 24 June 1863. [CH]

LORD:
Samuel, s/o George bp Sep. 1792. [CH]

LOVERING:
Anna, d/o Simon Bearborn bp 25 May 1775. [CH]
Clarissa Ballard, d/o Ebenezer & Clarissa bp 27 June 1824. [CH]
Daniel, s/o John bp 30 Nov. 1777. [CH]
Ebenezer, s/o Ebenezer bp 19 Oct. 1755. [CH]
Ebenzer, s/o John bp 7 Aug. 1786. [CH]
Edwin Otis, s/o Ebenezer & Clarissa bp 10 Dec. 1810. [CH]
Elizabeth, d/o Dr. John bp 8 Nov. 1789. [CH]
Henry Dearborn, s/o Simon bp 24 Feb. 1765. [CH]
Hannah, w/o Thomas bp 17 Nov. 1800. [CH]
John, s/o Ebenezer bp 12 Aug. 1755. [CH]
Joseph Augustus, s/o Ebenezer Jr. & Clarissa bp 1 Aug. 1813. [CH]
Lydia, d/o John bp 26 Apr. 1779. [CH]
Mary, d/o Simon & Anna bp 30 Nov. 1756. [CH]
Mary, d/o Ebenezer bp 12 Feb. 1758. [CH]
Mary Elizabeth, d/o Ebenezer & Clarissa bp 30 Aug. 1818. [CH]
Samuel, s/o Simon Dearborn bp 11 Oct. 1770. [CH]
Sarah, d/o Simon Dearborn bp 16 Oct. 1768. [CH]
Simon, s/o Simon bp 22 Oct. 1775. [CH]
Thomas, s/o Ebenezer bp 6 July 1760. [CH]

LOVITT/LOVETT:
Eleanor Carroll, d/o Roger S. & Lydia M. (Davis) 2d child, born 25 Dec. 1917.
   [AR]
Hazel, d/o Roger S, & Lydia (Davis) 3d child, born 7 Mar. 1922. [AR]
Nancy Louise, d/o Leslie L. & Louise (Lane) 1st child, born 27 Sep. 1921.
   [AR]
Robert Arthur, s/o Arthur R. & Barbara (Cole) 2d child, born 2 Sep. 1928.
   [AR]

LUCK:
Child of Robert & Mary A. (Roberts) born 21 June 1899. [AR]
Dau. of Robert E. & Mary A. (Roberts) born 31 Mar. 1895. [AR]
Dau. of Robert E. & Mary A. (Roberts) 4th child, born 31 May 1896. [TR][AR]
Dau. of Robert E. & Mary A. (Roberts) 5th child , born 18 May 1898. [AR]
Dau. of Robert & Nellie E. (Swim) 1st child, born 14 May 1905. [AR]

LUTHER:
Dau. of Francis J. & Mary (Macternary) 8th child, born 7 Sep. 1907.

MacANDREW:
Dorothy, d/o Ed. & Annie (Gavaghan) 3d child, born 18 Oct. 1922. [AR]

McCLURE:
Abigail, d/o David & Hannah b. 19 Nov. 1781. [TR][CH]
Rachel, d/o David & Hannah b. 29 Oct. & bp 2 Nov. 1785. [TR][CH]

MacKENZIE:
Alexander Frederick, s/o Walter A. & Edith (Littlefield) 4th child, born 17
   June 1940. [AR]
Barbara Margaret, d/o Walter & Edith (Littlefield) 1st child, born 14 Aug.
   1935. [AR]
Irma Sarah, d/o Walter A. & Edith M. (Littlefield) 3d child, born 9 Oct.
   1938. [AR]

McLANE:
Diane May, d/o William T. & Great M. (Storm) 3d child, born 28 Nov. 1943.
   [AR]

McLEAN:
Rita Arlene, d/o John A. & Martha (Simpson) 4th child, born 22 Oct. 1921.
   [AR]

McPHEE:
Son of Angus L. & Mary E. (Houghton) 3d child, born 24 July 1905. [AR]

MACK:
David Emmett, s/o Ernest H. & Katherine C. 1st child, born 25 July 1943. [AR]

MALEY:
Beatrice Sarah, d/o William J. & Sarah A. (MacNeil) 2d child, born 29 Aug.
   1917. [AR]

MARSH:
Stephenie Elizabeth, d/o William S. & Margaret E. (Pease) 1st child, born 31
   Dec. 1937. [AR]

MARSTON:
Abiel. d/o Constable Benjamin Jr. & Mary b. 13 Sep. & bp 22 Sep. 1745.
   [TR][CH]
Abigail, d/o Benjamin & Mary b. 7 June & bp 18 June 1749. [TR][CH]
Abigail, d/o John bp 6 Nov. 1768. [CH]
Abigail, d/o Jonathan bp 12 Apr. 1772. [CH]
Abigail, d/o Lt. Simeon bp 30 Sep. 1792. [CH]
Abigail, d/o Jonathan & Mary born 26 Feb. 1806. [TR]
Abigail, d/o Jeremiah & Abigail bp 22 July 1810. [CH]
Abraham, s/o Reuben & Mary born 10 June 1752. [TR]
Abraham, s/o Thomas bp 8 July 1759. [CH]
Alan Curtis, s/o Curtis D. & Louise (Webb) 1st child, born 25 Aug. 1940. [AR]
Alfred, s/o Dearborn & Sally bp 23 June 1811. [CH]

MARSTON Cont.

Ann, d/o Daniel & Sarah b. 28 Apr. & bp 5 May 1745. [TR][CH]
Anne, d/o Daniel & Anne b. 7 July 1734. [TR]
Anna, d/o Jonathan & Abigail bp 11 Oct. 1767. [CH]
Anna, d/o Simeon bp 27 Mar. 1774. [CH]
Anna, d/o Samuel & Hepzibah born 29 Apr. 1774. [TR]
Anna, d/o Samuel bp 28 Apr. 1776, [CH]
Asa, s/o Simon & Hannah b. 16 Mar. & bp 22 Oct. 1758. [TR][CH]
Bethial, d/o Benjamin & Mary born 9 June 1736. [TR]
Bracket, s/o John Jr. bp 3 Jan. 1748. [CH]
Carol Jean, d/o Norman E. & Gertrude (Durant) 1st. child, born 8 Apr. 1939.
    [AR]
Catherine, d/o Simon bp 19 Aug. 1759. [CH]
Clarence Dennett Jr., s/o Clarence D. & Doris M. (Woodburn) 5th child, born 5
    July 1927. [AR]
Clarissa, d/o Levi & Abigail b. 11 Aug. & bp 12 Aug. 1798. [TR][CH]
Clarissa D., d/o George A. & Carrie A. Drake, 1st child, born 16 Sep. 1898.
Clarissa L., d/o Jonathan & Mary born 15 Apr. 1810. [TR]
    [TR]
Cotton Ward, s/o Isaac bp 6 Aug. 1769. [CH]
Cynthia Locke, d/o Norman O. & Letitia (Mason) 4th child, born 10 May 1939.
    [AR]
Daniel, s/o Daniel & Sarah b. 18 July & bp 26 July 1741. [TR][CH]
Daniel, s/o Samuel & Hepzibah born 15 Sep. 1773. [TR]
Daniel, s/o Benjamin & Sarah bp 9 May 1789. [CH]
Dau. of Harvey D. & Martha A. born 2 Nov. 1867. [TR]
Dau. of Joseph A. & Charlotte D. (Brodine) born 11 Mar. 1872. [TR]
Dau. of Ashey & Lucinda born 4 Oct. 1877. [TR]
Dau. of Joseph A. & Charlotte (Brodine) born 17 Aug. 1879. [TR]
Dau. of James & Emily (Fogg), 2d child, born 17 Mar. 1882. [TR]
David, s/o Daniel & Sarah b. 24 Sep. & bp 9 Oct. 1757. [TR][CH]
David, s/o Isaac bp 28 Feb. 1780. [CH]
David, s/o David & Mary bp 18 Jan. 1784. [CH]
David, s/o Simeon bp 1794. [CH]
David, s/o Jonathan & Mary born 27 Sep. 1794. d.y. [TR]
David, s/o Thomas & Hannah born 20 Mar. 1797. [TR]
David, s/o Jonathan & Mary born 28 Feb. 1814. [TR]
David James, s/o Dearborn & Sally bp 29 May 1831. [CH]
David Knowles, s/o Thomas bp 10 sep. 1797. [CH]
Dearborn, s/o Levi born 3 Oct. 1781. [TR]
Deborah, d/o Benjamin & Esther b. 10 Aug. 1743. [TR][CH]
Deborah, d/o Thomas bp 19 May 1754. [CH]
Deborah, d/o Benjamin bp 20 July 1755. [CH]
Deborah, d/o John bp 12 Aug. 1764. [CH]
Deborah (twin), d/o Thomas & Hannah b. 15 Dec. 1799 & bp before July 1800.
    [TR][CH]
Dolly, d/o Benjamin Sr. bp 12 June 1743. [CH]

MARSTON Cont.

Dolly, d/o Dea. Benjamin Jr. bp 15 July 1746. [CH]
Dorothea, d/o Clarence & Doris (Woodburn) 7th child, born 30 July 1930. [AR]
Dorothy, d/o Benjamin & Mary born 7 May 1742. [TR]
Edward Everett, s/o Thomas E. & Margaret A. born 23 Jan. 1875. [TR]
Ebenezer, s/o Dea. Benjamin & Esther b. 17 Apr. 1745. [TR][CH]
Edwin Otis, s/o Dearborn & Sally bp 1 July 1827. [CH]
Elijah, s/o Benjamin bp 20 May 1753. [CH]
Elizabeth, d/o Thomas bp 15 May 1763. [CH]
Elizabeth, d/o Jonathan & Abigail bp 12 July 1767. [CH]
Elizabeth, d/o Thomas & Hannah born 26 Oct. 1784. [TR]
Elizabeth, d/o Dearborn & Sally bp 15 Aug. 1807. [CH]
Esther, d/o Benjamin Jr. bp 8 May 1757. [CH]
Fannie B., d/o Andrew A. & Nora F. (Mansfield) born 6 Nov. 1895. [TR][AR]
Fanny, d/o Simeon bp 4 Aug. 1799. [CH]
Floyd Franklin, s/o Clarence D. & Doris M. (Woodburn) 9th child, born 25 Mar. 1934. [AR]
Franklin Augustus, s/o Thomas J. & Elizabeth Abby bp 3 July 1851. [CH]
George Wilber, s/o Clarence & Doris (Woodburn), 3d child born 13 Apr. 1924. [AR]
Gloria Elizabeth, d/o Clarence D. & Doris (Woodburn) 1st child, born 14 Apr. 1922. [AR]
Hannah, d/o Winthrop bp 12 Feb. 1746. [CH]
Hannah, d/o Jonathan & Sarah b. 14 Aug. & bp 14 Aug. 1748. [TR][CH]
Hannah, d/o Simon bp 28 Mar. 1762. [CH]
Hannah, d/o Josiah & Hannah born 29 Aug. 1762. [TR]
Hannah, d/o Samuel & Hepzibah born 31 June 1768. [TR]
Hannah, d/o Thomas & Hannah born 11 Apr. 1788. [TR]
Henry Smith, s/o Dearborn & Sally bp 30 Mar. 1828. [CH]
Hepsibah, d/o Winthrop bp 22 May 1748. [CH]
Hermon Laroi, s/o Thomas F. & Eliz. A. bp 3 Sep. 1857. [CH]
Isaac, s/o Isaac & Mary bp 1 Mar. 1767. [CH]
Isodora Leota, d/o Sheldon & Georgia (Garland) 3d child, born 8 May 1919. [AR]
James,s /o Josiah & Hannah born 19 Jan. 1766. [TR]
James, s/o John bp 10 July 1768. [CH]
James L., s/o George Albert & Carrie A. born 23 Jan. 1900. [TR]
Jane, d/o Constable Benjamin Jr. & Mary b. 13 Sep. & bp 22 Sep. 1745. [TR][CH]
Jean, d/o Reuben & Mary born 17 Mar. 1749. [TR]
Jeremiah, s/o Thomas Jr. bp 7 Jan. 1753. [CH]
John, s/o John Jr. & Susanna bp 20 Jan. 1740. [CH]
John, s/o Daniel bp 19 Aug. 1753. [CH]
John, s/o Reuben of Nottingham bp 10 July 1757. [CH]
John, s/o Paul bp 10 Feb. 1771. [CH]
John Day, s/o Levi & Sarah bp 5 Nov. 1847. [CH]

MARSTON Cont.

John Leavitt, s/o John bp 31 Dec. 1760. [CH]

Jonathan, s/o David bp 19 Feb. 1769. [CH]

Jonathan, s/o Jonathan bp 29 sep. 1776. [CH]

Joseph, s/o Jonathan bp 17 July 1774. [CH]

Joseph Stacy, s/o Jonathan & Mary born 23 Sep. 1803. [TR]

Judith Anna, d/o Clarence D. & Doris (Woodburn) 13th child, born 19 Dec. 1940. [AR]

Katherine, d/o Simon & Hannah born 14 Aug. 1759. [TR]

Lavina, d/o Jeremiah & Abigail bp 6 Aug. 1809. [CH]

Leadey, d/o Jonathan & Mary born 11 Mar. 1793. [TR]

Levi, s/o Jeremy bp 2 Sep. 1781. [CH]

Levi, s/o Dearborn & Sally bp 4 June 1809. [CH]

Lizza, d/o Thomas Jr. bp 15 Apr. 1785. [CH]

Lucille, d/o Clarence D. & Doris M. (Woodburn) 4th child, born 11 Nov. 1925. [AR]

Lydia, d/o Jonathan born 11 Mar. 1795. [TR]

Lydia, an adult bp 7 Dec. 1817. [CH]

Lydia, d/o Jonathan & Mary born 11 Mar. 1793. [TR]

Martha, d/o Benjamin Jr. bp 7 Mar. 1747. [CH]

Mary, d/o Benjamin & Mary b. 13 June & bp 1739. [TR][CH]

Mary, d/o Jonathan & Sarah b. 2 Nov. & bp 8 Nov. 1745. [TR][CH]

Mary, d/o Josiah & Hannah born 31 Mar. 1758. [TR]

Mary, d/o Simon bp 10 Mar. 1765. [CH]

Mary, d/o John Jr. bp 26 Nov. 1769. [CH]

Mary, d/o Thomas & Hannah b. 31 Jan. & bp 3 June 1790. [TR][CH]

Mary, d/o Levi & Abigail b. 6 Apr. & bp 14 Apr. 1801. [TR][CH]

Mary, d/o Jonathan & Mary born 27 Feb. 1802. [TR]

Mary Appleton, d/o Levi bp 1842. [CH]

Mary Chapman, d/o Dearborn & Sally bp 22 Sep. 1816. [CH]

Mehitabel, gd/o Dea. Thomas & Deborah bp 1739. [CH]

Mehitable, d/o Benjamin & Mehitable born 17 Mar. 1739. [TR]

Miriam, d/o Daniel & Sarah b. 29 July 1749. [TR][CH]

Molly Wedgwood, d/o Samuel & Hepzibah b. 4 July 1764 & bp 10 Mar. 1765. [TR][CH]

Nabby, d/o Levi b. 18 Apr. & bp 15 May 1786. [TR][CH]

Nathaniel Batchelder, s/o Dearborn & Sally bp 1 July 1827. [CH]

Nellie, d/o Joseph A. & Charlotte E. (Brodine) born 24 Mar. 1881. [TR]

Norman Edward, s/o Edward J. & Addie (Burleigh) 2d child, born 31 Aug. 1918. [AR]

Norman E. Jr., s/o Norman E. & Gertrude M. (Durant) 2d child, born 1 may 1943. [AR]

Patience, d/o John bp 18 Mar. 1753. [CH]

Patience, d/o John bp 3 Jan. 1762. [CH]

Paul Stuart, s/o Curtis D. & Louise (Webb) 2d child, born 5 Jan. 1943. [AR]

Ralph Wayne, s/o Clarence D. & Doris M. (Woodburn) 12th child, born 28 Sep. 1938. [AR]

MARSTON Cont.
Rebecca Plummer, d/o Levi & Sarah A. bp 23 Apr. 1840. [CH]
Reuben, s/o Reuben & Mary born 19 Apr. 1746. [TR]
Robert, s/o Robert bp 26 July 1765. [CH]
Robie, s/o Daniel bp 2 Aug. 1747. [CH]
Sally, d/o Samuel bp 26 May 1765. [CH]
Sally (twin), d/o Thomas & Hannah b. 15 Dec. 1799 & bp before July 1800.
   [TR][CH]
Sally Eveline, d/o Dearborn & Sally bp 1 July 1827. [CH]
Samuel, s/o Daniel & Anne born 17 Jan. 1739. [TR]
Samuel, s/o Daniel bp 27 Mar. 1743. [CH]
Samuel, s/o Winthrop & Martha b. 19 Oct. & bp 23 Oct. 1743. [TR][CH]
Samuel, s/o Daniel & Sarah born 10 Mar. 1748. [TR]
Samuel, s/o Josiah & Hannah born 7 Oct. 1760. [TR]
Samuel, s/o Simeon bp 10 sep. 1780. [CH]
Sandra Mae, d/o Richard E. & Arelene E. (Inglis) 1st child, born 15 Sep.
   1943. [AR]
Sarah, d/o Benjamin & Mary born 23 June 1734. [TR]
Sarah, d/o Reuben & Mary b. 14 Oct. & bp 8 Nov. 1747. [TR][CH]
Sarah, d/o Daniel& Sarah b. 15 Aug. & bp 5 Oct. 1752. [TR][CH]
Sarah, d/o John bp 12 Feb. 1758. [CH]
Sarah, d/o Samuel & Hepzibah born 17 May 1765. [TR]
Sarah, d/o Simon bp 10 Jan. 1768. [CH]
Sarah, d/o John Jr. bp 28 Feb. 1773. [CH]
Sherburne, s/o Simon bp 24 May 1812. [CH]
Shirley Ann, d/o Clarence & Doris (Woodburn) 10th child, born 30 Sep. 1935.
   [AR]
Shubal, d/o John bp 2 May 1779. [CH]
Simeon, s/o John Jr. bp 22 Jan. 1755. [CH]
Simon, s/o Daniel & Sarah born 3 Feb. 1737. [TR]
Simon, s/o Isaac bp 14 Mar. 1773. [CH]
Simon, s/o Simon bp 24 Sep. 1775. [CH]
Son of James & Emily (Fogg), 1st child, born 3 Mar. 1864. [TR]
Son of James & Emily (Fogg), 2d child, born 28 Mar. 1866. [TR]
Son of James & Emily (Fogg), 3d child, born 5 July 1868. [TR]
Son of George & Ella, 1st child, born 7 Jan. 1874. [TR]
Son of Joseph A. & Charlotte born 26 Feb. 1877. [TR]
Son of Harry & Martha, 4th child, born 21 Jan. 1878. [TR]
Son of Harvey & Martha (Dow) born 3 Sep. 1883. [TR]
Son of George A. & Carrie A. (Drake) 1st child, born 16 Sep. 1898. [AR]
Son of George A. & Carrie A. (Drake) 3d child, born 12 Sep. 1902. [AR]
Son of Herman L. & Fannie A. (Rollins) 1st child, born 13 June 1903. [AR]
Son of George A. & Carrie A. (Drake) 4th child, born 16 June 1904. [AR]
Son of Irving W. & Bertha E. (Fogg) 1st child, born 8 Oct. 1905. [AR]
Son of Harry C. & Mabel J. (Dearborn) 1st child, born 23 Apr. 1914. [AR]
Son of Clarence & Doris (Woodburn) 8th child, born 28 Mar. 1932. [AR]
Sophia Elizabeth, d/o Thomas F. & Elizabeth A. bp 3 May 1860. [CH]

MARSTON Cont.

Stephen, s/o Reuben Sr. & Mary b. 1 Mar. & bp 24 Mar. 1751. [TR][CH]
Tabitha, d/o Simeon bp 19 Jan. 1783. [CH]
Theodore, s/o Daniel & Sarah b, 8 Sep. & bp 12 Oct. 1755. [TR][CH]
Thomas, s/o Thomas bp 21 Nov. 1756. [CH]
Thomas, s/o Jeremy bp 2 Sep. 1781. [CH]
Thomas, s/o Thomas & Hannah born 31 Mar. 1793. [TR]
Thomas Leavitt, s/o Jonathan & Mary born 24 Apr. 1797. [TR]
Walter Stanley, s/o Clarence D. & Doris (Woodburn) 6th child, born 8 Feb.
  1929. [AR]
Wise, s/o Simeon bp 2 May 1790. [CH]

MASON:

Benjamin, s/o Benjamin & Margeat b. 22 Mar. & bp 5 Apr. 1772. [TR][CH]
Billy Marshall, s/o Benjamin bp 27 Nov. 1785. [CH]
Dau. of J. Everett & Effie M. (Thompson) 6th child, born 23 Aug. 1912. [AR]
Dau. of J. Everett & Effie (Thompson) born 12 June 1916. [AR]
Edward, s/o Benjamin bp 13 Apr. 1783. [CH]
Love, d/o Banjamin & Margret b. 21 Jan. & bp 13 Mar. 1774. [TR][CH]
Samuel. s/o Benjamin & Margret b. 8 Sep. & bp 29 Sep. 1776. [TR][CH]
Son of J. Everett & Effie M. (Thompson) 2d child, born 4 Sep. 1906. [AR]
Son of Everett & Effie M. (Thompson) 4th child, born 18 Aug. 1909. [AR]
Son of J. Everett & Effie (Thompson) 5th child, born 21 Mar. 1911. [AR]
William Marshall, s/o Benjamin & Mary born 25 Nov. 1789. [TR]

MAXFIELD:

Eliphalet, s/o Eliphalet & Elizabeth born 4 Aug. 1744. [CH1]

MEADE:

Betty, d/o Benjamin & Sarah bp 29 Mar. 1767. [CH]
Francis Boardman, s/o John B. & Sarah bp 14 Oct. 1827. [CH]
John, s/o Benjamin of Newmarket bp 26 Apr. 1772. [CH]
Lucy Ann, d/o John B. & Sarah bp date missing. [CH]
Lucy Dearborn, d/o Benjamin of Newmarket bp 30 Sep. 1770. [CH]
Mary, d/o Benjamin of Newmarket bp 5 Oct. 1777. [CH]
Mary Eliza Mehitabel, d/o John B. & Sarah bp date missing. [CH]
Nanny, d/o Benjamin bp 2 Oct. 1768. [CH]
Nathaniel Blanchard, s/o John B. & Sarah bp 21 Sep. 1823. [CH]

MERCHANT:

Alice Louise, d/o Harold & Alice B. (Irving) 3d child, born 13 Apr. 1924.
  [AR]
Harold Oscar, s/o Harold & Alice B. (Irving) 2d child, born 5 Apr. 1923. [AR]
Mildred Eleanor, d/o Harold & Alice (Irving) 1st child, born 10 Feb. 1921.
  [AR]

MERRILL:

Affi, d/o James & Mary born 30 Oct. 1744. [CH1]
Benjamon, s/o Nathaniel & Hannah born 26 June 1744. [CH1]
James, s/o James & Mary born 16 Aug. 1745. [CH1]
Joseph, s/o Eliphalet & Mary born 4 May 1745. [CH1]

MEVIS:

Dau. of Martin F. & Mary K. (Adams) 2d child, born 22 June 1907. [AR]
Son of Martin F. & Mary K. (Adams) 3d child, born 6 Apr. 1909. [AR]

MOORE:

Arnold Leroy, s/o Melvin D. & Dorothy L. (Wilson) 1st child, born 10 Jan.
    1928. [AR]
Dau. of Edgar & Allis, 2d child, born 21 Nov. 1875. [TR]
Dau. of Edgar & Abba (Page) born 7 Sep. 1879. [TR]
Dau. of Edgar & Abbie (Page), 5th child, born 20 Nov. 1889. [TR]
Eleanor Irene, d/o George A. & Sarah (Bennett) 1st child, born 30 Sep. 1918.
    [AR]
Son of Edgar & Abbie, 1st child, born 25 Mar. 1874. [TR]
Son of Edgar & Abbie born 7 July 1878. [TR]
Son of Fred J. & Mary (Dow) born 12 Mar. 1880. [TR]
Son of Fred J. & Mary D. (Dow) born 10 Jan. 1895. [AR]
Son of Edgar & Abba (Page), 5th child, born 7 Apr. 1882. [TR]
Thomas S., s/o Edgar & Abbie (Page) born 5 May 1884. [TR]

MORGAN:

James, s/o Abigail Morgan, now Potter bp 17 July 1748. [CH]

MORRILL:

Abigail, d/o Abner & Lydia born 25 Feb. 1745. [CH1]
Abraham Leavitt, s/o Edmund & Abigail of Salisbury, Mass.bp 1 Sep. 1861. [CH]
Adam, s/o Joseph & Sarah born 2 July 1745. [CH1]
Ephraim, s/o Paul & Martha born 4 Sep. 1745. [CH1]
Mary Abby, d/o Edward & Abigail of Salisbury, Mass. bp 10 Sep. 1858. [CH]
Nathaniel, s/o Nathaniel & Elizabeth born 5 Apr. 1745. [CH1]

MORRISON:

Child of David A. & Lena B. (Shaw) born 22 Aug. 1899. [AR]

MORSE:

Sarah, d/o Jacob & Abigail born 21 Jan. 1744. [CH1]

MOULTON:

Abner, s/o Samuel bp 20 Nov. 1774. [CH]
Benjamin, s/o Thomas bp 29 Oct. 1754. [CH]
Bettina W., d/o Gilmas & Luella (Brown) born 9 Dec. 1883. [TR]
Betty, d/o Joseph, bp 9 Oct. 1795. [CH]

MOULTON Cont.

Charles William, s/o Charles T. & Josephine (Ross) 1st child, born 24 July 1921. [AR]
Child of William bp late 1798 or early 1799. [CH]
Child of Gilman, 2d child, born 14 Sep. 1886. [TR]
Child of George A. & Mary P. (Otis) born 1 Feb. 1899. [AR]
Cora Jane, d/o John & Eliza A. bp 27 Aug. 1854. [CH]
Daniel, s/o Samuel Jr. bp 15 Aug. 1779. [CH]
Daniel Nudd, s/o Joseph & Betsy bp 25 Jan. 1795. [CH]
Dau. of Robert bp 12 July 1772. [CH]
Dau. of Oliver & Lizzie (Sleeper), 1st child, born 13 Apr. 1895. [TR]
Dau. of Warren B. & Elvira B. (Briggs) 2d child, born 9 Aug. 1897. [AR]
Dau. of Orice J. & Jessie H. (Marston) 1st child, born 28 Nov. 1902. [AR]
Dau. of George E. & Mary F. (Otis) 8th child, born 8 Dec. 1904. [AR]
Dau. of J. Burt & Sarah L. (Wiggin) 1st child, born 5 Feb. 1907. [AR]
Dau. of Russell D. & Edith S. (Coffin) 1st child, born 29 Oct. 1911. [AR]
Dau. of Erwin B. & Maud A. (Dalton) 2d child, born 20 Nov. 1912. [AR]
David, s/o Thomas bp 19 Dec. 1762. [CH]
David, s/o Samuel Jr. bp 22 June 1777. [CH]
Dearborn, s/o Levi bp 30 May 1783. [CH]
Deborah, d/o William Jr. bp 6 Nov. 1757. [CH]
Elizabeth, d/o Samuel Jr. bp 6 Jan. 1771. [CH]
Ernest J., s/o Gilman H. & Luella (Brown), 3d child, born 28 Jan. 1886. [TR]
George Otis, s/o Reuben L. & Mary C. bp 1 July 1853. [CH]
Job bp 20 July 1746. [CH]
John, s/o Samuel bp 30 Sep. 1781. [CH]
John Mobs, s/o Thomas bp 15 Feb. 1756. [CH]
Jonathan, s/o Robert bp 19 Mar. 1769. [CH]
Jonathan Dearborn, s/o Reuben L. & Mary O. bp 2 May 1851. [CH]
Joseph, s/o Thomas, bp 29 Oct. 1754. [CH]
Joseph, s/o Joseph Jr. bp 13 Mar. 1774. [CH]
Joseph, s/o Joseph Jr. bp 19 Mar. 1803. [CH]
Joseph, s/o Jonathan & Olive bp 3 July 1814. [CH]
Josiah, s/o William Jr. bp 20 Jan. 1760. [CH]
Juldah, d/o William & Mary bp 12 Aug. 1801. [CH]
Martha, d/o Joseph bp 11 Apr. 1779. [CH]
May R. d/o William E. & Clara Anne (Rumery) born 1 May 1887. [TR]
Nathaniel, s/o Thomas bp 20 Sep. 1759. [CH]
Newhall, s/o Joseph Jr. & Elizabeth bp 12 Aug. 1801. [CH
Reuben Lamprey, s/o Jonathan bp 23 Mar. 1816. [CH]
Russell, s/o Gilman & Luella (Brown) born 7 Jan. 1890. [TR]
Sally, d/o N.G. bp 24 Nov. 1799. [CH]
Sarah, d/o Robert & Sarah bp 10 May 1767. [CH]
Sarah Adeline, d/o Reuben & Mary G. bp 26 Apr. 1846. [CH]
Simon, s/o Samuel Jr. bp 14 Mar. 1773. [CH]
Son of William & Anna born 1 Apr. 1878. [TR]
Son of Fremont & Annie (Brown), 1st child, born 19 Sep. 1882. [TR]

MOULTON Cont.
Son of Oliver d. & Emily J., 1st child, born 6 Apr. 1884. [TR]
Son of Justin C. & Katie R. (Cummins), 3d child, born 10 Feb. 1888. [TR]
Son of Warren & Elma B. (Briggs) 1st child, born 28 June 1892. [TR][AR]
Son of John B. & Elizabeth A. (Godfrey) 1st child, born 22 Nov. 1897. [AR]
Son of Gilman H. & Luelle (Brown) 4th child, born 28 May 1901. [AR]
Son of George E. & Mary (Fotes) 7th child, born 11 Feb. 1902. [AR]
Son of Warren B. & Elvira B. (Briggs) 3d child, born 25 June 1910. [AR]
Son of Erwin B. & Maud A. (Dalton) 1st child, born 27 Oct. 1910. [AR]
Steven Aaron, s/o Gilman M. & Veronica (Metrick) 2d child, born 20 Apr. 1943.
    [AR]
William, s/o William Jr. bp 22 May 1763. [CH]

MURDO: Murdough
Abigail, d/o Nathan bp 5 Nov. 1758. [CH]
Dorothy, d/o Nathan bp 10 May 1760. [CH]
Mary, d/o Nathan bp 5 June 1763. [CH]

MYERS:
Nancy bp 11 Sep. 1790. [CH]

NARY:
Charles M., s/o James W. & Georgette M., 1st child, born 16 Nov. 1884. [TR]

NEAL:
Deborah, d/o Ebenezer bp 10 Jan. 1768. [CH]
Levi, d/o Ebenezer bp 16 Sep. 1770. [CH]
Moses, s/o John & Mary born 19 Apr. 1766. [TR]
Olly, d/o Ebenezer bp 16 Jan. 1774. [CH]
Sophia, d/o Walter & Rachel b. 1 Aug. & bp 1 Sep. 1780. [TR][CH]

NEALLY/NEALLEY:
Dau. of Fred H. & Edith (Hally) 2d child, born 12 July 1902. [AR]
Dau. of F.H. & Edith M. (Halley) 3d child, born 5 Dec. 1903. [AR]

NORTON:
Child of Frank C. & Abbie (Breed) born 6 Feb. 1900. [AR]
Clarissa Perkins, d/o Joshua & Phebe J, born 8 Mar. 1869. [TR]
Clinton B., s/o Frank C. & Abbie F. (Breed) born 13 May 1890. [TR][AR]
Dau. of George & Ella, 2d child, born 5 Apr. 1876. [TR]
Dau. of Frank C. & Abbie F. (Breed) born 9 July 1895. [TR][AR]
James L., s/o Frank C. & Abbie F., 1st child, born 11 June 1892. [TR][AR]
Mabel Elizabeth, d/o Herman L. & Mary E. (Young) 1st child, born 28 aug.
    1918. [AR]
Nelson, s/o Joshua J. & Phebe A. (Perkins) born 18 Aug. 1870. [TR]
Ralph Ashton, s/o Nelson J. & Mary C. (Knowles) born 12 Oct. 1890. [TR]
Son of Nelson J. & May E. (Knowles) born 22 Oct. 1890. [AR][AR]

NORTON Cont.

Son of Frank C. & Abbie A. (Breed), 3d child, born 29 May 1893. [TR][AR]
Son of Nelson & Mae E. (Knowles) 2d child, born 20 June 1893. [TR]
Stillborn s/o Joshua J. & Phebe Ann (Perkins) born 25 Dec. 1871. [TR]

NUDD:

Abigail, d/o John bp 4 Apr. 1773. [CH]
Anna, d/o John bp 5 Sep. 1775. [CH]
Betty, d/o John & Ruth bp 22 Feb. 1767. [CH]
Deborah, d/o John bp 15 June 1777. [CH]
Edward, s/o John bp 1 July 1764. [CH]
Eliza, d/o David & Sarah bp 1 Jan. 1804. [CH]
Hannah, d/o John bp 19 Mar. 1769. [CH]
John, s/o James bp 15 May 1768. [CH]
Jonathan, s/o James bp 27 May 1770. [CH]
Levi, s/o James bp 1 Nov. 1772. [CH]
Lydia, d/o David bp 1794. [CH]
Mary, reputed d/o Nancy Nudd & Ebenezer Sanborn bp 1 Aug. 1808. [CH]
Mary Ann, d/o David & Sarah bp 3 May 1805. [CH]
Molly, d/o John bp 11 Nov. 1764. [CH]
Olivia, d/o John bp 21 May 1780. [CH]
Ruth, d/o David bp 21 May 1797. [CH]
Sarah, d/o John bp 31 Mar. 1771. [CH]
Sarah Smith, d/o David & Sarah bp before Aug. 1821. [CH]

ODELL:

Dau. of Joseph W. & Martha E. (Daniels) born 3 Feb. 1871. [TR]

O'SHEA:

Son of John & Elizabeth (O'Donnell) 2d child, born 21 June 1915. [AR]

OLESON:

Charles Harold, s/o Simon & Mary (Bohman) 2d child, born 11 Dec. 1919. [AR]

ORLANDINI:

Son of Vittorio & Mary F. (Johnson) 1st child, born 8 Aug. 1907. [AR]

PAGE:

Abigail, d/o Jeremy Jr. bp 2 Dec. 1770. [CH]
Abigail, d/o Joseph of Nottingham bp 9 June 1771. [CH]
Abigail, d/o David Jr. & Bethiel b. 17 Apr. bp 16 June 1771. [TR][CH]
Anna, d/o Daniel bp 25 Mar. 1770. [CH]
Anna, d/o D____d Jr. bp 1 June 1777. [CH]
Benjamin, s/o David Jr. & Bethiel b. 25 June & bp 21 Dec. 1758. [TR][CH]
Benjamin, s/o Coffin bp Sep. 1792. [CH]
Betty, d/o John bp 29 Oct. 1791. [CH]
Betty, d/o Wid. Betty bp 17 Feb. 1803. [CH]

PAGE Cont.

Beulah, d/o James B. & Florabel born 21 Jan. 1899. [TR]

Charles Stephens, s/o George William & Ellen Maria born 11 Jan. 1867. [TR]

Child of Coffin bp May 1791. [CH]

Child of James & Isabell (Hurd), 4th child, born 14 June 1886. [TR]

Child of James B. & Florabel (Hurd) 6th child, born 27 July 1897. [AR]

Child of James B. & Florabel (Hurd) born 21 Jan. 1899. [AR]

Child of James B. & Florabel (Hurd) born 14 Mar. 1900. [AR]

Christopher, s/o David Jr. & Bethiel b. 16 Sep. & bp 18 Sep. 1768. [TR][CH]

Dau. of James B. & Flora B. (Hurd) born 26 May 1891. [AR]

David, s/o Joseph Jr. bp 18 Nov. 1753. [CH]

David, s/o John bp 29 May 1757. [CH]

David, s/o David bp 20 Nov. 1774. [CH]

David Joseph, s/o Joseph Jr. bp 1 Sep. 1751. [CH]

Deborah, d/o David Jr. & Bethiel b. 18 June & bp 19 June 1763. [TR][CH]

Dolly, d/o Joseph of Northwood bp 5 June 1774. [CH]

Dudley, s/o Stephen bp 21 Feb. 1762. [CH]

Elijah, s/o Elijah & Meribah born 27 June 1745. [TR]

Eliza, w/o Stephen bp 5 May 1839. [CH]

George Edwin, s/o Edwin A. & Ola M. (Frost) 1st child, born 28 Mar. 1925. [AR]

Hannah, d/o Elisha & Meribah born 8 Oct. 1740. [TR]

Hannah, d/o Nathaniel bp 11 June 1769. [CH]

James, s/o Jeremy Jr. bp 23 Aug. 1772. [CH]

Jonah, s/o Elisha & Meribah born 27 June 1742. [TR]

Josiah, s/o David bp 5 Feb. 1749. [CH]

Josiah, s/o John bp 29 Oct. 1791. [CH]

Katherine Mary, d/o Leslie H. & K. (McDonough) 1st child, born 3 Dec. 1918. [AR]

Leslie Hurd, s/o James A. & Florabel (Hurd) born 27 July 1897. [TR]

Levi, s/o Elijah & Meribah born 17 Oct. 1747. [TR]

Lucy, d/o Francis bp 19 Apr. 1772. [CH]

Lydia, d/o Jeremiah bp 16 June 1751. [CH]

Mary, d/o David Jr. & Bethiel b. 16 Aug. & bp 31 Aug. 1760. [TR][CH]

Mary, Jonathan Jr. bp 21 Feb. 1762. [CH]

Mary, d/o Joseph bp 11 June 1769. [CH]

Mehitabel, d/o Simon bp 10 Dec. 1758. [CH]

Mehitabel, d/o Stephen bp 13 Dec. 1761. [CH]

Molly, d/o Nathaniel bp 29 Aug. 1773. [CH]

Odion, s/o Stephen bp 31 Mar. 1771. [CH]

Phebe, d/o Joseph bp 1 Mar. 1761. [CH]

Redman, s/o Coffin bp 12 Sep. 1784. [CH]

Reuben, s/o Christopher bp 7 Jan. 1770. [CH]

Reuben, s/o Nathaniel bp 15 Sep. 1771. [CH]

Ruth, d/o Robert bp 7 Nov. 1756. [CH]

Ruth, d/o David & Bethiel born 10 Mar. 1766. [TR]

Sarah, d/o Jonathan bp 24 Mar. 1747. [CH]

PAGE Cont.

Sarah, d/o Jonathan Jr. bp 12 June 1757. [CH]
Sarah, d/o Joseph bp 27 Aug. 1758. [CH]
Sarah, d/o Jonathan bp 17 Feb. 1765. [CH]
Sarah, d/o Jeremy Jr. bp 2 Dec. 1770. [CH]
Sarah, d/o David bp 29 May 1780. [CH]
Sarah, d/o Shubel bp 8 Feb. 1789. [CH]
Simon, s/o Jonathan born 15 June 1731. [CH]
Simon, s/o Soloman bp 11 May 1740. [CH]
Simon, s/o Jeremiah bp 2 June 1754. [CH]
Simon, s/o Stephen bp 6 Sep. 1762. [CH]
Son of William A. born 6 Dec. 1873. [TR]
Son of William, 3d child, born 7 Jan. 1875. [TR]
Son of James & Isabell (Hurd), 3d child, born 24 July 1884. [TR]
Susan, d/o John & Betsy bp 1 July 1827. [CH]
Susannah, d/o Joseph bp 4 Sep. 1763. [CH]
Tabitha, d/o Joseph bp 23 May 1756. [CH]
Taylor, s/o Simeon bp 12 June 1757. [CH]

PAIRE:

Newell Joseph Jr., s/o Newell J. Dorothy (Schurman) 1st child, born 18 Jan.
    1940. [AR]

PALMER:

Comfort, twin d/o Joseph & Lidy b. 19 Aug. & bp 26 Aug. 1770. [TR][CH]
David, twin s/o Joseph bp 26 Aug. 1770. [CH]
Debrah, d/o William & Hannah born 1 Oct. 1729. [TR]
Hannah, d/o Joseph & Lidy born 2 Feb. 1765. [TR]
Jeremiah, s/o Joseph & Lidy b. 7 May & bp 12 Oct. 1760. [TR][CH]
Jonathan, s/o Joseph & Lidy b. 10 Sep. & bp 1 Nov. 1772. [TR][CH]
Joseph, s/o William & Hannah born 1737. [TR]
Joseph, s/o Joseph & Lydia b. 15 Jan. & bp 29 Mar. 1767. [TR][CH]
Molly, d/o Joseph & Lidy b. 4 Sep. & bp 11 Oct. 1761. [TR][CH]
Simon, s/o Joseph & Lidy b. 10 Nov. 1768 & bp 15 Jan. 1769. [TR][CH]
William, s/o Joseph & Lidy b. 9 Oct. 1758 & bp 12 Oct. 1760. [TR][CH]
Zadok Sanborn, s/o Joseph & Lidy b. 31 July & bp 11 Sep. 1763. [TR][CH]

PARKER:

Charles David, s/o William E. & Mary E. (Hobbs) 1st child, born 20 Mar.
    1940. [AR]
Janet E., d/o William E. & Mary E. (Hobbs) 2d child, born 19 Dec. 1941. [AR]

PARSHLEY:

Dau. of Walter S. & Lu. E. (Marston) 1st child, born 12 Nov. 1911. [AR]
Dau. of Walter T. & Lou (Marston) 2d child, born 8 June 1913. [AR]

PARSON:
Sarah, d/o Rev. William & Sarah born 28 Mar. 1744. [CH1]
William, s/o Rev. William & Sarah born 1 Apr. 1745. [CH1]

PEARL:
Son of Ernest J. & Alice M. (Sanborn) 2d child, born 21 June 1915. [AR]

PEARSON:
Charles Albert, s/o Albert C. & Alice (Bellows) 2d child, born 13 Sep. 1934.
[AR]
Mary Anna, d/o Albert C. & Alice M. (Bellows) 1st child, born 7 June 1933.
[AR]
Robert Arthur, s/o Albert C. & Alice M. (Bellows) 3d child, born 3 Sep. 1936.
[AR]

PENMAN:
David Foster, s/o Ether & Bertha (Allen) 3d child, born 5 Aug. 1935. [AR]

PERKINS:
Alice, twin d/o Joseph bp 18 May 1771. [CH]
Bradley Arnold, s/o Edward A. & Judith (Drew) 2d child, born 8 May 1926. [AR]
James, twin s/o Joseph bp 3 Mar. 1768. [CH]
John, s/o Benjamin & Abigail bp 10 May 1767. [CH]
Joseph, twin s/o Joseph bp 18 May 1771. [CH]
Mary, twin d/o Joseph bp 3 Mar. 1768. [CH]
Mary, d/o Joseph bp 30 Apr. 1769. [CH]
Son of George S. & Edith G. (Bachelder) born 27 Apr. 1891. [AR]
Son of George E. & Edith G. (Batchelder), 5th child, born 8 Nov. 1892.
[TR][AR]
Son of George B. & Edith G. (Batchelder), 5th child, born 27 Jan. 1896.
[TR][AR]
Son of Percy & Grace (Rumford) 1st child, born 4 Apr. 1914. [AR]
Susan, d/o George E. & Edith (Batchelder), 6th child, born 8 Nov. 1884. [TR]
William, s/o Benjamin bp 16 Apr. 1769. [CH]

PEVEAR:
Norma Ruth, d/o Eben R. & Gladys A. (Hurlburt) 2d child, born 25 June 1930.
[AR]

PHILBRICK:
Anna Sarah, d/o Jonathan & Clarissa A. bp 2 May 1851. [CH]
Benjamin, s/o Josiah & Mary bp 17 June 1804. [CH]
Catherine Elizabeth, d/o Thomas & Margaret S. (Page) born 2 Jan. 1872. [TR]
Child of Charles W. & Sarah A. (Taylor) born 3 Dec. 1899. [AR]
Clara Nudd, d/o Jonathan & Clarissa bp 13 July 1860. [CH]
Dau. of William H. & Grace W., 2d child, born 2 July 1892. [TR]
Dau. of Charles W. & Sarah E. (Taylor) 3d child, born 10 July 1905. [AR]

PHILBRICK Cont.
David, s/o John bp 11 July 1742. [CH]
Frank Harry, s/o Woodbury (25) & Eliza (Jenness) (27) born 11 Jan. 1876. [TR]
Henry P. s/o Willard & Grace W. (Dunham), 1st child, born 18 Apr. 1890.
   [TR][AR]
John Leonard, s/o Jonathan & Clarissa bp 2 Sep. 1849. [CH]
John Warren, s/o Jonathan & Clarissa bp 2 Mar. 1855. [CH]
Jonathan, s/o Page bp 5 May 1793. [CH]
Lucy, d/o Page bp 17 Apr. 1795. [CH]
Martha Ann, d/o Jonathan & Clarissa bp 29 Apr. 1847. [CH]
Martha May, d/o John W. & Jennie S. (Berry) born 22 Dec. 1883. [TR]
Mary, d/o John bp 17 Oct. 1745. [CH]
Mary Ann, d/o Josiah & Mary bp 6 Sep. 1807. [CH]
Nabby, d/o Josiah bp 25 Sep. 1810. [CH]
Olive, d/o Josiah & Mary bp 8 June 1806. [CH]
Rhoda, d/o John bp 11 July 1742. [CH]
Sarah, d/o Benjamin bp 29 Apr. 1770. [CH]
Simeon, s/o Benjamin bp 10 June 1773. [CH]
Son of John Warren & Jennie S. (Berry), 3d child, born 15 Mar. 1894. [TR][AR]
Son of Charles W. & Sarah E. (Taylor), 1st child, born 17 Aug. 1896. [TR][AR]

PHILBROOK: Philbrick?
Allen Howard, s/o Joseph & Julia M. bp 2 Sep. 1864. [CH]
Daniel, s/o John bp 3 Mar. 1754. [CH]
Daniel, s/o John bp 23 Apr. 1758. [CH]
Harriet Leavitt, d/o Henry M. & Rebecca F. bp 2 Nov. 1860. [CH]
John, s/o John bp 13 Apr. 1746. [CH]
Jonathan, s/o John bp 21 May 1749. [CH]
Josiah bp 18 Mar. 1777. [CH]
Julia Elizabeth, d/o Joseph & Julia M. bp 1 July 1859. [CH]
Mabel Dunham. d/o Willard H. & Grace W. born 2 July 1892. [AR]
Mary, d/o John bp 4 Apr. 1756. [CH]
Penelope, d/o Benjamin bp 3 Aug. 1753. [CH]
·Willard Henry, s/o Henry M. & Rebecca F. bp 2 July 1857. [CH]

PHILLIPS:
Dau. of Miss Mary A. born 30 Jan. 1866. [TR]

PICKERING:
Ann Ringe, d/o Joshua bp 3 Oct. 1813. [CH]
Lydia, d/o Joshua & Elizabeth bp 14 Feb. 1802. [CH]
Mary Olive, d/o Joshua bp 3 Oct. 1813. [CH]
Rosamond, d/o Joshua & Elizabeth bp 28 Oct. 1804. [CH]
Rosamond, d/o Joshua & Elizabeth bp 26 July 1807. [CH]

PIPER:
James Edwin, s/o James C. & Olive J. (Young), 3d child, born 16 Oct. 1886.
[TR]

POTTER:
Benjamin, s/o Benjamin bp 26 June 1748. [CH]
Benjamin, s/o Benjamin bp 16 Apr. 1749. [CH]
Child of Benjamin bp 1 Dec. 1745. [CH]
Hepzibah, d/o Benjamin bp 26 June 1748. [CH]
James, s/o Abigail Morgan, now Potter bp 17 July 1748. [CH]
Joseph, s/o Benjamin bp 21 Apr. 1756. [CH]

POWERS:
Harold, s/o Harold & Madeline V. (Seavey) 1st child, born 17 July 1925. [AR]
Shirley Williams, d/o Harold E. & Madeline (Seavey) 3d child, born 27 Aug.
1926. [AR]

POWHATAN:
Dau. of Leslie F. & Mabel F. (Jenness) 2d child, born 10 Dec. 1909. [AR]

PURINGTON:
Dau. of Walter F. & Hazel M. (Chapman) born 30 Sep. 1941. [AR]

POWERS:
Harold, s/o Harold & Madeline V. (Seavey) 1st child, born 17 July 1925. [AR]
Shirley Williams, d/o Harold E. & Madeline (Seavey) 3d child, born 27 Aug.
1926. [AR]

POWHATAN:
Dau. of Leslie F. & Mabel F. (Jenness) 2d child, born 10 Dec. 1909. [AR]

PURINGTON:
Dau. of Walter F. & Hazel M. (Chapman) born 30 Sep. 1941. [AR]

RAND:
Alice, d/o Samuel & Sarah S. born 10 Sep. 1867. [TR]
Edith Barker, d/o Samuel & Sarah J. born 1 July 1872. [TR]

RICHARDSON:
Alayne Jayne, d/o Williard C. & Gertrude (Seavey) 1st child, born 9 Nov.
1943. [AR]

RILEY:
Dau. of James & Bbbie (Tucker) , 2d child, born 2 Feb. 1887. [TR]

ROBIE/ROBY:
Abigail, d/o Thomas bp 8 Sep. 1749. [CH]
Abigail, d/o James bp 11 July 1753. [CH]
Abigail Caldwell, d/o Simon & Lydia bp 19 Oct. 1838. [CH]
David Emery, s/o Simon & Lydia bp 19 Oct. 1838. [CH]
Hannah, d/o John bp 11 Oct. 1761. [CH]
Jeremiah Henry, s/o Thomas & Betsy bp 19 Oct. 1838. [CH]
John, s/o John bp 2 Mar. 1760. [CH]
John William, s/o Simon & Lydia bp 19 Oct. 1838. [CH]
Lydia, w/o Simon bp 2 June 1827. [CH]
Mary, d/o James bp 19 May 1754. [CH]
Mary Elizabeth Ann, d/o Thomas & Betsy bp 19 Oct. 1838. [CH]
Molly inf. bp June 1790. [CH]
Polly, d/o John bp 13 Mar. 1768. [CH]
Sarah, d/o John bp 4 Dec. 1763. [CH]
Simon, s/o Simon & Lydia bp 19 Oct. 1838. [CH]
Thomas,s /o John bp Oct. 1765. [CH]
Thomas, s/o John Jr. bp 18 July 1784. [CH]

ROBINSON:
Abigail Dow, d/o Lt. James (dead) & Dolly bp 5 Nov. 1815. [CH]
Jeremiah, s/o Lt. James (dead) & Dolly bp 5 Nov. 1815. [CH]
Jonathan Page, s/o Lt. James (dead) & Dolly bp 5 Nov. 1815. [CH]
Mary Smith, d/o Lt. James (dead) & Dolly bp 5 Nov. 1815. [CH]
Sarah Malvina, d/o Lt. James (dead) & Dolly bp 5 Nov. 1815. [CH]
Son of Albert C. & Helen C. (Larkin) born 29 June 1876. [TR]

ROWE:
John, s/o James bp 8 July 1764. [CH]
Mary, d/o Mary bp 3 Oct. 1762. [CH]
Mary an adult bp 19 July 1769. [CH]

ROWELL:
Elizabeth, d/o Thomas & Sarah born 16 Mar. 1745. [CH1]
Nathaniel, s/o Elijah & Jann born 22 Sep. 1744. [CH1]

RUNDLETT:
Abigail Sanborn, d/o Noah bp July 1792. [CH]
John, s/o Noah bp 5 Aug. 1791. [CH]
Sarah, d/o Noah bp 5 Aug. 1791. [CH]
Susanna, d/o Noah bp 5 Aug. 1791. [CH]

RYAN:
Son of Daniel & Margaret (Mullen) 3d child, born 17 Aug. 1913. [AR]

SADLER:
Edward Paul, s/o Edward P. & Gladys I. (Flanigan) 1st child, born 26 Feb.
1943. [AR]

SALTON:
Dau. of Albert & Fanny (Philbrick) born 4 Aug. 1879. [TR]

SAMPSON:
Dau. of Frank H. born 13 Feb. 1876. [TR]

SANBORN:
Aaron, s/o Daniel & Katherin b. 8 Feb. & bp 20 Feb. 1743. [TR][CH]
Abigail, w/o William born 5 Mar. 1754. [TR]
Abigail, d/o William & Abigail b. 11 Sep. & bp 15 Oct. 1780. [TR][CH]
Abijah, s/o Dea. bp 4 Mar. 1748. [CH]
Anna, d/o Ebenezer & Ruth born 9 Mar. 1737. [TR]
Anna, d/o William & Abigail b. 6 Nov. 1776 & bp 19 Jan. 1777. [TR][CH]
Anne, d/o Daniel & Katherin born 26 Feb. 1726/7. [TR]
Beath, d/o Ebenezer & Ruth born 26 Sep. 1740. [TR]
Behaiah, d/o Daniel Jr. bp 12 June 1757. [CH]
Benjamin, s/o Ebenezer & Ruth born 5 July 1746. [TR]
Betty, d/o Nathan bp 1 Mar. 1741. [CH]
Catherine, d/o Daniel bp 8 Mar. 1761. [CH]
Comfort, d/o Daniel Jr. bp 4 Nov. 1753. [CH]
Daniel, s/o Daniel & Katherin born 17 May 1734. [TR]
Daniel, s/o John bp 6 July 1760. [CH]
Daniel, s/o Daniel bp 5 Sep. 1762. [CH]
Daniel, s/o Thomas bp 12 Jan. 1772. [CH]
Ebenezer, s/o Ebenezer & Ruth born 15 Apr. 1755. [TR]
Elizabeth, d/o Ebenezer & Ruth born 22 Feb. 1745. [TR]
Enoch, s/o Enoch bp 9 July 1759. [CH]
Enoch, s/o Enoch bp 10 June 1764. [CH]
Ebenezer, s/o John bp 14 June 1767. [CH]
Jacob & wife, adults bp Nov. 1786. [CH]
James, s/o Daniel Jr. bp 8 Apr. 1764. [CH]
John, s/o Ebenezer & Ruth born 28 Jan. 1736. [TR]
John, s/o Enoch bp 27 Aug. 1758. [CH]
John, s/o Josiah bp 21 May 1764. [CH]
John, s/o Thomas bp 24 Sep. 1769. [CH]
John, s/o William & Abigail born 26 Mar. 1785. [TR]
Jonathan Hobbs, s/o Daniel Jr. bp 6 May 1759. [CH]
Joseph, s/o William & Abigail b. 5 Oct. & bp 11 Nov. 1782. [TR][CH]
Joseph Hobbs, s/o William & Abigail born 16 Dec. 1774. [TR]
Josiah, s/o Ebenezer & Ruth born 19 Aug. 1738. [TR]
Josiah, s/o Josiah bp 3 Nov. 1765. [CH]
Katherine, d/o Daniel & Katherin born 1 June 1728. [TR]
Lucy, d/o Daniel bp 4 May 1755. [CH]
Lydia, d/o Thomas bp 23 Aug. 1767. [CH]
Mary, d/o Daniel Jr. bp 12 Apr. 1752. [CH]
Molly, d/o Daniel of Sanbornton bp 17 Sep. 1769. [CH]
Moses, s/o Daniel & Catherine b. 8 June & bp 22 June 1740. [TR][CH]

SANBORN Cont.

Phebe, d/o Daniel & Katherin born 13 Dec. 1725. [TR]
Rachel, d/o Daniel & Katherin born 25 Apr. 1736. [TR]
Richard, s/o Enoch bp 31 Aug. 1760. [CH]
Ruth, d/o William & Abigail born 2 Sep. 1778. [TR]
Sally, d/o Mr. of Hampton bp 10 Sep. 1797. [CH]
Samuel, s/o Josiah of Sanbornton bp 24 June 1770. [CH]
Sarah, d/o Daniel & Katherin born 2 Nov. 1733. [TR]
Sarah, d/o Abijah bp 21 Apr. 1771. [CH]
Sarah, d/o Daniel bp 24 Feb. 1745. [CH]
Thomas. s/o Daniel & Katherin born 17 May 1738. [TR]
William, s/o Ebenezer & Ruth born 8 Jan. 1753. [TR]
William, s/o Ebenezer & Ruth born 9 Jan. 1758. [TR]

SCHULT:

Neil Craig, s/o Walter F. & Alice M. (Craig) 2d child, born 15 June 1939.
[AR]

SEAVEY:

Annie, d/o Cecil R. & Jennie (Eastman) 4th child, born 15 Apr. 1918. [AR]
Barbara Brown, d/o Chester E. & Margaret (Brown) 3d child, born 3 July 1920.
[AR]
Carrie Dora, d/o Frank & Abbie C. born 26 Aug. 1868. [TR]
Child of Charles & Cattie S. born 22 July 1877. [TR]
Dau. of Arthur E. & Hattie M. (Tarlton) 1st child, born 28 June 1901. [AR]
Dau. of Charles C. & Bertha G. (Sanborn) 1st child, born 2 June 1905. [AR]
Dau. of Cecil R. & Jennie (Eastman) 2d child, born 1 Nov. 1910. [AR]
George S., s/o Charles & Hattie, 3d child, born 4 Apr. 1875. [TR]
John Ashley, s/o John K. & Shirley M. (Hobbs) 1st child, born 5 Apr. 1943.
[AR]
John Kenneth, s/o Chester E. & Margaret (Brown) 2d child, born 3 Sep. 1918.
[AR]
Muriel Alice, d/o Donald R. & Alice (McKenzie) 1st child, born 5 Apr. 1932.
[AR]
Pamela, d/o Ralph B. & Esther J. (Scott) 5th child, born 25 Oct. 1943. [AR]
Son of Charles S. & Hattie (McDonald) born 8 July 1883. [TR]
Son of George L. & Mary A. (Bartlett) 2d child, born 25 Mar. 1911. [AR]
Son of George L. & Mary A. (Bartlett) 1st child, born 19 Aug. 1907. [AR]
Son of George L. & Mary A. (Bartlett), 2d child born 25 Mar. 1911. [AR]
Son of Cecil R. & Jennie (Eastman) 3d child, born 11 Dec. 1911. [AR]
Thelma Arlene, d/o Cecil R. & Jennie (Eastman) 5th child, born 10 Aug. 1922.
[AR]
Vernon Rand, s/o Chester E. & Margaret (Brown) 4th child, born 3 July 1923.
[AR]

SELLERS:

Son of Chester J. & Carrie (Marston) 2d child born 20 Jan. 1915. [AR]

SEYMOUR:
Carolyn Louise, d/o William T. & Mildred L. (Durgin) 2d child, born 19 Jan.
1943. [AR]

SHAW:
Child of Fred L. & Ethel B. (Parshley) born 16 Aug. 1899. [AR]
Comfort, d/o Edward bp 12 Mar. 1758. [CH]
Dau. of Frederick M. & Emma L. (Taylor), 1st child born 14 Sep. 1896. [AR]
John, s/o Edward bp 24 Mar. 1754. [CH]
John, s/o Edward bp 21 Sep. 1755. [CH]
John, s/o Edward bp 18 Nov. 1764. [CH]
Josiah, s/o Edward bp 13 Mar. 1763. [CH]
Luster Roland, s/o Frederick M. & Emma L. (Taylor) 1st child, born 19 Sep.
1896. [TR][AR]
Mary Abbie, d/o Fred L. & Ethel B. (Benchley), 3d child, born 7 Oct. 1895.
[TR][AR]
Richard, s/o Samuel bp 24 Mar. 1754. [CH]
Samuel, s/o John & Sarah born 21 Mar. 1723. [TR]
Sarah, d/o Samuel bp 6 June 1756. [CH]

SHEPARD:
Marey, d/o John & Comfort born 13 Aug. 1762. [TR]
Mercy, d/o John bp 14 Aug. 1765. [CH]

SIMPSON:
Dau. of Frank & Laura (Page), 7th child, born 18 Apr. 1887 . [TR]
Dau. of Frank P. & Laura A. (Page), 11th child, born 1 May 1894. [TR][AR]
Lucy Elizabeth, d/o Frank & Louise (Page) born 24 May 1884. [TR]
Son of Frank & Laura born 15 Nov. 1877. [TR]
Son of Frank & Laura (Page) born 25 Jan. 1880. [TR]
Son of Frank B. & Anne, 1st child, born 11 Apr. 1889. [TR]
Son of Benjamin F. & Laura A. (Page), 10th child, born 25 Dec. 1890. [TR][AR]

SLAVICEK:
Karoline, d/O Karoline, 1st child born 5 Sep. 1924. [AR]

SLEEPER:
Son of Frank & Alice (Moulton), 1st child, born 27 Dec. 1882. [TR]

SMALL:
Carl Bernard, s/o Bernard & Mary (Locke) 1st child, born 13 May 1922. [AR]
Mildred Emily, d/o Bernard C. & Mary A. (Locke) 2d child, born 27 Aug. 1927.
[AR]
Son of W.H. & Joise (Chaffee) 1st child, born 26 Mar. 1901. [AR]
Walter Harrison, s/o Bernard C. & Mary A. (Locke) 3d child, born 24 sep.
1927. [AR]

SMART:
Joseph, s/o Benjamin bp Nov. 1786. [CH]

SMITH:
Abigail, d/o John & Rachel born 9 June 1750. [TR]
Abigail, d/o Lt. Christopher bp 1 Feb. 1778. [CH]
Abigail, d/o Samuel bp before July 1800. [CH]
Andrew David, s/o David & Dolly born 13 Aug. 1821. [TR]
Benjamin, s/o Christopher bp 9 Oct. 1757. [CH]
Caroline, d/o Dearborn & Harriet born 24 Sep. 1807. [TR]
Christopher, s/o Christopher bp 11 Feb. 1775. [CH]
Christopher, s/o Ebenezer & Rachel born 6 Mar. 1805. [TR]
Dau. of Morris & Isabella, 3d child, born 11 Sep. 1874. [TR]
David Curtis, s/o Christopher & Eliza bp 9 June 1839. [CH]
David Stevens, s/o Ebenezer & Rachel born 13 Dec. 1796. [TR]
Dearborn, s/o Samuel bp 8 Sep. 1782. [CH]
Ebenezer, s/o Benjamin bp 7 May 1747. [CH]
Ebenezer, s/o Christopher bp 22 Apr. 1773. [CH]
Ebenezer, s/o Christopher born 25 Feb. 1793. [TR]
Edward Morris, s/o Morris H. & Belle bp 1 July 1866. [CH]
Eles, d/o John & Rachel born 6 June 1747. [TR]
Eliza, d/o Dearborn & Harriet born 20 Feb. 1817. [TR]
Eliza Gilman, d/o Dearborn & Harriet bp 17 Aug. 1823. [CH]
Elizabeth Dearborn, d/o Stephen & Rachel b. 15 Jan. & bp before July 1800.
   [TR][CH]
Ephraim, s/o Samuel bp 13 Oct. 1754. [CH]
Hannah, d/o Christopher bp 9 Dec. 1764. [CH]
Henry Cutts, s/o ___ & Sarah Ann bp 19 Oct. 1838. [CH]
Huldah, d/o Christopher bp 9 Dec. 1764. [CH]
John C., s/o Joshua & Belinda L. born 4 Sep. 1867. [TR]
John Leavitt, s/o Christopher & Eliza C. bp 19 July 1835. [CH]
John Parker, s/o Morris & Isabella bp 18 aug. 1864. [CH]
John Pickering, s/o Christopher & Eliza C. bp 19 July 1835. [CH]
John William, s/o ___ & Sarah Ann bp 19 Oct. 1838. [CH]
Joshua Pickering, s/o Christopher & Eliza C. bp 19 July 1835. [CH]
Josiah, s/o Samuel bp May 1790. [CH]
Martha Lila, d/o Morris H. & Isabella bp 6 Apr. 1862. [CH]
Mary, d/o Christopher & Mary bp 15 Feb. 1767. [CH]
Mary, d/o Samuel bp 7 Nov. 1779. [CH]
Mary C., d/o John L. & Rebecca P. born 22 Oct. 1867. [TR]
Mary Stevens, d/o Ebenezer & Rachel born 2 Mar. 1799. [TR]
Morris Hobbs, s/o Christopher & Eliza C. bp 27 Oct. 1833. [CH]
Oliver Leavitt, s/o Dearborn & Harriet born 25 Jan. 1814. [TR]
Paul Walker, s/o Ralph T. & Barbara P. (Bellatty) 2d child, born 20 Apr.
   1943. [AR]
Philip, s/o John & Rachel born 14Apr. 1746. [TR]
Ruth, d/o Samuel bp 5 Jan. 1794. [CH]

SMITH Cont.
Samuel, s/o Samuel bp 27 Sep. 1745. [CH]
Samuel, s/o Samuel bp 9 Aug. 1753. [CH]
Sarah, d/o Samuel bp 9 Aug. 1763. [CH]
Sarah, d/o Samuel bp 10 Sep. 1797. [CH]
Silvanus, s/o John & Rachel b. 4 Nov. 1745. [TR]
Son of Christopher bp 27 Jan. 1760. [CH]
Son of Charles F. & Lizzie M. (Drake), 1st child, born 1887. [TR]
Son of Charles F. & Lizzie (Drake), 2d child, born 1 Apr. 1889. [TR]
Son of Charles F. & Lizzie M. (Drake), 3d child, born 31 Mar. 1894. [TR][AR]
Son of George M. & Nellie S. (Barton), 1st child, born 20 Apr. 1894. [TR][AR]
Son of Edward M. & Martha E. (Leavitt) 1st child, born 31 Aug. 1904. [AR]
Thomas, s/o ___ & Sarah Ann bp 19 Oct. 1838. [CH]
Viana Morrill, d/o ___ & Sarah Ann bp 19 Oct. 1838. [CH]
William, s/o wife of Samuel bp 17 Mar. 1754. [CH]

SPEAR:
Gwendolyn Langtry, d/o Earl L. & Dorothy (Riley) 2d child, born 3 June 1931.
[AR]
Jackquilyn, d/o Earl L. & Dorothy (Riley) born 2 June 1934. [AR]

SQUIRE:
Richard, s/o George E. & Evelyn A. (Philbrick) 1st child, born 25 Oct. 1941.
[AR]

STEELE:
Son of Herbert & Anna A. (Lewis), 1st child born 20 July 1906. [AR]

STEWART:
Gail, d/o George F. & Eleanor (Moore) 1st child, born 16 Oct. 1939. [AR]

STOBARTH:
Dau. of Sadie L., 1st child, born 6 Sep. 1898. [AR]

STRAW:
Daniel, s/o Lawrence & Abia born 16 Apr. 1744. [CH1]

STURTEVANT:
Dau. of C. Raymond & Mollie F. (Adams) 2d child, born 26 Dec. 1912. [AR]
Son of C. Raymond & Mary F. (Adams) 1st child, born 26 June 1911. [AR]

SWEET:
Sarah Gee, d/o Benjamin & Gemime born 30 June 1790. [TR]

SWETT:
Benjamin, s/o Benjamin & Gemime born 5 June 1788. [TR]
Joseph, s/o Benjamin & Gimime born 8 June 1786. [TR]

TARLTON:

Dau. of Atanle? & Sarah, 1st child, born 5 Oct. 1874. [TR]
Dau. of George W. & Nellie (Moulton) born 5 Sep. 1879. [TR]
Son of George W. & Mary Frances (Moulton), 2d child born 2 July 1882. [TR]
Son of George W. & Nellie L.F., 3d child, born 11 Oct. 1884. [TR]
Son of George W. & Nellie F. (Moulton) born 22 July 1895. [TR][AR]

TAYLOR:

Abigail, d/o John & Abigail b. 4 Apr. & bp 13 Apr. 1755. [TR][CH]
Abigiel, d/o Joseph & Mary born 29 Nov. 1790. [TR]
Abraham, s/o John & Abigail b. 19 Dec. & bp 30 Dec. 1750. [TR][CH]
Alfred, s/o John Kr. & Betsy born 3 Sep. 1816. [TR]
Anna, d/o Joseph bp 3 Sep. 1797. [CH]
Anne, d/o John & abigail born 16 Mar. 1747. [TR]
Benjamin, s/o John bp 30 Oct. 1748. [CH]
Benjamin, s/o Joseph & Mary b. 28 Oct. 1777 & bp 4 Jan. 1778. [TR][CH]
Clarissa Adeline, d/o Thomas bp 21 Nov. 1824. [CH]
Dau. of John T. & Abbie T. (Chase) 4th child, born 15 June 1894. [TR][AR]
Ebenezer, s/o Joseph & Mary b. 8 Oct. & bp 11 Nov. 1781. [TR][CH]
Elisha Johnson, s/o John Jr. bp 24 Nov. 1782. [CH]
Elizabeth, d/o John & Mary b. 29 Apr. & bp 3 May 1760. [TR][CH]
Hannah, d/o John bp 1 May 1765. [CH]
Ira James, s/o John & Mary bp 15 May 1831. [CH]
John, s/o John & Mary b. 25 Aug. & bp 26 Aug. 1759. [TR][CH]
John, later Col. s/o Joseph & Mary b. 16 Dec. 1787 & bp Jan. 1788. [TR][CH]
John, s/o John bp 16 Sep. 1821. [CH]
John Fogg, s/o John & Mary bp 4 June 1820. [CH]
John Salter, s/o Thomas bp 24 Nov. 1805. [CH]
John Salter, s/o Thomas bp 4 June 1820. [CH]
Jonathan, s/o John bp 14 Jan. 1772. [CH]
Joseph, s/o John & Abigail b. 20 Oct. & bp 20 Dec. 1748. [TR][CH]
Lydia, d/o Joseph & Mary b. 26 Dec. 1783 & bp 3 May 1784. [TR][CH]
Mary, d/o Joseph & Mary born 27 Mar. 1785. [TR]
Mary Ann, d/o John Jr. & Betsy born 22 Oct. 1814. [TR]
Mary Elizabeth, d/o Thomas bp 7 May 1809. [CH]
Mercy, d/o John bp 29 Jan. 1769. [CH]
Richard, s/o John & Margaret b. 2_ Mar. & bp 25 Mar. 1753. [TR][CH]
Richard, s/o John & Mary bp 7 Sep. 1828. [CH]
Salle, d/o Joseph & Mary born 2 Jan. 1793. [TR]
Sarah, d/o John bp 30 Jan. 1763. [CH]
Sarah, d/o Joseph bp 31 Mar. 1793. [CH]
Sarah Ann, d/o John & Mary bp 18 Sep. 1828. [CH]
Son of James & Martha born 27 Dec. 1875. [TR]
Son of Edward & Nellie (Batchelder) born 22 Aug. 1880. [TR]
Son of John & Abbie born 25 Apr. 1883. [TR]
Son of John born 11 Aug. 1888. [TR]
Thomas, s/o Joseph & Mary b. 8 Feb. & bp 14 Feb. 1779. [TR][CH]

THOMAS:
Elisha, s/o Jonathan bp 14 Feb. 1748. [CH]
Enoch, s/o Jonathan bp 8 sep. 1745. [CH]
John, s/o Elisha bp 5 Feb. 1749. [CH]
Joseph Merrill, s/o Jonathan bp 7 Nov. 1742. [CH]
Leonard Hervey, s/o William H. & Evelyn R. (Gile), 2d child born 13 Feb.
   1943. [AR]
Mary, d/o Benjamin Jr. bp 10 Apr. 1745. [CH]
Mary, an adult bp 5 July 1807. [CH]
Nathaniel, s/o Benjamin Jr. bp 10 Apr. 1748. [CH].

THOMPSON:
George, s/o George of Parsonfield bp Sep. 1792. [CH]
Ruby Lillian, d/o Anson F.J. & Lillian J. (Smith) 4th child, born 5 July
   1898. [TR][AR]

THURSTON:
Benjamin, s/o Rev. Benjamin & Sarah born 22 June 1785. [TR]
Betsy, d/o B. bp 17 June 1786. [CH]
Betsy, d/o Rev. Benj. & Sarah born 23 June 1787. [TR]
Betsy, d/o Nathaniel bp 28 Nov. 1799. [CH]
Daniel, s/o Rev. Benjamin & Sarah born 7 May 1789. [TR]
Daniel, s/o Nathaniel bp 6 Feb. 1800. [CH]
John Phillips, s/o Rev. Benj. & Sarah born 29 Feb. 1781. [TR]
Sally, d/o Rev. Benjamin & Sarah born 12 Feb. 1783. [TR]

TILTON:
Edward James, s/o James S. & Rebecca A. bp 2 Sep. 1859. [CH]
Mary Betsey, d/o James S. & Rebecca A. bp 29 Feb. 1856. [CH]

TOURTILLOTT:
Dau of Herbert S. & Sarah I. (Fife) 1st child, born 8 May 1907. [AR]
Dau. of Herbert S. & Sarah L. (Fife) 4th child, born 19 Mar. 1911. [AR]
Dau. of Herbert S. & Sarah L. (Fife) 5th child, born 31 Jan. 1914.

TOWLE:
Abraham, s/o Zachariah & Anne born 19 June 1728. [TR]
Abraham, s/o Zachariah & Anne born 19 July 1732. [TR]
Abraham, s/o Zachariah Jr. & Marey b. 18 Oct. & bp 28 Oct. 1770. [TR][CH]
Anna, d/o Zachariah Jr. & Marey b. 18 Aug. 1768 & bp 30 July 1769. [TR][CH]
Benjamin Hobbs, s/o Nathan bp 15 Dec. 1765. [CH]
Elizabeth, d/o Isaac & Elizabeth, bp before Apr. 1764. [CH]
Issack, s/o Zachariah & Anne born 23 Feb. 1725. [TR]
Jane, d/o Zachariah & Marey born 25 Apr. 1780. [TR]
Jane, d/o Amos bp 10 Oct. 1802. [CH]
Jean, d/o Zachariah & Anne born 4 May 1730. [TR]
John, s/o Amos bp Sep. 1795. [CH]

TOWLE Cont.

Jonathan Dearborn, s/o Zachariah Jr. & Marey b. 23 Jan. & bp 30 May 1773.
[TR][CH]
Joseph Jr. bp 12 Aug. 1795. [CH]
Marah, d/o Zachariah & Anne born 21 July 1742. [TR]
Mary Marston, d/o Amos bp 15 Sep. 1795. [CH]
Molly, d/o Zachery Jr. bp 24 July 1785. [CH]
Nancy Jenness, d/o Amos bp 2 Oct. 1808. [CH]
Polly, d/o Joseph bp 12 Aug. 1795. [CH]
Sarah, d/o Zachariah & Marey b. 8 Apr. 1775 & bp 12 May 1776. [TR][CH]
Sarah, d/o Zachariah Jr. & Marey b. 22 Aug. & bp 26 Oct. 1777. [TR][CH]
Simon, s/o Zachariah & Anne born 11 May 1740. [TR]
Simon, s/o Isaac & Elizabeth bp before Apr. 1764. [CH]
Simon, s/o Zachariah Jr. bp 11 Nov. 1782. [CH]
Son of Ernest W. & Louise (Johnson) 4th child, born 30 Mar. 1913. [AR]
Zachariah, s/o Zachariah & Anne born 8 June 1736. [TR]
Zachary, s/o Zachary & Anne born 9 Dec. 1746. [TR]

TUTTLE:

Son of William E. & Mary E. (Johnson) 1st child, born 18 Feb. 1903. [AR]

TWOMBLY:

Son of Albert D. & Ellen L. (Freeman) born 7 Aug. 1915. [AR]

TYLER:

Dau. of H.W. & Florence M. (Johnson) 2d child, born 17 July 1902. [AR]
Son of Harrison W. & Florence M. (Johnson) 3d child, born 24 Feb. 1904. [AR]

VESZEY:

Anna, d/o _____ born 5 Apr. 1752. [TR]

WADLEIGH:

Simon Dearborn, s/o Benjamin bp 14 July 1754. [CH]

WALLACE:

Comfort, d/o Samuel bp 15 Nov. 1770. [CH]
Molly, d/o William bp 11 Aug. 1765. [CH]
Sarah, d/o William bp 11 Jan. 1761. [CH]

WARD:

Anna, d/o Simon & Abigail b. 8 Aug. & bp 20 Aug. 1797. [TR][CH]
Cotton, s/o Lt. Simon & Nabby b. 16 Apr. & bp 11 Sep. 1790. [TR][CH]
Dau. of Henry L. & Alice C. born 23 Sep. 1891. [AR]
John, s/o Lt. Simon & Nabby b. 23 Sep. & bp 30 Sep. 1792. [TR][CH]
Josephine, d/o Elizabeth, widow of Joseph bp 30 Apr. 1822. [CH]
Sarah, d/o Simon & Abigail b. 31 Aug. & bp 13 Sep. 1795. [TR][CH]
Simon, s/o Simon & Nabby b. 5 Aug. 1786 & bp 3 Oct. 1789. [TR][CH]

WARNER:
Abraham Robinson, s/o William S. & Elizabeth bp 2 Oct. 1825. [CH]
Albert Haven, s/o Samuel S. & Ann Elizabeth bp 4 Sep. 1846. [CH]
Alvaretta Maria, d/o Samuel S. & Ann Elizabeth bp 4 May 1849. [CH]
Andrew, s/o William S. & Elizabeth bp 30 Apr. 1822. [CH]
Dau. of Albert & Sarah? O. born 3 Nov. 1878. [TR]
Dau. of John & Estella (Garland), 3d child, born 4 May 1884. [TR]
Emily D., d/o William S. & Elizabeth bp 12 Jan. 1823. [CH]
Fanny Edith, d/o John W. & Estella (Garland) born 12 Dec. 1871. [TR]
Francelia Amanda, d/o Samuel S. & Ann Elizabeth bp 4 Sep. 1846. [CH]
La Fayette, d/o Samuel & Abigail bp 30 June 1839. [CH]
Lucy May, d/o John W. & Estella (Garland) born 13 Aug. 1874. [TR]
Mary Ann Matthews, d/o William S. & Elizabeth bp 30 Apr. 1822. [CH]
Mary Elizabeth, d/o Samuel & Abigail bp 30 June 1839. [CH]
Matilda Abby, d/o Samuel S. & Abigail bp 5 July 1840. [CH]
Nancy Knowles, d/o William S. & Elizabeth bp 30 Apr. 1822. [CH]
Samuel Clarence Rowe, s/o Samuel S. & Ann Elizabeth bp 29 Apr. 1853. [CH]
Samuel Sherburne, s/o William S. & Elizabeth bp 30 Apr. 1822. [CH]
Son of John W. & Estella (Garland) born 22 Jan. 1877. [TR]
William, s/o William S. & Elizabeth bp 30 Apr. 1822. [CH]
William Sherburne, an adult bp 5 Mar. 1843. [CH]

WASHBURN:
John Henry, s/o John R. & Ruth (Briggs) 3d child, born 28 May 1917. [AR]

WASON:
Betty, d/o Robert bp 4 Apr. 1773. [CH]

WATERS:
Samuel Dwight, s/o Dwight & Sarah bp 13 Aug. 1837. [CH]

WATSON:
Florence Pickering, d/o Charles A. & Elizabeth (French) born 25 Oct. 1871.
   [TR]

WEDGWOOD:
Bate, d/o James & Oly born 5 Mar. 1769. [TR]
Betsy, d/o James bp 10 Sep. 1769. [CH]
Catherine, d/o Jonathan bp 19 Aug. 1753. [CH]
Chase, s/o Samuel & Deborah b. 26 May & bp 7 June 1772. [TR][CH]
Cherstrin, d/o Jonathan & Mary born 3 July 1752. [TR]
David, s/o Jonathan & Mary born 11 Apr. 1740. [TR]
David, s/o David bp 20 May 1770. [CH]
David, s/o James & Oly b. 2 June & bp 7 July 1771. [TR][CH]
David, s/o David & Mary born 28 Feb. 1778. [TR]
Dearborn, s/o James & Oley b. 1 Sep. & bp 5 Sep. 1773. [TR][CH]
Hannah, d/o Jonathan & Mary born 9 Sep. 1738. [TR]

WEDGWOOD Cont.

Hepzibah, d/o Jonathan & Mary b. 28 Feb. & bp 18 Mar. 1744. [TR][CH]
James, s/o Jonathan & Mary b. 30 Mar. & bp 11 May 1746. [TR][CH]
Jane, d/o Jona. & Mary born 27 Mar. 1758. [TR]
John, s/o Jonathan & Mary b. 10 Aug. & bp 17 Aug. 1755. [TR][CH]
John, s/o Jonathan & Mary b. 4 Aug. & bp 5 Sep. 1762. [TR][CH]
Jonathan, s/o Jona. & Mary born 30 Sep. 1737. [TR]
Jonathan, s/o Jonathan & Mary b. 18 Mar. 1750 & bp 2 Apr. 1751. [TR][CH]
Jonathan, s/o born 27 Mar. 1756. [TR]
Jonathan, s/o Jonathan bp 2 Apr. 1758. [CH]
Jonathan, s/o David & Mary bp 19 Apr. 1767. [CH]
Josiah, s/o Jonathan & Mary b. 13 Sep. & bp 16 Sep. 1759. [TR][CH]
Lydia, d/o Samuel & Deabrah b. 28 July & bp 9 July 1764. [TR][CH]
Mary, d/o Jona. & Mary born 4 July 1748. [TR]
Mary, d/o David & Mary b. 16 Nov. 1763 & bp 22 Mar. 1764. [TR][CH]
Mary, d/o Samuel & Deborah bp 14 June 1767. [CH]
Nathan, s/o David & Mary born 15 Apr. 1767. [TR]
Olly/Ole, d/o Lt. James & Anne bp 27 May 1786. [TR][CH]
Polly, d/o Lt. James & Oley b. 22 Nov. & bp 24 Nov. 1776. [TR][CH]
Samuel, s/o Jonathan & Mary born 8 Sep. 1742. [TR]
Samuel, s/o Samuel & Deborah born 25 June 1767, [TR]

WELLS:

Daniel, s/o John bp 14 Feb. 1779. [CH]
Eliazbeth, d/o John & Elizabeth bp 6 Jan. 1771. [CH]
John, s/o John bp 17 Oct. 1773. [CH]
Robert Edwin, s/o Perley J. Jr. & Sadie Ola (Frost) 1st child, born 29 May
    1941. [AR]

WHENAL:

Beverly, d/o William T. & Katherine (Christie) 2d child, born 4 Apr. 1935.
    [AR]
Dau. of William & Jennie Brown born 30 Sep. 1879. [TR]
Dau. of Thomas B. & Isabel J. (White), 2d child born 4 June 1897. [AR]
Dau. of Thomas B. & Isabella J. (White) 4th child, born 11 June 1904. [AR]
Dau. of Thomas B. & Isabella J. (White) 6th child, born 10 Mar. 1915. [AR]
Henry Thomas, s/o Thomas & Esable J. White, 1st child, born 16 Mar. 1895.
    [TR]
Isabella Marilyn, d/o George F. & Esther L. (Gerry) 4th child, born 31 Mar.
    1925. [AR]
John William, s/o John & Carrie (Marston) 5th child, born 11 Jan. 1918. [AR]
John Leslie, s/o Martin W. & Hazel (Varney) 1st child, born 6 July 1928. [AR]
Marilyn Frances, d/o George E. & Esther L. (Gerry) 6th child, born 9 July
    1930. [AR]
Son of William & Jane born 8 May 1877. [TR]
Son of Thomas B. & Isabella J. (White) 3d child, born 24 Apr. 1902. [AR]
Son of John & Caroline A. (Marston) 2d child, born 22 Sep. 1904. [AR]
Son of John W. & Carrie A. (Marston) 3d child, born 16 Jan. 1907. [AR]

WHENAL Cont.

Sylvia Louise, d/o William T. & Katherine (Christie) 3d child, born 7 July 1936. [AR]

William Teele Jr., s/o William T. & Katherine R. (Christie) 1st child, born 28 Nov. 1933. [AR]

WHITE:

Son of Herbert A. & Mildred T. (Prescott) 2d child, born 1 sep. 1907. [AR]

WIGGIN:

Child of Fred B. & Alice (Robie) born 2 Nov. 1899. [AR]

Dolly, d/o David bp 23 May 1773. [CH]

Dau. of Daniel S. & Delia N. born 15 Sep. 1868. [TR]

Edwin G., s/o Enoch F. & Martha Berry born 18 Feb. 1853. [TR]

Elizabeth, d/o Widow bp 22 June 1783. [CH]

James, s/o David, bp 22 Sep. 1771. [CH]

Love, d/o David bp 8 May 1768. [CH]

Mary, d/o John Jr. bp 27 Aug. 1769. [CH]

Son of Fred B. & Alice L. (Robie) 2d child, born 1 Jan. 1901. [AR]

Sons, twins of Fred B. & Alice L. (Robie) 3d & 4th children, born 21 Feb. 1904. [AR]

Susanna, d/o David & Dorothy bp 30 Nov. 1766. [CH]

Susanna, d/o Widow bp 22 June 1783. [CH]

Thomas, s/o Widow bp 22 June 1783. [CH]

WILLS:

Elisabeth, d/o John born 9 Oct. 1760. [TR]

John, s/o John born 4 Oct. 1773. [TR]

WINCH:

Son of Herman L. & Edith V. (Thompson) 2d child, born 15 June 1914. [AR]

WIND:

Dau. of William & Jane born 31 Oct. 1874. [TR]

WOOD:

Alfred Frederick, s/o Alfred & Hope S. (Hart) 1st child, born 2 Mar. 1920. [AR]

WRIGHT:

Charles Sherman, s/o J.M. & Isabell, 2d child, born 18 Oct. 1886. [TR]

David Kaharl, s/o Maurice R. & Alice (Kaharl) 1st child,b orn 21 May 1917. [AR]

NORTH HAMPTON, N.H.

DEATHS

1742 - 1942

ADAMS:
Emily J. d/o John H. Adams died 22 Sep. 1938, ae 79-8-7. [AR]

AJEMIAN:
Ajem, s/o Harabed died 3 July 1929, ae 40-7-3. [AR]

ALEXANDER:
Martha, d/o Richard of Hampton bur. 8 Jan. 1850, ae 18. [CH]

ALLEN:
Rev. Henry of Falmouth, Nova Scotia died 2 Feb.1784, ae 35 yrs. [CEM]
Howard R. s/o Howard F. & Florence V. died 27 Oct. 1941, ae 0-0-9. [AR]

ALLINE:
Rev. Henry of Falmouth, N.S. bur. 2 Feb. 1784. ae 35-8/]CH]

ALLISON:
Celia Carrie, d/o Benj. & Sarah of Portsmouth died 18 Sep. 1858, ae 2. [CH]

ARMSTRONG:
Ellen M., d/o Enoch Carter died 27 Nov. 1915, ae 75-6-18. [AR]

AUSTIN/ASTON:
Mrs. Jemima, ae 73, md. died 17 June 1881. [TR]
Jennie Madel, d/o Charles, ae 0-0-17 died 24 Dec. 1881. [TR]
M. Jennie, d/o Clark, ae 0-8-9, died 24 Dec. 1881. [TR]

BACHELDER: See Batchelder.

BAILEY:
Sarah J., d/o Chas. Gould died. 13 Apr. 1943, ae 102-1-15. [AR]

BARNABY:
Charles R., s/o Charles T. died 4 Apr. 1943, ae 17-6-24. [AR]

BARTON:
Bessie Elizabeth, d/o Joseph Sayball died 31 Jan. 1929, ae 76-9-23. [AR]
Charles C. died 30 Sep. 1905, ae 91-7-21. [AR][CEM]
Charles L., s/o Charles C. died 30 Mar. 1940, ae 87-11-28. [AR]
Dorcus, d/o James Libby & w/o Charles C. b. 24 Dec. 1832, died 24 Mar. 1898,
    ae 77-3. [AR]
Eliza P., d/o Amos Jenness died 13 Nov. 1924, ae 73-7-24. [AR]
George E., s/o Charles C. died 10 Apr. 1938, ae 81-3-11. [AR]
Gertrude A, d/o Joseph Sayball died. 18 Apr. 1943, ae 78-4-6. [AR]
James W., s/o Chauncey died 14 Apr. 1931, ae 77-6-11. [AR]

BATCHELDER/BACHELDER:
Abigail, w/o Josiah bur, 27 Feb. 1810, ae 67. [CH]

BATCHELDER Cont.

Abigail died 19 Feb. 1845, ae 43 or 44 yrs. [CEM][CH]
Abigail died 21 Feb. 1845, ae 75. [CH]
Albert, s/o James died 7 Aug. 1923, ae 82-9-17. [AR]
Ambrose, s/o James died 6 Mar. 1920, ae 93-6-6. [AR]
Anna T., w/o Joseph Roberts b. 1819, d. 1896. [CEM]
Arthur, s/o Samuel H. bur. 15 May 1831, ae 23. [CH]
Arthur b. 3 July 1839, d. 14 Oct. 1914. [CEM]
Chapman bur. Aug. 1852, ae about 70. [CH]
Charles E., s/o Levi b. 1843, d. 18 Apr. 1922, 79-1. [CEM][AR]
Charles L., s/o Charles died 27 Mar. 1938, ae 53-1-24. [AR]
Child of Samuel bur. 19 Aug. 1826. [CH]
Clarissa, w/o Levi & d/o Jeremiah Marston, b, 1815, d. 5 Mar. 1896, ae 79-2.
  [CEM][AR]
Clarissa, Mrs. d/o Jeremiah Marston, ae 79-2-0 died 5 Mar. 1894. [AR][TR]
Mrs. Edward bur. 13 Mar. 1826, ae 36. [CH]
Eliza (Ward), w/o Nathaniel b. 1796, d. 21 May 1847. [CEM][CH]
Elizabeth, wid. bur. 27 Oct. 1842, ae 81. [CH]
Elizabeth died 17 Feb. 1856, ae 85. [CH]
Frank H., s/o George died 18 Feb. 1904, ae 40-11-14. [AR]
Frederick, ae 73, md. died 8 Oct. 1882. [TR]
Frederick A. died 22 Oct. 1852, ae 23-9. [CEM]
George, s/o Levi died 27 Oct. 1906, ae 67-6-18. [AR]
Georgianna, d/o Josiah Sanborn died 25 June 1907, ae 70-10-23. [AR]
Harriet, Mrs. d/o Moses Leavitt, ae 65, md. died 19 Nov. 1880. [TR]
Henry bur. Apr. 1791. [CH]
Infant of Jeremiah bur. 7 Sep. 1831. [CH]
Ivy S., d/o John Brown, ae 90, md. died 12 Aug. 1879. [TR]
James bur. 6 Feb. 1810, ae 77-9. [CH]
James bur. 22 Apr. 1869. [CH]
James Bell, s/o John & Mary A. died 4 Sep. 1859, ae 4. [CH]
James L., ae 70, s/o Samuel died 11 Mar. 1870. [TR]
James L., s/o Albert died 11 Oct. 1926, ae 42-7. [AR]
Jane, Mrs. died 5 Aug. 1824, ae 29. [CEM]
John bur. 18 Apr. 1770, ae 70-8. [CH]
John bur, 15 July 1809, ae 41-3. [CH]
John, s/o John & Patty bur. 1 Dec. 1817, ae 1-6. [CH]
John Jr., Mrs. bur. 1821, ae 50. [CH]
John bur. 7 Aug. 1855, ae 77-8. [CH]
John, s/o Nathaniel & Mary bur. 20 Jan. 1841, ae 1-1. [CH]
John died 14 Sep. 1846, ae 75. [CH]
John, died 22 Nov. 1868, ae 62-8. [TR][CEM]
John, s/o James, ae 73 wid. died 21 Sep. 1889. [TR]
John Martin, s/o Nathaniel b. 1840, d. 1841. [CEM]
John Taylor, s/o Josiah & Molly bur. 12 Mar. 1826, ae 2. [CH]
Jonathan, s/o Late Nathaniel & Wid. Elizabeth bur. 14 Nov. 1805. [CH]
Jonathan C. bur. 9 Aug. 1823, ae 29. [CH]
Jonathan Towle, s/o Josiah bur. 6 Sep. 1820, ae 0-2-2. [CH]

BATCHELDER Cont.
Josiah bur. 7 Apr. 1803, ae 58. [CH]
Josiah, s/o Edward Chapman bur. 2 Sep. 1826, ae 2. [CH]
Josiah died 5 July 1850, ae 68. [CH]
Josiah b. 1782, d. 1855, [CEM]
Julia Ann, d/o Thomas bur. 15 Sep. 1837, ae 3. [CH]
Levi, s/o John Jr. bur. 15 Oct. 1806, ae 13. [CH]
Levi, ae 72, md. born 1810, died 25 Dec. 1880. [TR][CEM]
Lillie, d/o Roderick McDonald died 6 dec. 1899, ae 45. [AR]
Lizzie A., w/o Arthur & d/o John Ring, b. 21 Sep. 1845, d. 6 Oct. 1894.
    [CEM][AR]
Lizzie, d/o John Rigg, ae 49-1-10 died 6 Oct. 1894. [TR]
Lydia, w/o Leavitt died 1 Jan. 1863, ae 49-5. [CH]
M. Abbie, d/o John Lamprey died 1 July 1937, ae 86-7-8. [AR]
Mark, ae 80, md. died 23 Jan. 1880, ae 80-2. [TR][CEM]
Martha M,, w/o Charles E. & d/o Nathan Brown b. 1844, d. 20 Dec. 1924,
    ae 80-4-17. [CEM][AR]
Mary, d/o James bur. 1784, ae 19. [CH]
Mary, w/o John bur. 4 Apr. 1807, ae 45. [CH]
Mary, d/o Samuel bur. 5 July 1831, ae 3. [CH]
Mary, w/o Josiah b. 1785, d. 4 Sep. 1862, ae 77. [CEM][CH]
Mary A., d/o James died 21 May 1901, ae 67-0-11. [AR]
Mary D., w/o Sylvester Jackson b. 1812, d. 1884. [CEM]
Mary J. (Powers), w/o Nathaniel b. 1812, d. 1908. [CEM]
Mary M., w/o Shubal Leavitt died 11 Apr. 1845, ae 42. [CH]
Mary Olive, w/o Fred. A. & d/o Joshua Pickering died 2 Oct. 1865, ae 55.
    [TR][CEM]
Mehitabel, widow bur. 24 Dec. 1819, ae 89-4. [CH]
Nathaniel died 12 Mar. 1803, ae 69. [CH]
Nathaniel Jr. b. 1807, d. 4 Mar. 1841, ae 35. [CEM][CH]
Nathaniel b. 1796, d. 1877. [CEM]
Nathaniel Frank, s/o Nathaniel & Mary J. died 23 July 1851, ae 8. [CH]
Olla, d/o Lt. Joseph bur. 1797. [CH]
Orrin, s/o Thomas died 10 Feb. 1900, ae 61. [AR]
Orren, Mrs. died 30 Sep. 1890. [TR]
Polly, d/o Josiah died 7 Feb. 1803, ae 6. [CH]
Polly, wid. of John died 30 Nov. 1868, ae 70. [TR][CH]
Polly, w/o John died 29 Nov. 1855, ae 59-10. [CEM]
Sally, w/o James bur. 8 Oct. 1821, ae near 27. [CH]
Samuel, Mrs. bur. 8 Nov. 1813, ae 69. [CH]
Samuel bur. 9 Jan. 1822, ae 79-6. [CH]
Samuel died 7 June 1857, ae 76. [CH]
Samuel died 11 Mar. 1870. [TR]
Samuel L. died 3 Apr. 1891, ae 74. [AR]
Sarah, d/o John bur. 1 Jan. 1785, ae 1. [CH]
Sarah widow bur. 26 July 1805, ae 85. [CH]
Sarah (Leavitt), w/o Samuel bur. 13 Sep. 1833, ae 55. [CH]
Sarah, d/o Chapman B. bur. 3 Oct. 1835, ae nearly 16. [CH]

BATCHELDER Cont.
Sarah, d/o Samuel B. bur. 14 Nov. 1835, ae 25. [CH]
Sarah, d/o James & Mehitabel bur. 4 Nov. 1847, ae 87. [CH]
Sarah, d/o Samuel Brown, ae 74-11-0, md. died 1 July 1883. [TR]
Sarah J., d/o James died 20 Dec. 1900, ae 81-7-1. [AR]
Simon bur. 13 Apr. 1806, ae 0-0-2. [CH]
Son of John H. ae 6 hours died 23 Sep. 1889. [TR]
Sophia, w/o Mark d. 6 May 1860, ae 59-10. [CEM][CH]
Sophia A., d/o Mark died 23 Aug. 1855, ae 21-8. [CEM][CH]
Thomas E., s/o John, ae 85-2 died 10 Oct. 1889. [TR]
Thomas L., s/o Jeremiah & Caroline (Chesley) died 26 Feb. 1897, ae 59-3-6.
  [AR]
Warren, s/o James died 28 Dec. 1899, ae 61. [AR]

BENNET:
Abel bur. 12 Mar. 1863, ae 79. [CH]

BERRY:
Arnold P. b. 1893, d. ____ [CEM]
Charles P. b. 1839, d. 1896. [CEM]
Clara, d/o Mr. Gibson died 26 Nov. 1924, ae 48-0-8. [AR]
D. Mabel b. 1886, d. ____ [CEM]
Earle M. b. 1888, d. ___ [CEM]
Ebenezer, ae 67½, died 25 Mar. 1880. [TR]
Emma E. (locke), w/o John W. b. 1867, d. ____ [CEM]
Esther B., d/o David P. Moulton died 31 Mar. 1931, ae 77-0-26. [AR]
Fred W., s/o John C. died 13 Nov. 1930, ae 76-1-6. [AR]
Infant of Ella died 20 Nov. 1912. [AR]
John S., s/o Frank E. & Susia G. (Perkins) died 24 Mar. 1907, ae 1-6-5. [AR]
John W., s/o Joseph b. 1867, d. 2 June 1926, ae 58-5-28. [CEM][AR]
Lawrence F. b. 1850, d. 1900. [CEM]
Lemora (Drinkwater), w/o Richard C. b. 1849, d. 1898. [CEM]
Otto W. b. 1865, d. 1917. [CEM]
Persey Franklin, d/o Frank P., ae 0-9-5, died 9 Apr. 1896. [TR][AR]
Richard C. b. 1845, d. 1911. [CEM]
Rose E., w/o Otto b. 1875, d. 1899. [CEM]
Seretta, w/o Charles P. b. 1848, d. 1926. [CEM]
Stillborn, d/o Edward H. & Addie C. Fogg died 23 Oct. 1884. [TR]
Thomas H. b. 5 Feb. 1841, d. 25 Sep. 1913. [CEM]

BETTON:
Albert Everett, s/o Wm T. died 4 Feb. 1925, ae 19-1-17. [AR]

BICKFORD:
Anna A., d/o Edwin H. Bickford died 23 Sep. 1939, ae 41-11-10. [AR]

BILLINGS:
Jesse E., s/o Robert B. died 13 June 1923, ae 51-6-12. [AR]

BINNEY:
Charles C., s/o Horace died 10 July 1913, ae 57-8-20. [AR]

BIRD:
James w., s/o Benj. C. died 23 Sep. 1937, ae 85-9-19.]AR]

BLEVINS:
John Ashley, s/o Joseph died 12 July 1941, ae 75-3-17. [AR]

BLOCK:
Caroline M. died 19 Dec. 1920, ae 79-2-10. [AR]

BLOOM:
George R., s/o Abraham died 26 May 1921, ae 30-10-19. [AE]

BOARDMAN:
George L., s/o George died 4 Mar. 1933, ae 84-1-23. [AR]
Maude G., d/o Ezra Reed died 28 June 1943, ae 63-7-26. [AR]
Sarah Ann died 24 Apr. 1925, ae 69-3-14. [AR]

BOYNTON/BOYTON:
Abbie L., d/o Michael Dalton died 19 June 1912, ae 69-11-22. [AR]
George W. died 25 June 1925, ae 80-4-9. [AR]

BRACKER:
M. Leon, s/o Charles died 25 Apr. 1937, ae 52-9-28. [AR]

BREED:
Elmenia T. (f) d/o William J., ae 9 mos. died 29 Jan. 1876. [TR]
Lydia A., w/o William b. 22 Sep. 1848, d. 25 Feb. 1902. [CEM]
William J., s/o Justin b. 17 May 1846, d. 20 May 1911, ae 65-2-4. G.A.R.
    [CEM][AR]

BRIGGS:
Elvira B., d/o Paul W. Briggs died 21 Mar. 1908, ae 77-2. [AR]
Harriet, d/o Jeremiah & Polly Jenness d. 16 Nov. 1881, ae 79 yrs. [CEM]

BRITTON:
Jennis, d/o John Britton died 6 July 1941, ar 73-3-27. [AR]

BROCK:
Susan Page died 4 Feb. 1914, ae 94 yrs. [CEM]

BROWN:

Abigail, w/o Jacob bur. 1801. [CH]

Abigail, w/o Jacob died 9 Sep. 1847. [CH]

Adner, s/o David, ae 65-0-12, wid. died 2 Feb. 1889. [TR]

Alfred, s/o Jeremiah died 29 June 1856, ae 27-7. [CH]

Alice Emma, w/o Horace died 13 Nov. 1885, ae 25-11. [CEM]

Alice S., d/o Edwin Snow died 10 Dec. 1938, ae 75-2-3. [AR]

Alvin C., s/o True died 15 Nov. 1924, ae 72-3-9. [AR]

Anna, d/o A. Dana & Merianna died 27 Feb. 1862, ae 1-11. [CH]

Benjamin bur. 11 May 1799. [CH]

Benjamin, s/o Wid. of Stephen bur. 12 June 1831, ae 27. [CH]

Benjamin, s/o Jeremiah bur. 24 Jan. 1832, ae 34-5. [CH]

Benjamin bur. 19 Dec. 1850. [CH]

Betsy, d/o Benjamin bur. 11 Dec. 1777, ae 10. [CH]

Betsey, w/o Jeremiah died 16 Feb. 1887, ae 81-5. [CEM]

Caroline Ward, d/o Jenness died 20 June 1851, ae 7 wks, 1 day. [CEM][CH]

Mrs. Charles bur. 8 Dec. 1840, ae 32. [CH]

Charles J., s/o Oliver died 24 Oct. 1914, ae 63-8-22. [AR]

Charlotte A., d/o Samuel Tarlton died 18 Mar. 1911, ae 83-1-19. [AR]

Child of Jacob bur. 12 July 1801. [CH]

Clara E., d/o Stephen Butler died 7 Jan. 1938, ae 80-10-29. [AR]

Clarissa, w/o Nathan Jr. d. 25 May 1858, ae 45-6. [CH][CEM]

Dau. of John H. d. 23 Sep. 1889, ae 6 hrs. [TR]

David died 16 Aug. 1854, ae 77. [CH]

Dolly, w/o Jacob H. bur. 20 Aug. 1848, ae 38. [CH]

Eddie Addison, adopted by True & Charlotte died 8 Nov. 1858, ae 11 wk. [CH]

Edwin L., s/o Simon Jr. died 24 Oct. 1905, ae 68-0-20. [AR]

Eliza A., d/o David P. Brown died 19 Oct. 1906, ae 74-2-25. [AR]

Elizabeth, w/o Jacob 3d bur. 9 July 1818, ae 26. [CH]

Elizabeth, d/o Raymon Jenness, ae 58-10-25 died 30 Jan. 1892. [TR]

Elizabeth A., w/o Nathan died 30 Jan. 1892, ae 68-10. [CEM]

Elizabeth M., w/o Capt. Jonah died 8 July 1815, ae 26 yrs. [CEM]

Elizabeth M., w/o Oliver & d/o Noah Marston, died 27 Jan. 1898, ae 81-7-20. [CEM][AR]

Emily Drake, d/o Nathaniel Drake, ae 74, md. died 26 Aug. 1880. [TR]

Emily, w/o Simon died 22 Sep. 1880, ae 74 yrs. [CEM]

Emma F., d/o Joseph Johnson died 16 May 1924, ae 74-6-17. [AR]

Emma Susan, d/o Jenness & Lydia N. died 23 Aug. 1856 ae 1-10-6. [CH][CEM]

Emmons T. d. 27 Nov. 1930, ae 76-4-4. [AR]

Ernest A., s/o Oliver A. died 28 dec. 1911, ae 33-7. [AR]

Eva M. died 15 Sep. 1943, ae 67-8-5. [AR]

Frank, ae 19, died 1 Jan. 1866. [TR]

Frederick A., s/o George D. died 14 Aug. 1939, ae 81-9-9. [AR]

Freeman, s/o Oliver & Elizabeth d. 18 Oct. 1840, ae 3-1. [CEM]

Freeman died 19 Nov. 1857, ae 1-9. [CH]

George D, s/o Reuben L. died 28 Nov. 1923, ae 89-9-21. [AR]

Hannah, d/o Wid. Jacob & dau. Morris Lamprey bur. 17 Mar. 1820, ae 76. [CH]

BROWN Cont.

Hannah, ae 24, died 29 July 1868. [TR]

Hannah J., d/o Nathan bur. 23 Oct. 1810, ae 3-3. [CH]

Harriet, d/o Oliver bur. 8 Feb. 1835, ae 4. [CH]

Harriet, Mrs., d/o Moses Leavitt, d. 19 Nov. 1880, ae 65. [TR]

Harriet Elizabeth, d/o Jeremiah died 12 Feb. 1925, ae 79-4-15. [CEM][AR]

Harvey, s/o David died 2 Feb. 1908, ae 65-0-1. [AR]

Hattie M., d/o Oliver Brown died 5 Jan. 1923, ae 70-11-29. [AR]

Helen Frances, d/o Oliver & Elizabeth died 23 May 1847, ae 0-11. [CH][CEM]

Hiram C. died 5 Sep. 1861, ae 20-6. [CH]

Horace S., s/o Joseph died 3 Sep. 1904, ae 58-4. [AR]

Howard B., s/o Warren died 23 Nov. 1934, ae 67-7-8. [AR]

Infant, c/o Stephen & Molly died 27 Jan. 1803, ae 0-0-5. [CH]

Infant, c/o Stacey & Polly bur. 28 Mar. 1808. [CH]

Infant, c/o Stacey bur. 8 Oct. 1809, ae 0-0-14. [CH]

Infant, c/o Stacey bur. 5 Dec. 1811, ae 6 wk. [CH]

Infant, c/o Joseph bur. 1 Mar. 1838, ae 0-0-7. [CH]

Infant, c/o Mary Jane died 8 Sep. 1850., ae 0-3. [CH]

Infant, c/o Simon bur. 11 Sep. 1850, 0-0-1. [CH]

Jacob bur. 22 July 1819, ae 78. [CH]

Jacob, s/o David bur. 25 Oct. 1840, ae 24. [CH]

Jacob died 3 Jan. 1851, ae 81. [CH]

Jake, Mrs., d/o Mr. Jenness, md. died 21 Feb. 1887. [TR]

James P., s/o O. Coleman died 15 Aug. 1939, ae 84-11-1. [AR]

Jenness died 17 Sep. 1876, ae 68 yrs.

Jennie O., d/o Martin Sleeper died 24 Aug. 1920, ae 64-7-6. [AR]

Jeremiah bur. 30 Dec. 1840, ae 78-10. [CH]

Jeremiah died 12 Feb. 1875, ae 64 yrs.

Jerusha, d/o Stephen bur. 25 Jan. 1819, ae 1. [CH]

John bur. 4 Mar. 1825, ae nearly 77. [CH]

John died 23 Aug. 1825, ae 50 yrs. [CEM][CH]

John, Capt. bur. 22 July 1831, ae 87. [CH]

John, s/o Jeremiah bur. 31 Dec. 1841, ae 4. [CH]

John, s/o John, ae 80-0-28, wid. died 30 Mar. 1893. [TR][AR]

John H., s/o Benjamin died 30 Oct. 1903, ae 62. [AR]

Jonathan, old Mr. bur. Sep. 1792. [CH]

Jonathan Jr. bur. 2 June 1833, ae 21. [CH]

Joseph, s/o Joseph died 9 Sep. 1806, ae 24. [CH]

Joseph, s/o Nathan bur. 28 Oct. 1814. [CH]

Joseph, s/o Nathan ae 63, md. died Dec. 1879. [TR]

Joseph, s/o William died 10 May 1931, ae 91-4-8. [AR]

Joshua Sr. bur. 10 Dec. 1783, ae 93-8. [CH]

Joshua bur. 26 May 1808, ae 83-11. [CH]

Josiah Livingston, s/o Jacob Jr. bur. 1837, ae 1. [CH]

Levi died 28 July 1861, ae 84. [CH][CEM]

Lucy, d/o Frank, ae 2-7-3, died 8 Oct. 1886. [TR]

Lydia, w/o Levi died 7 Feb. 1852, ae 70. [CEM][CH]

BROWN Cont.
Lydia Dalton, d/o Oliver & Lydia bur. 1837, ae 0-10. [CH]
Lydia (Ward), w/o Jenness died 2 Feb. 1876, ae 58 yrs. [CEM]
Mary, d/o John bur. 22 Mar. 1809, ae 19-8. [CH]
Mary died 25 Mar. 1810, ae 40 yrs. [CEM]
Mary, wid. of Benjamin bur. 12 Sep. 1823, ae near 84. [CH]
Mary w/o Capt. Simon died 25 Sep. 1837, ae 90-6. [CH][CEM]
Mary, d/o John bur. 30 Mar. 1840, ae nearly 40. [CH]
Mary, w/o Stacey bur. 5 June 1841, ae 52. [CH]
Mary, wid. of John died 25 Jan. 1847, ae 94-11. [CH]
Mary died 22 Dec. 1853, ae 79. [CH]
Mary, wid. of Benjamin died 17 Oct. 1854. [CH]
Mary, wid. died 27 Sep. 1863, ae 83-7. [CH]
Mary A., d/o Nathaniel Lock, ae 80-0-11, md. died 30 July 1889. [TR]
Mary A. died 21 Nov. 1923, ae 82-5-18. [AR]
Mary Adelaide, d/o Joseph & Sarah bur. 25 Aug. 1843, ae 0-5. [CH]
Mary C., s/o Jonathan died 13 Mar. 1902, ae 86-4-11. [AR]
Mary Webster, d/o David Jr. bur. 18 Oct. 1820, ae 6. [CH]
May E., d/o George A. Boynton died 27 Oct. 1908, ae 31-9-27. [AR]
Nancy, d/o Jacob bur 17 Feb. 1806, ae 19. [CH]
Nathan born 20 Mar. 1824, died 1 May 1859? [CEM]
Nathan died 20 July 1862, ae 89-7. [CH]
Oliver 2d, s/o Joshua, died 20 Feb. 1872, ae 81-1. [TR][CEM]
Oliver, died 8 Oct. 1882, ae 70-1-12. [TR]
Oliver A., s/o Oliver died 18 Apr. 1920, ae 76-0-23. [AR]
Oliver P. bur. 21 May 1837, ae 32. [CH]
Otis S., s/o Simon died 4 Apr. 1924, ae 77-1-11. [AR]
Polly, d/o widow died 9 May 1859, ae 81-4. [CH]
Polly, w/o John died 9 May 1859, ae 81 yrs. [CEM]
Polly, ae 75-11-7, md. died 21 Apr. 1882. [TR]
Polly H., d/o Samuel Hodges died 5 July 1933, ae 80-8-1. [AR]
Reuben, s/o David bur. 26 Oct. 1805, 3-6. [CH]
Reuben L., s/o David R. died 7 Feb. 1900, ae 93-1. [AR]
Rhoda J., d/o David Fogg died 26 Oct. 1919, ae 82-8-21. [AR]
Ruth, w/o Capt. David died 22 Apr. 1852, ae 72-4. [CH]
Sally, d/o Jacob bur. 1796. [CH]
Sarah, w/o Joshua Sr. bur. 19 Aug. 1783, ae 72. [CH]
Sarah, d/o Capt. David bur. 13 July 1819, ae 0-10. [CH]
Sarah, w/o Jeremiah bur. 29 Apr. 1840, ae 75. [CH]
Sarah, d/o Stacy Brown, ae 70-8-11, wid. died 3 Aug. 1885. [TR]
Sarah E., d/o Oliver & Elizabeth died 11 Oct. 1840, ae 19 mos. [CEM]
Simon, Capt. died 20 July 1831, ae 87 yrs. [CEM]
Simon, s/o John, ae 86-3-25, wid. died 23 Dec. 1890, ae 86-3-25.
    [TR][CEM][AR]
Simon died 29 July 1893, ae 85. [AR]
Stephen bur. 7 Oct. 1820, ae 50. [CH]
Stephen bur. 4 Dec. 1837, ae 30. [CH]

BROWN Cont.

Thomas Lovering, s/o Levi & Lydia died 24 Mar. 1835, ae 24-2. [CEM][CH]
Widow of Joshua bur. 8 Jan. 1814, ae near 90. [CH]
Walter Harriman, s/o Abel I. & Charlotte died 2 Aug. 1860, ae 0-5. [CH]

BUNKER:

Eli J., s/o Smith died 10 Sep. 1912, ae 71-9-13. [AR]
James A., s/o John C. b. 25 Mar. 1853, d. 6 Mar. 1911, ae 57-11-10. [AR][CEM]

BURLEIGH/BURLEY:

Sarah, d/o Benj. Jenness died 1 May 1932, ae 90-4-22. [AR]
Widow bur. May 1823, ae 72, [CH]
William W. b. 4 May 1859, d. 14 Jan. 1907. [CEM]

BURTON:

Charles C. b. 5 Jan. 1814, d. 30 Sep. 1905. [CEM]
Dorcus, w/o Charles b. 24 Dec. 1821, d. 24 Mar. 1898.
George W. died 1 May 1871, ae 30-8. [CEM]

CALAUM:

Katherine F., d/o Rensselaer Freeman died 21 Mar. 1939, ae 84-4-2. [AR]

CAMPBELL:

Edward L., s/o Wm C. died 17 July 1921, ae 38-7-21. [AR]

CANDAGE:

Hannah died 3 Mar. 1897, ae 69. [AR]

CANNON:

John, s/o Aaron died 27 Apr. 1938, ae 83-8-5. [AR]

CARD:

Elias Tarlton, s/o James W. died 20 Aug. 1929, ae 54-2-14. [AR]

CARLISLE:

Ida M., d/o Franklin Hayes died 11 June 1941, ae 71-2-15. [AR]

CARLSON:

John D., s/o Carl Anderson died 16 Oct. 1928, ae 44-4-22. [AR]

CARR:

Josette A., d/o Joseph H. Warren died 8 Mar. 1896, ae 36. [AR]

CARSWELL:

Frances A., w/o Samuel & d/o Wm Philips died 4 Jan. 1898, ae 75-0-12.
  [AR][CEM]
Mary, Mrs., d/o Mr. Greely, ae 72-0-25, wid. died 14 Dec. 1881. [TR]
Samuel G. died 25 June 1891, ae 81 yrs. [CEM][AR]

CARTER:
Ellen F., d/o Simon Fogg died 5 Jan. 1917, ae 75-1-29. [AR]
Horace W., s/o Enoch died 11 May 1917, ae 81-0-23. [AR]
John M., s/o Wm H. died 23 Nov. 1937, ae 72-0-26. [AR]
Martha, d/o George W. Page, died 16 Feb. 1933, ae 58-1-9. [AR]

CASEY:
Constance E., d/o E. Justin Rand died 3 Sep. 1943, ae 33-5-18. [AR]

CASWELL:
Hattie F., d/o George W. Johnson died 18 Apr. 1941, ae 76-4-1. [AR]
Lucy E., w/o Timothy & d/o Edward Simpson died 10 Dec. 1908, ae 86-3-17.
   [CEM][AR]

CHAPMAN:
Abigail, wid. of James died 23 Feb. 1852, ae 75-4. [CH]
Abigail, w/o David died 13 Dec. 1878, ae 83-10. [CEM]
Benjamin James, s/o Benjamin died 17 Jan. 1843, ae 8. [CH][CEM]
David died 9 Feb. 1826, ae 30. [CEM][CH]
Edward Nathan, s/o Samuel & Sarah E. died 27 Aug. 1859, ae 1-5. [CH][CEM]
Elizabeth, d/o Benjamin & Hannah died 26 Jan. 1828, ae 0-0-1. [CH]
Elizabeth J., w/o Leonard died 14 Nov. 1848, ae 24-7. [CEM][CH]
Hannah, w/o Benjamin died 25 Aug. 1848, ae 44-9. [CH]
Hattie died 22 Aug. 1857. [CEM]
Infant c/o Benjamin & Hannah bur. 8 Sep. 1819, ae 0-0-1. [CH]
Infant c/o Samuel Jr. bur. 24 Aug. 1867, ae 1. [CH]
James, s/o John & Mary died 15 Apr. 1740. [TR]
James, s/o James & Abigail bur. 5 Oct. 1805, ae 6 wk. [CH]
James, s/o Benjamin & Hannah bur. 22 Mar. 1822, ae 0-9. [CH]
James died 19 Mar. 1833, ae 71-9. [CH]
John died 9 Feb. 1885, ae 82-3. [CH]
John, s/o John born 25 May 1834, died 16 Apr. 1900, ae 65-11-20. [CEM][AR]
Leander, s/o Benjamin & Hannah died 20 Jan. 1842, ae 4. [CEM][CH]
Leander, s/o Leonard W. & Elizabeth J. died 13 Jan. 1849, ae 0-3-0. [CEM]
Leocada D., w/o John died 27 Sep. 1858, ae 54-4. [CH][CEM]
Lucretia A. born 13 Aug. 1839, died 11 Jan. 1899. [CH]
Martha Ann, d/o John & Leoceda O. died 8 Sep. 1839, ae 3 wk. [CH][CEM]
Martha W., wid. of Samuel died 17 Nov. 1848, ae 53. [CEM][CH]
Mary, d/o Samuel & Mary bur. 8 Apr. 1816, ae 21-11-0. [CH]
Mary, d/o Benjamin bur. 27 Aug. 1820, ae 5 wk. [CH]
Mary, sister James died 22 July 1844, ae 92-9. [CH]
Mary wid. of Samuel died 18 Oct. 1879, ae 75. [CH]
Mary W., d/o Winthrop Rowe & w/o Samuel, ae 73-6, wid. died 18 Oct. 1879.
   [TR][CEM]
Mercy, w/o Samuel died 11 May 1845, ae 76-2. [CH][CEM]
Polly, d/o Samuel & Mercy died 7 Apr. 1816, ae 22. [CEM]
Rachel, wid. bur. 19 Feb. 1798, ae 97. [CH]
Rosamond B., d/o John & Leoceda D. died 6 Apr. 1841, ae 4-10.]CEM]

CHAPMAN Cont.
Samuel died 17 Nov. 1804, ae 78. [CH]
Samuel died 6 Sep. 1840, ae 85-9. [CEM][CH]
Samuel died 24 May 1866, ae 41. [CEM]
Samuel, s/o Samuel, md. died 29 Mar. 1876, ae 84. [TR][CH][CEM]
Sarah, wid. of John died 6 Oct. 1829, ae 25. [CH]
Sarah E. born 15 Jan. 1832, died 24 Nov. 1922. [CEM]
Sarah Leavitt, w/o John died 6 Oct. 1829, ae 25. [CH]
Thomas M. died 20 Aug. 1868, ae 41-4. [CEM]

CHASE:
Roy J., s/o Fred N. & Emma (Bolke) died 13 Nov. 1924, ae 13-9-8. [AR]

CHEVALIER:
Hazel L., d/o Lewis A. & Grace L. (Morse), b. 1908, d. 4 Sep. 1910, ae 2-6-27. [CEM][AR]
Julia E., d/o Joseph L. Philbrick died 11 Mar. 1943, ae 84-10-15. [AR]
Wilfred J., s/o Louis died 12 Oct. 1937, ae 81-9-10. [AR]

CINNSON?
Olive Cotton, d/o Frank B., ae 1-5-6 died 19 Mar. 1889. [TR]

CLARK:
Abigail (Hinkley), wid. of James of Georgetown, Me. died 26 Jan. 1849, ae over 85. [CH]
Mary Lizzie, d/o Albion S., ae 0-0-13 died 6 June 1895. [TR][AR]
Mary Frances, Mrs., d/o Jere. Marston died 4 May 1849, ae 22. [CH]
Rachel, w/o Mayhew bur. 29 Dec. 1775. [CH]
William of Portland, Me. bur. 10 Apr. 1850, ae 26. [CH]

COLEMAN:
George A., s/o George E. died 19 Dec. 1928, ae 73-6-1. [AR]

COREY:
Lydia H.B., d/o Jacob H. Brown died 2 Feb. 1932, ae 89-3-29. [AR]
Orrin R., s/o Ira R. died 12 Aug. 1905, ae 72-2-16. [AR]

CORLISS:
Martin C., s/o Martin J., b. 1918, d. 3 Sep. 1926, ae 8-2-15. [CEM}[AR]
Martin J. died 8 Oct. 1943, ae 58-2-16. [AR]

COTTON:
Abigail, w/o Jonathan bur. 2 July 1832, ae 24. [CH]
Anna, d/o Thomas bur. 1800. [CH]
Elizabeth, d/o Thomas Jr. bur. 30 July 1801, ae 15. [CH]
George D., s/o Jonathan died 11 Aug. 1918, ae 72-8-20. [AR]
John bur. 13 July 1778, ae 3. [CH]
Jonathan bur. 20 Aug. 1799. [CH]

COTTON Cont.

Jonathan, s/o Morris, ae 78, single died 24 Dec. 1880. [TR]
Levi, infant bur. 22 Mar. 1769. [CH]
Mary bur. 16 Apr. 1803, ae 48. [CH]
Mary W., ae 74-6, md. died 24 Sep. 1880. [TR]
Morris died 27 Mar. 1804, ae 28. [TR][CH]
Morris, s/o Jonathan died 3 Apr. 1921, ae 93-7-2. [AR]
Sarah, widow bur. 2 Sep. 1810, ae 88-8. [CH]
Thomas Jr. died 31 Dec. 1801, ae 46. [CH]
Thomas bur. 24 Sep. 1803, ae 78. [CH]
Thomas, s/o Morris died 18 May 1804, ae 20-11-17. [TR][CH]

COULTER:

Alice D., d/o George L. & Alice M. (Arnold) died 4 Aug. 1906, ae 0-1-16. [AR]

CRAIG:

George P.A., s/o Alexander died 11 Geb. 1919, ae 44-8-13. [AR]
Peter David, s/o George A. & Roberta J. (Taylor) died 9 Jan. 1939, ae 0-0-3.
  [AR]
Robert A., s/o James died 9 Sep. 1917, ae 48-9-21. [AR]

CREASEY:

Stephen H., s/o Enoch P. & Eliza D. died 1 Nov. 1863, ae 2-9. [CEM]

CRIMBAL/CRIMBLE:

Abigail H., w/o Benjamin died 25 May 1862, ae 53, [CH][CEM]
Abigail, d/o Eben Taylor died 6 Aug. 1900, ae 83. [AR]
Abraham bur. 14 Nov. 1814, ae 53. [CH]
Abraham bur. 19 Jan. 1827, ae 30. [CH]
Mary bur. Jan. 1801, ae 83. [CH]
Miriam bur. 24 Oct. 1814, ae 21. [CH]
Sarah, w/o Benjamin died 5 Mar. 1855, ae 55. [CEM][CH]
Widow died 10 Sep. 1851, ae 88-11. [CH]

CROCKETT:

George L., s/o Thomas died 14 July 1930, ae 36-10. [AR]

CRONK:

John Henry, gs/o Stephen bur. 28 May 1836. [CH]

CUMMINGS:

Betsey, w/o James & d/o Paul Long bur. 6 Apr. 1805, ae 18. [CH]

CURRIER:

James E., s/o Gilbert died 7 Oct. 1939, ae 24-2-6. [AR]

DALTON:

Abby S., d/o Eben L. & Alvena bur. 24 Mar. 1863, ae 0-4. [CH]

Abigail bur. 25 Dec. 1802, ae 76. [CH]

Albert, s/o Rufus & W.L. died 4 Apr. 1851, ae 4 dy. [CEM]

Benjamin, s/o Tristram bur. 19 Aug. 1824, ae 24. [CH]

Benjamin, s/o Morris C. & Ursula bur. 24 Sep. 1828, ae 1-3. [CH]

Celia A., w/o Eben H. & d/o Samuel Warner, b. 22 Feb. 1846, d. 31 Dec. 1906,
   ae 60-10-10. [CH][AR]

Charles Edwin, s/o rufus & Mehitabel died 27 June 1846, ae 5-0-17. [CH][CEM]

Child of Ebenezer bur. 19 aug. 1799. [CH]

Child of Rufus bur. 3 Apr. 1851, ae 0-0-23. [CH]

Daniel W., s/o Daniel died 27 Mar. 1918, ae 69-10-6. [AR]

Dolly, w/o Tristram died 14 Feb. 1802, ae 27. [CH]

Dolly Brown, d/o Tristram bur. 20 July 1811, ae 1-11. [CH]

Eben H., s/o Rufus, b. 31 Aug. 1842, d. 5 Nov. 1913. [CH][AR]

Eben L., s/o Morris C. died 7 June 1924, ae 88-3-27. [AR]

Ebenezer Marden died 12 Nov. 1846, ae 78. [CH][CEM]

Ellen L., d/o George E. ae 0-3-0 died 11 Sep. 1889. [TR]

Emily A., d/o Ruel Shapleigh died 24 Mar. 1898, ae 63-10. [AR]

George Rufus, twin s/o Rufus died 14 Sep. 1848, ae 11 wk. [CH][CEM]

Georgiana Esther, twin d/o Rufus died 15 Sep. 1849, ae 14 mo. [CH][CEM]

Infant, s/o Irving & Emma Jenness, ae 3 died 25 Mar. 1880. [TR]

John bur. 18 Oct. 1767. [CH]

Joseph Franklin, s/o Rufus & Mehitable died 5 Aug. 1845, ae 14 mo. [CH][CEM]

Josiah bur. 10 Nov. 1812, ae 72. [CH]

Love, wid of Ebenezer M. died 7 Aug. 1848, ae 76. [CH][CEM]

Maria, d/o Ebenezer M. bur. 10 Dec. 1820, ae 19. [CH]

Maria, w/o Rufus died 13 Mar. 1887, ae 73. [CEM]

Martha died 8 Dec. 1820, ae 18. [CEM]

Mary, d/o Samuel bur. 30 June 1769. [CH]

Mary Hannah, d/o Jonathan Cotton, ae 41, md. died Apr. 1880. [TR]

Mehitable L., w/o Rufus died 7 Sep. 1873, ae 60. [CEM]

Michael bur. 4 May 1846, ae 82. [CH]

Philemon, infant bur. 2 Feb. 1770. [CH]

Rienzi L., d/o George E. died 24 July 1937, ae 51-7-8. [AR]

Rufus died Sep. 1864. [TR]

Rufus, s/o Ebenezer, ae 80-2-21, wid. died 29 Feb. 1888, ae 80. [TR][CEM]

Rufus J., s/o Rufus & W.L. died 2 Sep. 1861, ae 9-9. [CEM]

Samuel, s/o Samuel bur. 23 July 1770, ae infant. [CH]

Samuel R. b. 1863, d. 1909. [CEM]

Thomas, s/o Ebenezer bur. 29 Dec. 1797. [CH]

Tristram died 21 Nov. 1854, ae 80. [CH]

DAVIS:

Child of Reuben bur. Apr. 1799. [CH]

Child of Benjamon bur. 1801. [CH]

Child of Oliver bur. 1814, ae 0-6. [CH]

DAVIS Cont.
Child of Simon bur. 26 Dec. 1826, ae 0-0-2. [CH]
Child of Joseph bur. 26 May 1841, ae 0-0-1. [CH]
Elijah bur. 8 Jan. 1856, ae 68. [CH][CEM]
J. Hamilton, s/o Elijah died 29 Mar. 1913, ae 68-2-20. [AR]
Lydia, w/o Elijah died 26 Apr. 1869, ae 92-5. [CEM]
Lydia A., d/o Joseph Kelley died 29 Nov. 1909, ae 74-8-5. [AR]
Mary, wid. of Samuel died 30 May 1804, ae 78. [CH]
Myrtle E., d/o Chester A. died 24 Aug. 1923, ae 11. [AR]
Nelson S., s/o Thomas N. died 22 Aug. 1932, ae 66-10-13. [AR]
Samuel bur. before Apr. 1804, ae 83. [CH]
Sarah Frances, d/o Orin L. & Sarah bur. 30 Mar. 1839, ae 5-3. [CH][CEM]
Widow & mother of Dosty bur. 9 Feb. 1789. [CH]
Widow of Simon of Winnecut bur. 20 Jan. 1815, ae 37. [CH]
Widow of James bur. 17 Feb. 1836, ae 88-5. [CH]
Widow of Benjamin bur. 27 Apr, 1850. [CH]
Willie Stone, s/o Jacob, single died 11 Dec. 1870, ae 12. [TR][CH]

DEARBORN:
Abigal (Batchelder), w/o John b. 28 Dec. 1667, d. 14 Nov. 1736, ae 69. [CEM]
Abigail, w/o Capt. John bur. 21 Jan. 1830, ae 69. [CH]
Abner, s/o John bur. 2 Sep. 1779, ae 17. [CH]
Affiah, Mrs. d/o John Hobbs d. 1 Oct. 1885. [TR]
Alvah died 6 June 1869, ae 72-9. [CEM]
Angeline Parker, d/o John & Sarah died 22 Apr. 1846, ae 2-3. [CH]
Ann Maclay, d/o Benjamin bur. 10 Oct. 1807, ae 2-6. [CH]
Anna, w/o Simon died 22 Oct. 1765, ae 52. [CEM]
Bethiah, w/o Capt. John bur. 14 July 1807, ae 66. [CH]
Charles H. b. 1858, d. 1863. [CEM]
Child of Reuben bur. Apr. 1799. [CH]
Child of Benjamin bur. 1801. [CH]
Child of Oliver bur. 1814, ae 0-6. [CH]
Child of Simon bur. 26 Dec. 1826, ae 0-0-2. [CH]
Child of Joseph bur. 26 May 1841, ae 0-0-1. [CH]
Daniel bur. 24 Dec. 1783, ae 33-3. [CH]
Daniel bur. 18 Aug. 1842, ae 42, [CH]
Dolly, w/o Nathaniel died 24 Apr. 1809, ae 28-6-24. [CH][CEM]
Dolly G., d/o Nathaniel, b. 7 July 1812, d. 26 Dec. 1906, ae 94-5-19.
   [CEM][AR]
Edmund B,. s/o Samuel b. 28 Nov. 1806, d. 25 Jan. 1886. [CEM]
Elizabeth Tabor, 3nd w/o Joseph bur. Nov. 1845. [CH]
Elizabeth, Miss. old bur. 18 Dec. 1869. [CH]
Esther, widow bur. 24 July 1798. [CH]
George b. 1859, d. 1892. [CEM]
George, s/o Jeremiah, b. 1834, d. 15 Feb. 1907, ae 72-6-15. [CEM][AR]
George Washington, s/o Joseph bur. Sep. 1800. [CH]

DEARBORN Cont.

Hannah, wid. of Oliver bur. 2 Apr. 1832, ae 44. [CH]

Hannah, wid. of Samuel died 20 Feb. 1841, ae 88. [CH][CEM]

Hannah, w/o Jeremiah died 20 Mar. 1884, ae 85. [CEM]

Henery died 14 Feb. 1882, ae 42. [CEM]

Henry, s/o Simon bur. 19 July 1798. [CH]

Henry Washington, s/o Simon & Mary died 21 Jan. 1803, ae 1-8-17. [CH]

Herbert b. 1855, d. 1864. [CEM]

Horatio Gates, s/o Capt. John died 23 Apr. 1802, ae 23. [CH][CEM]

Isaac Hurd, s/o Jeremiah & Hannah died 19 Jan. 1840, ae 58? [CH][CEM]

James died 18 Feb. 1809, ae nearly 66. [CH]

James, s/o Lt. bur. 1789, ae 1-8. [CH]

Jamima, native of stratham died 10 May 1848. [CH]

Jeremiah bur. 27 Jan. 1784, ae 57. [CH]

Jeremiah bur. 15 Feb. 1829, ae 14-8. [CH]

Jeremiah died 5 Oct. 1856, ae 62. [CH][CEM]

John, s/o Simon & Sarah died 28 Apr. or 26 Dec. 1736, ae 4. [CEM]

John b. 10 Oct. 1666, d. 28 Nov. 1750. [CEM]

John, Capt., bro. of Gen. Henry D., died 18 Jan. 1830, ae 92. [CH][CEM]

John died 20 Oct. 1880, ae 59. [CEM]

Jonathan, s/o Joseph bur. 7 July 1778. [CH]

Jonathan, s/o Simon bur. 3 July 1837. [CH]

Jonathan died 13 Feb. 1847, ae 64. [CH]

Joseph, s/o Joseph & Anna died 13 Feb. 1738, ae 13. [CEM]

Joseph bur. 15 Jan. 1768, ae 72. [CH]

Mrs. Joseph of Ossipee, d/o Lt. James Wedgwood bur. Sep. 1801. [CH]

Joseph of Ossipee, s/o Capt. John bur. 6 Nov. 1891, ae 33. [CH]

Joseph died 4 Apr. 1811, ae 56. [CH][CEM]

Joseph, single bur. 16 Mar. 1826, ae 54. [CH]

Joseph bur. 16 Sep. 1857, ae 45. [CH]

Josephine, d/o Joseph & Late Eliz. Tabor Shaw died 30 Dec. 1845, ae 0-8½. [CH]

Lawrence , s/o Nathaniel died 14 Nov. 1895, ae 78. [AR]

Leocarda died 28 Nov. 1804, ae 21. [CH][CEM]

Levi, Dr. died 8 Mar. 1792. [CH][CEM]

Levi, Dr. died 5 Mar. 1902, ae 62. [CH][CEM]

Levi W., s/o Jeremiah, b. 1832, d. 17 Nov. 1918, ae 86-10-11. [CEM][AR]

Lucy, w/o Nathaniel died 8 June 1867, ae 85-0-26. [CEM][CH]

Lucy Frances, d/o John & Sarah died 29 Jan. 1846, ae 0-6. [CH]

Lucy Parker, Mrs. died 18 Nov. 1848, ae 27-9. [CEM][CH]

Lydia (Marston), wid. of Samuel died 28 June 1851, ae 58-3. [CH][CEM]

Marcia Adeline, d/o John & Sarah died 11 Sep. 1849, ae 8 wk. [CH]

Martha J. (Philbrick) b. 1838, d. 1898. [CEM]

Mary, wid. bur. 20 Dec. 1796. [CH]

Mary, wid. of Joseph died 1 Jan. 1835, ae 76-7. [CH][CEM]

Mary, w/o Simeon died 5 Jan. 1845, ae 68. [CEM]

Mary, w/o Samuel died 5 Jan. 1848, ae 68. [CEM]

DEARBORN Cont.

Mary, w/o Simon died 7 Nov. 1848, ae 68. [CH]
Mary, wid. of Simon died 28 Apr. 1859, ae 90-5. [CH][CEM]
Mary, w/o John died 29 Apr. 1901, ae 82-6-4. [CEM]
Mary Ann, d/o Joseph & Mary died 14 Jan. 1802, ae 7. [CH]
Mary Ann H., w/o Joseph bur. 10 July 1842, ae 28. [CH]
Mary Ann Angeline, d/o Joseph bur. 10 Sep. 1843, ae 1-2. [CH]
Mary E., d/o Jeremiah & Hannah died 4 Nov. 1862, ae 26-8. [CEM][CH]
Mary E., d/o Nathaniel Batchelder died 13 July 1905, ae 69-6-6. [AR][CEM]
Mary Frances, d/o Joseph of Hampton died 20 Nov. 1852, ae 0-7. [CH]
Mary H. b/ 1838, d. 1906. [CEM]
Nancy, d/o Levi bur. 26 Mar. 1778, ae 16. [CH]
Nancy, d/o Simeon bur. 16 July 1798. [CH]
Nathaniel, Deacon died 30 Nov. 1854, ae 77-3-2. [CEM][CH]
Oliver, s/o Joseph bur. July? 1778. [CH]
Oliver, s/o Simeon bur. 7 Jan. 1805, ae 1-7-0. [CH]
Oliver bur. 1814, ae 29-6-19. [CH]
Oliver bur. 30 Jan. 1833, ae 25. [CH]
Reuben Jr., Mrs., bur. 16 Apr. 1786. [CH]
Reuben bur. 25 Jan. 1790. [CH]
Reuben Gove bur. 15 June 1797. [CH]
Reuben Gove bur. 18 June 1823, ae 71. [CH]
Richard Greenlief, s/o Samuel Jr. & Ruth bur. 25 Apr. 1810, ae 1-6. [CH]
Ruth, w/o Samuel died 19 Dec. 1817, ae 35-5. [CH][CEM]
Sally died 3 Apr. 1891, ae 90. [AR]
Samuel, s/o Reuben bur. 16 July 1778, ae 18. [CH]
Samuel died 11 Nov. 1838, ae 84. [CEM][CH]
Samuel died 21 Nov. 1846, ae 65-10. [CH][CEM]
Sarah, d/o Joseph & Anna died 13 Feb. 1736, ae 4. [CEM]
Sarah, d/o R.G. bur. 11 June 1775. [CH]
Sarah, wid., bur. 18 Sep. 1777, ae 72-9. [CH]
Sarah of Concord, wid. of True W.G. bur, 21 Sep. 1843, ae 70. [CH]
Sarah, w/o Alvah died 4 Nov. 1861, ae 61-10. [CEM][CH]
Sarah A., w/o George & d/o Nathaniel Batchelder, b. 1837, d. 15 Dec. 1932, ae 95-3-3. [CEM][AR]
Seth, d/o George, ae 90-10-8 died 3 Apr. 1891. [TR]
Simeon died 23 Aug. 1856, ae 77. [CH][CEM]
Simon died 3 Nov. 1843, ae 77. [CEM]
Sylvester died 31 Dec. 1861, ae 24. [CH]
Widow died 9 Feb. 1789. [CH]
Widow of Simon of Winnecut d. 20 Jan. 1815, ae 30. [CH]
Widow of James d. 17 Feb. 1836, ae 88-5. [CH]
Widow of Benjamin d. 27 Apr. 1850. [CH]

DELANEY:

Mary A., d/o James Sanborn, died 2 Oct. 1933, ae 83-10. [AR]

DEMBRACK:

Lizzie Bachelder, d/o James L., ae 32, md. died 9 June 1879. [TR]

DeMERITTE:

Edwin, s/o Stephen died 27 Nov. 1936, ae 90-8-24. [AR]

DINSMORE:

Althea, w/o Rev. John & d/o Late Rev. Nathan Cobb, b. 14 Feb. 1830 in
Portland, Me., died 11 July 1859, ae 29-5. (CEM][CH]

DOW:

Abbie L., w/o David died 19 Oct. 1885, ae 64. [CEM]
Abram C., s/o David M. died 7 May 1939, ae 77-3-6. [AR]
Abraham D. died 24 Nov. 1840, ae 75. [CEM][CH]
Affish, Mrs., d/o John Hobbs, ae 63-11-5 died 1 Oct. 1885. [TR]
Anna, d/o David G. bur. 12 Oct. 1849, ae 1-7. [CH]
Child of John bur. 16 Nov. 1835, ae 2. [CH]
Child of Simon bur. 16 Nov. 1798. [CH]
Daniel, s/o Simon, md. died 6 Apr. 1869, ae 79. [TR][CH][CEM]
David M. died 12 Apr. 1870, ae 49. [CEM]
Emily A., w/o Samuel & d/o James Marston, b. 1848, d. 2 June 1919,
ae 73-0-28. [AR][CEM]
Frank P., s/o David M. & Abbie L., ae 24-5 single died 27 Aug. 1876.
[TR][CEM]
Fred L. b. 1873, d. _____. [CEM]
George H. died 5 Apr. 1883, ae 28-8. [CEM]
George O. died 27 Sep. 1856, ae 38-7. [CH][CEM]
Gertrude E., w/o Fred L. b. 1871, d. 1907. [CEM]
Hebsibah bur. July 1785, ae 82. [CH]
J. Russell, s/o Samuel A. died 20 Feb. 1934, ae 47-10-12. [AR]
John died 9 June 1851. [CH]
Lottie F., d/o Samuel A., b. 24 May 1878, d. 3 Jan. 1899. [CEM][AR]
Love, Mrs. wid. of Abram H. died 10 Feb. 1855, ae 81. [CH][CEM]
Lucinda, w/o Daniel died 1 Oct. 1831, ae 29. [CH]
Martha G., w/o David M. died 4 Dec. 1844, ae 21, [CH][CEM]
Mary H., w/o George O. died 4 May 1877, ae 51-7. [CEM]
Rachel, widow bur. 26 Mar. 1807, ae 75. [CH]
Rachel b. 1801, d. 29 May 1889. [CEM]
Samuel A., s/o Samuel, b. 1847, d. 15 Mar. 1933, ae 85-6-10. [CEM][AR]
Simon bur. 2 Feb. 1805. [CH]
Simon died 8 Aug. 1840, ae 33. [CEM]
Widow of Simon & d/o late Coffin Page bur. 31 May 1821, ae 33. [CH]
Widow bur. Dec. 1867. [CH]

DOWNING:
Anna J., d/o John Mysen died 16 June 1912, ae 23-3-27. [AR]
Daisy A., d/o Oliver Page died 7 Jan. 1900, ae 30-9-9. [AR]
Isabel, d/o Jonas & Anna J. (Myson) died 14 June 1912, ae 0-2-7. [AR]

DRAKE:
Abigail (Weare), w/o Abraham, sister of 1st Gov. of NH, b. 17 May 1716, d. 2
     Oct. 1746. [CEM]
Abigail (Dearborn), w/o Abraham b. 19 Oct. 1720, d. 1 July 1811. [CEM][CH]
Abraham, b. 4 Dec. 1715, bur. 1 Aug. 1781, ae 65-8. [CH][CEM]
     [Prov. Congress, Lt. Col. Rev. War, French & Indian War.]
Abraham, Cornet, died 11 May 1819., ae 74-3. [CH][CEM]
Abraham bur. 16 Feb. 1865, ae 82. [CH][CEM]
Abraham, s/o Francis, ae 57½, md. died 14 Apr. 1874. [TR][CEM]
Adaline N., w/o Dea. Abraham died 28 June 1892, ae 75-11 [CEM]
Annie M., w/o Walter L. died 20 Nov. 1909, ae 74. [CEM]
Annie T., w/o Nathaniel & d/o Amos Seavey, b. 14 Oct. 1824, d. 23 Dec. 1900,
     ae 76-2-9. [AR][CEM]
Betsy bur. 8 Jan. 1853. [CH]
Child of Samuel & Mehitabel bur. 3 Feb. 1818, ae 3 wk. [CH]
Climena (Hodsdon), w/o Francis b. 7 Apr. 1854, d. 10 Jan. 1918. [CEM]
Elizabeth, wid. of Nathaniel died 8 Jan. 1853, ae 91-8-11. [CH][CEM]
Emma S., d/o Freeman, ae 25-6-0, single died 12 Aug. 1887. [TR]
Fabyan bur. 14 Nov. 1841, ae 22-10. [CH][CEM]
Francis bur. 21 June 1843, ae 57-10. [CH]
Francis R., s/p Nathaniel, b. 5 Nov. 1845, d. 18 May 1902. [CEM][AR]
Freeman, s/o Samuel died 24 Nov. 1901, ae 66-10-27. [AR]
Henry F., s/o Freeman died 26 Oct. 1926, ae 71-1-10. [AR]
Herman Edwards, s/o Joshua & Sarah died 24 Dec. 1852, ae 0-7-16. [CH][CEM]
Joseph, s/o Weare & Anne d. 19 Jan. 1765. [TR]
Joshua P., s/o Samuel, b. 22 Jan. 1823, d. 19 Nov. 1901. [CEM][AR]
Justin E., s/o Joshua P. died 5 May 1939, ae 82-9-275. [AR]
Martha A., d/o Joshua & Sarah b. 8 Oct. 1853, d. 25 July 1875. [CEM]
Mary, w/o Cornet Abraham died 8 Feb. 1815, ae 66 [CEM]
Mary, Mrs. bur. 4 Feb. 1868, ae 77. [CH]
Mary H., d/o John Hobbs died 23 June 1909, ae 77-4-19 .[AR]
Mary J. died 19 Nov. 1848, ae 27. [CH]
Mary L., w/o Samuel J. died 15 Oct. 1882, ae 61-5. [CEM]
Mehitabel, w/o Samuel bur. 8 June 1850, ae 51-5. [CH][CEM]
Minnie W., d/o Freeman died 8 Nov. 1917, ae 50-9-3. [AR]
Nathaniel, s/o Francis bur. 7 July 1816, ae 1-2. [CH]
Nathaniel Jr. bur. 25 Apr. 1823, ae 25. [CH][CEM]
Nathaniel died 5 Nov. 1828, ae 68-9. [CH][CEM]
Nathaniel died 6 June 1850, ae 85. [CH]
Nathaniel, s/o Francis, b. 21 Aug. 1825, died 22 May 1895. [TR][CEM][AR]
Nellie F., d/o Freeman died 23 Nov. 1941, ae 77-5-29. [AR]
Robert Weare, s/o Clifford S., b. 25 Dec. 1919, d. 14 May 1923, ae 3-4-17.
     [CEM][AR]

DRAKE Cont.
Ruth Elizabeth, b. 11 June 1912, d. 24 Oct. 1917. [CEM]
Samuel, husband of Mehitabel bur. 3 Nov. 1835, ae 42-6. [CH][CEM]
Samuel J. died 15 Oct. 1891, ae 70-5. [CEM]
Sarah died 25 Feb. 1850, ae 75. [CH][CEM]
Sarah Abigail, d/o Francis bur. 24 Mar. 1821, ae 2-6. [CH]
Sarah E., w/o Samuel J. b. 24 Aug. 1826, d. 12 June 1915. [CEM]
Sarah L., w/o Joshua P. b. 16 Mar. 1825, d. 16 Dec. 1885. [CEM]
Theodate, d/o Abraham bur. 23 May 1769, ae 5. [CH]
Walter L. died 25 Oct. 1901, ae 53-5. [CEM]

DRAPER:
John C., s/o Gideon F. died 13 Oct. 1912, ae 87-1-10. [AR]

DREW:
Ada B., d/o Stephen Tarlton died 8 Apr. 1932, ae 64-8-2, [AR]
Albert C., s/o Willie, ae 0-16-0 died 2 Oct. 1887. [TR]
Elwell P. died 1 Sep. 1891, ae 0-0-12. [AR]
Emily A., d/o Fred A. died 15 Mar. 1928, ae 32-7-13. [AR]
Fred A., s/o Nathaniel died 15 Oct. 1924, ae 54-4-29. [AR]
Willie P., s/o Nathaniel died 22 May 1899, ae 37-8. [AR]

DRINKWATER:
C.S. b. 1898, d. 1899. [CEM]
Gladys M. b. 1882, d. 1899. [CEM]
Howard L. b. 1877, d. ____ [CEM]
Jennie W. b. 1875, d. ____ [CEM]
Lemira L., w/o Richard A. Berry, b. 1849, d. 1898. [CEM]
Lottie b. 1870, d. ____ [CEM]
Millie H. b. 1879, d. ____ [CEM]
Pearl E. b. 1884, d. ____ [CEM]

DRYSDALE:
William, s/o Joseph died 26 Oct. 1940, ae 72-13-17. [AR]

DUNHAM:
Augusta A., w/o William H. & d/o Jeremiah Brown, b. 10 Oct. 1840, d. 6 May
    1910. [CEM][AR]
George H. b. 8 June 1838, d. 12 Apr. 1916, Navy Civil War. [CEM]

DURGIN:
Marcia P., w/o Arthur H. b. 18 Oct. 1858, d. 13 May 1919. [CEM]

DUSTIN:
Clara B., d/o John S.R. Brown died 18 May 1941, ae 86-2-15. [AR]

EATON:
Mary, wid. bur. 10 Oct. 1818, ae 53. [CH]

EGAN:
Thomas , s/o Michael died 18 Feb. 1941, ae 44. [AR]

ELKING/ELKINS:
Henry died 7 Mar. 1852, ae 77. [CH]
Henry, s/o Jeremiah, ae 65, md. died 19 Jan. 1871. [TR]
Mrs. Marjorie. ae 81 wid. died 1883. [TR]

EWER:
Louis Cass died 4 Feb. 1925, ae 79. [AR]

FENWICK:
Harriet F., d/o James Marston died 2 Apr. 1941, ae 91-7-1/ [AR]
Joseph Allen, s/o Ezekiel, b. 1852, d. 11 Apr. 1918, ae 66-0-21. [CEM][AR]

FERNOLD:
Joanna A., d/o James Butler died 19 June 1937, ae 88-5-3. [AR]
Lavinia, d/o Jonathan Dore died 28 Aug. 1923, ae 80-1. [AR]

FISHER:
Daniel, s/o Brewster died 12 Aug. 1918, ae 80-4-6. [AR]

FLANDERS:
Margery E., d/o Ernest R. & Georgie R. (Day) died 23 Dec. 1920, ae 1-6-4.
  [AR]

FLEMING:
George, s/o John died 22 Apr. 1930, ae 57-11-23. [AR]

FOGG:
Abbie M., d/o Cyrus Fogg, b. 23 Aug. 1879, d. 8 May 1917, ae 37-8-15.
  [AR][CEM]
Abigail bur. 8 Apr. 1767. [CH]
Abigail bur. 13 Sep. 1854, ae 93-11-23. [CH]
Abner, Capt. bur. Aug. 1788. [CH]
Almira (Haines) w/o Richard b. 14 Mar. 1806, d. 2 Oct. 1888. [CEM]
Andrew J. died 26 Jan. 1891, ae 62-3-3. [AR]
Bathsheba, d/o Joshua Shaw, ae 77, wid. died 1870. [TR]
Bethia, Miss d/o Samuel Roby died 8 Oct. 1845, ae 71-8. [CH]
Bethiah, w/o Abner bur. 26 July 1773, ae 65. [CH]
Betty, Miss bur. 28 June 1852, ae 88. [CH]
Child, twin of Dr. John bur. 17 Nov. 1803, ae 0-0-1. [CH]
Child of Ebenezer bur. 16 Aug. 1828, ae 2. [CH]
Child of Ebenezer bur. 14 Nov. 1828, ae 0-0-1. [CH]

FOGG Cont.

Cyrus, s/o Simeon b. 21 June 1845, d. 26 Sep. 1912, ae 67-3-5. [CEM][AR]
Daniel, s/o Samuel bur. 15 Jan. 1770, ae 1-9. [CH]
Dearborn of Hampton died 13 Dec. 1841, ae 85. [CH][CEM]
Deborah, w/o Ransom died 5 Sep. 1854, ae 23. [CH]
Dolly, widow of Dearborn died 16 May 1847, ae 76, [CH]
Dorothy, widow of Dearborn died 15 May 1847, ae 76. [CEM]
Ebenezer C. died 25 Jan. 1854, ae 52. [CH]
Edward bur. 27 July 1845, ae 50. [CH]
Elizabeth (Batchelder) w/o Richard b. 3 Dec. 1804, d. 7 Sep. 1838. [CEM]
Emery, s/o Simon died 21 June 1901, ae 48-6. [AR]
Emma A., d/o Elvin Locke died 9 Mar. 1921, ae 72-3-10. [AR]
Emma A., d/o Jonathan Locke, died 22 June 1941, ae 91-6-7. [AR]
Esther, infant d/o Dearborn bur. 1788. [CH]
Frank P., s/o Ransom died 22 Jan. 1857, ae 3. [CH]
Jemima, w/o Ebenezer died 1 Mar. 1846. [CH]
Jennie, d/o Simon & Lavinia b. 21 Sep. 1850, d. 20 Apr. 1887. [CEM]
Jeremiah, Mrs. bur. Apr. 1790. [CH]
Jeremiah bur. 28 Oct. 1810, ae 47. [CH]
Jeremiah William, s/o Dr. bur. 9 Nov. 1812, ae 6. [CH]
John, Dr. bur. 8 Mar. 1816, ae 52. [CH][CEM]
John D. Dr., s/o Dr. John drowned at Kittery 28 Nov. 1830, ae 32. [CH][CEM]
John bur. 21 Nov. 1840, ae 74-9. [CH]
L. Woodbury b. 1845, d. 1918. [CEM]
Lavinia, w/o Simon & d/o Jeremiah Marston, died 29 Sep. 1898, ae 89-10.
   [AR][CEM]
Levi W., s/o David died 31 May 1918, ae 72-11-13. [AR]
Lewis, s/o Simon & Lavinia died 19 Apr. 1854, ae 11. [CH][CEM]
Lucinda B. Fogg, w/o John H. Ferguson b. 2 June 1828, d. 8 May 1850. [CEM]
Lydia, d/o Tristram Dalton died 22 Oct. 1898, ae 85-8-16. [AR]
Margaret, ae 22 died Apr. 1867. [TR]
Mary, wid. bur. 1 Dec. 1815, ae 85-10. [CH]
Mary, d/o Ebenezer died 14 Aug. 1828, ae 2-0-23. [CEM]
Mary Ellen, d/o Nathaniel Tarlton died 3 Aug. 1941, ae 90-7-19. [AR]
Minah H., w/o Ebenezer C. died 22 Feb. 1848, ae 42 yrs. [CEM]
Moses bur. 1796. [CH]
Orice, shot at Bull Run, died 6 Oct. 1862, ae 23. [CH]
Polly, d/o John bur, 1795. [CH]
Ransom, s/o Ransom died 15 Aug. 1848, ae 5. [CH]
Rhoda, Mrs. died June 1857, ae 71. [CH]
Rhoda died 16 Mar. 1886, ae 68 yrs. [CEM]
Rhoda Ann, d/o Ransom died 19 Oct. 1849, ae 12. [CH]
Richard b. 7 Aug. 1799, d. 12 Mar. 1852, ae 52-7. [CH][CEM]
Richard Jr. b. 20 July 1841, d. 8 Sep. 1872. [CEM]
Ruth, w/o John bur. 28 Feb. 1818, ae 53. [CH]
Samuel, s/o Samuel bur. 28 Sep. 1820, ae 0-11. [CH]
Samuel bur. 28 Apr. 1825, ae 47-7. [CH]

FOGG Cont.

Samuel Dearborn, s/o David & Eliza bur. 20 Nov. 1840, ae 8. [CH]
Samuel Roby bur. 23 Feb. 1826, ae 82-11. [CH]
Sarah, widow of Dr. John died 15 Apr. 1858, ae 85-4. [CH][CEM]
Sarah N., d/o George F. Clayton died 24 May 1940, ae 82-10-0. [AR]
Seth, Mrs. of Leavittown bur. 9 Feb. 1789. [CH]
Simon bur. 25 Feb. 1798. [CH]
Simon died 8 Sep. 1881, ae 57-6. [CEM]
Widow of Samuel bur. 27 Oct. 1818, ae nearly 70. [CH]
William Cutter, s/o Dr. John & Sally bur. 21 June 1805, ae 7 wk. [CH]

FOLSAM:

Hannah, w/o John D. of Exeter & d/o Abrahm Leavitt died 31 May 1858, ae 46.
   [CH]

FOSS:

Clark bur. 9 Sep. 1825, ae 43. [CH]
Edward S. died 1 Sep. 1908, ae 79-2-28. [AR]
Eunice, wid. bur. 29 Mar. 1867, ae 75. [CH]
William, eldest s/o widow Eunice, d. army, Mexico Sep. 1847. [CH]

FOWLER:

Carrie S. (Smith), w/o Nathan b. 1867, d. 1930. [CEM]
George b. 1834, d. 1889. [CEM]
Gertrude M. (Strout), w/o Nathan & d/o Frank H. Strout, b. 1876, d. 12 Aug.
   1901, ae 25-0-23. [AR][CEM]
Mary A. (Hicks), w/o George b. 1841, d. 1900. [CEM]
Nathan b. 1868, d. _____. [CEM]
William P., s/o Asa died 3 July 1918, ae 67-9. [AR]

FRENCH:

Ann R., w/o Samuel F. & d/o Joshua Pickering died 9 Aug. 1883, ae 70. [CEM]
Charles bur. 17 Sep. 1869, ae 28. [CH]
Charles H., s/o Samuel F. died 16 Sep. 1869, ae 28-3-11. [CEM]
Emma Blood, d/o Aretas Blood died 23 Sep. 1932, ae 78-10-8. [AR]
John F., s/o Jonathan died 2 Oct. 1900, ae 82. [AR]
Jonathan, Rev. husb. of Rebecca, b. Andover, Mass. 25 Aug. 1778, Grad.
   Harvard 1795, died 13 Dec. 1856, ae 78-3-27. [CH][CEM]
Rebecca, d/o Samuel, ae 83-1, md. died 3 Feb. 1869. [TR]
Rebecca (Farrar), wid. of Rev. Jonathan born Lincoln, Mass. 21 Dec. 1785,
   died 3 Feb. 1869, ae 83-1-13. [CH][CEM]
Rebecca M., d/o Jonathan, ae 63 single died 8 Mar. 1870. [TR][CH]
Samuel F. s/o Jonathan died 10 Feb. 1899, ae 90-0-28. [AR][CEM]
Samuel F. s/o Jonathan died 2 Oct. 1900, ae 82. [AR]
Samuel Speery, s/o Rev. James bur. 12 Jan. 1851, ae 3. [CH]
William Harris, s/o Rev. James bur. 12 Jan. 1851, ae 2-0-13. [CH]

FREND:
Charles H. ae 72 died 16 Sep. 1869. [TR]

FRISSALL:
Anthony W. b. 1866, d. 1929. [CEM]
Ellen B. (Locke), w/o Anthony b. 1865, d. ____. [CEM]

FROST:
Eva Edna, d/o Franklin Storer died 19 May 1935, ae 55-0-9. [AR]
George E., s/o Pepperal died 29 Dec. 1937, ae 81-1-28. [AR]
Hannah L., d/o James Libby, ae 78-9-9 md. died 23 Dec. 1895. [TR][AR]
Isabella M., d/o Peter Taylor died 8 Oct. 1915, ae 89-1-14. [AR]
Levi William, s/o Pepperell & Lydia d. 17 Aug. 1859, ae 8. [CEM][CH]
Lydia, w/o Pepperell died 28 Nov. 1878, ae 67-10. [CEM]
Maria Hall, d/o Ephraim Hall died 6 Dec. 1937, ae 82-5-13. [AR]
Mary Frye, d/o George Frost died 5 Jan. 1939, ae 82-9. [AR]
Pepperell, s/o William, b. 8 Dec. 1815, d. 2 June 1903, ae 87-5-26. [CEM][AR]
Thomas B., s/o Pepperell & Lydia, single died 23 Apr. 1867, ae 22-0-5.
    [TR][CEM]

FULLER:
Walter L., s/o Llewyllyn died 4 Nov. 1934, ae 62-5-13. [AR]

GALLOWAY:
Mrs. Harriet, d/o William Emory, ae 66, md. died 29 Jan. 1881. [TR]

GARLAND:
Abiah Harriet, d/o Samuel & Sarah died 1 Oct. 1852, ae 1-5. [CH]
Alfretta, d/o Samuel & Sarah died 6 Sep. 1857, ae 3-7. [CH]
Annah A., d/o Samuel Whidden died 7 Dec. 1937, ae 81-11-6. [AR]
Bessie G., w/o Webster d. Hobbs b. 1874, d. 1899. [CEM]
C. Osgood, s/o Charles L.A. died 20 Oct. 1918, ae 17-2-19. [AR]
C. Thompson, s/o John C. died 11 July 1898, ae 59-1. [AR]
Eliza J., d/o John B. Downs died 8 Dec. 1914, ae 70-2-20. [AR]
George L., s/o Samuel, b. 1852, d. 15 Apr. 1921, ae 68-6-23. [CEM][AR]
Georgie R., w/o Sheldon Marston b. 1877, d. 1924. [CEM]
Hannah, w/o Samuel, died Boston 3 Jan. 1848, ae 36-8. [CEM]
Isadora, w/o George L. & d/o Simon Page b. 1855, d. 14 Jan. 1913,
    ae 58-11-21. [CEM][AR]
J. Calvin, s/o John, ae 95, md. died 28 Dec. 1889. [TR]
John, Mrs. bur. 22 Feb. 1843, ae 64. [CH]
Joseph died 5 May 1805, ae 71. [CEM][CH]
M. Abbe b. 5 Mar. 1834, d. 4 Apr. 1918. [CEM]
Mary, w/o Simon died 17 July 1858, ae 57-8. [CEM][CH]
Mary, d/o Edward Bachelder, ae 79-2-22, wid. died 25 May 1890. [TR][AR]
Moses C., s/o George W. died 2 Mar. 1903, ae 68-7-1. [AR]
Samuel b. 1813, d. 1885. [CEM]

GARLAND Cont.
Sarah T., w/o Samuel b. 1817, d. 1888. [CEM]
Simon died 8 Feb. 1840, ae 74-8. [CH][CEM]

GERSTACKER:
Mary, single died 10 Aug. 1893, ae 65-6-15. Native of Bavaria, Germany.
[TR][CEM]

GIBSON:
Charles K. b. 1921, d. 1924. [CEM]

GILLIS:
Alice M., d/o George H. died 5 Jan. 1919, ae 47-4-7. [AR]

GILMAN:
Mary L., d/o Joseph T. Gilman died 21 Sep. 1917, ae 56-10-27. [AR]

GILPATRICK:
Mrs. Sarah E. b. 29 May 1836, d. 12 Sep. 1892. [CEM]

GRIMBALL:
Benjamin, s/o Abraham, ae 85-2-0 died 16 Nov. 1885. [TR]

GODFREY/GODFREE:
Charles, s/o Dearborn bur. 16 Dec. 1845, ae 29. [CH]
Dearborn bur. 14 Nov. 1828, ae 40-10. [CH]
Georgie Ellen, d/o James & Nancy died 5 Mar. 1862, ae 0-1. [CH]
James bur. 13 Aug. 1799. [CH]
Jeremiah bur. 24 Mar. 1807, ae 40-11. [CH]
Jeremiah died 11 Feb. 1853, ae 46. [CH]
Mary Ann, d/o Joseph & Sally died 7 Feb. 1803, ae 3 wk. [CH]
Mary Ann, w/o James died 7 Sep. 1854, ae 54. [CH]
Patience bur. 27 Mar. 1767, ae 58. [CH]
Priscilla bur. 31 Aug. 1768, ae 88. [CH]
Sarah, widow of Dearborn bur. 6 Aug. 1851, ae 72-5. [CH]
William A., s/o Wm C. died 30 May 1918, ae 34-3-22. [AR]

GOOKIN:
Anna (Fitch), w/o Rev. Nathaniel bur. 14 Feb. 1746/7. [TR][CH]
Anna, d/o Rev. N. & Love (Wingate) died 3 Oct. 1754, ae 2-2. [TR][CH]
Daniel of Scarboro, Me. bur. 25 Oct. 1812. [CH]
Dorothy, d/o Rev. N. & Love W. died 4 Oct. 1754, ae 5-0-23. [TR][CH]
Elizabeth, d/o Rev. Nathaniel d. 12 Nov. 1745. [TR]
Love, wid. of Rev. Nathaniel died 11 Aug. 1809, ae 89. [CH][CEM]
Martha, Miss d/o Rev. Nathaniel bur. 6 June 1838, ae 80. [CH]
Mary, d/o Rev. N. & Love W. died 18 Oct. 1754, ae 3-10-6. [TR][CH]
Nathaniel, Rev. b. 18 Feb. 1713, died 22 Oct. 1766. 1st pastor of N. Hpt.
[CH][CEM]

GOOKIN Cont.

Sarah, d/o Rev. Nathaniel & Love bur. 12 Feb. 1803, ae 43-1-1. [CH]

GOSS:

Fannie B. (Knowles), w/o Walter & d/o Edward Knowles, b. 1877, d. 22 Oct. 1911, ae 34-8-14. [AR]

Louise S. (Varney), w/o Richard T. b. 1904, d. 1925. [CEM]

GOULCH:

Abba, d/o David Moulton, ae 50, wid. died 15 Nov. 1882. [TR]

GOULD:

George, gs/o Daniel Moulton died 22 Aug. 1857, ae 2. [CH]

GOVE:

Abbie P., w/o Ebenezer & d/o Jonathan Philbrook, b. 27 Sep. 1824, d. 9 Feb. 1901. [CEM][AR]

Ebenezer b. 17 Feb. 1814, d. 28 May 1897, ae 79-11. [CEM]

GOWELL:

Laura E., w/o Eugene E., b. 6 Aug. 1865, d. 30 Sep. 1914. [CEM]

GRANT:

Eleanor L., d/o Charles H. & Isabel (Leavitt) died 19 July 1922, ae 0-1-14. [AR]

Frederick H., s/o Nathaniel, b. 27 Nov. 1839, d. 6 Aug. 1917. [CEM][AR]

Sarah A., w/o Fred H. b. 10 Aug. 1857, d. 21 Mar. 1890. [CEM]

GREEN:

Elsie E., w/o Harry P. died 11 Nov. 1885, aw 28-6. [CEM]

Ephraim bur. 16 Apr. 1803., ae 16. [CH]

Marietta, d/o late Jacob bur. 4 Feb. 1842, ae 23. [CH]

GROUARD:

George Edwin, s/o John P. & Hannah L. d. 28 June 1855, ae 23-4. [CH][CEM]

Hannah L., w/o John P. died 10 April 1871, ae 54. [CEM]

John P. died 13 Apr. 1870, ae 54-5. [CEM]

HAINES:

Abigail bur. 26 June 1772, ae 85-6. [CH]

Abigail, Miss died 13 Nov. 1816, ae 81-10. [CH]

Abigail died 23 Oct. 1877, ae 76-7. [CEM]

Abner bur. 9 July 1823, ae 77. [CH]

Deborah, d/o wid. Deborah bur. 9 Dec. 1771, ae 4. [CH]

Elizabeth died 14 Apr. 1871, ae 75. [CEM]

Joshua bur. Oct. 1782, ae 32. [CH]

Lucy, d/o Wid. Lucy bur. 13 Jan. 1783, ae 0-1. [CH]

HAINES Cont.

Mary F., d/o Reuben French died 21 Jan. 1908, ae 71-6-14. [AR]

Priscilla, widow of Abner bur. 15 May 1840, ae 86. [CH]

Thomas bur. 10 May 1767, ae 40-6. [CH]

Thomas bur. 25 Mar. 1770, ae 85. [CH]

Thomas V., s/o Thomas J. died 9 May 1903, ae 69-4-14. [AR]

HAM:

John died 26 Apr. 1840, ae 18. [CH]

HAMILTON:

Frank E., s/o Ishmael died 18 Feb. 1943, ae 21-7-1. [AR]

HANSCOM:

Allan F. Jr., s/o Allan F. died 1 Jan. 1943, ae 9-9-11. [AR]

HAMSON:

Elna, d/o Sven Olson died 24 Sep. 1928, ae 78-6-7. [AR]

HARMAN:

Infant of Orin & Jean, ae 0-0-24, died 16 Dec. 1881. [TR]

HARRIS:

Elizabeth E., d/o Nicholas Fleming died 25 Sep. 1940, ae 71-9-0. [AR]

Orinda A. (Jewell), w/o Wm H. & d/o Levi Jewell, b. 1825, d. 13 June 1905, ae 77-2-6. [AR] [CEM]

William H., s/o Daniel, b. 1825, d. 21 June 1903, ae 78-2-19. [AR][CH]

HARVEY:

Martha W., d/o George Williams did 28 Aug. 1914, ae 66-10-11. [AR]

HAVEN:

Anne, w/o John b. 1781, d. 1855. [CH]

James W. b. 1808, bur. 7 Feb. 1837, ae 27-2. [CH][CEM]

John, Capt. s/o Rev. Joseph of Rochester b. 1789, bur. 15 Feb. 1843, ae 68. [CH][CEM]

John W., s/o John, b. 1822, d. 5 June 1899, ae 76-10-2. [AR][CEM]

Nancy died 16 Nov. 1855, ae 74. [CH]

HAYDON:

Abbie F., d/o George Frost died 26 Dec. 1919, ae 40-4-1. [AR]

HEATH:

Gordon H, s/o George A. & Lily A. (Bunn) died 14 Sep. 1910, ae 6-7-5. [AR]

Lilly A., d/o Henry Bunn died 28 Oct. 1910, ae 35-1-15. [AR]

HENDAY:

Carrie B.M., d/o Clinton L., ae 0-10-14, died 20 Mar. 1884. [TR]
Clinton C., s/o John, b. 19 Oct. 1851, d. 28 June 1922. [CEM][AR]
Cora A., w/o Clinton d. 7 Sep. 1883, ae 27-11. [CH]
Emily C., w/o Clinton d. 1 May 1886, ae 23-7. [CH]

HERRON:

Daniel F., s/o Peter died 14 Oct. 1913, ae 75-0-19. [AR]

HILLIARD:

Wendell P., s/o Francis died 21 Oct. 1935, ae 63-4-13. [AR]

HOBBS:

Abigail, Mrs. bur. 5 May 1775, ae 80. [CH]
Abigail, d/o Benjamin died 22 Mar. 1829, ae 51-4. [CH][CEM]
Abigail, w/o Morris died 14 Sep. 1842, ae 68. [CH][CEM]
Abram D., s/o Oliver died 10 Nov. 1910, ae 74-5-25. [AR]
Annie (French), w/o Joseph O. & d/o John French, b. 11 Sep. 1856, d. 3 May
    1900. [CEM][aR]
Annie (Hoyt), w/o Joseph O. b. 29 Mar. 1883, d. 13 June 1912. [CEM]
Azalia, d/o J.W.F. of Boston died 1 Aug. 1858, ae 14-3. [CH][CEM]
Benjamin, s/o D. died 23 Apr. 1804, ae 76. [CH][CEM]
Benjamin bur. 16 July 1825, ae 86-5. [CH][CEM]
Benjamin died 24 Aug. 1865, ae 70-5-9. [CEM]
Bessie F., d/o George Garland died 28 Jan. 1899, ae 24-1-6. [AR]
Bessie V., d/o Walter D. died 14 Feb. 1899, ae 0-0-19. [AR]
Caroline D., Mrs. ae 78, wid. died 17 Dec. 1890. [TR][CEM][AR]
Carrie W., d/o Joseph S. died 28 Oct. 1935, ae 83-0-4. [AR]
Charles Paron, s/o Thomas D. died 8 July 1854, ae 3 wk. [CH]
Child of John S. & Josephine died 23 May 1845, ae 3 wk. [CH]
Christopher bur. Aug. 1792. [CH]
Data, w/o Lt. Jonathan bur. 16 Feb. 1807, ae 34-8. [CH][CEM]
Dau. of Josiah & Mabel died 11 Mar. 1868, ae 24-10. [CEM]
David, Capt. died 4 May 1849, ae 88-10. [CH][CEM]
David L., s/o Dr. died 3 Oct. 1854, ae 23-2-14. [CH][CEM]
Deborah, w/o Morris bur. 29 Sep. 1822, ae 73-7. [CH][CEM[
Edson C., s/o John W.F., b. 1 June 1850, d. 20 Aug. 1915. [CEM][AR]
Edward Whellock, s/o Joseph S. & Mary D. died 29 May 1860, ae 0-8. [CH]
Eliza Sarah, d/o Joseph S. & Mary bur. 8 Feb. 1852, ae 2-10. [CH]
Elizabeth, w/o Dea. Benj. died 12 June 1812, ae 76-6. [CH][CEM]
Elizabeth, d/o Capt. David bur. 24 Jan. 1844, ae 56. [CH][CEM]
Elizabeth H., d/o Joseph Towne & w/o James F. died 22 Nov. 1921, ae 72-3-5.
    [AR][CEM]
Elizabeth J., w/o J.W.F. Hobbs & d/o Mrs. Mary Drake died 14 Sep. 1856,
    ae 38. [CH][CEM]
Elizabeth J., w/o James F. b. 1849, d. 1921. [CEM]
Emeline, w/o Horatio D. died 26 Dec. 1897, ae 82. [CEM]

HOBBS Cont.

Emily, d/o J. & M.H. died 4 Sep. 1862, ae 20-8. [CH][CEM]
Emma M., d/o Thomas, ae 14-7, single died 15 Sep. 1867. [TR]
Fanny, w/o Jonathan Jr. died 5 Oct. 1826, ae 50-3. [CH][CEM]
Fanny, Mrs. bur. 20 Aug. 1864. [CH]
Fannie, d/o Thomas, ae 59-7-18 single died 23 Sep. 1895. [TR][AR]
Fanny Dearborn, d/o Jonathan Jr. & Fanny, died 8 Oct. 1802, ae inf. [CH]
Fannie F. died 21 May 1873, ae 15. [CEM]
Fanny M. died 30 June 1851, ae 51-11-9. [CEM]
Grace Lougks, w/o J. Harold b. 17 Aug. 1888, d. 21 Jan. 1917. [CEM]
Hannah (Chapman), wid. died 27 Jan. 1850, ae 81-9. [CH]
Hannah died 2 June 1859, ae 66. [CH]
Harriet Newell, d/o John Jr. & Fanny bur. 30 July 1822, ae 2-3-15. [CH][CEM]
Hattie, d/o Oliver & Sarah b. 2 May 1846, d. 13 Dec. 1876. [CEM]
Hattie A., d/o Oliver, ae 30, single died 13 Dec. 1876. [TR]
Henry, s/o John Jr. & Lucinda bur. 23 July 1822, ae 2-0-11. [CH][CEM]
Horatio D. md. died 6 Apr. 1888, ae 89. [TR][CEM]
J.W.F. b. 3 Jan. 1815, d. 27 Apr. 1890. [CEM]
James F., s/o Jonathan died 6 Apr. 1923, ae 79-7-27. GAR [AR][CEM]
John, infant bur. 24 Aug. 1768, [CH]
John bur. 17 Mar. 1783, ae 24-3. [CH]
John Alden, s/o Jonathan 3d & Mary b. 4 July 1852, d. 21 Nov. 1931, ae 79-8
   in Oregan, [CH]
John Dow bur. 19 sep. 1839, ae 40. [CH]
John F., s/o John W.F., b. 4 Feb. 1859, d. 27 Aug. 1881. [TR][CEM]
John L., s/o Morris, ae 68-4 single died 10 Oct. 1877. [TR][CEM]
John S., s/o John died 19 Feb. 1900, ae 82-10-25. [AR]
John W., only child of W.J.C. & N.F. died 15 Oct. 1864, ae 26. [CH]
John W., s/o John S., b. 1846, d. 18 Apr. 1923, ae 76-6-2. [AR][CEM]
John W. F. ae 75, died 27 Apr. 1890. [TR][AR]
Jonathan, Lt. died 21 Sep. 1844, ae 75. [CH][CEM]
Jonathan, s/o Thomas & husb. of Fanny died 23 Nov. 1852, ae 78-6. [CH][CEM]
Jonathan died 2 May 1872, ae 67-2. [CEM]
Jonathan F. bur. 21 June 1867, ae 35. [CH][CEM]
Joseph, s/o Nathaniel bur. Apr. 1777, ae 1. [CH]
Joseph, Mrs. bur. 1790. [CH]
Joseph bur. 6 July 1820, ae 94. [CH]
Joseph, s/o Benjamin died 22 Mar. 1847, single, ae 74-8. [CH][CEM]
Joseph H. died 19 Mar. 1870, ae 36-8-17. [CH][CEM]
Joseph Oliver, s/o Joseph S., b. 1855, d. 16 Jan. 1927, ae 71-7-12. [AR][CEM]
Joseph S. s/o Oliver died 20 Aug. 1907, ae 80-4-23. [AR]
Joseph W. b. 1846, d. 1917. [CEM]
Josephine W., d/o Joseph Ward died 3 Feb. 1901, ae 81-1-12. [AR]
Josiah bur. 10 Oct. 1767, ae 57. [CH]
Judith, w/o Benjamin bur. 26 Mar. 1818, ae 75-9. [CH]
Leavitt, s/o Thomas Jr. died 30 Jan. 1859, ae 25-8. [CH]
Lizzie A., d/o J. & M.H. died 4 Apr. 1865, ae 25-5. [CH][CEM]

HOBBS Cont.

Lizzie B., d/o Thomas, ae 12-10, singled died 20 Sep. 1867. [TR]

Lizzie D. died 22 Oct. 1890, ae 22-10. [CEM]

Lizzie May, d/o John W.F., died 7 Oct. 1865, ae 2-5. [TR][CEM]

Lucinda, d/o John & Lucinda bur. 27 Apr. 1816, ae 1-9-2. [CH][CEM]

Lucinda, Mrs. bur. 16 Feb. 1868, ae 77. [CH]

Martha A.C., w/o Simon S. died 25 Feb. 1848, ae 20. [CH]

Mary, d/o Benjamin bur. 23 Nov. 1781, ae 0-0-6. [CH]

Mary died 7 Apr. 1806, ae 79. [CEM]

Mary (Neal) w/o John died 18 Oct. 1805, ae 61. [CEM]

Mary w/o Jonathan died 24 May 1825, ae 40. [CEM]

Mary, Mrs. w/o John died 3 Dec. 1832, ae 99-0-9. [CH][CEM]

Mary, Mrs., sister of Daniel Marston died 29 Dec. 1856, ae 93-6. [CH]

Mary, w/o Jonathan d. 5 May 1889, ae 76-5. [CEM]

Mary D., d/o John Andrews died 23 June 1898, ae 72-2-8. [AR]

Mary E., w/o Thos. Philbrick & d/o Oliver & Sarah Hobbs b. 30 May 1841, d. 7 May ____. [CEM]

Mary F., w/o William G.F. Wright, b. 1 July 1847, d. 23 Nov. 1914. [CEM]

Mary F., d/o James Folsam, ae 42, md. died 14 Oct. 1865. [TR][CEM]

Mary H., w/o W.J.C. died 3 Feb. 1888, ae 73. [CEM]

Mary Jane, d/o Thomas died 19 Jan. 1926, ae 88-0-19. [AR]

Maurice died 1698, ae 89, [CEM]

Maurice b. in England 1611, d. 1702, ae 91. [CEM]

Maurice died 6 Apr. 1740, ae 88. [CEM]

Maurice b. 1714, d. 1 May 1756. [CEM]

Melissa Caskaline, d/o John W.F. & Eliz. of Boston died 28 Jan. 1850, ae 3-5. [CH][CEM]

Mercy, w/o Jonathan died 24 May 1825, ae 46. [CEM]

Nina A., d/o Joseph Seavey & w/o John W. died 25 Dec. 1916, ae 69-6-8. [AR][CEM]

Molly, w/o Josiah died 29 Dec. 1857, ae 92-6. [CEM]

Morris Jr. died 20 Jan. 1776. [CEM]

Morris, s/o Morris Jr. & Abigail died 11 Jan. 1815, ae 16-0-12. [CH][CEM]

Morris died 24 Mar. 1830, ae 83. [CH][CEM]

Morris died 9 July 1830, ae 54. [CH][CEM]

Morris died 26 Sep. 1841, ae 27. [CH][CEM]

Moses L. died 1 June 1915, ae 77-7. [CEM]

Moses L., Mrs. w/o Dr. died 30 June 1854, ae 55. [CH]

Moses L., Dr., died 25 May 1885, ae 84-11. [CEM]

Nancy died 1 Feb. 1887. [TR]

Nancy F., w/o W.J.C. died 3 Feb. 1888, ae 73. [CEM]

Nancy J., d/o Thomas Felch died 9 July 1901, ae 59-5-25. [AR]

Nina A. (Seavey), w/o John W. b. 1847, d. 1916. [CEM]

Olive died 30 Mar. 1874, ae 84. [CEM]

Oliver b. 19 Sep. 1802, d. 13 Jan. 1848, ae 45-4. [CH][CEM]

Oliver S., s/o Abram D. died 15 Apr. 1930, ae 62-0-16. [AR]

Orville Cutter, s/o John W. Fogg & Eliz. J. now of Boston died 11 Jan. 1849, ae 0-5. [CH][CEM]

HOBBS Cont.

Philip T. b. 1879, d. 1917. [CEM]
Poly died 17 Oct. 1805. [CEM]
Polly, d/o Lt. Jonathan & Date bur. 19 Dec. 1806, ae 11. [CH][CEM]
Polly, w/o Lt. Jonathan bur. 25 May 1825, ae 47. [CH]
Polly, 3d w/o Lt. Jonathan, d/o Dudley Page bur. 8 Oct. 1830, ae 42. [CH]
Rachel bur. 15 May 1767, ae 65-11. [CH]
Ruby Moore, d/o Jeremiah Moore, died 11 Jan. 1930, ae 87-11-17. [AR]
Samuel Farrar, s/o Jonathan 3d died 28 Mar. 1852, ae 2-0-5. [CH][CEM]
Sarah died 1696, ae 89. [CEM]
Sarah died 13 Sep. 1731. [CEM]
Sarah, wid. of Thomas died 28 Oct. 1826, ae 74. [CH][CEM]
Sarah, w/o Oliver b. 18 July 1806, d. 14 Feb. 1874. [CEM]
Sarah D. died 22 Oct. 1890, ae 22. [TR]
Simon, inf. bur. 19 Mar. 1767, [CH]
Simon bur. 27 Aug. 1771. [CH]
Theodate, w/o Jonathan d. 1823. [CEM]
Thomas bur. 2 Sep. 1822, ae 73. [CH][CEM]
Thomas died 3 Mar. 1862, ae 60-4. [CH][CEM]
Thomas died 27 Jan. 1900, ae 94. [AR]
Thomas Albert, s/o Thomas, ae 20-10, singled died 24 Sep. 1867. [TR][CEM]
Thomas D. died 6 Oct. 1868, ae 38. [CH]
Victory, Dr. died 2 July 1873, ae 33-10. [CEM]
W.J.C. b. 3 Jan. 1815, d. 2 Jan. 1891. [CEM][AR]
Woodbury, s/o Horatio & Emeline died 31 Jan. 1857, ae 20. [CEM]

HOBSON:

Clifton, s/o Arthur & Alice (Gale) died 25 Aug. 1900, ae 0-0-1. [AR]

HOWE:

Chester L., s/o LaForest D. died 18 Mar. 1939, ae 53-5-16. [AR]
Harry G., s/o John W. died 25 July 1922, ae 67-2-18. [AR]
Jeanne Stott, d/o Charles A. Stott died 11 July 1934, ae 67-8-29. [AR]

HOYT:

Agnes M. (Beckwith), w/o Charles W. b. 11 May 1852, d. _____. [CEM]
Charles W. b. 2 Oct. 1851, d. 17 July 1894. [CEM]

HUNT:

Minot E., ae 68-7-0 died 21 Mar. 1893. [TR]

ILSLEY:

William of Stratham bur. 11 June 1833, ae 45. [CH]

INMAN:

Ellen A., w/o William N. died 6 Feb. 1892, ae 42. [CEM]

IRELAND:
George A., s/o John M. died 29 June 1922, ae 19-6-4. [AR]

JACKSON:
Charles, s/o John A. died 6 Aug. 1910, ae 18-9-8. [AR]

JAMES:
Child of George & Eliza of Exeter died 11 Apr. 1859, ae 2 wk. [CH]
Infant d/o John A., ae 4, died 23 July 1870. [TR]

JENNESS:
Abigail, w/o Richard b. 1718, d. 1755? [CEM]
Abigail, d/o Jeremiah & Molly died 20 Feb. 1805, ae 0-0-5. [CH]
Alphonse G. s/o Orrin H. died 19 Mar. 1934, ae 53-7-5. [AR]
Benjamin died 4 Aug. 1875, ae 84. [CEM]
Betsy, w/o Richard b. 1783, d. 1835. [CEM]
Betsy D., w/o Richard b. 1780, d. 1859. [CEM]
Charles E., s/o Nathan B. & Julia A. died 24 Feb. 1876, ae 0-9-7. [CEM]
Charles W., s/o Edwin, b. 7 Nov. 1846, d. 6 Apr. 1903. [CEM][AR]
Dorothy, d/o Nathan Brown, ae 70-3-15, wid. died 7 Dec. 1893, ae 89-10-12? [TR][AR]
Dorothy, w/o Benjamin died 7 Dec. 1896, ae 89-10. [CEM]
Edwin, s/o Benjamin, b. 8 Sep. 1818, d. 16 Dec. 1902. [AR][CEM]
Elizabeth A. (Davis), w/o Charles W. b. 5 July 1849, d. ____. [CEM]
Elizabeth A. died 30 Jan. 1892, ae 58-10-25. [AR]
George Edwin, s/o Edwin & Mary died 19 May 1862, ae 3-10. [CH][CEM]
George Warren, s/o Benjamin & Dolly bur. 30 June 1846, ae 0-7. [CH][CEM]
Hannah, w/o Isaac bur. 22 Apr. 1840, ae 87-6. [CH]
Hannah bur. 9 Apr. 1863, ae 81. [CH]
Huldah, ae 76½, died 23 Aug. 1880. [TR]
Isaac bur. 8 Dec. 1841, 86. [CH]
Jeremiah, lately of Boston died 8 Feb. 1849, ae 73. [CH][CEM]
John B. b. 1765, d. 1840. [CEM]
Joseph B., s/o Benjamin, died 9 Jan. 1923, ae 86-7-28. [AR][CEM]
Josiah E., s/o N.B. & J.A. died 1 July 1862, ae 3-8. [CEM]
Julia A. (Merrill), w/o Nathan B. b. 1 Mar. 1834, d. 15 Mar. 1897. [CEM]
Langdon b. 1815, d. 1878. [CH]
Marian D., d/o Ivan D. & D.H. b. 7 May 1807, d. 19 July 1911. [CEM]
Martha (Brown), w/o S. Alonzo b. 5 Jan. 1853, d. 6 Nov. 1922. [CEM]
Martha Elizabeth, d/o Edwin & Mary died 19 Dec. 1848, ae 0-3. [CH][CEM]
Mary, w/o Samuel died 11 Dec. 1833, ae 78. [CEM]
Mary C., w/o Edwin, d/o Samuel Chapman, b. 24 July 1820, d. 21 Dec. 1901. [AR][CEM]
Mary P., w/o Henry & d/o Stacey Page, died 6 Jan. 1854, ae 19-6. [CH]
Molly, w/o Jeremiah bur. 25 Nov. 1806, ae 28. [CH][CEM]
Nathan H. b. 11 Mar. 1832, d. 2 Jan. 1896. [CEM]
Olive, w/o John B. b. 1765, d. 1823. [CEM]

JENNESS Cont.

Olive A., w/o Joseph & d/o Mark Batchelder, md. died 30 May 1891, ae 54-8-1. [TR][CEM][AR]

Rebecca, Mrs. d/o Samuel Rowe, ae 42, md. died 2 Feb. 1881. [TR]

Richard b. 1715, d. 1785. [CEM]

Richard b. 1786, d. 1869. [CEM]

Richard b. 1825, d. 1885. [CEM]

Roswell French, s/o Edwin & Mary died 19 May 1862, ae 11. [CH][CEM]

Rufus E. b. 1823, d. 1847. [CEM]

Samuel died 29 Dec. 1806, ae 54. [CEM]

Samuel, widow of bur. 13 Dec. 1833, ae 78. [CH]

Sarah bur. 30 Dec. 1806, ae 54. [CH]

Sarah, w/o Richard b. 1840, d. 1906. [CEM]

JEWELL:

Abbie M. (Locke), w/o Dewitt b. 1829, d. 1911. [CEM]

Abbie M. (Dow), w/o E. Bloomer b. 1849, d. 1927. [CEM]

Child of Levi & Hannah bur. 30 Aug. 1809. [CH]

David, infant bur. 8 Aug. 1767. [CH]

Dewitt G. b. 1825, d. 1918. [CEM]

E. Bloomer b. 1851, d. _____. [CEM]

Levi, s/o Capt. Daniel bur. 15 May 1783, ae 3. [CH]

JOHNSON:

John, Mrs. bur. 3 Feb. 1815, ae 85. [CEM]

John bur. 15 Feb. 1816, ae 93. [CH]

Martha, Mrs. bur. 14 Feb. 1775. [CH]

William of Greenland bur. 14 July 1825, ae nearly 49. [CH]

JOHNSTON:

Rachel S., w/o Rufus S. died 30 July 1859, ae 34-4. [CH]

JONES:

Frank, s/o Fred died 17 July 1935, ae 56-1-15. [AR]

Fred died 25 Oct. 1929, ae 80. [AR]

KEENE:

Harry C., s/o Daniel died 1 Oct. 1934, ae 55-2-9. [AR]

KENNEDY:

Edward J., s/o James died 14 Apr. 1940, ae 63-0-14. [AR]

KEOUS:

Deborah, w/o William bur. 7 May 1804, ae 47. [CH]

William T. died 30 Mar. 1825, ae 50-1. [CH][CEM]

KEYS:

Julia B., d/o John Baker died 12 Aep. 1915, ae 88-1-19. [AR]
Mary Eva, d/o Samuel B. died 22 Sep. 1926, ae 73-5-14. [AR]

KINGSFORD:

William Rowland, s/o Dr. William died 12 Oct. 1842, ae 0-4-10. [CH][CEM]

KINSMAN:

Child of John bur. Sep. 1831, ae 8 wk. [CH]

KNOWLES:

Abigail, d/o Samuel Tarlton, ae 61-10, wid. died 4 Dec. 1887. [TR]
Anna, w/o Samuel died 19 Mar. 1826, ae 62. [CEM][CH]
Bell G., d/o David & Sarah A. died 1 Dec. 1867, ae 20-6. [CEM]
Charles Woodbury, s/o Levi W., 5-11-0, died 15 July 1883. [TR]
Charlie, s/o Levi & Emma E. b. 10 Aug. 1877, d. 19 July 1883. [CEM]
Child of Oliver & Fanny bur. 16 Nov. 1828, ae 2 wk. [CH]
Clarence H., s/o Samuel H. died 9 Jan. 1935, ae 78-11-18. [AR]
Cora E., w/o Edward & d/o Simon Page, b. 12 Aug. 1859, d. 3 Nov. 1925.
   [AR][CEM]
Data, w/o Reuben died 11 May 1895, ae 85-3. [CEM]
Data, d/o Jonathan Hobbs, ae 85-0-3, wid. died 12 May 1895. [TR][AR]
David, Mrs. bur. 1799. [CH]
David bur. 10 Mar. 1806, ae 79. [CH]
David died 29 Oct. 1889, ae 74. [CEM]
David S., s/o Nathan, ae 73-0-17, died 11 July 1890. [AR][TR]
David Webster, s/o Thomas S. died 28 May 1934, ae 47-11-12. [AR]
Edward E., s/o Samuel, ae 36-9-20, md. died 12 Sep. 1892, [TR][AR]
Edward E. b. 23 Nov. 1855, d. 13 Sep. 1892. [CEM]
Elanor J., d/o John Leavitt died 16 June 1899, ae 81-9-6. [AR]
Eleazer L., s/o Amos, ae 66-6-8 died 3 Mar. 1888. [TR]
Elizabeth M., d/o Levi Jewell, & w/o Samuel died 23 Sep. 1894, ae 74-6.
   [TR][CEM][AR]
Emily C., d/o George F. Marston, ae 23-7-0, md. died 1 May 1883. [TR]
Emma E. (Courson?), w/o Levi W. b. 21 Jan. 1851, d. ____. [CEM]
Frances D., w/o Oliver died 25 Mar. 1882, ae 78. [CEM]
George W. died 26 Mar. 1923, ae 80-8-22. [AR]
Hannah, wid. bur. 18 Apr. 1828, ae 55. [CH]
Infant of Samuel bur. 30 Sep. 1801. [CH]
John, s/o Oliver & Frances died 7 Dec. 1845, ae 21-5. [CH]
John F. died 7 Dec. 1845, ae 21. [CEM]
Jonathan, s/o Simon bur. 26 July 1822, ae 1-6. [CH]
Jonathan bur. May 1825, ae 85. [CH]
Jonathan, wid. of bur. 18 Dec. 1829, ae 89. [CH]
Jonathan bur. 5 Mar. 1849, ae 24. [CH]
Josiah J., s/o Simon died 8 Aug. 1900, ae 71-4. [AR]
Katherine, w/o Jospeh bur. 30 May 1773, ar 65-2. [CH]

KNOWLES Cont.

Lemira, d/o Robert Billings died 21 June 1923, ae 81-2-13. [AR]
Leon M. Sr., s/o Levi W. died 4 May 1943, ae 50-0-8. [AR]
Levi Woodbury, s/o Samuel, b. 14 Sep. 1850, d. 26 July 1922. [CEM][AR]
Lucy E., d/o Rev. Henry Pottle, died 4 Dec. 1902, ae 82-6-3. [AR]
Mary Emma, d/o Samuel & Elizabeth, single died 23 July 1883, ae 21-10-3.
    [TR][CEM]
Maurice G., s/o Charley, ae 1-2-0 died 17 Sep. 1886. [TR]
Minnie Pearl, d/o Levi W. & Emma E., ae 0-0-7, died 30 July 1884. [TR][CEM]
Miss died June 1869. [TR]
Nancy, d/o Samuel bur. 6 Nov. 1820, ae 13. [CH]
Nancy, d/o Samuel & Anna died 4 Oct. 1821, ae 13-8. [CEM]
Nancy, w/o E.Q. died 24 Mar. 1889, ae 68-6. [CEM]
Nathan died 21 Sep. 1839, ae 88-6. [CEM]
Nathan, widow of died 3 Aug. 1848, ae 68. [CH]
Nathan bur. 29 Sep. 1859, ae 69. [CH]
Nathan, s/o Nathan, ae 77-0-8, died 23 Jan. 1890. [TR][AR]
Oliver bur. 7 July 1837, ae 35-8. [CH]
Oliver, Mrs. died 5 July 1837, ae 35. [CEM]
Reuben bur. 22 Jan. 1776, ae 85. [CH]
Reuben died 30 Oct. 1857, ae 58. [CH][CEM]
Reuben C. b. 26 Oct. 1849, d. 11 Jan. 1896. [CEM]
Robert E., s/o Leon M. & M.D., b. 12 May 1919, d. 29 May 1923. [CEM][AR]
S. Jewell, d/o Samuel, b. 19 Mar. 1845, d. 2 July 1918, ae 68-4-5. [AR][CEM]
Samuel died 28 Jan. 1803, ae 31-0-4. [CH]
Samuel died 23 Aug. 1846, ae 83. [CEM][CH]
Samuel, s/o Simon, ae 63-3, md. died 27 Mar. 1882. [TR]
Samuel, s/o Samuel died 9 July 1895, ae 82-6-4. [CEM][AR]
Sarah, w/o Reuben C. b. 7 Oct. 1840, d. 13 Sep. 1892. [CEM]
Sarah A., w/o Craig C. Lindsey b. 2 July 1852, d. 7 Feb. 1912. [CEM]
Sarah A., w/o David died 5 Nov. 1881, ae 58. [CEM]
Sarah Abbie, w/o S. Jewell & d/o David S. Knowles, b. 25 June 1850,
    d. 21 Sep. 1929. [AR][CEM]
Sarah L., d/o Mrs. Nancy died 19 Jan. 1854, ae 22-10. [CH]
Simon died 22 Apr. 1753. [TR]
Stanley J., s/o S. Jewell died 28 May 19443, ae 53-5-13. [AR]
Thomas J., s/o David died 12 Mar. 1928, ae 85-8-8. [AR]
Thomas L., s/o David & Sarah A. died 25 Oct. 1898. Co. I, 18th NH Inf. [CEM]
William J., s/o Levi W., ae 3-7-0 died 23 July 1883. [TR]
Willie J., s/o Levi W. & Emma E. b. 24 Oct. 1879, d. 23 July 1883. [cEM]

LAMPREY:

Abigail, w/o Benjamin bur. 27 Jan. 1771, ae 39-10. [CH]
Abigail, d/o John bur. 29 Jan. 1838, ae 35. [CH]
Clara M., d/o Oliver Nudd died 30 Apr. 1936, ae 89-6-26. [AR]
Dau. of John Jr. bur. Nov. 1806, ae 6. [CH]

LAMPREY Cont.

David, s/o John bur. 31 Jan. 1840, ae 23. [CH]

David J., s/o Hezekiah died 18 Apr. 1923, ae 78-7-1. [AR]

David Marks, s/o John Jr. & Mary died 21 Mar. 1848, ae 0-4. [CH]

Edwin M., s/o John, b. 17 Sep. 1836, d. 10 June 1912, ae 75-8-23. [CEM][AR]

George H., s/o Jonathan, b. 25 Aug. 1845, d. 17 Sep. 1915, ae 70-0-23. [AR][CEM]

Grace A., d/o Simon O. died 25 Dec. 1934, ae 62. [AR]

Hannah M., d/o Samuel Garland, b. 1839, d. 17 Mar. 1922, ae 82-8-20. [AR][CEM]

Hattie R., d/o Simon O. died 1 Nov. 1938, ae 75-4-20. [AR]

Hezekiah, s/o Morris, ae 73-8, died 9 July 1886. [TR]

Irving H., s/o Hezekiah B. died 27 Apr. 1908, ae 60-6-24. [AR]

John bur. 12 May 1835, ae 86. [CH]

John Jr., husb. of Mary died 10 Sep. 1848. [CH]

John died 1 Oct. 1850, ae 74-1. [CH]

John b. 13 Dec. 1804, d. 29 Kuly 1873. [CEM]

Jonathan died 4 Feb. 1854, ae 49-5. [CH]

Jonathan R. b. 24 June 1834, died 14 Aug. 1860, ae 26. [CH][CEM]

Josephine D., d/o Chester A. Davis died 26 Aug. 1923, ae 52-3-27. [AR]

Lydia, w/o John died 28 Feb. 1846, ae 31. [CH]

M.E. b. 5 Sep. 1840, d. 26 June 1903. [CEM]

Mary, ae 64, md. died 8 Mar. 1881. [TR]

Mary E., d/o Oliver Brown died 26 June 1903, ae 62-9-18. [AR]

Mary S., d/o Jonathan Robinson & w/o John died 2 Apr. 1899, ae 89-1-27. [AR][CEM]

Morris died 27 Oct. 1809, ae 97-9-27. [CH]

Morris bur. 5 July 1841, ae 63. [CH]

Molly, w/o John Sr. bur. 30 May 1825, ae 76. [CH]

Moses Jr. bur. 11 Jan. 1827, ae 20-10. [CH]

Nancy died 17 Oct. 1853, ae 68. [CH]

Polly, wid. died 4 Sep. 1862, ae 82. [CH]

S. Oliver b. 1839, d. 1912. [CEM]

Sally, Miss died 15 Mar. 1853, ae 46. [CH]

Simon, Mrs. died 1778, ae about 40. [CH]

Simon Dearborn, an infant bur. 8 Aug. 1767. [CH]

Simon O., s/o John died 13 Dec. 1912, ae 73-10-16. [AR]

Willis Oliver, s/o Simon O., b. 1837. d. 25 Apr. 1929, ae 1-6. [AR][CEM]

LANE:

Anna L.R., d/o J.D. & Margaret died 13 July 1852, ae 2-3. [CEM]

Alpheus C., s/o William, ae 33-3, md. died 1 Oct. 1882. [TR][AR]

Apphia, w/o Joseph died 20 Dec. 1893, ae 80-8. [AR][CEM]

Anna, d/o John & Margaret of Boston bur. 22 July 1852. [CH]

Christopher F. b. 3 Jan. 1844, d. _____.[CEM]

David b. 26 June 1817, d. 16 July 1890. [CEM]

Deborah, w/o Edward died 10 Apr. 1871, ae 71. [CEM]

LANE Cont.
Edward died 10 Apr. 1856, ae 68. [CEM]
Eleanor J., w/o David b. 10 Sep. 1817, d. 16 June 1899. [CEM]
Ida B., d/o Nathaniel Tarlton died 25 Dec. 1923, ae 68-4-4. [AR]
John D. b. 26 Mar. 1808, d. 23 May 1892. [CEM]
Lamira F. b. 8 Apr. 1842, d. ____. [CEM]
Lewis K.H., s/o Samuel D. died 16 Oct. 1897, ae 41-5-10. [AR]
Linnie A. b. 29 Jan. 1872, d. 6 Oct. 1878. [CEM]
Linnie J. b. 29 Jan. 1872, d. 6 Oct. 1878. [CEM]
Luthers J., w/o Christopher b. 27 Feb. 1843, d. 13 Sep. 1907. [CEM]
Margaret Dow b. 5 Oct. 1811, d. 22 Jan. 1889. [CEM]
Nancy died 29 June 1891, ae 68. [AR]
Samuel D., s/o John, ae 85-9-3, wid. died 8 Sep. 1895. [TR][AR]
Thomas J. b. 4 July 1840, d. ____. [CEM]

LANG/LANGE:
Frank E., s/o Karl died 8 Sep. 1937, ae 75-6-16. [AR]
Nancy bur. Sep. 1792. [CH]

LANHAM:
William F., s/o Frank died 4 July 1934, ae 44. [AR]

LAWRENCE:
Infant of Dr. Ebenezer & Abigail died 8 May 1802. [CH]

LEA:
Nina, d/o Henry C. Lea died 26 Aug. 1927, ae 72-3-13. [AR]

LEACH:
Francis H., s/o William died 25 June 1919, ae 64-2-13. [AR]

LEAVITT:
Abiah, wid. of John bur. 21 Jan, 1781. [CH]
Abigail, w/o John Esq. died Jan. 1782, ae 64. [CEM]
Abigail, w/o Simon 3d, died 21 Oct. 1822, ae 28-10. [CH][CEM]
Abigail, widow of Simon died 18 May 1844, ae 91. [CH][CEM]
  [Her 1st husband was Thomas Cotton]
Abigail, widow of Benjamin died 18 sep. 1857, ae 92-7-17. [CH][CEM]
Abraham, s/o Abraham & gs/o Simon died 22 Dec. 1857, ae 32. [CEM]
Abraham died 17 Aug. 1868, ae 83-6. [CH][CEM]
Addie (Philbrick), w/o John E. b. 1849, d. ____. [CEM]
Adelaide Sarah, d/o Tappan & Lucinda died 29 Oct. 1859, ae 1-1. [CH]
Alfred Johnson, s/o Samuel F. bur. 2 Nov. 1814, ae 12. [CH]
Amanda N., d/o E.A. & M.C. died 19 Mar. 1880, ae 32-1. [CEM]
Anna, w/o Capt. Samuel F. bur. 12 June 1816, ae 48. [CH][CEM]
Benjamin bur. 15 Mar. 1801, ae 64. [CH]
Benjamin, Capt & tavern keeper died 8 Nov. 1835, ae 68. [CH][CEM]

LEAVITT Cont.

Benjamin Jr., s/o Benjamin the taverner bur. 22 Mar. 1836, ae 31. [CH][CEM]
Betsy, wid. of John died 15 Dec. 1828, ae 43-6. [CH][CEM]
Carr b. 1806, d. 1863. [CEM]
Child of Ebenezer bur. Mar. 1801. [CH]
Child of John & Elizabeth bur. 13 Aug. 1809, ae 0-0-½. [CH]
Child of John & Elizabeth bur, 6 Aug. 1810, ae 0-0-½. [CH]
Child of John & Betsy bur. 20 July 1811, ae 0-0-½. [CH]
Child of Tappan died 15 Oct. 1847, ae 0-0-1. [CH]
Child of Eldridge bur. 7 July 1850. [CH]
Daisy Elisa, d/o Tabilion? & Lucinda Marston, ae 44 days died 2 Sep. 1875.
    [TR]
Daniel, s/o Ebenezer died 1801, ae 3. [CH]
Daniel, s/o Ebenezer bur. 14 Mar. 1803, ae 3-3. [CH]
Daniel, s/o Luther bur. 6 Sep. 1920, ae 0-0-6. [CH]
David M. bur. 1 June 1820, ae 44. [CH]
D. Curtis bur. 10 July 1869, ae 30. [CH]
Dearborn, Col. bur. 24 Jan. 1831, ae nearly 53. [CH]
Dolly, d/o Amos Towle, ae 94-3, md. died 8 May 1879. [TR]
Dolly Ann, d/o Simon L. Jr. & Dolly bur. 11 Nov. 1823, ae 5. [CH]
Dorothy died 8 May 1879, ae 94-3. [CEM]
Dorothy, w/o Ira James & former w/o Philip Leavitt died 16 Dec. 1879,
    ae 53-4. [CEM]
Dorothy Abby, d/o James B. & Elizabeth died 25 Nov. 1849, ae 6-8-19.
    [CH][CEM]
Dorothy Adeline, d/o Simon & Juliana died 12 Sep. 1846, ae 5. [CH][CEM]
Dorothy Frances, d/o James R. & Elizabeth M. died 30 Sep. 1856, ae 3-11.
    [CH][CEM]
E. Warren, s/o E.A. & M.C. died 19 June 1871, ae 25-4. [CEM]
Eben Joshua, s/o Carr & Eliza b. 1854, d. 1854. [CEM]
Eben True, s/o Carr & Eliza b. 1844, d. 1848. [CEM]
Ebenezer bur. 18 Apr. 1770, ae 1-8-3. [CH]
Ebenezer, s/o Moses bur. 1 Sep. 1771, ae inf. [CH]
Ebenezer, Rev. b. 1771 bur. 16 Dec. 1843, ae 72-9. [CH][CEM]
Ebenezer, Widower, d. 18 Aug. 1851, ae 77-6. [CH]
Ebenezer, Capt. b. 1796, d. 1875. [CEM]
Elbridge A. b. 24 Mar. 1813, d. 27 Sep. 1887. [CEM]
Eliza J. (Perkins), w/o John Esq. b. 1807 died 2 Feb. 1845, ae 38. [CH][CEM]
Eliza Jane, d/o Jacob Rowe, died 29 Jan. 1925, ae 61-7-9. [AR]
Eliza J.F. (Lane), w/o Carr b. 1815, d. 1898. [CEM]
Elizabeth, widow of Gen. Moses bur. 1 Apr. 1822, ae 77-1. [CH][CEM]
Elizabeth A., d/o Thomas C. Leavitt, b. 4 Sep. 1834, d. 31 May 1905.
    ae 70-8-27. [AR][CEM]
Elizabeth M., d/o James R. & Elizabeth M. died 1 Oct. 1856. [CH]
Elizabeth N,. w/o James R. & d/o Jeremiah Marston, b. 2 Feb. 1812, d. 30 Sep.
    1898. [CEM][AR]
Elizabeth S., w/o Simon died 3 Sep. 1904, ae 85-4-21. [CEM]

LEAVITT Cont.
Francis C. bur. 21 May 1868, ae 60. [CH]
Fred Lyman, s/o Homer, ae 0-1-7, died 9 July 1892. [TR]
Hannah, w/o John D. Folsam died 31 May 1858, ae 46. [CEM]
Horace, s/o Thomas C., b. 19 Nov. 1837, d. 19 June 1917, Sgt. Co. M 1st Cav.
    [AR][CEM]
Infant of Carr of Rye bur. Sep. 1855. [CH]
James A. b. 3 Oct. 1838, d. 8 June 1901. [CEM]
James Cornelius, s/o James R. & Elizabeth bur. 18 July 1837, ae 3 wk. [CH]
James R., s/o Philip, b. 22 Sep. 1815, d. 24 Dec. 1897. [AR][CEM]
John Esq. died May 1751, ae 79. [CEM]
John bur. 14 Jan. 1767, ae 3-6. [CH]
John Esq. bur. 11 May 1779, ae 73. [CH]
John died 14 Dec. 1802, ae 39. [CH]
John, s/o Col. Thomas & Mary died 4 Sep. 1820 at Cambridge, ae 34. [CH][CEM]
John died 25 Oct. 1820, ae 38. [CEM]
John, b. 1804, died 22 June 1848, ae 44. [CH][CEM]
John died 14 Apr. 1891, ae 67-9-1. [AR][CEM]
John b. 15 July 1823, d. 14 July 1891. [CEM]
John C., s/o Elbridge S. & Mary S. of Exeter died 22 July 1859, ae 20-6. [CH]
John E. b. 1848, d. 1923. [CEM]
John G., s/o E.A. & M.C. died 22 July 1859, ae 20-5. [CEM]
John L., s/o Tappan died 14 July 1933, ae 83-3-7. [AR]
John T. died 16 Sep. 1914, ae 61. [CEM]
Joseph, s/o Ebenezer b. 1811, bur. 6 July 1844, ae 35. [CH][CEM]
Joseph Benning, s/o Joseph b. 1836, died 19 Feb. 1854, ae 18. [CH][CEM]
Joseph Stacey at Hampton died 25 Sep. 1803, ae 32-6-22. [CH][CHEM]
Julia, Mrs. d/o clergman, ae 80-3, died 17 May 1885. [TR]
Juliana, 2d w/o Simon died 16 May 1885, ae 80-2. [CEM]
L. Cotton, Mrs. d/o Thomas Hobbs, ae 84-2-12, died 29 July 1894. [TR]
Laura Ann, d/o Simon Jr. & Dorothy died 19 Feb. 1831, ae 4-2? [CH][CEM]
Laura Jane, d/o Simon & Juliana died 25 Mar. 1851, ae 14-2. [CH][CEM]
Lavina, d/o Abraham died 17 May 1851, ae 35. [CH][CEM]
Lizzie W. died 29 Oct. 1911, ae 62. [CEM]
Louisa, twin d/o Abraham & Sarah died 10 Sep. 1840, ae 33. [CH]
Luther, s/o Benj., the taverner died 30 Apr. 1837, ae 38. [CH][CEM]
Margaret E., w/o Simon H. & d/o Thos. Berry, b. 12 Oct. 1845, d. 24 Aug.
    1921. [AR][CEM]
Martha Ann, d/o Simon & Juliana & d/o Simon L. Hobbs died 26 Feb. 1848,
    ae 26-6. [CEM]
Martha Ann, d/o James R. & Eliz. N. died 1 Oct. 1856, ae 1-9. [CEM]
Mary, d/o Thomas bur. 8 Feb. 1770, ae inf. [CH]
Mary, widow of Col. Thomas died 1 May 1840, ae 91. [CH][CEM]
Mary Ann, tiwn d/o James R. & Eliz. M. died 24 Dec. 1854, ae 2 ds.. [CH][CEM]
Mary C. (Marston), w/o Elbridge b. 9 Dec. 1814, d. 3 June 1897. [CEM]
Mary E., w/o James A. b. 10 Feb. 1838, d. 27 Jan. 1909. [CEM]
Mary B. (Chase), w/o Thomas b. 1878, d. 1913. [CEM]

LEAVITT Cont.

Mary E. (Dow), w/o Horace & d/o David M. Dow, b. 29 Aug. 1847, d. 19 June 1918. [AR][CEM]

Mary H., w/o Thomas G. & d/o Thos. Hobbs, died 29 July 1894, ae 84-2-12. [AR][CEM]

Mary O. (Drake), w/o Orin B. & d/o Francis Drake, b. 9 Oct. 1859, d. 16 May 1924. [CEM][AR]

Melvina died 19 Mar. 1859, ae 22. [CH]

Miriam, w/o Luther bur. 5 Jan. 1821, ae 25-7. [CH]

Moses, General, s/o John died 1 Sep. 1803, ae 60. [CH][CEM]

Moses, s/o Gen. Moses bur. 28 Nov. 1825, ae 56-8. [CH]

Oliver, s/o Simon Jr. & Dorothy bur. 23 Feb. 1826, ae 7. [CH]

Orin B., b. 3 Oct. 1848, d. 18 Feb. 1929. [CEM]

Orin Benjamin, s/o James R. died 15 Feb. 1929, ae 80-4-8. [AR]

Payson, s/o Thomas G. & Mary died 5 Sep. 1863, ae 22-5. [CH][CEM]

Philip died 1 Sep. 1829, ae 38. [CH][CEM]

Rachel, widow of Joseph died 28 Mar. 1887, ae 76. [CEM]

Rebecca F., d/o Simon 4th & Juliana died 10 Mar. 1833, ae 0-6½. [CH][CEM]

Rebecca F. b. 27 Jan. 1834, d. 1 Feb. 1899. [CEM]

Rufus, s/o Abraham died 21 Apr. 1863, ae 55. [CH][CEM]

Ruth, d/o Benjamin bur. 18 Feb. 1781, ae 0-5. [CH]

Ruth, wid. of Benjamin bur. 23 June 1821, ae 80-3. [CH]

Sally, w/o Capt. Simon bur. 27 Oct. 1842, ae 67. [CH]

Sally (Jewell), w/o Rev. Ebenezer b. 1775, d. 18 Aug. 1851, [CEM][CH]

Samuel, s/o Thomas Esq. bur. 22 Aug. 1834, ae 4. [CH]

Samuel F., Capt. bur. 20 Apr. 1829, ae 61-7. [CH][CEM]

Sarah, w/o Simon died 23 June 1802, ae 46. [CEM]

Sarah, d/o Gen. Moses & Eliz. bur. 7 Apr. 1822, ae 38-2. [CH]

Sarah, w/o Simon died 26 June 1856, ae 46. [CH]

Sarah, d/o Abraham, ae 71-6-12, single died 8 Feb. 1882. [TR][CEM]

Sarah Abbie, d/o Carr & Eliza b. 1855, d. 1855. [CEM]

Sarah E., w/o Tappan died 26 June 1856, ae 332 [CH]

Sarah J., w/o Abraham died 7 Aug. 1858, ae 72. [CH][CEM]

Simon 3d died 11 Jan. 1841, ae nearly 51. [CH][CEM]

Simon died 20 Aug. 1842, ae 89. [CH][CEM]

Simon died 19 Sep. 1873, ae 83-6. [CEM]

Simon died 29 Apr. 1874, ae 62-5. [CEM]

Simon H., s/o Simon H., b. 8 July 1848, d. 1 July 1916, ae 70. [AR][CEM]

Simon Oliver, s/o Simon Jr. bur. 5 FEb. 1831, ae 1-3. [CH][CEM]

Sophia, d/o Thomas & Polly died 16 Jan. 1831, ae 7-10. [CH][CEM]

Tappan bur. 17 Dec. 1817, ae 24. [CH]

Tappan, s/o Tappan died 21 May 1902, ae 83-9-23. [AR]

Thomas Jr. died 21 Nov. 1800, ae 27. [CEM]

Thomas, Col. died 20 Mar. 1830, ae 85-5. [CH][CEM]

Thomas b. 1872, d. 1926. [CEM]

Thomas C., s/o James R. & Eliz. M. died 14 July 1857, ae 20 ds. [CEM]

Thomas C., s/o John, ae 61, md. died 1868. [TR]

Thomas G. died 19 May 1868, ae 61. [CEM]

LeFEBVRE:
Alfred P., s/o Alfred died 28 Nov. 1936, ae 62-3-27. [AR]

LeHENAFF:
Frances E., d/o John Fitzgerald died 22 Dec. 1930, ae 86-8-27. [AR]

LEMICK?
Abigail, d/o Nathan Knowles, ae 72-0-4, wid. died 4 Feb. 1888. [TR]

LERNED:
Clifford F., s/o Walter h. died 21 Aug. 1938, ae 59-9-14. [AR]

LEWIS:
Margaret C., d/o Dr. James H. Candow died 24 Feb. 1943, ae 75-1-6. [AR]

LIBBY:
James Henry, s/o James, ae 27-6-0 died 22 July 1884. [TR]

LINABERRY:
Frederick Ralph, s/o Wm L. d. 10 Mar. 1927, ae 45-2-22. [AR]
Laura L., d/o Mr. Leflin died 24 Nov. 1941, ae 89-6. [AR]
William L., s/o Wm H. died 8 Feb. 1941, ae 83-10-22. [AR]

LINDSEY:
Sarah A., d/o David Knowles died 7 Feb. 1912, ae 59-8-5. [AR]

LITTLE:
Priscilla, formerly Haines bur. 18 May 1837, ae 45. [CH]

LOCKE:
Albert E. b. 1860, d _____. [CEM]
Almira, d/o Samuel & Mary died 23 Nov. 1841, ae 3-4. [CH][CEM]
Amanda, d/o Joseph Batchelder, md. died 16 Oct. 1881. [TR]
Charles W., s/o David died 20 Jan. 1941, ae 85-1. [AR]
Elvira G., d/o Nathaniel Marden died 17 Sep. 1936, ae 78-10-9. [AR]
Harold R. b. 1835, d. 1914. [CEM]
John died 15 Aug. 1845, ae 45. [CEM]
John b. 1826, d. 1893. [CEM]
Lille E. b. 1883, d. 1883. [CEM]
Mary, w/o Samuel died 5 Aug. 1872, ae 65-7. [CEM]
Mary E., w/o Morris & d/o Chas. Dow, b. 1870, d. 21 Jan. 1916, ae 75.
   [AR][CEM]
Morris, s/o Samuel. b. 1825, d. 8 Nov. 1920, ae 91-11-11. [AR][CEM]
Robert P., s/o John W. died 12 Oct. 1909, ae 90-0-12. [AR]
Samuel bur. 12 Aug. 1843, ae 44. [CH][CEM]
Sarah A., d/o Daniel Harris, b. 20 Oct. 1827, d. 8 June 1903, ae 75-7-19.
   [AR][CEM]

LOCKE Cont.

Susie (Berry), w/o Albert b. 1804, d. _____. [CEM]
Walter E., s/o Robert died 4 June 1933, ae 77-5-23. [AR]

LONG:

Alice, d/o Paul & Phebe bur. 24 June 1804, ae 17. [CH]
Nancy, d/o Paul & Phebe bur. 12 Nov. 1804, ae 12. [CH]

LOUGEE:

Sarah A., w/o George died 18 Aug. 1857, ae 25. [CH]

LOVERING:

Daniel died 15 May 1850, ae 83. [CH]
Ebenezer bur. 12 Dec. 1806, ae 87. [CH]
Ebenezer died 31 Aug. 1843, ae 87-5, Rev. War. [CEM][CH]
Hannah, w/o Thomas bur. 12 May 1801, ae 38. [CH]
Infant of John & Sally bur. 10 dec. 1814, ae 3 wk. [CH]
John, Lt. bur. 9 Dec. 1835, ae 82. [CH]
Lydia, w/o John bur. July 1829, ae 74. [CH]
Mehitable H., w/o Ebenezer died 2 June 1840, ae 68-6. [CH][CEM]
Miriam, wid. of Col. Thomas bur. 24 Feb. 1842, ae 80. [CH]
Rhoda, w/o Daniel & d/o David Batchelder died 6 Feb. 1847, ae 71-6. [CH]
Thomas, Col., Rev. War died 24 Nov. 1834, ae 74-4. [CH][CEM]

LOVETT:

Francis S., s/o Francis S. died 23 Feb. 1940, ae 75-10-28. [AR]
Mary Louise, d/o William Morgan died 14 Mar. 1923, ae 58-7-9. [AR]

LUCK:

Clements Frank. s/o Robert & Mary died 12 Feb. 1900, ae 7-0-26. [CEM][AR]
Mary A. (Rand), w/o Robert E. b. 29 Sep. 1871, d. 21 Aug. 1900. [CEM][AR]

McCAFFREY:

Thomas died 13 Sep. 1903, ae 40. [AR]

McDONALD:

Eliza, d/o David, ae 84-3-0, single died 22 July 1885. [TR]
Mary E., d/o Dennis Regan died 16 June 1943, ae 61-4-7. [AR]

McDONOUGH:

Frances K., d/ o Thos. Mahoney died 5 June 1940, ae 65-1-23. [AR]

McFADDEN:

Alice C., d/o Isaac Cutter died 14 Nov. 1935, ae 59-10-18. [AR]
Clara, d/o Thos. Stevens died 31 July 1935, ae 95-11-28. [AR]

McKENZIE:
Angus J., died 4 May 1940, ae 81-6-8. [AR]
Margaret, d/o Alex MacLeod died 15 Feb. 1939, ae 72-7-19. [AR]

McLAUGHLIN:
Charles F. died 5 Nov. 1874, ae 31. [CEM]
Clark died 22 Dec. 1891, ae 35-8. [CEM]
Emma F. died 9 May 1917, ae 64-10. [CEM]

McLEOD:
Ella d/o John W. McLeod died 4 July 1925, ae 33-8-5. [AR]

McNEAL:
Alice, w/o John bur. 7 July 1852, ae 56. [CH]
Alice Augusta bur. 25 May 1839, ae 0-2. [CH]
John, s/o John bur. 16 Apr. 1837, ae 5-8. [CH]
Rebecca, d/o John bur. 8 June 1838, ae 3. [CH]

MACE:
Beniah F., d/o Wm H. Douglas died 4 Apr. 1943, ae 28-6-26. [AR]
Clarence H., s/o John died 4 Apr. 1943, ae 32-7-4. [AR]
Henry died 4 July 1855, ae 57. [CH]
John Henry, s/o Henry bur. 14 Aug. 1839, ae 12-4-4. [CH]
Simon B., s/o Henry bur. 17 June 1846, ae 4. [CH]

MAGRAW:
James M. s/o John W. died 28 sep. 1936, ae 79-0-29. [AR]

MALOON:
Sylvester died 8 Dec. 1850. ae 27. [CH]

MARDEN:
Almira (Marston), w/o James & d/o Simon died 20 Jan. 1900, ae 82-9-15.
   [AR][CEM]
George A., s/o George E. died 13 Apr. 1909, ae 63-3. [AR]
James, s/o James, ae 72-5-8, died 15 June 1885. [TR][CEM]
Mary Lowell of Rye bur. 13 Aug. 1857, ae 0-8. [CH]

MARSH:
Alice M. Gillis b. 1871, d. 1919. [CEM]
Della, d/o Mr. Tenney died 21 Mar. 1929, ae 73-9-11. [AR]
G. Roscoe b. 1852, d. 1923. [CEM]
George R. died 25 Apr. 1923, ae 70-5-10. [AR]
Lurana (Rowe), w/o G. Roscoe b. 1866, d. 1912. [CEM]

MARSTON:

Abigail, d/o Jonathan bur. 20 May 1773, ae 0-0-12. [CH]
Abigail, wid. bur. 26 Oct. 1813, ae 92. [CH]
Abigail, Miss died 4 Dec. 1833, ae 52. [CH][CEM]
Abigail, wid. of Lt. Simeon & d/o Gen. M. Leavitt died 16 Apr. 1849, ae 83. [CH]
Abigail died 12 Oct. 1856, ae 94-10. [CH]
Abigail, w/o Jeremiah died 26 Jan. 1858, ae 72. [CH][CEM]
Abigail died 4 Sep. 1887, ae 75-8. [CEM]
Addie C., d/o Nathaniel B. Marston died 12 Jan. 1935, ae 77-7-6. [AR]
Adaline, d/o David bur. 1 Mar. 1843, ae 7. [CH]
Adeline Sarah, d/o Wm Burleigh died 28 Nov. 1927, ae 45-6-14. [AR]
Alfred L. s/o Nathaniel B. died 22 Mar. 1924, ae 72-4-17. [AR]
Almira died 3 Sep. 1870, ae 66. [CEM]
Andrew Jackson died 15 Nov. 1852, ae 37. [CH]
Ann, w/o Sherburne died 15 Mar. 1864, ae 54. [CEM]
Anna bur. 28 Apr. 1771, ae 35. [CH]
Anna Augusta, d/o Andrew bur. 30 Dec. 1849, ae 0-10. [CH]
Benjamin bur. 20 Oct. 1781, ae 74. [CH]
Benjamin died 15 July 1802, ae 86. [CH]
Benjamin, s/o wid. Abigail bur. 11 Nov. 1825, ae 21. [CH]
Benjamin died 5 Aug. 1862, ae 55. [CH][CEM]
Benjamin Franklin, s/o David died 27 Oct. 1851, ae 26. [CH]
Bertha E., d/o Cyrus Fogg died 20 Jan. 1940, ae 68-3-25. [AR]
Betsy, Miss died 4 Nov. 1855, ae 93. [CH]
Caleb bur. 7 Feb. 1778, ae 78-6. [CH]
Charles Augustus, s/o Thomas L. died 1 Sep. 1834, ae 3-3-27. [CH][CEM]
Charles H., s/o Joseph L. died 23 June 1909, ae 57-3-13. [AR]
Charles K. shot at Bull Run died 30 Sep. 1862, ae 17. [CH]
Charlotte, w/o Simon bur. 17 Dec. 1867, ae 75. [CH][CEM]
Child of Levi bur. 1788. [CH]
Child of Simeon bur. Jan. 1801. [CH]
Child of Simon & Charlotte bur. 2 Apr. 1811, ae 0-0-½. [CH]
Child of Daniel Jr. bur 6 Apr. 1828, ae 0-0-3. [CH]
Child bur. 3 May 1835, ae 7 wk. [CH]
Child of Daniel Jr. bur. 17 Aug. 1838, ae few wk. [CH]
Child of David bur. 22 Feb. 1843, ae 3 wk. [CH]
Child of Nathan bur. 20 Feb. 1843, ae 0-10. [CH]
Clarissa, w/o David bur. 10 Feb. 1843, ae 44. [CH]
Clarissa Hobart, d/o David & Clarissa bur. 14 Feb. 1843, ae 4. [CH]
Comfort, w/o Cotton W. died 4 Aug. 1832, ae 51-3. [CH][CEM]
Cotton W. bur. 29 Dec. 1839, ae 70-5. [CH][CEM]
Daniel Jr. b. 1805, bur. 28 Aug. 1849, ae nearly 44. [CH][CEM]
Daniel bur. 18 Dec. 1864, ae 91-5. [CH][CEM]
David, Cornet bur. 12 Feb. 1779, ae 70. [CH]
David, s/o Jonathan & Mary died 5 Aug. 1809, ae 14-11. [TR][CH][CEM]
David bur. 12 Mar. 1810, ae 30-2. [CH]

MARSTON Cont.

David, s/o Daniel Jr. bur. 7 Oct. 1844, ae 0-8. [CH]

David Co. K 2d D.C. Inf. [CEM]

David, s/o Jonathan, ae 79-11-23, single died 1 Jan. 1894. [TR][AR]

David S., s/o Cotton died 1 May 1897, ae 79-11. [AR]

David James, s/o Dearborn, b. 1830, d. 23 Mar. 1908, ae 77-5-4. [AR][CEM]

Dearborn died 23 Oct. 1860, ae 79. [CH]

Deborah bur. 24 Sep. 1824, ae 69. [CH]

Deborah, d/o Thomas died 14 Nov. 1852, ae 98-6. [CH][CEM]

Dolly bur. 10 Nov. 1812, ae 70. [CH]

E. Everett b. 23 Jan. 1875, d. 6 Dec. 1906. [CEM]

E. Josephine, d/o James died 21 Mar. 1936, ae 76-11-22. [AR]

Edward Seymour b. 1864, d. 1920. [CEM]

Edward S., s/o Joseph died 4 Apr. 1938, ae 64-7-3. [AR]

Elizabeth, d/o Thomas bur. Mar. 1786, ae 22. [CH]

Elizabeth A., w/o Thomas F. b. 5 Dec. 1827, d. 12 Jan. 1917. [CEM]

Elizabeth A., d/o Mark Bachelder died 12 June 1911, ae 83-6-9. [AR]

Elvira F., d/o Wm Judkins died 14 Sep. 1912, ae 80-5-20. [AR]

Emily, d/o Simon Fogg & w/o David J. b. 1840, d. 22 Mar. 1913, ae 73-0-1. [AR][CEM]

Emma O., d/o Edwin Marston died 23 Feb. 1937, ae 83-3-13. [AR]

Esther, wid. of Benjamin bur. 23 May 1809, ae 91-8. [CH]

Fanny, d/o Thomas, single died 15 May 1882, ae 79-6. [TR][CEM]

Fanny S., w/o George F. & d/o Thos. Cheswell, b. 22 Aug. 1840, d. 7 Sep. 1913. [AR][CEM]

Frank A., s/o Thos. R. died 19 Feb. 1938, ae 87-0-15. [AR]

George A., s/o James died 9 Apr. 1931, ae 80-2-15. [AR]

George F., s/o Thos. L. & Mary (Bailey) b. 9 Dec. 1833, d. 26 Mar. 1914. [AR][CEM]

Georgie E., d/o George Garland died 26 Aug. 1924, ae 45-8-26. [AR]

Hannah bur. 14 Oct. 1769, ae 21. [CH]

Hannah, w/o Thomas died 28 Feb. 1820, ae 59. [CH][CEM]

Hannah died 8 Jan. 1855, ae 88. [CEM]

Hannah K., d/o Jeremiah Batchelder died 13 Aug. 1914, ae 90-3-11. [AR]

Harry B., ae 64-1-16, died 6 May 1894. [TR]

Harvey B. b. 22 Mar. 1820, d. 6 May 1894, ae 64-1-16. [AR][CEM]

Henry died 6 June 1842, ae 62, [CEM]

Henry S., s/o Dearborn, b. 21 Mar. 1833, d. 18 Feb. 1911, ae 82-10-27. [AR][CEM]

Hepzibah, wid. of Samuel died 17 Feb. 1841, ae 96-11-17. [CH][CEM]

Herman Leroy, s/o Thomas F. & Eliz. A. died 1 Aug. 1864, ae 7-2-10. [TR][CEM]

Herman L. b. 21 Mar. 1866, d. 17 Mar. 1922. [CEM]

Hitty died 1801, ae 63. [CH]

Ida F., d/o Joshua Norton died 26 Apr. 1936, ae 80-5-7. [AR]

Isaac bur. 3 Mar. 1805, ae 62. [CH]

Isadora, d/o Simon Fogg died 14 Jan. 1913, ae 58-11-21. [AR]

J. Frank b. 6 July 1888, d. 13 Feb. 1932. [CEM]

MARSTON Cont.
James died 20 Nov. 1891, ae 71-10. [AR][CEM]
Jeremiah died 20 Aug. 1870, ae 85. [CEM]
Jonathan died in army 11 Sep. 1777. [CH]
Jonathan, s/o J. Stacey bur. 29 Oct. 1836, ae 1-3. [CH]
Jonathan died 27 Mar. 1845, ae 76. [CH][CEM]
Joseph, twin s/o Wid. Abigail bur. 4 Dec. 1808, ae 4-2. [CH]
Joseph L., s/o Thos. L. died 10 Apr. 1906, ae 76-18-7. [AR]
Joseph Stacy d. 20 Mar. 1876, ae 72-6. [CEM]
Katie W., d/o Henry S., b. 28 Jan. 1866, d. 6 Oct. 1938, ae 73-8-8. [AR][CEM]
Levi bur. 8 Nov. 1834, ae 76-7. [CH]
Levi, ae 76, md. died 27 Oct. 1880. [TR]
Linda M., b. 1843, d. 1929. [CEM]
Lucy A., w/o James & d/o Mark Dennett, ae 81-10-25, md. died 14 Dec. 1894.
    [TR][CEM]]AR]
Lydia A., d/o Joseph Palmer died 5 may 1908, ae 78-1-19. [AR]
Margaret A., d/o George D. Dow died 24 Sep. 1897, ae 49. [AR]
Margie A., w/o Thomas E. b. 17 Apr. 1848, d. 23 Sep. 1897. [CEM]
Martha bur. 12 Mar. 1769. [CH]
Martha A., w/o Harvey B. & d/o David M. Dow, b. 14 Mar. 1846, d. 14 June
    1914. [CEM][AR]
Martha D., d/o Nathan Brown, ae 90-4-22, died 2 Feb. 1892. [TR][AR]
Mary, d/o Jonathan & Mary bur. 3 Oct. 1818, ae 16. [CH]
Mary, w/o Levi & d/o John Lamprey bur. 4 Feb. 1838, ae 28. [CH]
Mary, w/o Isaac bur. 28 Apr. 1838, ae 91-4. [CH]
Mary, Mrs. bur. 5 Sep. 1854, ae 87-11. [CH]
Mary, Mrs. formerly of Hampton died 19 May 1855, ae 66. [CH]
Mary died 20 June 1871, ae 81. [CEM]
Mary, w/o Jonathan died 5 Apr. 1884, ae 87. [CEM]
Mary A. died 8 Dec. 1878, ae 72-8. [CEM]
Mary A., d/o Levi Marston, b. 14 Mar. 1842, d. 29 May 1896. [AR][CEM]
Mary Ann, d/o Peter Moore, ae 73, md. died 8 Dec. 1878. [TR]
Mary B., w/o T.L. d. 18 Feb. 1869, ae 74. [CEM]
Mary L., d/o Jonathan & Mary d. 2 Oct. 1810, ae 17. [CEM]
Mary L. died 18 May 1874, ae 79. [CEM]
Mehitabel died 1801. [CH]
Nabby, d/o Simon died 1795. [CH]
Nancy died 5 Oct. 1825, ae 36-5. [CEM[
Nancy (Garland) bur. 6 Oct. 1828, ae 36. [CH]
Nathaniel B., s/o Dearborn died 9 July 1903, ae 77-5-29. [AR]
Nora F., d/o Mr. Mansfield died 5 Mar. 1936, ae 71. [AR]
Olive L., w/o Sherburne died 15 Apr. 1893, ae 70-3-1. [AR][CEM]
Olive S., d/o Elisha Brown, ae 70-3-15, wid. died 15 Apr. 1893. [TR][AR]
Payson H., s/o Henry S., b. 31 Aug. 1881, d. 25 Apr. 1932. [CEM][AR]
Rachel C. (Lane), w/o Henry S. & d/o Thomas Lane, ae 56-9-22, died 26 Feb.
    1892. [TR][CEM][AR]
Sally, w/o Dearborn died 21 May 1845, ae 61. [CH]

MARSTON Cont.

Sally, w/o Daniel b. 1806, d. 1853. [CEM]
Sally, d/o Thomas, ae 82 single died 15 May 1882. [TR][CEM]
Sally A., d/o Jacob Brown died 27 Nov. 1901, ae 76-7-25. [AR]
Sarah bur. 7 Oct. 1767, ae 73. [CH]
Sarah died 29 Mar. 1851, ae 88. [CEM]
Sarah, Miss, sister of Daniel bur. 30 Mar. 1852, ae 86. [CH]
Sarah died 25 Jan. 1853, ae 46. [CH]
Sarah died 7 Jan. 1860, ae 72. [CH][CEM]
Sarah A., d/o Daniel & Sally b. 1834, d. 1860. [CEM]
Sarah A., d/o John Philbrick, ae 57, md. died 3 May 1875. [TR]
Sarah D., w/o Joseph died 15 May 1867, ae 62-4. [TR][CEM]
Sarah D., d/o John Nutter died 16 July 1898, ae 86-5-4. [AR]
Sarah H., w/o Frank A. & d/o Josiah b. 18 Feb. 1840, d. 8 Oct. 1900.
    [AR][CEM]
Sarah J. d/o James Batchelder died 20 Dec. 1900, ae 81-7-1. [AR]
Sherburne, s/o Simon, ae 72-2-16, died 9 Apr. 1884. [TR][CEM]
Simeon, Lt. Mrs. bur. Jan. 1797. [CH]
Simeon, ae 79-1, md. died 25 Oct. 1867. [TR][CH]
Simon d. 7 Jan. 1805, ae 56. [CH]
Simon died 29 Dec. 1867, ae 79. [CH][CEM]
Son of Clarence D. died 28 Mar. 1932. [AR]
Stephen, s/o Reuben & Mary died 8 July 1751, ae 0-4-7. [TR]
Thomas, Ens., Mrs. bur. Sep. 1796. [CH]
Thomas bur. 7 Apr. 1807, ae 78. [CH]
Thomas died 17 May 1847, ae 90-6. [CH][CEM]
Thomas died 17 Dec. 1870, ae 78-8. [CEM]
Thomas E., s/o Benjamin died 27 Oct. 1935, ae 87-7-25. [AR]
Thomas F., s/o Thos L., b. 10 Aug. 1825, d. 20 May 1920. [AR][CEM]
Thomas J. b. 1841, d. 1902. [CEM]
Thomas L. died 31 Dec. 1888, ae 91-3. [CEM]
Weare died 11 Sep. 1870, ae 80. [CEM]
Widow bur. Jan. 1795. [CH]
Wilbur Hayes b. 1861, d. 1915. [CEM]
Wilber H., s/o David J. died 11 Dec. 1915, ae 53-3. [AR]

MASON:
William P., s/o James died 25 Jan. 1937, ae 83-3-13. [AR]

MEADE:
John B. bur. 13 Dec. 1830, ae 35. [CH]
Nathaniel B., s/o John B. & Sarah bur. 14 Nov. 1823, ae 0-3. [CH]
Sarah, w/o John B. bur. Mar. 1832, [CH]
W. B. b. 7 Aug. 1825, d. 13 Nov. 1825. [CEM]

MERRILL:
Georgianna, d/o David Stevens died 27 Nov. 1928, ae 73-3. [AR]
Grace H., d/o George F. died 13 Feb. 1936, ae 56-2-23. [AR]

MESSER:
Mary (Hill), wid. of Nathaniel bur. 23 July 1847, ae 72. [CH]

MEVIS:
Mary O., w/o Rev. M.F. & d/o Daniel Adams, b. 1868, d. 2 May 1909, ae 41.
     [AR][CEM]

MITCHELL:
Mina , d/o Samuel Rand died 23 Oct. 1937, ae 74-9-2. [AR]

MOORE:
Abbie C. (Jenness), w/o Christopher & d/o Amos Jenness, b. 10 Sep. 1821,
     d. 6 Nov. 1910, ae 89-2-6. [AR][CEM]
Abbie J., d/o Oliver Page died 30 Dec. 1938, ae 85-10-15. [AR]
Abiah, w/o Peter died 5 Feb. 1870, ae 91-5-18. [TR][CEM]
Arnold Leroy, s/o Melvin D. died 13 Jan. 1928. [AR]
Christopher T., s/o Peter, ae 69-3-10, md. died 25 June 1892. [TR][CEM][AR]
Edgar S., s/o Thomas died 22 Apr. 1935, ae 86-10-28. [AR]
Frederic Jewell b. 1881, d. 1918. [CEM]
George A. b. 30 Nov. 1892, d. _____. [CEM]
Infant of Edgar & Abbie, ae 3 days died 10 July 1878. [TR]
Jennie A. died 1 Sep. 1877, ae 1-10. [CEM]
John Albion, s/o John bur. 15 Mar. 1843, ae 2. [CH]
Mary Olive (Dow), w/o Frederic b. 1885, d. 1917. [CEM]
Melvin J., s/o Christopher T. died 20 Apr. 1855, ae 10-0-26. [CH][CEM]
Mrs. bur. 7 Feb. 1870, ae 91-5-13. [CH]
Peter died 17 Mar. 1858, ae 80-6-12. [CH][CEM]
Sarah A., d/o Samuel Bennett & w/o George A., b. 7 Apr. 1897, d. 12 Oct.
     1918. [AR][CEM]
Sarah F. died 25 Sep. 1888, ae 64-8. [CEM]
Thomas, s/o Peter M. bur. 8 Apr. 1833, ae 20. [CH]
Thomas B., s/o Peter & Abiah died 1 Apr. 1855, ae 20. [CEM]

MORRILL:
Ruth, wid. & d/o Gen. Moses Leavitt bur. 16 Feb. 1844, ae 70. [CH]

MORRISON:
Emma S., d/o Isaac Stevens died 22 June 1930, ae 49-1-9. [AR]

MORSE:
James, s/o Edgar, ae 3-0-0 died 7 Aug. 1885. [TR]

MOSES:
Mary Anne, d/o Richard, ae 60, single died 8 Apr. 1884. [TR]

MOULTON:

Abner M., s/o William E., ae 0-8-16 died 5 Mar. 1884. [TR]

Abigail, wid. died 4 Feb. 1803, ae 73. [CH]

Annie M. died 3 Aug. 1908, ae 52-1-8. [AR]

Bethiah died 1801, ae 21. [CH]

Detsy, w/o Samuel died 1 June 1846, ae 23. [CH]

Charles Ridion, s/o Morris died 5 Jan. 1929, ae 52-2-17. [AR]

Child of William bur. 16 Dec. 1797. [CH]

Child of Jonathan bur. June 1812. [CH]

Child, twin of David bur. 29 Dec. 1844, ae 7 wk. [CH]

Daniel bur. 18 Mar. 1868, ae 67. [CH]

Daniel G. died 12 May 1893, ae 67. [AR]

Daniel P. died 17 Mar. 1869, ae 69. [CEM]

David P., s/o Daniel N. wid. died 18 Mar. 1896, ae 77-0-8. [TR][AR]

Ebenezer bur. 26 Jan. 1797. [CH]

Eliza A., w/o John & d/o David Fogg, died 23 Jan. 1916, ae 85-3. [CEM][AR]

Elizabeth A., w/o John B. & d/o Jeremiah Godfrey, died 21 Feb. 1902,
    ae 33-10-13. [AR][CEM]

Elizabeth H., d/o Mark Sleeper died 2 Dec. 1938, ae 74-3-8. [AR]

Fremont P., s/o John died 22 Feb. 1916, ae 60-5. [AR]

George, s/o Joseph bur. 27 Jan. 1842, ae 0-10.]CH]

George E. died 12 Nov. 1930, ae 70. [AR]

George O., s/o Reuben died 30 Oct. 1923, ae 70-1-22. [AR]

Gilman H., s/o Daniel died 30 Oct. 1923, ae 62-7-15. [AR]

Harriet, w/o Morris H. & d/o David Fogg, b. 14 Apr. 1842, d. 4 June 1915.
    ae 73-1-21. [CEM][AR]

Huldah, d/o William bur. 21 Apr. 1803, ae 2. [CH]

Jessie M., w/o Edwin O. b. 1 June 1860, d. 27 Dec. 1925, ae 65-6-26.
    [AR][CEM]

John, ae 52, md. died 25 Mar. 1879. [TR]

John died 2 Apr. 1879, ae 53-3. [TR][CEM]

John Burt, s/o John died 17 June 1927, ae 58-0-27. [AR][CEM]

John L., s/o Daniel, ae 68-2-13, died 22 June 1893. [TR][AR]

Jonathan bur. 10 Nov. 1843, ae 61. [CH]

Jonathan, s/o Jonathan bur. 26 Dec. 1843, ae 22-6. [CH]

Jonathan D., s/o Reuben L. died 7 Oct. 1900, ae 49-3-15. [AR]

Joseph, Mrs. bur. 4 May 1771. [CH]

Joseph bur. 29 June 1809, ae 73. [CH]

Joseph, ae 66, md. died 12 Oct. 1875. [TR]

Julia S. died 9 May 1860, ae 21. [CH]

Luella C., d/o Dearborn Blake d. 10 Aug. 1919, ae 62-8-22. [AR]

Martha, w/o Jeremiah bur. 10 Mar. 1770, ae 79. [CH]

Mary, w/o Daniel W. died 26 Dec. 1857, ae 60-7. [CH]

Mary C., d/o Dearborn Moulton, ae 72-7-0, md. died 2 Mar. 1889. [TR]

Mary E., d/o Monroe Otis died 8 June 1937, ae 69-7-3. [AR]

Melvin died 12 Aug. 1891, ae 1. [AR]

Molly, w/o William bur. 31 May 1845, ae 87-6. [CH]

MOULTON Cont.

Morris Hobbs, s/o Jonathan, b. 26 Nov. 1829, d. 16 May 1914. [AR][CEM]

Nehemiah bur. 17 Aug. 1816, ae 81. [CH]

Nellie F., d/o Eliza A. died 20 Jan. 1885, ae 28-9. [CEM]

Olive, wid. of Jonathan died 26 Oct. 1844, ae 56. [CH]

Oliver, d/o Daniel bur. 25 Oct. 1859, ae 16. [CH]

Oliver D., s/o David P. died 8 Jan. 1919, ae 66-6-27. [AR]

Orise J., s/o Morris H., b. 19 Oct. 1861, d. 19 Oct. 1943. [AR][CEM]

Phebe S., d/o Daniel Buxton or Norril Ruston, died 20 June 1894, ae 75-3-16.
   [TR][AR]

Reuben Lamprey, s/o Jonathan bur. 28 Mar. 1816, ae 0-7-8. [CH]

Reuben L., s/o Jonathan, died 12 June 1895, ae 72-11-0. [TR][AR]

Ruby M., d/o David P. Moulton died 17 Mar. 1921, ae 72-6-14. [AR]

Sally, d/o Mark Bachelder died 19 Feb. 1900, ae 71. [AR]

Sarah, w/o Nehemiah bur. 18 Apr. 1805, ae 66. [CH]

Sarah, wid. of Joseph bur. 5 May 1846, ae 91-3-15. [CH]

Sarah, d/o late Jonathan died 25 Apr. 1850, ae 25. [CH]

Warren B., s/o John died 24 Mar. 1941, ae 79-4-26. [AR]

William, Rev. War died 18 Mar. 1851, ae 95. [CH]

William E., s/o Daniel G. died 6 May 1906, ae 50-3-3. [AR]

MOWE:

Nellie Emma, d/o Ephraim, ae 12, died Jan. 1876. [TR]

MUNSEY:

Mary, d/o Eben, ae 7 died 11 Oct. 1880. [TR]

MURPHY:

Michael A. died 10 Aug. 1937, ae 40-6-3. [AR]

NARY:

Charlotte, w/o James E. died 30 Apr. 1890, ae 71-7. [CEM]

Elise, d/o F.E. & M.F. b. 19 June 1896, d. 11 May 1897. [CEM]

James E. b. 26 July 1816, d. 30 Oct. 1906. [CEM]

Murle, s/o F.E. & M.F. b. 12 Oct. 1892, d. 27 Sep. 1899. [CEM]

NASH:

Bennett H., s/o Joshua died 20 July 1906, ae 72-0-14. [AR]

NEAL:

Ebenezer died in army 20 Nov. 1777, ae 17. [CH]

Mary, w/o John Esq. d. 18 Oct. 1808, ae 61. [CEM]

Molly, wid. of John bur. 21 Oct. 1800, ae 62. [CH]

NEWCOMB:

Abby C., w/o Francis J. died 9 May 1864, ae 35-11-11. [CEM]

NEWMAN:
Infant of Thomas bur. 10 Feb. 1813. [CH]

NICHOLS:
John T.G., s/o George H. died 25 Apr. 1911, ae 74-0-14. [AR]

NORRIS:
Joseph bur. 12 Apr. 1803, ae 23. [CH]

NORTON:
Alonzo J. Smith b. 1842, d. 1916. [CEM]
Annie P., w/o Joshua J. died 8 Nov. 1891, ae 57-11-18. [CEM][AR]
Charles N. b. 1835, d. 1907. [CEM]
Clarence P., s/o Joshua J. & Phebe A. died 3 Sep. 1870, ae 1-3. [CEM]
Effie A., d/o Joshua J. & Phebe A. died 27 June 1859, ae 0-6-3. [CEM]
Elizabeth E.W., w/o Alonzo J. Smith b. 1843, d. 1891. [CEM]
Esther, wid. bur. 18 May 1783, ae 88-11. [CH]
Frank C., s/o Joshua died 4 June 1936, ae 81-10-26. [AR]
Hannah J. (Randell) b. 1828, d. 1853. [CEM]
Horace N. b. 1831, d. 1896. [CEM]
Joshua Johnson, s/o Robert W., ae 57-2 died 2 Jan. 1884. [TR][CEM]
Laura Pickins, d/o Joshua, ae 1-4, died 3 Sep. 1870. [TR]
Mae E., d/o Nelson J. or Samuel J, b. 11 May 1871, died 27 June 1893.
    [TR][CEM][AR]
Mary Olive, d/o Albert Kimball died 1 Nov. 1941, ae 70-7-29. [AR]
Mary W. b. 1823, d. 1858. [CEM]
Nathan b. 1797, d. 1875. [CEM]
Olive J., w/o Thomas M., died 9 Oct. 1853, ae 30. [CEM]
Sarah, w/o Nathan b. 1801, d. 1879. [CEM]
Sarah A. b. 1840, d. 1926. [CEM]
William, Mrs. bur. 24 Feb. 1827, ae 69-10. [CH]
William died 4 Apr. 1840, ae 78. [CH]

NUDD:
Caroline, d/o Mary Ann bur. 5 Sep. 1829, ae 1. [CH]
David bur. 16 May 1827, ae 65-8. [CH]
Infant twins of David bur. 22 Mar. 1811, ae 0-0-1. [CH]
John bur. 14 May 1806, ae 65. [CH]
Mary, wid. bur. 21 May 1841, aw 70 to 80. [CH]
Sarah, w/o David bur. 7 Dec. 1812, ae 42. [CH]
Sarah bur. 29 Sep. 1837, ae 37. [CH]
Sarah, widow of David bur. 31 Oct. 1841, ae 63. [CH]

O'BRIAN:
Mary A., d/o Daniel Kilkenny died 3 Dec. 1919, ae 71-7. [AR]

ODELL:

Infant of Dr. George bur. 10 Oct. 1819, ae 0-0-3. [CH]
Infant of Dr. George died 4 Aug. 1822, ae 0-0-3. [CH]

ODIORNE:

Joseph bur. 19 Jan. 1835, ae 16. [CH]
Martha Abigail, d/o Joseph bur. 29 Aug. 1835, ae 5-3. [CH]

OLESON:

Charles H., stillborn s/o Simon & Mary (Bohman) died 11 Dec. 1919. [AR]

OSGOOD:

Abigail, wid. d/o Samuel Chapman died 28 Apr. 1841, ae 82. [CH]

OSTERLUND:

Hilbert, s/o August died 8 July 1936, ae 56-8-21. [AR]

PAGE:

Abby T. d/o Elisha Rollins, w/o David J. b. 17 June 1824, d. 23 July 1897.
　[CEM][AR]
Abner, s/o David bur. 11 Sep. 1822, ae 2-6. [CH]
Alonzo D. b. 1840, d. 1903. [CEM]
Benjamin bur. 23 Oct. 1837, ae 45. [CH]
Betsy, d/o Dearborn bur. Sep. 1800. [CH]
Betsy, wid. of Dearborn died 15 Dec. 1852, ae 81-8. [CH][CEM]
Betsey died 16 Aug. 1886, ae 85-3. [CEM]
Betsy, w/o John died 12 Feb. 1879, ae 93. [CEM]
Betty, d/o Wid. Betty bur. 16 Mar. 1803, ae 1-3. [CH]
Betty, widow of Noah died 16 Apr. 1851, ae 87-6. [CH]
Charles S., s/o George W., b. 11 June 1867, d. 15 Apr. 1921. [AR][CEM]
Coffin bur. 12 July 1801, ae 46. [CH]
Coffin, s/o wid. Betty died 18 Mar. 1803, ae 8. [CH]
Cyrus Merrill, s/o Stacy died 13 June 1859, ae 3-2. [CH]
Daniel bur. Oct. 1782, ae 39. [CH]
Daniel bur. 9 June 1795, ae 82. [CH]
Daniel D., s/o Abner, ae 87, single died 16 May 1878. [TR]
Daisy A., w/o James G. Downing b. 29 Mar. 1869, d. 7 Jan. 1900, ae 30-9-9.
　[CEM]
Dau. of Dearborn bur. Sep. 1800. [CH]
David, s/o David Jr. bur. 20 Dec. 1781, ae 7-3. [CH]
David, s/o wid. Betty died 18 Mar. 1803, ae 6. [CH]
David died 16 May 1878, ae 86-7. [CEM]
David J. b. 25 Apr. 1825, d. 2 Jan. 1893. [AR][CEM]
Dearborn died 20 Dec. 1844, ae 76-4. [CH][CEM]
Eliza, w/o Stephen died 6 Feb. 1822, ae 33-9. [CH][CEM]
Ellen M., d/o Chas. Treletlon & w/o George W. b. 16 Oct. 1845, d. 25 Oct.
　1909, ae 64-0-9. [AR][CEM]

PAGE Cont.

Forabel, d/o Charles Hurd died 19 Mar. 1909, ae 46-10-7. [AR]

Francis died 1 May 1802, ae 78. [CH]

George A., s/o David J., b. 18 June 1847, d. 6 June 1909, ae 61-11-18. [AR][CEM]

George E., s/o Edwin A. died 30 May 1943, ae 18-2-12. [AR]

George W., s/o Stephen & Eliza died 11 Apr. 1837, ae 23-3. [CH][CEM]

George W., s/o Stephen, b. 12 Aug. 1845, d. 29 Apr. 1912. [AR][CEM]

Georgia M., w/o Charles S. b. 11 Apr. 1868, d. 6 July 1922. [CEM]

Gertrude F. d. 2 Mar. 1892, ae 0-9-6. [AR]

Grace M., d/o Chas. McLaughlin died 6 July 1922, ae 54-2-25. [AR]

Harriet, w/o David died 27 Oct. 1871, ae 78-4. [CEM]

Harriet N. died 24 Feb. 1879, ae 55-7. [CH]

Huldah, w/o Stacy died 15 June 1856, ae 46-11. [CH]

James B., s/o Oliver C. died 11 Feb. 1934, ae 77-8-7. [AR]

John bur. 28 Sep. 1822, ae 65. [CH]

John, wid. of bur. 28 Jan. 1851. [CH]

John died 26 Apr. 1851, ae 64-8. [CEM]. [CH]

Jonathan died 1770, ae 70. [CEM]

Jonathan, Mrs. bur. Dec. 1792. [CH]

Jonathan 2d, Lt. died 11 Dec. 1811, ae 84-7½. [CH][CEM]

Joseph bur. 5 Feb. 1773, ae 86-2. [CH]

Josiah died 1814, ae 27. [CH]

Josiah, s/o David bur. 23 Sep. 1822, ae 6. [CH]

Judith, w/o Simon D. & d/o Jonathan Rollins, b. 19 Oct. 1814, d. 21 May 1898. [AR][CEM]

Lucy bur. 15 June 1826, ae 52

Lydia F. (Hart), w/o George A. b. 12 Apr. 1849, d. 6 Mar. 1920. [CEM]

Lydia S., d/o Samuel Rowe, died 20 Sep. 1905, ae 74-11-10. [AR][CEM]

Mary (Towle), widow of Jonathan died 14 Nov. 1783, ae 82-8. [CH][CEM]

Mary (Smith), w/o Jonathan died 2 Dec. 1793, ae 61. [CEM]

Mary, w/o Francis died 6 Mar. 1802, ae 72. [CH]

Mary, w/o Benjamin bur. 5 Aug. 1859, ae 35-4. [CH]

Mary Frances, d/o Jewett died 12 Apr. 1855, ae 0-0-2. [CH]

Mehitabel died 31 Dec. 1818, ae 59. [CH]

Molly, wid. of Stephen P. bur. 9 Feb. 1826, ae 85-11. [CH]

Noah died 8 Dec. 1848, ae 82-4. [CH]

Odlin bur. 5 Jan. 1823, ae 53. [CH]

Oliver O., s/o Samuel C., md. died 17 Sep. 1895, ae 75-9-25. [TR][CEM][AR]

Ruth, w/o David bur. 8 July 1769, ae 66. [CH]

Sarah, d/o David bur. 4 June 1780, ae 0-0-7. [CH]

Sarah, widow bur. 27 Nov. 1826, ae 89. [CH]

Simon, s/o Jonathan bur. 12 July 1806, ae 75. [CH]

Simon D. b. 14 Nov. 1815, d. 16 June 1890. [AR][CEM]

Son of John bur. July 1791. [CH]

Stacy, s/o Noah, ae 57 or 87-11-4, widower, died 4 May 1894. [TR]

Stephen bur. 20 June 1805, ae 70. [CH]

PAGE Cont.

Stephen died 30 Mar. 1866, ae 71-6. [CEM]
Theodate, w/o Samuel bur. 3 July 1770, ae 26-3. [CH]
Widow bur. 3 Mar. 1783, ae 86. [CH]

PAIGE:

Gertrude F., d/o James B., ae 6-9-6 died 2 Mar. 1892. [TR][AR]
David J., s/o David, ae 67-8-8 died 2 Jan. 1893. [TR]
Simon Dearborn, s/o Stephen, ae 71-6-25, died 7 Feb. 1890. [TR]

PALMER:

David, s/o Joseph bur. 5 Sep. 1771, ae infant. [CH]
Hannah, w/o William bur. 8 Dec. 1776, ae 76. [CH]
William bur. 19 Nov. 1776, ae 79. [CH]

PARKER:

Allen Douglas, s/o Walter L. d. 7 Sep. 1929, ae 42-9-1. [AR]
Mary E.A., w/o Washington died 16 Dec. 1864, ae 34-11-11. [CEM]
Percy, s/o John M.J. died 7 Feb. 1923, ae 66-11-3. [AR]
Washington died 10 June 1866, ae 45-8. [CH]

PARSHLEY:

Rufina, d/o Ebenezer Smith died 29 Jan. 1917, ae 76-11-17. [AR]

PATTERSON:

Andrew H., s/o Rufus L. died 9 Sep. 1928, ae 57-11-12. [AR]

PEARSON:

Mary, d/o Albert C. & Alice M. (Bellows) died 13 Apr. 1939, ae 5-10-6. [AR]

PEPPER:

George Norris, s/o Henry died 8 Oct. 1898, ae 45-11-21/ [AR]

PERKINS:

George E., s/o George D. died 10 Feb. 1909, ae 46-4-22. [AR]
James, twin bur. 4 Mar. 1769. [CH]
Jonathan died 10 Apr. 1880, ae 87. [CEM]
Mary Abby, twin bur. 4 Mar. 1769. [CH]
Phebe, w/o Jonathan died 4 Apr. 1872, ae 74-7. [CEM]
Stephen G., s/o George E. died 22 Feb. 1903, ae 15-0-23. [AR]

PHILBRICK:

Allen, s/o Joseph L. ae 3, died 18 Sep. 1867. [TR]
Annah S., d/o Jonathan & Clara A. died 20 May 1865, ae 14-3. [CEM]
Betsy, wid. of Reuben bur. Aug. 1840, ae 33. [CH]
Charles W., s/o David J. died 16 Aug. 1941, ae 92-4-30. [AR]
Clara A., w/o Jonathan & d/o Moses Nudd, ae 73-7-16, died 15 Mar. 1894.
    [TR][CEM][AR]

PHILBRICK Cont.

Clara N. b. 10 May 1860, d. 19 Mar. 1914. [CEM]
Earl H., s/o Charles W. died 8 May 1934, ae 37-8-21. [AR]
Elizabeth, w/o Jonathan bur. 24 Jan. 1870. [CH]
Elizabeth L., d/o Joseph Lane, ae 73, md. died 20 Jan. 1870. [TR]
Emma L., d/o Abel Brown died 12 June 1938, ae 81-9-13. [AR]
Jennie S, w/o John W. & d/o James Parker, b. 1862, d. 7 Apr. 1928, ae
   66-1-18. [AR][CEM]
John Leonard, s/o Jonathan & Clara died 24 Apr. 1850, ae 1. [CH][CEM]
John W. b. 1954, d. _____. [CEM]
Jonathan, s/o Page, ae 77, md. died 16 Jan. 1870. [TR][CH]
Jonathan died 28 Aug. 1881, ae 66-7. [CEM]
Mark, ae 80, md. died 23 Jan. 1880. [TR]
Martha A., d/o Jonathan & Clara A. died 10 July 1864, ae 17-7. [CEM]
Martha J., d/o Jeremiah Dearborn died 17 July 1898, ae 62. [AR]
Mary Abby, d/o Jonathan & Clarissa died 12 Jan. 1846, ae 5 wk. [CH][CEM]
Nathan bur. 25 Feb. 1781, ae 26. [CH]
Sarah A., d/o Josiah Cram, ae 45-1-22, md. died 14 Mar. 1889. [TR]
Sarah E., d/o James Taylor died 10 Aug. 1936, ae 72-2-29. [AR]

PHILBROOK:

Allen Howard, s/o Joseph L. & Julia M. died 18 Sep. 1867, ae 3-2. [CEM]
Elizabeth, w/o Jonathan died 21 Jan. 1870, ae 73. [CEM]
Grace W., d/o Wm Dunham & w/o Willard H. died 9 May 1906, ae 35-6-22.
   [AR][CEM]
Henry M. b. 5 Aug. 1830, d. 5 Feb. 1865, ae 34. [CH][CEM]
Jonathan died 16 Jan. 1870, ae 76-11. [CH][CEM]
Joseph L., s/o Jonathan died 27 Aug. 1904, ae 77-7-1. [AR][CEM]
Julia M., w/o Joseph L. & d/o Simon Leavitt died 2 Sep. 1927, ae 97-6-8.
   [AR][CEM]
Margaret, d/o Simon Page d. 2 Apr. 1880, ae 32. [TR]
Margaret D., w/o Thomas died 26 Nov. 1879, ae 32-6. [CEM]
Mary E., d/o Oliver Hobbs died 7 July 1921, ae 79-11-6. [AR]
Page died 28 Sep. 1855, ae 92-11. [CH]
Rebecca P., d/o Simon Leavitt died 1 Feb. 1899, ae 65. [AR]
S. Page died 29 Sep. 1855, ae 92-11. [CEM]
Thomas, s/o Jonathan died 30 Apr. 1912, ae 79-9-18. [AR][CEM]

PICKERING:

Elizabeth (Fabyan) , w/o Joshua Esq. died 16 Nov. 1833, ae 61. [CH][CEM]
John, s/o Joshua & Elizabeth died 22 Mar. 1866, 71-1-12. [CH][CEM]
John P., ae 71, died 24 Mar. 1866. [TR]
Joshua, Esq. died 25 Jan. 1852, ae 83-10-17. [CH][CEM]
Joshua, s/o Joshua, ae 74, wid. died 4 Dec. 1870. [TR][CEM]
Lydia P., w/o Lyford Thyng of Iowa & d/o Joshua Esq. died 7 Sep. 1871, ae 70.
   [CEM]
Nancy C., w/o Joshua & d/o Morris Hobbs died 9 Jan. 1851, ae 46-2. [CH][CEM]

PICKERING Cont.
Rosamond, d/o Joshua & Elizabeth died 21 Nov. 1805, ae 23. [CEM]

PICKINS:
Mrs. Phebe Robinson, d/o David Pobinson, ae 74½, md. died 14 Apr. 1872.

POTTER:
John bur. 8 July 1833, ae 82. [CH]

POWERS:
Harold infant s/o Harold & Madeline (Seavey) died 17 July 1925. [AR]
Mary Abby, d/o Cyrus & Mary Jane b. 21 June 1835, d. 9 July 1853, ae 18.
   [CEM]
Mary S. died 9 July 1853, ae 18. [CH]

POWHATTAN:
Mabel F., d/o Herman Jenness died 19 May 1941, ae 54-0-21. [AR]

PRATT:
Hazel H., d/o Chas. Hook died 21 July 1943, ae 52-5-27. [AR]

PRECKLE:
Ada, d/o William F. & Emma of Manchester died 27 May 1855, ae 2-3. [CH]
Freddie, s/o William F. & Emma of Boston bur. 4 Dec. 1861, ae 3. [CH]

PRESCOTT:
Amos W., s/o Joseph died 13 Aug. 1940, ae 84-6-22. [AR]

PROSCHOLD:
Charles b. 1841, d. 1907. [CEM]
Elizabeth, w/o Charles b. 1841, d. 1925. [CEM]

PURINGTON:
Charles C., s/o George died 7 Feb. 1928, ae 74-2-26. [AR]
Francis, s/o George died 18 Oct. 1919, ae 81-8-18. [AR]

RAND:
Addie, d/o Samuel & Sarah b. 1855, d. 1862. [CEM]
Alice, d/o Samuell, ae 0-9-29, died 4 July 1868. [TR][CEM]
Eleanor P., d/o James Locke, ae 76-4, md. died 24 Sep. 1882. [TR]
Emily N., d/o Joshua, ae 66-7-0, single died 23 Jan. 1889. [TR]
Emma, d/o Samuel & Sarah b. 1856, d. 1862. [CEM]
Joseph, s/o Joseph, ae 89-10-25, wid. died 16 Dec. 1885. [TR]
Mary A., d/o Samuel & Sarah b. 1865, d. 8 July 1931, ae 65-11-5. [AR][CEM]
Samuel b. 1812, d. 1880. [CEM]
Samuel, s/o Samuel, ae 67, md. died 24 Jan. 1880. [TR]
Sarah J., w/o Samuel & d/o John Rand, b. 1836, d. 29 Nov. 1904, ae
   68-9-23. [AR][CEM]

REDMAN:
Tristram bur. June 1797. [CH]

REMICK:
John A., s/o John died 11 June 1911, ae 25-3-19. [AR]

RICE:
Thirza M., d/o Hazen Merrill died 9 Mar. 1899, ae 44-4-3. [AR]

RIDLOW:
Nathaniel T., s/o Samuel died 8 Apr. 1924, ae 86-5-2. [AR]
Rhoda A., d/o Ezra Fluent died 1 June 1919, ae 78-1-2. [AR]

RILEY:
Abby S. (Tucker), w/o Henry b. 24 Dec. 1855, d. 21 Dec. 1925. [CEM]
Henry b. 17 July 1852, d. 4 Apr. 1909. [CEM]
Margaret O., d/o Henry & Sarah A. (Tucker) b. 2 Feb. 1887, d. 14 Jan. 1902.
     ae 15. [AR][CEM]

RING:
Clara A., d/o Levi Batchelder & w/o Henry A. b. 6 Dec. 1844, d. 20 July 1927.
     [AR][CEM]
Henry A., s/o John & Rachel, b. 10 Jan. 1837, d. 26 June 1897. [CEM][AR]

ROBERTS:
Anna Towle, d/o Josiah Batchelder, died 20 June 1896, ae 77-6-22. [TR][AR]

ROBY/ROBIE:
Abigail, widow bur. 11 Jan. 1808, ae 81-9. [CH]
Betsey S., w/o Thomas died 5 June 1855, ae 61. [CH][CEM]
Child of Josiah died 1801. [CH]
David E. died 25 Oct. 1863, ae 38-1. [CEM]
Elizabeth, widow bur. 3 Sep. 1806, ae 70. [CH]
Elizabeth died 17 Oct. 1849, ae 63. [CH]
Hannah P., w/o Jeremiah & d/o Ephraim Seavey, b. 24 June 1830, died 17 May
     1892. [TR][CEM][AR]
Infant of Simon bur. 29 Nov. 1824, ae 2 wk. [CH]
Jeremiah H., s/o Thomas, b. 15 July 1828, d. 15 May 1901. [AR][CEM]
John bur. 17 Nov. 1794. [CH]
John, s/o Thomas & Betsey died 15 Oct. 1827, ae 3 mo. [CEM]
John, Mrs. bur. 31 Oct. 1829, ae 73. [CH]
John died 16 Sep. 1842, ae 84. [CH][CEM]
John Henry, s/o Thomas bur. 6 Oct. 1827, ae 0-3. [CH]
Lydia E., w/o Simon died 10 Aug. 1856, ae 56-1. [CH][CEM]
Mary, w/o John died 28 Oct. 1839, ae 73. [CEM]
Mary died 5 Sep. 1849, ae 59. [CH]
Ruth died 27 Dec. 1773, ae 26-10. [CH]

ROBY/ROBIE Cont.
Sarah bur. 16 May 1772. [CH]
Sarah, w/o John bur. 12 Apr. 1782, ae 56. [CH]
Simon died 4 Oct. 1845, ae 45-9. [CH][CEM]
Thomas bur. 4 Mar. 1767, ae 68-4. [CH]
Thomas died 4 Apr. 1872, ae 88-7. [CEM]

ROBINSON:
Jonathan, Lt. died 1 June 1814, ae 29-7. [CH]
Jonathan died 5 Jan. 1815, ae 29-7. [CEM]
Jonathan P. b. 30 May 1807, d. 29 Oct. 1897. [CEM[
Oliver died 20 Mar. 1826, ae 7-2. [CEM]

ROGERS:
Caroline, d/o Caroline formerly Smith bur. 14 Dec. 1825, ae 1-8. [CH]

ROLLINS:
Frances H., w/o Jonathan b. 27 Oct. 1839, died 22 Sep. 1881. [TR][CEM]
Greenlief D., s/o Jeremiah bur. 1 Oct. 1841, ae 1-4. [CH]
Jeremiah died 17 Apr. 1853, ae 45. [CH]
Jonathan, s/o Jeremiah died 5 Aug. 1902, ae 68-3-5. [AR]
Jonathan b. 30 Apr. 1834, d. 18 Sep. 1912. [CEM]
Mary Arabella, d/o Jeremiah died 22 Aug. 1845, ae 2. [CH]

ROWE:
Abigail, w/o Jacob & d/o Jeremiah Marston bur. 20 sep. 1846, ae 35. [CH]
Ella Jane bur. 6 July 1854. [CH]
Jacob, s/o Samuel died 3 Dec. 1900, ae 80. [AR]

RUMERY?
William Albion, s/o Albion R. & Ann died 10 July 1856, ae 2-10. [CH]

SAMMIS:
Charles F. b. 1909, d. 1917. [CEM[
Edward A. b. 1872, d. 1919. [CEM]
Frances D, w/o Edward b. 1873, d. 1912. [CEM]

SANBORN:
Anna, d/o William died 1795. [CH]
Anna bur. 30 May 1823, ae 20. [CH]
Anna, wid. of Thomas bur. 27 Aug. 1823, ae 80-5. [CH]
Betsy died 13 July 1862, ae 67. [CH]
Caleb bur. 11 Jan. 1795. [CH]
Catherine, w/o David bur. 23 Apr. 1775, ae 73. [CH][CEM]
Child of Caleb died 1790. [CH]
Child of John bur. Feb. 1798. [CH]
Child of John bur. 6 Apr. 1806, ae 0-0-10. [CH]

SANBORN Cont.

Child of Sewell bur. 1 Nov. 1824, ae 0-0-2. [CH]
Daniel died 30 Mar. 1767. [CEM]
Daniel died 9 Mar. 1787. [CEM[
Daniel bur. Feb. 1798. [CH]
Ebenezer, Mrs. bur. 16 July 1778. [CH]
Ebenezer died 1794. [CH]
Frank H. died 5 July 1891, ae 38. [AR]
Joanna Waterman, d/o Sewell bur. 20 Jan. 1842, ae 3-9. [CH]
John died 1807, ae 69, bur. at Sanbornton. [CH]
Jonathan died 25 Jan. 1857, ae 37. [CH]
Sarah, d/o Daniel & Katherine died 19 Sep. 1742. [TR]

SAYBALL:

Betsey E., w/o Joseph & d/o Paschel Martin, b. 22 Jan. 1829, d. 28 Oct. 1910.
  ae 84-4-6. [CEM][AR]

SCOTT:

Hannah, widow bur. 25 Feb. 1781, ae 74. [CH]

SEARS:

Garrett D. b/ 1871, d. _____. [CEM]
Laleah (Fowler), w/o Garrett b. 1866, d. 1929. [CEM]

SEAVEY:

Abbie E., w/o Frank b. 8 Oct. 1850, d. 14 Dec. 1903. [CEM]
Anna H., d/o A. Willis Bartlett & w/o George L. b. 17 Oct. 1882, d. 7 Feb.
  1919. [AR][CEM]
Bettis, w/o Charles b. 4 Feb. 1840, d. 7 June 1920. [CEM[
Carra Dora, d/o Frank & Abbie d. 15 Oct. 1868. [CEM]
Charles C., s/o Charles died 29 July 1940, ae 59-7-21. [AR]
Charles E., s/o Joseph, b. 10 June 1834, died 28 Dec. 1895. [TR][CEM][AR]
Charles, Mrs. died 16 Sep. 1864. [TR]
Della E., w/o Charles b. 26 Apr. 1835, d. 16 Sep. 1864. [CEM]
Donald R., s/o Cecil P. died 2 Sep. 1933, ae 31-3-11. [AR]
Frank H., b. 16 Dec. 1843, d. 28 Apr. 1926. [CEM]
George L., s/o Chas. E., b. 11 Apr. 1875, d. 21 Aug. 1943, ae 68-4-10.
  [AR][CEM]
Hattie S., d/o Noah McDaniel died 14 June 1920, ae 80-4-10. [AR]
Infant, s/o C.E. & H.S. b. 22 July 1877, d. 28 July 1877. [CEM]
Infant s/o Charles , ae 5 days died 1878. [TR]
Margaret B., d/o George Brown died 17 Sep. 1943, ae 56-10-22. [AR]
Sidney J., widow of John L. died 3 Mar. 1858, ae 68-6. [CEM]

SHAFTER:

Mary Ann Hazen, ae 67-3-10, died 6 Aug. 1886. [TR]

SHAW:

Andrew died 14 July 1869, ae 88-2. [CEM][CH]
Clara L., d/o Jonathan Marston, single died 9 Jan. 1894, ae 83-9-0. [AR][TR]
Edward bur. 3 July 1777. [CH]
Elmary, w/o Moses & d/o Daniel Dow, ae 62-10-8, wid. died 11 July 1883
   [TR][CEM]
George Bradbury, s/o Andrew died 29 Aug. 1845, ae 1-9. [CH]
Henry died 15 Jan. 1853, ae 60. [CH]
Jonathan died 7 July 1860, ae 70. [CH]
Judith, w/o Andrew died 5 Aug. 1841, ae 61. [CEM][CH]
Miss of Kensington bur. 26 Jan. 1816, ae 45. [CH]
Moses, s/o Benjamin & Abigail died July 1864. [TR]
Moses died 15 Jan. 1876, ae 51. [CEM]
Dau. of Reuben, md., died 13 Nov. 1885, ae 25-11-9. [TR]
Polly, w/o Andrew died 20 Apr. 1836, ae 53-4-12. [CEM][CH]
Stephen bur. 19 Feb. 1783, ae 66. [CH]
Thomas Brackett, s/o Edward died 24 July 1925, ae 74-7-20. [AR]

SHERBURNE:

Daniel, s/o John, ae 87-4-3, died 11 Sep. 1895. [TR][AR]
Infant od Daniel bur. Aug. 1841, ae 0-0-1. [CH]
Infant of Daniel bur. 28 Dec. 1842, ae 0-0-1. [CH]
Sarah, Mrs. d/o Nathan Knowles, ae 78-6-4, died 4 Feb. 1890. [AR][TR]

SHEPARD:

John bur. 8 Aug. 1767, ae 32. [CH]

SIMPSON:

Benjamin F., s/o Lucy E. Simpson, b. 1850, d. 28 June 1922, ae 72-0-9.
   [AR][CEM]
Joseph S. died 5 Feb. 1891, ae 0-1-11. [AR]
Laura A., w/o Benjamin & d/o Oliver Page, b. 1850, d. 15 Feb. 1919,
   ae 68-8-28. [AR][CEM]
Maggie J., w/o Willie P. & d/o Thos. Scott died 6 Apr. 1900, ae 35-8-11.
   [AR][CEM]
Oliver C. died 17 Sep. 1890, ae 1-5-6. [AR]
William F., s/o Benjamin F. died 31 Dec. 1926, ae 54-1-20. [AR]

SINNETT:

George, s/o Michael died 23 Aug. 1940, ae 78-0-5. [AR]

SLAFTER:

Edmund F., s/o Sylvester died 22 Sep. 1906, ae 90-3-23. [AR]

SLEEPER:

Alice F., d/o David P. Moulton died 8 May 1908, ae 44-1-2. [AR]
Ruth T., d/o Thomas, ae 80, single died 10 Mar. 1880. [TR]

SLEEPER Cont.
Sarah, d/o Francis Broadman, ae 79, died 25 Mar. 1883. [TR]
Theophilus W. died 16 Nov. 1856, ae 49. [CEM][CH]

SMITH:
Abigail, d/o John & Rachel died Feb. 1754. [TR]
Abigail, wid. died 1797. [CH]
Abigail, w/o Deacon bur. Feb. 1801, ae 59. [CH]
Alonzo J. b. 1828, d. 1916. [CEM]
Anna, w/o Samuel bur. 14 Sep. 1820. ae 49. [CH]
Arnold Drake, s/o Charles P., b. 1887, d. 3 Apr. 1920, ae 33-2-9. [AR][CEM]
Charles Fremont, s/o Joshua P., b. 1857, d. 28 Jan. 1930, ae 72-1-14.
   [AR][CEM]
Christopher, Mrs. bur. 28 Mar. 1778, ae 45. [CH]
Christopher died 7 Dec. 1814, ae 78, Rev. War. [CEM][CH]
Christopher, s/o Ebenezer, ae 76-6-24, md. died 20 Sep. 1881. [TR][CEM]
David, s/o Jonathan died 16 Feb. 1903, ae 82-9-2. [AR]
David Curtis, s/o Christopher died 1 July 1869, ae 30. [TR][CEM]
David Curtis, s/o John L. & R.F. b. 22 July 1872, d. 7 Sep. 1908. [AR][CEM]
Dearborn bur. 31 Mar. 1839, ae 57. [CH]
Ebenezer died 28 Oct. 1844, ae 71. [CH]
Edward M., s/o Morris H. died 29 Nov. 1943, ae 77-10-1. [AR]
Eles, d/o John & Rachel died 31 Jan. 1754. [TR]
Eliza, d/o Stephen & Rachel bur. 15 Mar. 1803, ae 3. [CH]
Eliza E., w/o Christopher & d/o Morris Hobbs, ae 83-10-8, died 13 Oct. 1884.
   [TR][CEM]
Elizabeth E.W., w/o Alonzo b. 1843, d. 1891. [CEM]
George E., s/o John L. & Rebecca, ae 1-4, died 5 July 1865. [TR][CEM]
George M. b. 15 Aug. 1864, d. 5 June 1915. [AR][CEM]
Infant of Samuel bur. 29 June 1785. [CH]
Infant of William bur. 3 July 1811, ae 0-0-9. [CH]
Infant of Christopher & Eliza bur. 28 May 1837, ae 0-0-2. [CH]
Isabella, w/o Morris Hobbs & d/o Simon Leavitt , b. 17 Feb. 1839, d. 6 May
   1905, ae 66-2-19. [AR][CEM]
Jedediah bur. 6 Oct. 1775. [CH]
Jesse C., s/o John died 27 May 1907, ae 67-11-12. [AR]
John bur. 23 Dec. 1769, ae 57-8. [CH]
John died 21 May 1853, ae 45. [CH]
John, s/o Morris H. & Isabella died 17 Sep. 1864, ae 0-3.
John E. b. 4 Sep. 1887, d. 24 Mar. 1911. [CEM]
John L., s/o Christopher b. 15 June 1835, d. 7 Nov. 1924, ae 89-4-22. [CEM]
Joshua P., s/o Christopher, ae 59-1-14, md. died 29 July 1894. [TR][CEM]
Josiah bur. 11 Dec. 1823, ae 33-7-10. [CH]
Linda B., w/o Joshua P. & d/o Samiel Berry died 9 Dec. 1919, ae 83-7-5.
   [AR][CEM]
Lucy Maria, d/o John Snell, ae 78, md. died 6 Nov. 1878. [TR]
Lydia, widow bur. 5 Oct. 1829, ae 83. [CH]

SMITH Cont.

Lydia bur. 5 Nov. 1842, ae 55. [CH]

Martha, d/o Morris H. & Isabella died 28 July 1864, ae 2-10. [CEM]

Maurice Leavitt, s/o Edward M. & Estelle b. 31 Aug. 1904, d. 1 Feb. 1905. [CEM]

Morris Hobbs, s/o Christopher, b. 1 July 1833, d. 28 Jan. 1904 ae 70-6-27. [AR][CEM]

Oliver, s/o Dearborn bur. 15 Nov. 1819, ae 5-10. [CH]

Philip, s/o John & Rachel died 24 Jan. 1754. [TR]

Philip, s/o Lt. Samuel bur. Aug. 1788. [CH]

Rachel, widow of Stephen died 11 May 1844, ae 68. [CH]

Rachel, widow died. 11 Mar. 1852, ae 85. [CH]

Rebecca P, w/o John L.& d/o Levi Marston, b. 5 July 1840, d. 22 Aug. 1905. ae 65-1-17. [AR][CEM]

Samuel bur. 11 Oct. 1812, ae 75. [CH]

Samuel died 19 Apr. 1847, ae 80. [CH]

Sarah, widow bur. 20 Apr. 1779, ae 89. [CH]

Silvanus, s/o John & Rachel died 8 Jan. 1754. [TR]

Son of John bur. 9 May 1852, ae 25 or 30. [CH]

Sophia S., d/o Mr. Safford, ae 82-8-6, wid. died 4 Apr. 1892. [TR][AR]

Stephen bur. 5 aug. 1830, ae 56. [CH]

Theodosia died 23 July 1933, ae 60-9-13. [AR]

SOUTHWORTH:

Robert A., s/o Alex died 25 Aug. 1920, ae 68-3-19. [AR]

SPERRY:

Mabel A., d/o James L. Nicholson died 9 May 1939, ae 71-5-8. [AR]

Mary H., wid. of Rev. E.F. & sister of Rev. J. French b. 6 Aug. 1751, d. 6 Jan. 1858, ae 76-4. [CH][CEM]

SPEAR:

Louisa A., d/o George Lutz died 15 Mar. 1932, ae 60-6-2. [AR]

George A., s/o George W. died 19 Sep. 1920, ae 83-10-7. [AR]

SQUIRE:

Richard, s/o George E. died 24 Oct. 1941. [AR]

STEVENS:

Anna, wid. of Nathaniel bur. 11 Sep. 1809, ae 61. [CH]

Infant of John bur. 1820. [CH]

Infant of David bur. 27 June 1842. [CH]

Sally, d/o Joseph bur. 25 Nov. 1817, ae 22-3. [CH]

STANLEY:

Fred D., s/o Thomas died 28 Oct. 1933, ae 75-11-28. [AR]

STOCKER:
Child of Margaret died 1811. [CH]

STONE:
Herbert A., s/o Abriel H. died 23 Sep. 1931, ae 59-8-20. [AR]

STORER:
Dora M., d/o Chas. Fitzgerald died 26 May 1926, ae 69-0-23. [AR]

STOTT:
Edith, d/o Charles A. Stott died 15 May 1943, ae 74-6-26. [AR]

STRAW:
Thomas B. b. 1841, d. 1925. [CEM]

TARLTON/TARLETON:
Arianna E., d/o Josiah smith died 21 June 1906, ae 67-3-1. [AR]
Byron, s/o George W. & Nellie (Moulton) died 31 Dec. 1899, ae 15-7. [AR]
Elias Albion, s/o Samuel died 17 July 1851, ae 12-6. [CH]
Elmer C., s/o Stephen P., ae 23-7-21, single died 25 Feb. 1885. [TR]
Infant of Samuel bur. 22 Jan. 1832, ae 0-1. [CH]
Joseph A., s/o Samuel died 2 Jan. 1908, ae 71-7-5. [AR]
Justin H., s/o George W. & Nellie F. (Moulton) died 19 May 1898, ae 15-10-15.
   [AR]
Lester, s/o Herbert J. died 30 June 1914, ae 29-2-26. [AR]
Margaret died 23 Mar. 1900, ae 63-4. [AR]
Nellie Frances, d/o Curtis Moulton died 30 June 1926, ae 63-9-20. [AR]
Sarah A., d/o Oliver Leavitt died 26 Mar. 1900, ae 59-3-21. [AR]
Stephen B., s/o Samuel died 17 Mar. 1921, ae 87-9-11. [AR]
Walter E., s/o John F. died 13 Jan. 1919, ae 33-8-20/ [AR]

TAYLOR:
Abbie F., w/o John F. & d/o George Chase. b. 24 Feb. 1857, d. 12 Oct. 1912.
   ae 55-8-18. [CEM][AR]
Abraham, single died 27 Mar. 1830, ae 79. [CH]
Betsy, w/o Col. John died 3 Oct. 1848, ae 59. [CEM]
Charles W., s/o Ira K. died 3 May 1941, ae 65-4-5. [AR]
Clementine, d/o Col. John & Elizabeth died 11 June 1842, ae 17. [CH][CEM]
Edward J. b. 10 Sep. 1856, d. 17 Mar. 1929. [CEM]
Elizabeth E., d/o Alfred died 10 Mar. 1854, ae 2-7. [CH]
Eva M., w/o Edward & d/o Eben H. Dalton, b. 19 Dec. 1865, d. 19 Mar. 1914.
   ae 48-3. [AR][CEM]
Fred L., s/o Richard, b. 9 July 1862, d. 10 Feb. 1904, ae 41-7-1. [AR][CEM]
George E., s/o Ira J., b. 10 Feb. 1859, d. 5 Apr. 1928. [AR][CEM]
Hannah, Miss bur. 1 Feb. 1840, ae 74. [CH]
Infant of John & Mary bur. 15 Nov. 1817, ae 0-0-12, [CH]
Infant of John & Mary bur. 26 Feb. 1827, ae 0-0-0. [CH]

TAYLOR Cont.
Infant of Ebenezer bur. Sep. 1831, ae 0-6. [CH]
Infant of John bur. Dec. 1836. [CH]
Infant of James died 16 Feb. 1858, ae 0-1. [CH]
Ira J., s/o John, b. 7 Aug. 1830, d. 11 Sep. 1904, ae 74-1-4. [AR][CEM]
John bur. 16 Jan. 1795. [CH]
John 4th died 16 Aug. 1846, ae 25. [CH][CEM]
John, Mrs. of Col. died 4 Oct. 1848, ae 60. [CH]
John died 7 May 1852, ae 63. [CH][CEM]
John, Col., s/o Joseph died 17 Feb. 1855, ae 67. [CH][CEM]
John F., s/o Richard, b. 28 Jan. 1853, d. 25 May 1908, ae 55-3-26. [AR][CEM]
John Fogg, s/o John & Mary bur. 16 Feb. 1821, ae 1-8. [CH]
John Salter, s/o Thomas & Elizabeth died 14 Oct. 1817, ae 12. [CH][CEM]
Jonathan, s/o John bur. 22 Mar. 1773, ae 0-9. [CH]
Joseph died 27 Mar. 1824, ae 74. [CH][CEM]
Lydia, d/o Joseph bur. 11 Dec. 1797. [CH]
Martha A., d/o Leon Knowles died 5 June 1923, ae 87-10-9. [AR]
Martha S. (Locke), w/o Ira b. 27 July 1835, d. 5 June 1928. [CEM]
Mary, w/o Joseph bir. 30 Mar. 1806, ae 48. [CH]
Mary, widow bur. 7 Apr. 1806, ae 79. [CH]
Mary, w/o John died 16 Aug. 1882, ae 85. [CEM]
Mary E. died 19 Nov. 1875, ae 54. [CEM]
Mary J., d/o Reuben Rand died 2 Oct. 1913, ae 80-8-5. [AR]
Mary J., w/o Richard b. 1853, d. 1918. [CEM]
Mary Lydia, d/o Richard & Sarah b. 22 Jna. 1855, d. 15 May 1864. [CEM]
Nathaniel, s/o Joseph, ae 65-2-0, single died 6 Oct. 1885. [TR][CEM]
Polly died 27 Oct. 1854, ae 79. [CEM]
Richard, s/o John, b. 5 Apr. 1825, d. 11 May 1899. [AR][CEM]
Sally bur. 22 June 1829, ae 66. [CH]
Sarah, w/o Richard died 8 Nov. 1858, ae 36. [CH][CEM]
Son of James bur. 1 July 1867, ae 5. [CH]
Sophia E., w/o George F. & d/o Thos. Marston, b. 25 Feb. 1860, d. 24 Feb.
    1924, ae 63-11-30. [CEM][AR]
Walter E. b. 28 Apr. 1883, d. 13 Jan. 1919. [CEM]
Warren E., s/o Ira & Martha died 30 June 1867, ae 5-1. [CEM]

THOMAS:
Ann, w/o Elisha bur. 4 May 1771. [CH]
Benjamin bur. 13 Nov. 1766, ae 89. [CH]
Elisha bur. 13 June 1782, ae 58. [CH]
James H. d. 8 June 1928. [AR]
Mary bur. 29 May 1823, ae 80. [CH]

THORTON:
Eliza (Gookin) bur. 2 July 1854, ae 59. [CH]

THURSTON:
Daniel, s/o Rev. bur. 3 Nov. 1816, ae 27-6. [CH
Sarah, w/o Rev. Benjamin died 22 May 1787 or 1798, ae 35. [CH][CEM]

TILTON:
Elizabeth, d/o Mary Ann bur. 25 Sep. 1846, ae 1. [CH]

TISDALE:
Caroline, d/o George Tisdale, died 13 Nov. 1919, ae 61-8-5. [AR]

TOBAY:
Esther Sayward b. 25 Mar. 1854, d. 27 Mar. 1906. [CEM]
Ethlyn, w/o Justin b. 4 July 1866, d. ____. [CEM]
Hiram b. 30 Nov. 1838, d. 25 Mar. 1924. [CEM]
Justin B. Drake b. 8 July 1855, d. ____. [CEM]

TOURTILLETT:
Emma A. (Ingalls), w/o George A. b. 18 Mar. 1858, d. 13 July 1903. [CEM]
George A. b. 9 Dec. 1854, d. 11 July 1923, ae 68-7-2. [AR][CEM]
John N, s/o George & Emma b. 25 Apr. 1896, d. 25 Jan. 1909. [CEM]

TOWLE:
Abraham bur. 20 Mar. 1823, ae 54. [cH]
Abraham, Mrs. bur. 20 Apr. 1835, ae 27. [CH]
Amos, Mrs. bur. 15 Apr. 1815, ae 38. [CH]
Amos died 15 Feb. 1855, ae 90-11-15. [CH][CEM]
Betsy, w/o Jonathan bur. 11 Dec. 1808, ae 35. [CH]
Infant of Zachariah Jr. died 1776. [CH]
Infant of Simon of Boston bur. 27 Nov. 1815, ae 0-0-2. [CH]
Isaac, s/o Zachariah died 1785 or 1796. [CH]
Jane, d/o Amos bur. 8 Oct. 1820, ae 18. [CH]
Jane, d/o Zachariah bur. 18 Apr. 1803, ae 23. [CH]
John died 11 Oct. 1849, ae 55. [CH][CEM]
John, s/o Joshua died 13 Sep. 1906, ae 90-4-21. [AR]
Jonathan D. bur. 17 Dec. 1817, ae 44. [CH]
Joseph A., s/o John, b. 1825, d. 30 Apr. 1899, ae 73-4. [AR][CEM]
Mary, wid.of Zachariah bur. 24 Apr. 1828, ae 80. [CH]
Mary bur. 9 May 1830, ae 87-11. [CH]
Mary M., d/o late Amos died 7 Sep. 1855, ae 63. [CH][CEM]
Nancy Jenness, d/o Amos bur. 3 Feb. 1809, ae 0-5. [CH]
Sally, d/o Amos bur. 26 Sep. 1820, ae 21. [CH]
Sarah, d/o Zachariah died 22 Feb. 1802, ae 23. [CH]
Sarah died 22 Feb. 1859, ae 59. [CH]
Zachariah died 28 May 1803, ae 57. [CH]

TREADWAY:
Edward H. died 26 Nov. 1883, ae 37. [CEM]

TREADWELL:
Annie P., d/o Thos. Treadwell died 4 Aug. 1903, ae 73-6. [AR]

TUCKER:
Caroline M., d/o John A. Tucker died 11 Oct. 1912, ae 53-10-5. [AR]

TUCKERMAN:
Kittery, s/o Kittery & Peg. bur. 27 Dec. 1781, ae 1. [CH]

TUTTLE:
Mary Elizabeth, d/o Richard Horne died 28 Apr. 1934, ae 82-2-29. [AR]

TYLER:
Newell B., s/o Harrison W. & Florence M. (Jenness) died 12 Feb. 1907,
   ae 2-11-19. [AR]

VINCIGUERRA:
Louis, s/o Francesco died 10 Feb. 1941, ae 62-10-4. [AR]

WAYNE:
Elizabeth, d/o John Hurley died 6 July 1941, ae 87-4-11. [AR]

WARD:
Alice (Birchall), w/o Leverett b. 4 June 1868, d. ____. [CEM]
Leverett H. b. 11 Sep. 1855, d. ____. [CEM]
S. Content, d/o Leverett & Alice b, 22 Sep. 1891, d. 3 May 1915. [CEM]

WARNER:
Abigail, w/o Samuel S. b. 18 June 1814, d. 15 Mar. 1842, ae 27-9. [CH][CEM]
Albert, s/o William bur. 20 Feb. 1813, ae 1-5. [CH][CEM]
Albert H., s/o Samuel S. died 23 Apr. 1917, ae 72-5. [AR]
Alpheretta, d/o Samuel S. & Ann E. died 23 Aug. 1855, ae 7. [CH]
Alvaretta M. b. 30 Mar. 1848, d. 29 Aug. 1855. [CEM]
Andrew Rubern, s/o William L., ae 62, md. died 3 Apr. 1876. [TR][CEM]
Ann died 21 Feb. 1903. [AR]
Ann E. b. 7 Sep. 1818, d. 11 Mar. 1908. [CEM] ????
Charles A. b. 12 July 1836, d. 27 May 1837. [CEM]
Elizabeth, d/o William bur. 23 Nov. 1809, ae 1-3. [CH]
Elizabeth, d/o William bur. 25 Sep. 1810, ae 0-3. [CH]
Elizabeth, w/o William died 23 Dec. 1827, ae 49. [CEM]
Elizabeth, w/o William bur. 26 Dec. 1835, ae 50. [CH]
Emily, d/o Andrew bur. 30 Sep. 1841, ae 1-8. [CH]
Emily D., d/o William & Eliz. died 19 Nov. 1839, ae 16-10. [CH][CEM]
Emily Malissa, d/o Andrew & Olivia died 28 Sep. 1842, ae 1-8. [CEM]
Estella G., d/o Daniel Garland died 18 Oct. 1919, ae 74-5-14. [AR]
Ethel G., w/o John W. b. 1845, d. 1919. [CEM]
Fannie E. b. 1871, d. 1872. [CEM]

WARNER Cont.

Infant of Samuel & Abigail bur. 29 May 1837. [CH]

John W., s/o Andrew S., b. 1848, d. 25 May 1919, ae 76-2-17. [AR][CEM]

Lucy M., d/o John W., b. 1874, d. 30 Jan. 1916, ae 42-5-8. [AR][CH]

Malissa Ellen, d/o Andrew & Olivia died 4 July 1851, ae 0-6-15. [CH][CEM]

Marion F. b. 1884, d. 1885. [CEM]

Mary, w/o William died 10 Apr. 1864, ae 73. [CH][CEM]

Mary Ann, d/o William bur. 28 Oct. 1822, ae 4-4. [CH][CEM]

Matilda Abby, d/o Samuel S. b. 15 May 1840, d. 30 Sep. 1841. [CH][CEM]

Nancy Knowles, d/o William died 4 Nov. 1822, ae 1-10. [CH][CEM]

Olivia R., w/o Andrew S. died 24 Apr. 1885, ae 66-7. [CEM]

Samuel Clarence Howe, s/o Samuel S. & Ann E. b. 18 July 1852, died 3 Apr. 1854, ae 2. [CH][CEM]

Samuel J. b. 18 Jan. 1807, d. 8 Apr. 1882. [CEM]

Samuel S., s/o William, ae 73-3, md. died 8 Apr. 1882. [TR]

Susan L., d/o James Bachelder died 7 Aug. 1898, ae 61-1. [AR]

William S. died 14 Apr. 1864, ae 78. [CH][CEM]

WARREN:

Christina E., d/o James Sawyer d. 23 Mar. 1898, ae 65-7-15. [TR]

WATSON:

Charles A. died 28 Oct. 1902, ae 87-10-23. [AR]

WATTS:

Alice J., d/o Joseph Pottle, ae 37-2-23, died 11 Oct. 1883. [TR]

WAYNE:

Elizabeth, d/o John Hurley d. 6 July 1941, ae 87-4-11. [AR]

WEDGWOOD:

Catherine, d/o Jonathan & Mary died 2 Oct. 1754. [TR]

Clark, Mrs. died 1790. [CH]

David bur. 6 May 1770, ae 30. [CH]

Hannah died 9 Aug. 1755. [TR]

John died 31 July 1733. [TR]

John, s/o Jonathan & Mary d. 7 Oct. 1759. [TR]

Jonathan, s/o Jonathan & Mary died 21 Sep. 1754. [TR]

Jonathan, s/o Jonathan & Mary died 31 aug. 1758. [TR]

Jonathan bur. 11 June 1806, ae 90. [CH]

Mary, w/o Jonathan died 9 July 1790. [TR]

Olivia, w/o James bur. 28 July 1783, ae 35-9. [CH]

WELLS:

Infant of John died before Apr. 1777. [CH]

WENTWORTH:
Infant of Joshua & Ann died 9 Mar. 1849, ae 9-7. [CH]
Mary Ann, w/o Joshua died 15 Oct. 1849, ae 20-9. [CH]

WETHERBEE:
Abigail, w/o Elder died 17 Sep. 1854, ae 68. [CH]

WHENAL:
Carrie A., d/o Harvey Marston died 5 Oct. 1936, ae 56-7-9. [AR]
Jane, d/o Wm Brown & w/o William b. 15 June 1839, d. 18 July 1922. [AR][CEM]
John, s/o William died 2 Apr. 1940, ae 70-9-7. [AR]
John Winthrop, s/o John & Carrie b. 16 Jan. 1907, d. 19 June 1909. [CEM]
Josephine P., d/o Thos. B. & Isabel L. (White) b. 1904, d. 17 Apr. 1906,
    ae 1-10-7. [AR][CEM]
Louis C., s/o William & Jane (Brown) died 14 Jan. 1896, ae 18-8-5. [AR][CEM]
Robert b. 2 Feb. 1865, d. _____. [CEM]
William, s/o William, ae 62-4-20 died 9 Oct. 1893. [TR][CEM][AR]

WHITE:
Alice E., d/o Joseph Lambert died 5 Feb. 1937, ae 80-4-25. [AR]
Nathaniel G., s/o Nathaniel, ae 65-4, md. died 12 Sep. 1886. [TR]

WHITTIER:
John of Newfields, Me. died 24 Apr. 1840, ae 34. [CH]
Martha, w/o Sargeant bur. 10 Sep. 1772. [CH]

WIGGINS:
Aaron, Mrs. of Stratham bur. 5 Jan. 1815, ae 44. [CH]
Ave M., d/o E.F. & M.O. died 11 June 1864, ae 2-3. [CEM]
Bertie F., s/o E.F. & M.O. died 29 Oct. 1875, ae 11-4. [CEM]
Edwin G., s/o Enoch F. & Martha Berry, ae 26-3, single died 13 Apr. 1879.
    [TR][CEM]
Ella C., d/o E.F. & M.O. died 25 Oct. 1862, ae 2-11. [CEM]
Elizabeth, widow died Dec. 1857. [CH]
Enoch Frank, s/o Andrew, died 25 May 1878, ae 52-1. [TR][CEM]
Infant of Andrew died 2 Jan. 1848, ae 3 wk. [CH]
Martha O., w/o William C. Garland & wid. of Enoch died 6 June 1889, ae 53.
    [CEM]
Nathaniel, s/o William bur. Mar. 1816, ae 4. [CH]

WILLIAMS:
Norman, s/o Norman died 19 June 1899, ae 64-4-18. [AR]

WILLSON:
Lydia single died 18 Aug. 1881. [TR]

WILMOT:
Huldah bur. 4 Nov. 1804. [CH]

WILTBANK:
William M., s/o Wm W. died 10 July 1905, ae 35-6-5. [AR]

WINCH:
Edith I., d/o Herman L. & Edith (Thompson) died 17 Apr. 1913, ae 0-0-5. [AR]

WINGATE:
Annie, d/o Wm J. Breede died 21 Sep. 1943, ae 71-3-16. [AR]
John died 4 Sep. 1812, ae 87-8. [CH][CEM]
Joshua bur. 9 Feb. 1769, ae 89-11. [CH]
Mary bur. 27 May 1772, ae 90-3. [CH]
Oliver S., s/o Henry P. & Sarah A. b, 25 Aug. 1870, d. 5 Sep. 1906. [CEM]

WINSLOW:
Thirsa, d/o George Hill died 5 Apr. 1937, ae 51-9-5. [AR]

WOOD:
Anna P., d/o Jonathan Towle died 23 Nov. 1932, ae 81-10-10. [AR]
Helen G., d/o Benjamin Grant died 29 July 1905, ae 40-9-25. [AR]

WRIGHT:
David P., s/o John A., b. 24 Feb. 1844, d. 6 May 1909, ae 65-2-12. [AR][CEM]
David K., s/o Maurice R. died 5 Sep. 1938, ae 21-3-15. [AR]
John A., s/o James, ae 71-1-7 died 14 Nov. 1895. [TR][CEM][AR]
Margaret H., d/o Maurlee Adams d. 17 Dec. 1938, ae 89. [AR]
Willey J. b. 27 Mar. 1894, ae 18-9. [CEM]

YOUNG:
Mary, d/o Isaac bur. 29 Aug. 1781, ae 0-0-7. [CH]

YURAN:
John died 31 Aug. 1884, ae 80-9. [CEM]
Lauranda, w/o John died 23 June 1860, ae 51. [CH][CEM]
Lorinda, w/o John died 13 June 1860, ae 50. [CEM]

NORTH HAMPTON, N.H.

MARRIAGES

1742 - 1942

ABBOTT:

Alice - Dudley Chase, both of Hampton Falls md. 19 Apr. 1770. [CH]
Rev. Sereno Timothy of Hampton Falls - Sarah French, d/o Rev. Jonathan md. 15
Aug. 1839. [CH]

ACKERMAN/AKERMAN:

Frank R. (19), s/o Frank D. - Eunice G. Haines (19), d/o Matthias md. 8 Sep.
1860. [TR]
Solome - Henry Cate, both of Portsmouth md. 5 Jan. 1806. [CH]

ADAMS:

Daniel E. (76) Wellesly Hills, MA. - Ella M. Haines (47) md. 7 Apr. 1909.
[AR]
Emma O. (22) - Rienze Ridge (25) md. 12 Jan. 1884. [TR]
Nathaniel S. - Elizabeth M.J., both of Exeter md. 10 Nov. 1836. [CH]

ALLEN:

Abigail of Greenland - Titus Philbrick of Rye md. 22 Oct. 1767. [CH]
Allison A. (21) - Laura A. Booker (22) md. 12 Jan. 1935. [AR]
Bertha E. (24) - Ether Penman (27) md. 22 Sep. 1933. [AR]
Deborah of Stratham - John Weels Jr. of Greenland md. 28 Oct. 1773. [CH]
Herbert M. (42) - Elizabeth Proschold (43) md. 28 Apr, 1908. [AR]
Irvin (23) Dartmouth - Helen M. Bolton (22) md. 20 May 1936. [AR]
Jeremiah - Abigail Currier md. 24 Dec. 1751, [CH]
Raymond Marshall (21) - Amy May Fogg (20) md. 23 Dec. 1938. [AR]

ALPAUGH:

Ruth B. (25) Orange, NJ - Maurice B. Smith (27) md. 2 Sep. 1933. [AR]

APPLETON:

Benjamin A. (37) Newburyport - Bertha E. Brown (24) md. 29 Oct. 1902. [AR]

ARMSTRONG:

Beatrice Louise (19) - Willard Chandler White (21), both of Newton, Mass.
md. 23 Nov. 1929. [AR]

ASHFORD;

Bertrum Wm (35) - of Newburyport - Mabel Louise Carter (22) md. 12 Oct. 1940.
[AR]

AUSTIN:

Charles E. (21) - Sarah J. Gould (20) md. 24 June 1880. [TR]

AYERS:

Ann - Eliphalet Johnson, both of Green;and md. 3 Aug. 1794. [CH]
Phebe of Greenland - Nathaniel Huggins md. 29 July 1778. [CH]
William - Deborah Weeks, both of Greenland md. 8 Jan. 1795. [CH]

BACHELDER/BATCHELDER:
Addie (38), d/o Levi - Henry A. Ring (39), s/o John md. 16 Sep. 1877. [TR]
Albert (25), s/o James - Abbie M. Lamprey (19), d/o John md. 22 June 1869.
  [TR][CH]
Almira - Sheriden Jenness of Rye md. 30 Dec. 1845. [TR][CH]
Annie C. (23), d/o James & Elizabeth - George A. Hill)22), s/o James & Mary
  A. md. 24 Nov. 1859. [TR]
Annie M. (23) - George A. Hill (22) s/o James md. 24 Nov. 1859. [TR][CH]
Asenath H. - David Perkins of Hampton md. 1 Mar. 1825. [TR][CH]
Bartlett A. (21) - Bernice E. Downes (23) Boston md. 25 Nov. 1922. [AR]
Bartlett A. (32) - Katherine Rand (22) Brentwood md. 1 Jan. 1934. [AR]
Bessie L. (22) - R. Jenness Locke (34) of Rye md. 22 Feb. 1898. [AR]
Betsy - Josiah Perkins of Rye md. 13 Sep. 1807. [CH]
Betsy (64), d/o Nathaniel & Elizabeth - John Clay (62), s/o John & Abigail
  md. 31 May 1864. [TR]
Carrie L. (18) - Frank Dearborn (23) of Portsmouth md. 24 Sep. 1868.]CH]
Charles E. (19) - Martha M. Brown (18) md. 12 Jan. 1863. [TR][CH]
Charles L. (22) - Jessie F. Butler (25) md. 15 June 1907. [AR]
Clarabell (19) - Frank P. Brown (20) md. 12 Sep. 1885. [TR]
Confort of Hampton - Joseph Hennison of Deerfield md. 12 Aug. 1793. [TR]
Dora C. (23) - Walter P. Plummer of Newbury, MA. (23) md. 21 Oct. 1903. [AR]
Edith G. (18), d/o Thos. - Edgar G. Perkins (21), s/o George md. 27 Oct.
  1883. [TR]
Eleanor C. (20) - Prentice F. Moulton (22) md. 3 Nov. 1933. [AR]
Elesebeth - John Samborn of Hampton Falls md. 2 Jan. 1792. [TR]
Elizabeth - James Batchelder md. 27 Mar. 1823. [TR][CH]
Elizabeth Abigail (23) - Thomas Franklin Marston 6 Oct. 1850. [CH]
Emily - John S. Bancroft of Bradford, Mass. md. 22 Oct. 1855. [CH]
Eunice - Oliver Leavitt md. 13 Apr. 1814. [TR][CH]
Frederick A. - Mary C. Pickering md. 3 Nov. 1842. [TR][CH]
George A. (20) - Ethel M. Locke (21) md. 30 June 1888. [TR]
Helen E. (18) - Ralph B. Hussey (24) md. 28 Nov. 1934. [AR]
Increase of Nottingham - Anna Taylor md. 25 Feb. 1770. [CH]
James - Saley/Sally Bachelder md. 23 May 1816. [TR][CH]
James - Elizabeth Batchelder md. 27 Mar. 1823. [TR][CH]
James L. (24) - Viola M. Redden (23) of Portsmouth md. 27 Oct. 1909. [AR]
Jeremiah Jr. (28) - Martha H. Fogg (22) md. 27 Mar. 1834. [CH]
John - Mary Cotton md. 30 Nov. 1780. [CH]
Jonathan of Northwood - Sarah Shaw md. 27 June 1786. [CH]
Jonathan C. - Mary Ann Jenness md. 21 Nov. 1816. [TR][CH]
Josephine A. (24) - Wm Macpherson Wiltbank (27) of Phila. md. 2 Sep. 1897.
  [AR]
Josiah - Abigail Cotton md. 5 Dec. 1770. [CH]
Josiah - Molly Towle md. 6 Mar. 1806. [CH]
Levi of Kensington - Susanna Gilman of Exeter md. 1 Apr. 1793. [TR][CH]
Levi - Clarissa Marston md. 24 Oct. 1837. [CH]
Martha - Bickford L. Rand of Ipswich, Mass. md. 9 Oct. 1842. [TR][CH]

BACHELDER Cont.

Martha L. (23) - Charles W. Goodwin (29) md. 16 June 1896. [TR][AR]

Mary - Reuben Marston md. 28 Mar. 1745. [TR]

Mary - Jonathan Brown md. 16 Sep. 1807. [CH]

Mary - David B. Elkins of Hampton md. 3 June 1828. [TR][CH]

Mary D. - Sylvester H. Jackson of No. Berwick, Me. md. 30 Nov. 1842. [CH]

Mary I. - Robert A. Southworth, Boston md. 25 Apr. 1916. [AR]

Minerva (32), d/o Nathaniel - Rev. Levi L. Fay of Lawrence, Ohio md. 25 Oct. 1855. [CH]

Mira B. (23) - John McGrad (25) md. 4 June 1865. [TR]

Mira W. (23), d/o Robert & Sophia - Joh H. Grant (23), s/o John M. & Alice M. md. 4 June 1865. [TR]

Molly of Hampton - ____ Samuel Garland md. 1 June 1794. [TR]

Nathaniel - Elizabeth Taylor md. 10 Jan. 1782. [CH]

Nathaniel - Mrs. Eliza Ward md. 18 Oct. 1822. [TR][CH]

Nellie N. (21), d/o B.P. - Edward J. Taylor (20), s/o Ira J. md. 12 July 1876. [TR]

Olive A. (42), s/o Mark - Joseph B. Jenness (42), s/o Benj. md. 25 Feb. 1879. [TR]

Patience - Isaac Godfrey of Hampton md. 21 July 1783. [CH]

Polly - Edward Chapman Cotton of Effingham md. 5 Jan. 1800. [CH]

Polly - John Hobbs 3d md. 19 Jan. 1815. [TR][CH]

Richard Alden (22) - Marion Elizabeth Rideout (20) md. 10 Jan. 1941. [AR]

Ruth I. (19) - James W. Taylor (26) Calif. md. 26 June 1932. [AR]

Sally - Dearborn Marston md. 27 Nov. 1805. [CH]

Sally - James Bachelder md. 23 May 1816. [TR][CH]

Sarah - Francis Jenness of Rye md. Sep. 1778. [CH]

Sarah - Jeremiah Godfree md. 1 Oct. 1788. [TR]

Sarah - Simon Wills of Rye md. 16 Nov. 1797. [CH]

Stephen of Deerfield - Sarah Cotton md. 22 Apr. 1779. [CH]

Thomas I. (24) - Hattie Brown (23) md. 26 Nov. 1862. [CH]

Thomas J. (43), s/o Jeremiah - Lillie McDonald (23) md. 18 Oct. 1880. [TR]

BAKER:

Harold W. Jr. (23) of Boston - Elizabeth F. Hanson (21) of Swampscott, Me. md. 29 Jan. 1933. [AR]

Susan R. (19) of Boston - Robert Winsor Jr. (35) of Weston, MA. md. 27 Sep. 1919, [AR]

BALSLEY:

Alfred H. (33) of Reidsville, NC - Margaret M. Moody (33) of Los Angeles md. 11 July 1925. [AR]

BANCROFT:

John S. of Bradford, Mass. - Emily Batchelder md. 22 Oct. 1855. [CH]

BARDENSTEIN:
Jeannette P. (24) - Irving Kams (25) both of Dorchester, MA. md. 27 Feb. 1937. [AR]

BARKER:
Abigail - William Robinson, both of Stratham md. 26 Nov. 1807. [CH]
Charles M. (22), s/o Nathan - Annie Church (22), d/o Noah md. 16 Oct. 1872. [TR]
Nathan of Greenland - Molly Marston md. 4 Oct. 1770. [CH]
Samuel - Dolly Blake, both of Hampton md. 24 Nov. 1807. [CH]

BARNARD:
Andrew - Phebe Dow md. 25 Apr. 1752. [CH]
Mary - Moses M. Tuxbury md. 25 Sep. 1823. [CH]
Sarah - Theophilus Morrill md. 25 Dec. 1755. [CH]

BARTLETT:
Cyrus R. (23) - Josephine E. Moulton (19) of Kittery md. 20 Nov. 1902. [AR]
Hon. Josiah of Stratham - Hannah Weeks of Greenland md. 5 Apr. 1812. [TR][CH]
Mary A. (22) of Salisbury - George L. Seavey (29) md. 27 Sep. 1904. [AR]
Perley - Patience Locke, both of Hampton md. 15 Jan. 1818. [TR][CH]
Sally (of E.K.) - Lt. Jacob French md, 30 May 1913. [CH]

BARTON:
Barbara Helen (16) - Paul Edwin Brewster (17) md. 8 Jan. 1937. [AR]
Charles E. (32), s/o Charles E - Gertie W. Sabell (24), d/o Joseph md. 20 Nov. 1889. [TR]
Charles W. (36) - Mildred E. Hobson (25) of Concord, NH md. 6 Oct. 1926. [AR]
Chauncey (35) - Agnes D. Fitts (40) of Pittsfield md. 7 July 1926. [AR]
Goldie M. (22) - William D. Bridge (21) of Haverhill md. 8 Jan. 1910. [AR]
James? M. s/o Charles - Addie E. Spears, d/o Samuel md. 17 Feb. 1877. [TR]
James W. (34) - Eliza P. Philbrick (37) md. 9 May 1888. [TR]
Maud E. (28) - Harry A. Mathers (42) of Rockland, Me. md. 15 Nov. 1916. [AR]

BATCHELDER: See Bachelder.

BAVIS:
Thomas F. (22) of Jamaica Plains, MA. - Marion Hunnewell (19) of Roxbury, MA. md. 1 Mar. 1937. [AR]

BEACON:
Emmons L. (24), s/o Abel - Susan Palmer (20), d/o John M. md. 20 ___ 1878. [TR]

BEALE:
Grace (31) of Greenville Jnt, Me. - Frank Elmer Smith (32) md. 9 June 1928. [AR]

BEAMAN:
Charles Ellery (21) - Eleanor Wilson (22) both of Gloucester, MA. md. 16 June
1938. [AR]

BECK:
Catherine - Nathaniel Walker, both of Portsmouth md. 4 July 1810. [TR][CH]

BELLOW:
Alice M. (33) of Hampton Falls - Albert C. Pearson (33) md. 9 Nov. 1932. [AR]

BENNEHOFF:
Olton Rader (32) of Ohio - Priscilla Louise Merrill (20) md. 15 Dec. 1928.
[AR]

BENNETT:
Gwendolyn A. (19) Orland , Me. - Winslow R. Fogg (22) Hampton md. 27 June
1936 at Newfields. [AR]

BENSON:
Charles Robert (21) of Beverly, MA - Phebe Alverna Woodward (20) of Brockton
MA. md. 12 June 1938. [AR]

BERNARD:
Theodore F. (22) - Theresa Cuddy (20) both of Roxbury, MA. md. 3 July 1937.
[AR]

BERRY:
Alberta E. (20) of Hampton - Howard M. Jenness (24) md. 16 Nov. 1910. [AR]
Amanda (21), d/o Ebenezer - Joseph B. Hobbs (30) s/o Moses md. 9 Sep. 1863.
[TR]
Edwin M. (25) - Addie C. Fogg (19) md. 20 June 1882.[TR]
Enoch J. (26) - Jennie S. Wright (19) md. 14 Dec. 1885. [TR]
Frank E. (26) - Susy G. Perkins (19) md. 27 June 1904. [AR]
Frank E. (47) - Wolberg L. Peterson (46) of W. Watertown, MA. md. 21 Oct.
1925. [AR]
Fred W. (21), s/o John C. - Esther S. Moulton (22), d/o David D. md. 5 June
1876. [TR]
Haven S. (22), s/o Chas. P. - Mabel J. Dow (19), d/o Samuel A. md. 7 June
1890. [TR][AR]
Janice S. (22) - J. Warren Philbrick (23) md. 29 Oct. 1883. [TR]
John M. (26), s/o Thos. & Lottie - Valorie H. Brown (22), d/o Nathan &
Clarissa md. 12 Sep. 1860. [TR]
John W. (21), s/o Joseph E. - Emma E. Locke (21) md. 30 Jan. 1889. [TR]
Joseph J. - Betsy Wedgwood , both of Rye md. 24 Feb. 1813. [TR][CH]
Joshua of Greenland - Abigail Drake md. 15 Feb. 1810. [TR][CH]
Leon M. (20) - Emma A. Tourtilott (19) md. 31 Oct. 1909 at Rye. [AR]
Mary A. (21), d/o E.H. - Perley Watson (32), s/o Henry md. 26 Dec. 1871. [TR]

BERRY Cont.
Mary S. (32) of Stratham - Frank W. Jenness (27) md. 16 June 1899. [AR]
Olive - Joseph Locke 4th, both of Rye md. 4 Aug. 1811. [TR][CH]
Otto W. (25) - Rose Sanford (18) md. 1 Mar. 1893. [TR][AR]
Samuel Bracket - Abigail Webster, both of Rye md. 7 Feb. 1796. [CH]
Susie A. (19) - Albert E. Locke (22) md. 4 Apr. 1883. [TR]

BIANCO:
Angelo Del (33) of Concord - Irene Craven (25) md. 5 Sep. 1940. [AR]

BILLINGS:
Marland Pratt (36) of Roslindale, MA. - Katherine Fowler Lunn (35) md. 23
Apr. 1938. [AR]

BIRSHALL:
Alice C. (22) - Henry L. Ward (33) md. 21 Mar. 1889. [TR]

BISBEE:
Mary A. of N. Livermore, Me. - Russell P. Hutchins of Wells, Me. md. 21 Apr.
1913. [AR]

BISSELL:
Sherman (35) of Exeter - Ida B. Tilton (23) of Manchester md. 6 Oct. 1935 at
Portsmouth. [AR]

BLAIR:
Glenn Warren (30) of Bath, Me. - Iola Ellis Moulton (24) of Wells River, Vt.
md. 17 May 1941. [AR]

BLAISDELL:
David - Judith Jewell md. 24 Dec. 1755. [CH]
John (28), s/o Albert - Patty Jenness (25) md. 8 June 1871. [TR]

BLAKE:
Almira of Hampton - Benjamin Grover of Exeter md. 13 Mar. 1825. [TR][CH]
B. Herbert (20), s/o Benj. P. - Hanna Felch (24), d/o Caleb Jones md. 7
Apr. 1876 at Hampton Falls. [TR]
Dolly - Samuel Barker, both of Hampton md. 24 Nov. 1807. [CH]
Frances - Daniel H. Rundlett, both of Exeter md. 1 Oct. 1826. [TR][CH]
Francis - Mary Prescott, both of Hampton md. 20 Mar. 1832. [TR][CH]
George W. (26), s/o Wm - Sandra A. Lamprey (24), d/o Thos. L. md. 23 May
1878. [TR]
Jethro Jr. - Betsy Cilley both of Hampton md. 12 Sep. 1820. [TR][CH]
John - Hannah Palmer, both of Hampton md. 7 Nov. 1792. [TR]
Leland L. (32) of Saco, Me. - Louise M. Mater (33) of N. Kennebectport, Me.
md. 14 Mar. 1937. [AR]
Mary Ann - James Lane, both of Hampton md. 1 Feb. 1838. [CH]

BLAKE Cont.

Sarah of Kensington- Samuel Hobbs md. 28 Jan. 1829. [TR][CH]

Simon - Mary Towle, both of Hampton md. 29 Mar. 1795. [CH]

BLANEY:

Adelbert Stanley (23) - Ethel Marie Degan (20) md. 12 Apr. 1941 at
Portsmouth. [AR]

Ester L. (28) of Kittery, Me. - George B. Whenal (22) md. 6 Sep. 1924. [AR]

Kenneth Gerry (25) - Thelma Mann (23) md. 14 June 1941. [AR]

BLAY:

Ann - Samuel Carter md. 11 Feb. 1751. [CH]

BOBSON:

Juanita J. (36) of Indianapolis - David A. Lane (34) of Institute, W. Va. md.
12 Aug. 1935 at Rye. [AR]

BOGGS:

Evelyn L. (25) - Wallace H. Ellis (22) of W. Medford, MA. md. 28 Aug. 1937.
[AR]

BOISVERT:

Robert Fred (21) of Portsmouth - Barbara Rose Wentworth (18) md. 1 May 1940
at Kittery, Me. [AR]

BOLTON:

Helen M. (22) - Irvin Allen (23) of Portsmouth md. 20 May 1936. [AR]

BOOKER:

Asa A. (23) - Emma S. Brown (21) md. 16 Oct. 1907. [AR]

Laura A. (22) - Allison A. Allen (21) md. 12 Jan. 1935. [AR]

Louise (21) - Richard I. Goss (31) md. 14 Feb. 1932. [AR]

BOURGESS:

George (23) of Lynn, MA - Carrie M. Heading (17) md. 3 Dec. 1903. [AR]

BOOTH:

George A. (30) - Octivia L. Millikan (20) md. 30 Oct. 1895. [AR]

BOUTHBY:

George A. (20) - Octavia L. Williken (20) md. 30 Oct. 1895. [TR][AR]

BOYD:

Austin D. (27) - Louise T. Dow (19) both of Stratham md. 23 Jan. 1932. [AR]

BOYNTON:

Mary E. - Irving W. Brown (32) md. 16 Jan. 1902. [AR]

BRADSTREET:
Emma F. (21) of Danvers, MA. - Charles R. Chevalier (23) md. 8 June 1904.
[AR]
Moses (35) of Rowley, Mass. - Sarah I Hobbs (19) md. 6 Aug. 1857. [CH]

BREED:
Abbie T. (19) - Frank C. Norton (34) md. 24 Dec. 1888. [TR]
William J. (25), s/o Otis J. - Lydia A. Frost (23), d/o Peperill md. 29 Nov.
1871. [TR]

BREWSTER:
Paul Edwin (17) - Barbara Helen Barton (16) md. 8 Jan. 1937. [AR]

BRIDGE:
William D. (21) of Haverhill - Goldie M. Barton (22) md. 8 Jan. 1910. [AR]

BRIDLE:
William (33) - Clara L. McIntire (28) both of Portsmouth md, 27 July 1899.
[AR]

BRIGGS:
Elvira B. (22) - Warren B. Moulton (29) md. 3 Sep. 1841. [TR][AR]

BROOKS:
Joshua - Ruth L. Dearborn, both of Portsmouth md. 17 Dec. 1839. [CH]

BROWN:
Abbott (32) - Eleanor Lane (21) of Hampton md. 31 Oct. 1929. [AR]
Abel Jr. - Ruth Fellows, both of Kensington md. 17 June 1824. [TR][CH]
Abigail - Theodore Coosing? md. 6 Apr. 1790. [TR]
Abigail - Benjiman Philbrook md. 4 Oct. 1794. [TR]
Abigail - Samuel Tarlton md. 26 Jan. 1819. [TR][CH]
Abigail, Mrs. (30) - Edmund Morrill (49) of Salisbury, Mass. md. 8 Apr. 1857.
[CH]
Abraham - Hannah Morrill, widow md. 24 Dec. 1755. [CH]
Adeline - Abraham Drake Jr. md. 30 Nov. 1842. [CH]
Almira A. (40) - Henry Jenness (55) md. 15 Dec. 1881. [TR]
Alvin C. (23), s/o Abel T. - Jennie O. Sleeper (20), d/o Martin md. 18 Apr.
1876. [TR]
Amy A. (20), d/o Adam - Fremont R. Moulton (24), s/o John md. 1 Jan. 1880.
[TR]
Anne A. (40) - Arthur G. Leacock (43) of Exeter md. 24 Aug. 1911. [AR]
Arthur W. (28) - Maud M. Carr (24) of Portsmouth md. 26 Oct. 1908 at
Portsmouth. [AR]
Benjamin - Mary Page md. 18 Feb. 1768. [CH]
Benjamin - Mary Brown md. 24 Aug. 1797. [CH]
Bertha E. (24) - Benjamin A. Appleton (37) of Newburyport md. 29 Oct. 1902.
[AR]

BROWN Cont.

Charles - Abigail Leavitt md. 16 Mar. 1841. [TR][CH]

Charles H. (31) of Salisbury, MA. - L. Blanche Knowles (32) md. 17 Sep. 1919.
[AR]

Daniel - Hannah Jewell md. 17 Jan. 1754. [CH]

David Jr. - Abigail Hobbs md. 2 Mar. 1813. [TR][CH]

Dolly - Benjamin Jenness of Rye md. 27 May 1827. [TR][CH]

Dorothy - Tristram Dalton md. 11 Nov. 1798. [CH]

E. Gertrude (23) of Berwick, Me. - Melvin P. Locke (25) md. 29 June 1921.
[AR]

Elesebeth - Ruben Philbrook of Sanbornton md. 21 Feb. 1791. [TR]

Eliza - Joseph Ward of Hampton md. 24 Jan. 1819. [TR][CH]

Eliza - Abraham P. Towle Jr., both of Hampton md. 14 Nov. 1824. [TR][CH]

Elizabeth M. (21) - Charles W. Taylor (27) md. 24 June 1903. [AR]

Emma L. (26), d/o Abel L. - Walter S. Philbrick (27), s/o Rufus md. 14 Dec.
1882. [TR]

Emma S. (21) - Asa A. Booker (23) md. 16 Oct. 1907. [AR]

Eunice L. (23) of Rye - Harrison W. Dalton (23) md. 1 Jan. 1933. [AR]

Evan D. (28) - Edith W. Pelton (26) of Winchester, MA. md. 8 June 1931. [AR]

Frank P. (20) - Clarabell Bachelder (19) md. 12 Sep. 1885. [TR]

Frank P. (28) - Eva M. Horne (18) md. 30 Mar. 1893. [TR][AR]

Fred A. (31) - Lizzie A. Knowles (19) md. 3 Oct. 1890. [TR][AR]

George Henry (21), s/o Langdon - Cora Jane Moulton (21), d/o John md. 21 Dec.
1876. [TR]

George L. of Hampton Falls - Joanna M. Perkins of Hampton md. 7 Nov. 1849.
[CH]

Hannah - Daniel Newman of Newburyport md. 26 Dec. 1811. [TR][CH]

Hannah L. - John P. Grouard? md. 12 July 1829. [TR][CH]

Hattie)23_ - Thomas I. Batchelder (24) md. 28 Nov. 1862. [CH]

Hayden M. (22) - Margaret E. Nesbitt (19) of Exeter md. 27 May 1932. [AR]

Helen H. (22) - George A. Ward (30) of S. Hamilton, MA. md. 1 June 1935. [AR]

Helen V. (24) of Rye - Joshua F. Drake (26) md. 20 Apr. 1924. [AR]

Herbert T. (25) - Viva M. Nesbitt (19) of Exeter md. 17 Feb. 1931. [AR]

Hiram (26), s/o Jacob & Dolly - Ellen A. Lamprey (22), d/o Mary A. md. 13
Mar. 1865. [TR]

Horace L. (22), s/o Joseph - Norma Garland (16), d/o Rufus md. 10 Nov 1868.
[TR]

Irving W. (32) - Mary E. Boynton md. 16 Jan. 1902. [AR]

Irving W. (43) - Clara W. Wentworth (42) of Rochester md. 12 Oct. 1912. [AR]

Jacob Jr. - Abigail Lamprey md. 21 Feb. 1797. [CH]

Jacob Jr. - Debra L. Keous md. 19 Mar. 1820. [TR][CH]

Jeremiah 3d - Betsy Sanborn of Hampton Falls md. 12 Apr. 1837. [CH]

John - Olive Dalton, both of Leavitts Town md. 19 Sep. 1773. [CH]

John - Polly Jenness md. 5 June 1798. [CH]

John - Anna Jones md. 3 Apr. 1825. [CH]

John Jr. - Rachel Philbrook, both of Hampton md. 19 Feb. 1803. [CH]

John H. (21) - Hannah M. Godfrey (19) md. 7 Aug. 1862. [TR][CH]

BROWN Cont.

John Henry (56), s/o Simon - Mrs. Mary Abby Davis (27), d/o David Fogg md. 27 July 1873. [TR]

John I. (25) - Mildred C.S. Tuttle (22) of Watertown, MA. md. 4 Sep. 1908. [AR]

Jonathan - Mary Batchelder md. 16 Sep. 1807. [CH]

Joseph - Ruth Hoyt md. 29 Nov. 1756. [CH]

Joseph Jr. - Sarah Brown md. 17 Apr. 1842. [TR][CH]

Julia L. (25) - Charles T. Marden (24) md. 2 Aug. 1888. [TR]

Levi of Hampton Falls - Sarah Drake of Hampton md. 15 Dec. 1792. [TR]

Levi - Lydia Lovering md. 17 Nov. 1803. [CH]

Louisa C. - Benjamin Chapman md. 3 Jan. 1849. [CH]

Luella M. (24) - Gilman H. Moulton (22) md. 18 Oct. 1883. [TR]

Lydia H. (48) - Orrin R. Corey (50) of Derby, Vt. md. 8 Jan. 1891. [TR][AR]

Martha (22), d/o William - S. Alonzo Jenness (31), s/o Edwin md. 5 Jan. 1875. [TR]

Martha M. (18) - Charles E. Batchelder (19) md. 1 Jan. 1863. [TR]

Martha P. (27) - George W. Tarbell (29) md. 3 Sep. 1881. [TR]

Nathan of Hampton Falls - Rosemond Pickering md. 13 Nov. 1828. [TR]

Mary - Jacob Worthen md. 28 Sep. 1756. [CH]

Mary - Humphry Hook of Salisbury md. 15 Oct. 1777. [CH]

Mary - Simon Dearborn md. 9 Aug. 1787. [CH][TR]

Mary - Denjamin Brown md. 24 Aug. 1797. [CH]

Mary of E.K. - James Doton of Canaan, NH md. 21 Apr. 1817. [CH]

Mary H. of Hampton - William Marsh of Newburyport md. 6 Sep. 1831. [CH]

Nathan of Hampton Falls - Rosamond Pickering md. 13 Nov. 1828. [CH]

Nathan Jr. (45) - Elizabeth A. Jenness (36) md. 20 Mar. 1859. [CH]

Nathan P. (27) - George W. Tarbell (29) md. 3 Sep. 1881. [TR]

Nutter - Margaret Simpson, both of Greenland md. 12 Mar. 1812. [CH]

Olive - Capt. David Simpson, both of Greenland md. 18 June 1813. [TR][CH]

Oliver A. (32), s/o Oliver - Polly Hodges (24), d/o Samuel md. 19 Sep. 1876. [TR]

Otis G. (26), s/o Simon - Emma P. Johnson (22), d/o Joseph md. 24 June 1872. [TR]

Polly - Stacey Brown md. 25 May 1807. [CH]

Rachel - Samuel Smith of Stratham md. 1 Feb. 1773. [CH]

Sarah - James Sawyer Lampre(y) of Rye md. 17 Aug. 1793. [TR]

Sarah - John Rundlet, both of Stratham md. 4 July 1812. [TR][CH]

Sarah - Joseph Brown Jr. md. 17 Apr. 1842. [TR][CH]

Sewell of Hampton Falls - Eliza Nudd md. 20 Sep. 1821. [TR][CH]

Sewell - Hannah Johnson, both of Hampton md. 24 Dec. 1834. [TR][CH]

Simon - Esther Dalton md. 27 Oct. 1793. [TR]

Simon - Emily Drake md. 6 Nov. 1827. [TR][CH]

Stacey - Polly Brown md. 28 May 1807. [CH]

Stephen - Molly Pitts Jarrel md. 13 Jan. 1795. [CH]

Susanna of Hampton - Thomas Nudd md. 25 Oct. 1796. [CH]

Valarie M. (22), d/o Nathan & Clarissa - John M. Berry (26), s/o Thomas & Lottie md. 12 Sep. 1850. [TR]

BROWN Cont.
Verina M. (18) - Meade Jenness (28) md. 24 Dec. 1884. [TR]
Waity - Ezra Nichols Jr., both of Seabrook md. 4 July 1814. [TR]
Walter - Margaret Simpson, both of Green;and md. 12 Mar. 1812. [TR]
Warren (28), s/o D.P. & N.C. Perkins - Mary A. Garland (23), d/o M.L. & L.
   Lock md. 24 May 1865. [TR]
William of Hampton - Nancy Downing md. 9 Dec. 1810. [TR][CH]
William P. (21), s/o Stacy - Laura P. Garland (18), d/o Joseph md. 17 Nov.
   1869. [TR]

BRYANT:
Joseph - Hannah Smith md. 16 May 1771. [CH]
Sukey - William Smith md. 4 July 1809. [TR][CH]

BUNN:
Lily A. (25) of Phila, PA. - George W. Heath (31) md. 8 Oct. 1900. [AR]

BURGESS:
Carrie M. (27) - Chester J. Sellers (31) of Boston md. 27 Dec. 1913. [AR]

BURKE:
Edwin (25), s/o David - Olaran Johnson (21), d/o Mathew md. 21 Apr. 1876.
   [TR]

BURLEIGH/BURLEY:
Adeline s. (21) - Edward S. Marston (28) md. 27 July 1902. [AR]
Caleb - Sarah Flanders md. 7 Feb. 1752. [CH]
Edward - Polly Scammons, both of Stratham md. 8 Aug. 1783. [CH]
Hattie (20), d/o Henry - David Jewell Jr., s/o David md. 2 Mar. 1869. [TR]
Mary - Ezra Smith, both of Newmarket md. 17 July 1794. [CH]
William H. (37), s/o Henry - Sarah M. Jenness (35), d/o Benj. md. 28 Jan.
   1877. [TR]

BURN:
Philip - Elizabeth Dow, both of Hampton Falls md. 19 Apr. 1770. [CH]

BURNHAM:
James of Rochester - Abigail Pickering of Newington md. 25 Apr. 1783. [CH]

BUTLER:
Jessie F. (25) - Charles L. Bachelder (22) md. 16 June 1907. [AR]
Yvone Rose Alma (18) of Waterville, Me. - Frank Hamilton Moulton (22) md. 11
   May 1929. [AR]

CAIT: ?
Daniel of Northwood - Nancy Jenness md. 27 Nov. 1788. [TR]

CALDER:
Nathaniel H. of Boston - Ethelinda Clark of Hampton md. 20 July 1834.
[TR][CH]

CAMERON:
Reatha M. (28) - William G. Lavoic (33) both of Manchester md. 7 Sep. 1930.
[AR]

CAMMETT:
Samuel S. - Betsey Coons, both of Exeter md, 18 Dec. 1828. [TR][CH]

CANTLEY:
James Vernon (25) - Beatrice May Hobbs (22) both of Beverly, MA. md. 6 Sep.
1930. [AR]

CARD:
Elias T. (48) - Ruth B. Haynes (27) of Kingston, NY md. 19 June 1924. [AR]

CAREY:
Frank W. (24) of Palmer, MA. - Emilia Kapiec (19) of Ware, MA. md. 10 Mar.
1935. [AR]

CARLSON:
Arthur (25) - Dorothy Ward (30) of Rye md. 30 June 1934. [AR]
Augusta N. (24) of Lexington, MA. - Philip A. Warner (62) md. 17 July 1900 at
Hampton. [AR]

CARPENTER:
Mildred A. (20) of Hampton - Thomas E. Murrey (22) md. 3 Mar. 1935 at
Hampton. [AR]

CARR:
Mary E. (45) - Robert Pike (55) md. 20 June 1881. [TR]
Maud M. (24) of Portsmouth - Arthur W. Brown (28) md. 28 Oct. 1909 at
Portsmouth. [AR]
Sarah (21) - Joel Chamblin (25) md. 3 Jan. 1880. [TR]

CARROLL:
Greenland of Union, Me. - Eliza Clark of Stratham md. 1 Nov. 1848. [CH]

CARSTON:
Olive J. (40), d/o Elisha & Elizabeth - Sherburne Marston (53), s/o Simon &
Charlotte md. 25 Apr. 1865. [TR]

CARTER:
Dorothy Lois (22) - Ralph Arnold Collins (25) of Groton, Ct. md. 29 Dec. 1940
at Mystic, Ct. [AR]

CARTER Cont.

Frank O. (57) - Lottie M. Lee (39) both of Amesbury md. 30 June 1926. [AR]
George G. (24) - Martha E. Page (28) md. 6 Jan. 1904. [AR]
George J. (57) - Marion Lane (49) md. 1 June 1937. [AR]
George Wesley (29) - Eleanora Mary Zarnowski (22) md. 31 Dec. 1938 ar
    Hampton. [AR]
Mabel Louise (27) - Bertrum William Ashford (35) of Newburyport md. 12 Oct.
    1940. [AR]
Samuel - Ann Blay md. 11 Feb. 1751. [CH]
Stanley Page (33) - Gladys Hayes (22) of Manchester md. 19 Nov. 1938 at
    Candia NH. [AR]
William E. (28), s/o Mitchell - Fannie W.P. Salter (33), d/o John C.
    Philbrick md. 29 Jan. 1887. [TR]

CASSELMAN:

Arthur V. (31) of Pittsburg, PA. - Nina H. Drake (24) md. 26 July 1905. [AR]

CASWELL:

Nellie S. (21), d/o Samuel - Frank P. Rand (25), s/o William W. md. 21 Sep.
    1878. [tR]

CATE:

Anna - Benjamin Dearborn, both of Sanborn Town md. 9 Nov. 1768. [CH]
Hannah - Jeremiah Dennett, both of Portsmouth md. 9 Aug. 1815. [TR][CH]
Henry - Salome Akerman, both of Portsmouth md. 5 Jan. 1805. [CH]
Mary D. of Hampton - Enos (Amos?) Collins of Springfield md. 10 Dec. 1828.
    [TR][CH]

CHAMBERS:

Wilfred J. (24), s/o Lewis - Lizzie J. Philbrook (20), d/o Joseph md. 14 Apr.
    1880. [TR]

CHAMBLIN:

Joel (25) - Sarah Carr (21) md. 3 Jan. 1880. [TR]

CHANDLER:

Sarah - Reuben Spaulding md. 2 Jan. 1755. [CH]

CHAPMAN:

Abigail - John Seavy md. 16 Oct. 1800. [CH]
Abigail - Simon Leavitt 3d md. 7 June 1818. [TR][CH]
Benjamin - Hannah Chapman md. 15 Sep. 1818. [TR][CH]
Benjamin - Louisa C. Brown md. 13 Jan. 1849. [CH]
David - Abigail Keous md. 24 Nov. 1822. [TR][CH]
Elizabeth J. - Leonard W. Chapman md. 28 Dec. 1847. [CH]
Hannah - John Hobbs md. 26 Mar. 1792. [TR][CH]
Hannah - Benjamin Chapman md. 5 Sep. 1818. [TR][CH]

CHAPMAN Cont.

Hazel M. (22) of Stratham - Walter F. Purington (21) md. 22 Oct. 1932. [AR]

John - Sarah L. Hobbs md. 18 Jan. 1824. [TR]

John - Leocenda D. Hobbs md. 5 Jan. 1831. [TR][CH]

John (62), s/o Martha - Mrs. Nancy B. (Baker) Moore, d/o Joseph & Hannah Baker md. 3 Jan. 1865. [TR]

Juliana - Simon Leavitt 3d md. 18 Jan. 1824. [TR][CH]

Lauranda - John Yuran of Tunbridge, Vt. md. 15 Nov. 1832. [TR]

Leonard W. - Elizabeth J. Chapman md. 26 Dec. 1847. [CH]

Lillian S. (19), d/o DeWitt - Charles N. (22), s/o Uri A. md. 18 Sep. 1900. [TR]

Mary - Edwin Jenness md. Apr. 1842. [TR][CH]

Rachel - Samuel Towle of Rye md. 26 Oct. 1769. [CH]

Ruth - John Fogg md. 15 Jan. 1796. [CH]

Samuel (29) of Bath, Me. - Sarah E. Cobb (24) md. 23 Feb. 1857. [CH]

CHASE:

Abbie J. (24) - John J. Taylor (28) md. 22 Dec. 1881. [TR]

Dudley - Alice Abbot, both of Hampton Falls md. 19 Apr. 1770. [CH]

Hepsa - Thomas Flanders md. 21 May 1755, [CH]

Jonathan - Mary Harris, both of Stratham md. 17 Oct. 1773. [CH]

Lucy of Stratham - Joshua Hill of Exeter md. 1 Oct. 1789. [TR]

Mary of Hampton Falls - Jacob Rowe of Seabrook md. 12 Nov. 1826. [TR][CH]

Nancy - Theophilus Smith Jr., both of Stratham md. 14 Dec. 1820. [TR][CH]

Patty of Stratham - James Conner of Toptonborough md. 1 Oct. 1794. [TR]

Robert - Eliza Jewell md. 13 FEb. 1827. [CH]

Thomas - Tabitha Piper, both of Stratham md. 15 Aug. 1790. [CH]

Capt. Thomas Jr. - Lucinda Perkins Locke, both of Seabrook md. 29 Nov. 1830. [TR][CH]

CHECKERING:

Mary M. (38), d/o Abel Corconon? - Ranson Fogg (48), s/o Samuel md. 11 Oct. 1875. [TR]

CHESWELL:

Thomas E. (32), s/o Thos. J. - Angela M. Davis (29), d/o Anderson md. 22 May 1875. [TR]

CHEVALIER:

C. Russell (26) - Francis W. Goodhue (30) of Concord md. 28 Nov. 1935 at Concord. [AR]

Charles R. (23) - Emma F. Brodstreet (21) of Danvers, MA. md. there 8 June 1904. [AR]

Lewis A. (20) - Grace L. Morse (18) of Hampton md. 6 Oct. 1902. [AR]

Raymond Morse (23) - Gladys Mina Hobbs (21) of Beverly, MA. md. 6 Aug. 1927, at Exeter [AR]

CHOATE:
Abigail - Jesse Samborn of Kensington md. 17 Aug. 1790. [TR]

CHRISTIE:
Catherine I. (22) of Minn. - Elroy T. Clark (22) md. 30 Sep. 1909. [AR]
Katherine R. (22) of Dover - William T. Whenal (24) md. 6 May 1934 at Dover.
   [AR]

CHURCH:
Annie (22), d/o Noah - Charles M. Barker (22), s/o Nathan md. 16 Oct. 1872.
   [TR]

CILLEY/CILLIY:
Amos of Hampton - Ruth Nudd md. 26 Jan. 1809. [TR][CH]
Betsy - Jethro Blake Jr., both of Hampton md. 12 Sep. 1820. [TR][CH]

CIOFFI:
Jean (16) of Everett, MA. - Alfrod E. Farese (21) of Lynn, MA. md. 25 Aug.
   1935. [AR]

CLARK:
Abigail - Joseph Smith, both of Newmarket md. 9 Sep. 1783. [CH]
Anna - Sergeant Whittier, both of Newmarket md. 25 Nov. 1773. [CH]
Deborah - Samuel Shaw, both of Hampton md. 11 Feb. 1808. [CH]
Elizabeth of Stratham - Greenland Carroll of Union, Me. md. 1 Nov. 1848. [CH]
Elroy T. (22) - Catherine I. Christie (22) of Minn. md. 30 Sep. 1909. [AR]
Ethelinda of Hampton - Nathaniel H. Calder of Boston md. 20 July 1834.
   [TR][CH]
Evelyn L. (30) - David F. Colt (46) of Hampton md. 11 July 1937. [AR]
John of Stratham - Elizabeth Neal md. 16 Dec. 1773. [CH]
Marvis June (19) of Roslindale, MA. - Harold Ernest Hunt (21) of Higham, MA.
   md. 28 Aug. 1938. [AR]
Mayhew - Rachel Robinson md. 21 Dec. 1773. [CH]
Polly - Reuben Dow md. 25 Jan. 1797. [CH]
Raymond W. (31) - Jeanette R. White (28) of Hampton md. 20 June 1936 at
   Alfred, Me. [AR]

CLAY:
John (67), s/o John & Abigail - Betsy Batchelder (64), d/o Nathaniel &
   Elizabeth md. 31 Mar. 1864. [TR]

CLIFFORD:
William of Raymond - Mary Fitts md. 9 May 1823. [CH]

CLOUGH:
Elizabeth (25), d/o Nathan - Albian R. Rumary (39), s/o William md. 18 Nov.
   1866. [TR]

CLOUGH Cont.

Sarah, d/o Samuel & Sarah - Daniel Marston, s/o Simon & Hannah md. 30 Dec.
1730. [TR]
Sarah - Jonathan Currier md. 15 Dec. 1753. [CH]
William Brown - Eleanor Page md. 24 Sep. 1751. [CH]

COATES:

William T. (60) - Nellie A. Keach (42) both of Malden, MA. md. 2 Jan. 1943.
[AR]

COBB:

Katie (26), d/o Nathan & Catherine - Rev. John Dinsmore (40), s/o Thos. &
Sarah md. 20 May 1861. [TR][CH]
Sarah E. (24) - Samuel Chapman (29) md. 23 Feb. 1857. [CH]

COFFIN:

Edythe S. (23) of Hampton - Russell D. Moulton (20) md. 4 Jan. 1911. [AR]

COKER:

Elizabeth - John Silver md. 14 Dec. 1755. [CH]

COLBY:

Elizabeth - Moses Straw md. 17 Oct. 1751. [CH]
Thomas Eliot - Sausannh Ring md. 29 Mar. 1755. [CH]

COLE:

Simon of Sanbornton - Abigail Piper of Stratham md. 23 Mar. 1789. [TR]

COLEMAN:

Emma F. (23) of Greenland - Percy T. Perkins (22) md. 25 Oct. 1913 at
Greenland. [AR]
Mercy of Greenland - Josiah Weeks md. 22 June 1809. [TR][CH]

COLLINS:

Enos (Amos?) of Springfield - Mary D. Cate of Hampton md. 10 Dec. 1828.
[TR][CH]
Margaret A. (37) - George W. Witherell (45) md. 8 July 1864. [TR]
Ralph Arnold (25) of Groton, Ct. - Dorothy Lois Carter (22) md. 29 Dec. 1940
at Mystic, Ct. [AR]
Sarah - John Hoyt md. 21 Nov. 1751. [CH]

COLT:

David F. (46) of Hampton - Evelyn L. Clark (30) md. 11 July 1937. [AR]

CONNER:

James of Toptonborough - Patty Chase of stratham md. 1 Oct. 1794. [TR]

CONSTABLE:
Ella F. (35) of Dorchester, MA. - Addison F. Crafts (42) of Brockton, MA. md.
   23 June 1928. [AR]

COOMES:
Betsey - Samuel S. Cammett, both of Exeter md. 18 Dec. 1828. [TR][CH]
David of Stratham - Anna Godfree md. 2 Sep. 1810. [TR][CH]

COOSING: ?
Theodore - Abigail Brown md. 6 Apr. 1790. [TR]

COREY:
Orrin R. (50) of Derby, Vt. - Lydia H. Brown (48) md. 4 Jan. 1891. [TR][AR]

CORLIS/CORLISS:
Hiram - Elizabeth Langdon Hart, both of Portsmouth md. 8 Jan. 1823. [TR][CH]
Martin J. (33) - Annie M. Dalton (20) md. 29 Oct. 1917 at Hampton. [AR]

CORNELL:
Anne M. (20), d/o William Moulton - Daniel W. Elkins (41), s/o David B. md.
   26 May 1874. [TR]

COTES:
Martha - Sergeant Whittier md. 7 May 1771. [CH]

COTTON:
Abigail - Josiah Batchelder md. 6 Dec. 1770. [CH]
Abigail, Mrs. - Simon Leavitt md. 12 Dec. 1805. [CH]
Betsy/Betty, Mrs. of Rye - James Foss of Barrington md. Jan. 1787. [TR][CH]
Edward Chapman of Effingham - Polly Batchelder md. 5 Jan. 1800. [CH]
Huldah, Mrs. - Tristram Dalton md. 7 Oct. 1804. [CH]
John - Sally Philbrick md. 22 July 1805. [CH]
John - Sally Marston, both of Hampton md. 7 July 1818. [CH]
John - Polly Marston, both of Hampton md. 7 July 1818. [TR] (same as above?)
Jonathan - Abigail C. Hobbs md. 24 Nov. 1825. [TR][CH]
Mary - John Batchelder md. 30 Nov. 1780. [CH]
Sarah - Stephen Batchelder of Deerfield md. 22 Apr. 1779. [CH]

COURSON/CORSON:
Emma E. - Levi W. Knowles md. 7 Aug. 1876 at Newmarket. [TR]

COUSENS:
Octavia H. (27) - Hosea W. Gough (27) of Waltham md. 19 July 1910. [AR]
Ruth B. (22) - Daniel G. Goodwin (23) of Saco, Me. md. 18 Sep. 1907 at
   Hampton. [AR]

CRAFTS:
Addison F. (42) of Brockton, MA. - Ella F. Constable (35) of Dorchester, MA.
md. 23 June 1928. [AR]

CRAIG:
George A. (19) - Roberta Taylor (18) md. 31 Aug. 1935. [AR]

CRAVEN:
Irene (25) - Angelo Del Bianco (33) of Concord md. 5 Sep. 1940. [AR]

CROFT:
Richard (55) of Peabody, MA. - Alice Maud Dow (53) md. 14 Dec. 1929. [AR]

CROSS:
Clayton (25) - Marguerite Cunningham (18) md. 10 Mar. 1934 at Plaistow. [AR]

CROWELL:
Dora B. (18) of Greenland - Frank H. Philbrick (24) md. 12 Dec. 1900. [AR]
Effie L. (27) - E. Everett Marston (31) md. 9 Sep. 1906 at Greenland. [AR]
Mina (38) - Mortin R. Malone (40) both of Everett, MA. md. 12 Aug. 1925. [AR]

CROWLEY:
Cortlandt R. (41) of Topsfield, MA. - Augusta J. Nelson (29) of Middleton,
MA. md. 20 June 1937. [AR]

CUDDY:
Theresa (20) - Thomas F. Bernard (22) both of Roxbury, MA. md. 3 July 1937.
[AR]

CUNNINGHAM:
Marguerite (18) - Clayton Cross (25) md. 10 Mar. 1934 at Plaistow. [AR]

CURRIER:
Abigail - Jeremiah Allen md. 24 Dec. 1751. [CH]
Abigail - Daniel Fitts md. 4 Dec. 1755. [CH]
Ann - Nahum French of Northwood md. 7 ___ 1821. [CH]
George W. (37), s/o William - Maria L, Leman (34), d/o Jacob B. Johnson md.
15 May 1879. [TR]
Hannah - Ephraim Page md. 13 Dec. 1753. [CH]
Henry - Sarah True md. 19 Feb. 1755. [CH]
John Jr. - Abigail Merrill md. 28 Oct. 1756. [CH]
Jonathan - Sarah Clough md. 13 Dec. 1753. [CH]
Judith - Obadiah Eastman md. 28 Dec. 1752. [CH]
Miriam - Moses Morrill md. 18 Feb. 1755. [CH]

CURTIS:
Sarah Dodge (31) - N. Dearborn Marston (30) md. 31 Jan. 1893. [TR][AR]

DALTON:

Annie M. (20) - Martin J. Corliss (33) md. 29 Oct. 1917 at Hampton. [AR]

Charles C. (22) - Jennie Weave (22) md. 4 July 1895. [TR][AR]

Charlotte - Simon Marston md. 31 Mar. 1811. [TR][CH]

Clara L. (17), d/o Michael - Alonzo M. Stevens (23), s/o David md. 23 Jan. 1867. [TR]

Ebenezer Marden - Love Hobbs md. 22 May 1796. [CH]

Elizabeth - Benjamin Johnson of Epping md. 14 Nov. 1786. [TR][CH]

Esther - Simon Brown md. 27 Oct. 1793. [TR]

Esther - John B. James of Deerfield md. 15 Sep. 1829. [TR][CH]

Eva M. (36) - Edward J. Taylor (45) md. 2 Apr. 1902. [AR]

Fred G. (25) - Alice A. White (22) of Hampton md. 7 June 1932 at Hampton. [AR]

George C. (18), s/o J.G. - Emma P. Jenness (17), d/o J.R. md 15 Jan. 1879. [TR]

Hannah - Samuel Murrey of Rye md. 4 May 1769. [CH]

Harrison W. (23) - Eunice L. Brown (23) md. 1 Jan. 1933 of Hampton. [AR]

Mary W. (28), d/o Michael - William H. Garland (29), s/o William md. 12 Nov. 1867. [TR]

Maude A. (26) - Erwin B. Moulton (25) md. 5 Feb. 1908. [AR]

Micall - Mary Palmer md. 27 May 1786. [CH]

Olive - John Brown, both of Leavitts Town md. 19 Sep. 1773. [CH]

Rufus (68) - Mrs. Maria Harvey (63) md. 9 May 1878. [TR]

Samuel R. (26) - Katie E. Philbrick (19) md. 23 Oct. 1890. [TR][AR]

Tristram - Dorothy Brown md. 11 Nov. 1798. [CH]

Tristram - Mrs. Huldah Cotton md. 7 Oct. 1804. [CH]

DANIELS:

George - Betsy Towle, both of Exeter md. 15 Oct. 1820. [TR][CH]

DARBORN: See Dearborn

DAVIES:

Mary - Thomas Sleeper, both of Kingston md. 27 Aug. 1771. [CH]

Reginald H. (26) - Gladys Belle Keene (29) md. 11 Aug. 1928 at Rye Beach. [AR]

DAVIS:

Angela M. (29), d/o Anderson - Thomas E. Cheswell (32), s/o Thos. J. md. 22 May 1875. [TR]

Charles E. (26), s/o William A. - Minsani Marston (27) md. 2 Dec. 1860. [TR]

Eliza A. (21), d/o Jerry - Charles W. Jenness (24), s/o Elwin md. 3 Jan. 1871. [TR]

Jacob (30), s/o Jacob & Betsy - Mary J. Fogg (26), d/o David & Eliza md. 15 Oct. 1861. [TR][CH]

Lucinda - James Jenness, both of Exeter md. 15 Mar. 1826. [TR][CH]

Mary Abby, Mrs. (37), d/o David Fogg - John Henry Brown (56), s/o Simon md. 27 July 1873. [TR]

DAVIS Cont.

Lydia M. (17) - Roger S. Lovett (21) md. 1 Jan. 1915 at Kensington. [AR]
Reuben of Poplin - Sarah Jewell of Stratham md. 3 Dec. 1772. [CH]
Samuel - Mary Nutter, both of Stratham md. 8 Sep. 1819. [TR][CH]
Sarah A. - Joseph Swasey, both of Exeter md. 2 Sep. 1839. [CH]
Warren M. (24) - Helen R. St. Clair (24) of Springfield, MA. md. 10 Mar. 1934
   at Hampton. [AR]

DAY:

Georgie R. (29) of Portsmouth - Ernest R. Flanders (34) md. 6 Nov. 1918 at
   Portsmouth. [AR]

DEAL:

Chester A. (34) of Stratham - Idella A. Gatis (18) of Exeter md. 10 Aug.
   1927. [AR[

DEAN:

Dorothy (24) of Millis, Me. - Marshal S. Hilman (22) md. 23 Apr. 1920 at
   Millis, MA. [AR]

DEGAN:

Ethel Marie (20) - Adelbert Stanley Blaney (23) md. 12 Apr. 1941 at
   Portsmouth. [AR]

DEARBORN:

Abigail, d/o Dr. Levi - Daniel Gookin md. 14 Nov. or 6 Dec. 1787. [CH][TR]
Abigail - John Locke of Portsmouth md. Sep. 1800. [CH]
Anna - John Dearborn md, 6 July 1783. [CH]
Anna of Greenland - Edward Varrell of Me. md. 2 Mar. 1820. [TR]
Benjamin - Sarah Pachering of Greenland md. 14 Oct. 1792. [TR]
Betsy - James Johnson, both of Hampton md. 31 Mar. 1818. [TR][CH]
Carr L. - Mary Ann Taylor md. 4 Apr. 1839. [CH]
Daniel - Anna Veazey of Stratham md. 4 Feb. 1770. [CH]
Elizabeth - Simon Marston md. 13 Sep. 1770. [CH]
Fanny - Jonathan Hobbs Jr. md. 2 July 1797. [CH]
Frank (23) of Portsmouth - Carrie L. Batchelder (18) md. 24 Sep. 1862. [CH]
Freese of Hampton - Nabby Drake md. 6 Nov. 1799. [CH]
Harriet - Simon Sanborn, both of Epsom md. 1- Mar. 1811. [TR][CH]
Jacob - Betsy Wedgwood md. July 1789. [CH]
John - Anna Dearborn md. 6 July 1783. [CH]
John of Stratham - Mrs. Susanna Wiggin of Greenland md. 1787. [CH]
John 3d - Mary Ann Towle, both of Hampton md. 12 July 1828. [TR][CH]
Levi - Patience Godfree, both of Hampton md. 21 Nov. 1793. [TR]
Lucinda - John Hobbs Jr. md. 9 Nov. 1808. [TR][CH]
Mabel J. (20) of Hampton - Harry C. Marston (27) md. 8 Nov. 1910. [AR]
Mary - Joseph Stace Leavitt md. 11 Sep. 1792. [TR]
Mary - Samuel Lock md. 3 July 1825. [TR][CH]

DEARBORN Cont.

Miriam - Winthrop Johnson of Greenland md. 30 Jan. 1781. [CH]
Nathan - Lydia Nudd md. 10 Nov. 1813. [TR][CH]
Nathaniel - Lucy Parker md. 11 Sep. 1810. [TR][CH]
Olive - James Wedgwood md. 14 July 1788. [CH]
Phineas - Anna Neal md. 19 Sep. 1771. [CH]
Polly P. - Daniel Veasey of Stratham md. 10 dec. 1807. [CH]
Polly - Andrew Shaw md. 4 Jan. 1808 by Elias Smith. [TR]
Rachel - Stephen Smith md. 22 June 1799. [CH]
Reuben of Effingham - Comfort Hobbs of Hampton md. 7 Apr. 1793. [TR][CH]
Reuben Gove Jr. - Elizabeth Dow md. 30 Jan. 1778. [CH]
Ruth - John Foss of Stratham md. 14 May 1770. [CH]
Ruth L. - Joshua Brooks, both of Portsmouth md. 17 Dec. 1839. [CH]
S. Lucasta - George H. Pearson of Saugus, Mass. md. Apr. 1856. [CH]
Sally - Michael McClary of Epsom md. 7 Oct. 1778. [CH]
Sally - Simon Leavitt md. July 1794. [CH]
Sally/Sarah - Dr. John Fogg md. 24 July 1793. [TR][CH]
Sally - Joseph Kingsbury md. 26 Feb. 1797. [CH]
Sally - Joseph Godfrey md. 6 Sep. 1808. [CH]
Samuel Jr. - Lydia Marston md. 2 Aug. 1818. [TR][CH]
Sarah - Levi Jenness of Rye md. 3 Mar. 1782. [CH]
Sarah of Hampton- James Sanborn md. 25 Dec. 1786. [CH][TR]
Sarah, Widow - Phillips White md. 16 June 1798. [CH]
Sarah - Abraham Leavitt md. 4 June 1807. [CH]
Sarah Ann - Dwight Waters md. 30 May 1835. [CH]
Simeon - Betsy Nudd md. 14 Dec. 1794. [CH]
Simeon - Mary Smith md. 27 Nov. 1799. [CH]
Simon - Mary Brown md. May 1787. [CH][TR]

DENING:

William - Sarah M. Moulton md. 9 Nov. 1878. [TR]

DENNETT:

Jean - Samuel Norris, both of Portsmouth md. 23 Mar. 1812. [TR][CH]
Jeremiah - Hannah Cate, both of Portsmouth md. 9 Aug. 1815. [TR][CH]

DIMOND:

Judith - Joseph French 3d md. 12 Dec. 1752. [CH]

DINSMORE:

Emily C. (28) of Anson, Me. - Robert C. Stanwood (38) of Portland, Me. md.
    27 July 1853. [CH]
Rev. John (40), s/o Thos. & Sarah - Katie Cobb (26), d/o Nathan & Catherine
    md. 20 May 1861. [TR][CH]
John (26) - Katie Scott (21) md. 22 May 1861. [TR]

DOLIBER:

W. Francis (22) of W. Lebenon, Me. - Bessie A. May (20) md. 19 May 1917. [AR]

DONKE:
Delia A. of Hampton - Henry Robie of Hampton Falls md. 1 Feb. 1821. [TR]

DORE:
Abraham of Milton - Comfort Talton of Rye md. 22 Apr. 1816. [TR][CH]

DOTON:
James of Canaan, NH - Mary Brown of E.K. md. 21 Apr. 1817. [CH]

DOUCET:
Marguerite Rosella (23) - Harry Wallace Maxim (20) both of Lewiston, Me. md.
3   July 1928

DOUCETTE:
Gertrude (29) of Peabody, MA. - Lyman Elliot (29) md. 17 Jan. 1936. [AR]

DOUST:
Ozem - Martha Webster md. 3 Nov. 1796. [CH]

DOW:
Abbie C. (21), d/o Levi - George C. Lowell (23), s/o Oliver C. md. 30 May
    1875. [TR]
Abbie M. (25), d/o George O. - E. Bloomer Jewell (24), s/o DeWitt C. md. 10
    Sep. 1874. [TR]
Abraham B. - Mrs. Love Dow md. 17 Aug. 1805. [CH]
Abram C. (36) - Addie F. Tuttle (23) of Lawrence, MA. md. 22 June 1899 at
    Lawrence. [AR]
Alice Maud (53) - Richard Craft (55) of Peabody, MA. md. 14 Dec. 1929 at
    Portsmouth. [AR]
Daniel - Lucinda Marston md. 9 Jan. 1821. [TR][CH]
David M. - Abby L. Hobbs md. 24 Apr. 1845. [TR][CH]
Eliza - Stephen Page md. 24 June 1813. [TR][CH]
Elizabeth - Philip Burn, both of Hampton Falls md. 19 Apr. 1770. [CH]
Elizabeth - Reuben Gove Dearborn Jr. md. 30 Jan. 1772. [CH]
Fred L. (23), s/o Samuel A. - Gertrude L. Robinson (25) md. 27 Oct. 1896.
    [TR][AR]
George Edgar (19), s/o George O. - Fannie Wesley Jenness (18), d/o Wesley md.
    22 Dec. 1873. [TR]
Gertrude (22) - D. Morris Lamprey (24) md. 1 Dec. 1934. [AR]
Gordon S. (28) - Edith G. Golter (23) of Portsmouth md. 1 Nov. 1933 at
    Portsmouth. [AR]
Isaac - Lydia Pickering, both of Portsmouth md. 25 Feb. 1809. [TR][CH]
J. Russell (21) - Grace J. Wright (27) of Greenland md. 9 Oct. 1907. [AR]
John Jr. of Hampton - Deborah Page md. 10 Dec. 1807 by Elias Smith. [TR]
Joseph of Pembroke - Abby French d/o Rev. Jonathan md. 14 Apr. 1835. [CH]
Josiah Jr. - Mrs. Eunice Moulton, both of Hampton md. 29 Apr. 1835. [CH]
Louise T. (19) - Austin D. Boyd (27) md. 23 Jan. 1932. [AR]

DOW Cont.

Love, Mrs. - Abraham B. Dow md. 17 Aug. 1806. [CH]

Mabel J. (19), d/o Samuel A. - Haven S. Berry (27), s/o Chas.P. md. 7 June 1890. [TR][AR]

Margaret A. (26), d/o George - Thomas C. Marston (26), s/o Benj. md. 4 Jan. 1869. [TR]

Martha of Rye - Simon Lamprey md. 15 July 1780. [CH]

Mary E. (22), d/o David - Horace Leavitt (33), s/o Thos C. md/ 1 Feb. 1871. [TR]

Meream - John Leavitt md. 23 Aug. 1790. [TR]

Mildred F. (20) - Eugene H. Roberts (24) md. 28 May 1932 at Exeter. [AR]

Miriam - Luther Leavitt md. 17 or 27 June 1819. [TR][CH]

Moses of Seabrook - Margraet Downs of Hampton md. 16 Sep. 1812. [TR][CH]

Phebe - Andrew Barnard md. 23 Apr. 1752. [CH]

Phebe - Reuben Page, both of Hampton md. 26 Dec. 1811. [TR][CH]

Rachel - Ezekiel Knowles of Deerfield md. 12 Dec. 1783. [CH]

Reuben - Polly Clark md. 26 Jan. 1797. [CH]

Samuel A. (22), s/o Samuel - Emily A. Marston (23), d/o James md. 29 Dec. 1869. [TR]

Simon - Mrs. Love Mason md. 23 Nov. 1788. [CH]

Simon B. (26) - Elizabeth C. Fogg (18) md. 3 Oct. 1852. [CH]

DOWNING:

James G. (26) of Newcastle - Daisy A. Page (23) md. 11 Nov. 1891. [TR][AR]

Jonas T. (26) - Anna J. Mysen (22) of Boston md. 1 Nov. 1911. [AR]

Nancy - William Brown of Hampton md. 9 Dec. 1810. [TR][CH]

DOWNS/DOWNES:

Bernice E. (23) of Boston - Bartlett A. Bachelder (21) md. 23 Nov. 1922. [AR]

Charles N. (21) - Georgiana H. Kean (18), both of Portsmouth md. 29 June 1851. [CH]

Eliza J. (19), d/o John b. & Martha O. of Gosport - Moses C. Garland (28), George & Polly md. 6 July 1863. [TR]

Erna L. (22) of Havverhill - Charles R. Hutchinson (22) of Brighton, MA. md. 6 Sep. 1919. [AR]

Margaret of Hampton - Moses Dow of Seabrook md. 16 Sep. 1812. [TR][CH]

DRAKE:

Abby - Orren Smith md. 24 Apr. 1845. [TR][CH]

Abigail - Peter Jenness of Rye md. 25 Dec. 1782. [CH]

Abigail - Joseph Richardson of Moultonboro md. 25 Feb. 1784. [CH]

Abigail - Joshua Berry of Greenland md. 15 Feb. 1810. [TR][CH]

Abraham Jr. - Adeline Brown md. 30 Nov. 1842. [CH]

Betsy - John Leavitt Jr. md. 21 Oct. 1806. [TR][CH]

Carrie A. (17), d/o Morris - George H. Foster (22), s/o Chas. W. md. 23 July 1890 at Portsmouth. [TR]

Carrie A. (31) of Hampton - George A. Marston (46) md. 13 Oct. 1897. [AR]

DRAKE Cont.

Clara B. (21), d/o Nathaniel - Oliver S. French (24), s/o John F. md. 6 Dec. 1875. [TR]

Data - Jonathan Hobbs Jr. md. 5 Mar. 1792. [TR][CH]

Delia B. of Hampton - Henry Roby of Hampton Falls md. 1 Feb. 1821. [CH][TR]

Elizabeth J. - John W.T. Hobbs of Boston md. 17 Nov. 1841. [TR][CH]

Elmer E. (32), s/o Joshua - Ella E. Haines (26), d/o Joseph W. md. 14 Feb. 1894. [TR][AR]

Emily - Simon Brown md. 6 Nov. 1827. [TR][CH]

Esther P. (21) - Harvey J. Kyser (25) of Portsmouth md. 4 Nov. 1915 at Kittery Point. [AR]

Frances H. (34) - Edward A. Sammis (36) of Stanford, Ct. md. 12 Aug. 1908 at Portsmouth. [AR]

Francis - Mary Drake md. 17 Mar. 1814. [TR][CH]

Hannah of Hampton - Robey Marston of Stratham md. 4 Jan. 1768. [CH]

Jane - Joshua Towle, both of Hampton md. 31 Oct. 1771. [CH]

Josephine M. (32) - Austin Lamprey (36) md. 20 Jan. 1904. [AR]

Joshua F. (26) - Helen V. Brown (24) of Rye md. 26 Apr. 1924 at Rye. [AR]

Joshua P. (28) - Sarah D. Leavitt (26) md. 23 Apr. 1851. [CH]

Lizzie M. (22), d/o Charles - Charles F. Smith (27), s/o Joshua md. 4 Feb. 1886. [TR]

Marion T. (15) - Leon M. Knowles (21) md. 30 Jan. 1915 at Kensington, [AR]

Marey - John Lang of Rye md. 1788. [TR]

Mary - Lt. Johanthan Hobbs md. 26 Jan. 1808. [CH]

Mary - Francis Drake md. 17 Mar. 1814. [TR][CH]

Mary O. (29) - Orrin B. Leavitt (40) md. 20 Oct. 1888. [TR]

Nabby - Frees Dearborn of Hampton md. 6 Nov. 1799. [CH]

Nina H. (24) - Arthur V. Casselman (31) of Pittsburg, PA. md. 26 July 1905. [AR]

Samuel - Mehitabel Pickering md. 1 Feb. 1818. [TR][CH]

Samuel J. - Mary Leavitt md. 19 Apr. 1842. [TR][CH]

Sarah - Simon Leavitt md. 25 Dec. 1777. [CH]

Sarah of Hampton - Levi Brown of Hampton Falls md. 15 Dec. 1792. [TR]

Wear, s/o Abraham & Abigail - Anna Taylor, d/o _____ & Elizabeth md. 2 Dec. 1760. [TR]

DREW:

Fred A. (22), s/o Nathaniel - Ella M. Tarlton (18), d/o Artwell md. 28 Mar. or 23 Apr. 1893. [AR][TR]

Leon Stephen Jr. (25) - Laura Henriette Filley (19) of Hampton md. 19 Apr. 1941 at Hampton. [AR]

Wilber S. (20) - Lila C. Moulton (24) md. 19 Apr. 1919 at Hampton. [AR]

Willie P. (22), s/o Nathan - Ada B. Tarlton (17), d/o Stephen md. 2 Apr. 1884. [TR]

DRYSDALE:
Jessie Dodge (22) - Irving Knight Strout (31) md. 29 June 1929. [AR]
John (33) - Minnie M. Eugley (27) of Exeter md. 6 June 1943 at Exeter. [AR]
Walter J. (31) - Fanny J. Towle (31) md. 24 Sep. 1932. [AR]

DUDLEY:
Florence L. (25) of Wakefield - Leonard P. Philbrick (26) md. 23 Oct. 1920 at
   Union. [AR]

DUNHAM:
Grace W. (18), d/o William H. - Willard H. Philbrick (31), s/o Henry md. 31
   July 1888. [TR]

DUNN:
Ethelda G. (34) of Auburn, Me. - Roland Lake Lefebvre (40) md. 1 Oct. 1941 at
   Nashua, NH. [AR]

DURAND:
Flora M.L. (31) - Clarence E. Symonds (36) both of Salem, MA. md. 18 Dec.
   1932. [AR]

DURANT:
Ethel R. (17) of Hampton - Harold I. Grant (20) md. 19 Oct. 1935 at Hampton.
   [AR]
Flora M.L. (31) - Clarence E. Symonds (36) both of Salem, MA. md. 18 Dec.
   1932. [AR]
Gertrude Mae (18) of Hampton - Norman Edward Marston (19) md. 25 June 1938 at
   Hampton. [AR]

DUSTIN:
Cedric H. (25) - Bertha Robinson (23) of Pittsfield md. 9 May 1925 at
   Newmarket. [AR]

DYER:
Lillie G. (51) - Edward J. Taylor (61) md. 10 Sep. 1918 at Hampton. [AR]

EASTMAN:
Elizabeth, widow - Joseph Jewell md. 18 Dec. 1753. [CH]
Jacob - Sarah Jones md. 14 Feb. 1817. [CH]
Obadiah - Judith Currier md. 28 Dec. 1752. [CH]
Thomas - Eliizabeth French, widow md. 24 Jan. 1751. [CH]

EATON:
Dorothy L. (21) of Kingston - Francis S. Lovett Jr. (24) md. 18 Sep. 1915 at
   Kingston. [AR]
Eunise Wells of Newbury, Mass. - Clark Foss md. 10 Nov. 1818. [TR]
Maria - James Doton of Canaan, N.H. md. 22 Dec. 1818. [CH]

EATON Cont.
Mary - William S. Warner md. 19 July 1838. [CH]
Oliver - Caroline Hull, both of Seabrook md. 15 Dec. 1831. [CH]

EDWARDS:
Harvey R. (37) of Danvers - Eva V. Harrington (36) md. 13 Jan. 1935. [AR]

ELKINS:
David B. of Hampton - Mary Batchelder md. 3 June 1828. [TR][CH]
Daniel W. (41), s/o David B. - Anne M. Cornell (20), d/o William Moulton md.
    26 May 1874. [TR]
John P. (28) of Hampton - Mary A. Marston md. 13 Sep. 1851. [CH]

ELLIOT/ELIOT:
Hannah - Samuel Kimball md. 18 May 1753. [CH]
Jacob - Dorothy Jones md. 29 Dec. 1752. [CH]
Lyman (29) of Salem, MA. - Gertrude Doucette (29) of Peabody, MA. md. 17 Jan.
    1936. [AR]

ELLIS:
Wallace H. (26) of W. Medford, MA. - Evelyn M. Boggs (25) of Arlington
    Height, MA. md. 28 Aug. 1937. [AR]

ELSWORTH:
John of Brentwood - Jenny Rundlett of Stratham md. 9 Dec. 1783. [CH]

EMERY:
Clement of Oxford - Mary Page md. 23 Apr. 1771. [CH]
Harriet - Johnson Lamprey md. 9 Jan. 1837. [CH]

EUGLEY:
Minnie M. (27) of Exeter - John Drysdale (33) md. 6 June 1943 at Exeter. [AR]

EWENS:
Betsey - Jacob Jones md. 23 Apr. 1826. [CH]
Mildred J. (32) of Twin Mt., NH - Forrest E. Knowles (52) md. 2 June 34 at
    Twin Mountain. [AR]

FAIRBANKS:
Wilson H. (25), s/o Washington - Martina L. Johnson (19), d/o Rufus S. md. 1
    July 1873. [TR]

FAIRFIELD:
Sarah W. (25) of Greenland - John B. Moulton (36) md. 3 June 1905 at
    Greenland. [AR]

FARESE:
Alfred P. (21) of Lynn, MA. - Jean Cioffi (18) of Everett, MA. md. 25 Aug.
1935. [AR]

FARRAR:
John W. of Lincoln, Mass. - Elizabeth D. French, d/o Rev. Jonathan md. 25
Oct. 1848. [CH]

FAY:
Rev. Levi L. (42) of Lawrence, Ohio - Minerva Batchelder, d/o Nathaniel md.
25 Oct. 1855. [CH]

FEELY:
Annie M. - Horace A. Moulton (25) md. 8 June 1882. [TR]

FELCH:
Hanna (24), d/o Caleb Jones - B. Herbert Blake (20), s/o Benj. P. md. 7 Apr.
1876 at Hampton Falls. [TR]

FELLOWS:
Ruth - Abel Brown Jr., both of Kensington md. 17 June 1824. [TR][CH]

FENNY:
Samuel, Dr. - Tabitha Gilman of Exeter md. 28 Sep. 1786. [TR]

FENWICK:
Allan (26), s/o E.B. - Hattie F. Marston (26), d/o James md. 1 Mar. 1878.
[TR]
Edith M. (35) - Frank L. Mackinlay (35) of Medford, MA. md. 1 Dec. 1913. [AR]
Jack (26) - Elizabeth J. Seavey (23) of Portsmouth md. 17 Oct. 1906. [AR]

FIFE:
Sadie S. (24) - Herbert S. Tourtillott (20) md. 10 Mar. 1907. [AR]

FIFIELD:
Benjamin J.? - Caroline Young, both of Exeter md. 19 Aug. 1829. [TR][CH]
Betty - Jesse Merrill, both of Stratham md. 7 Nov. 1781. [CH]
Jonathan - Margaret Sanborn md. 9 Mar. 1768. [CH]
Lydia - Josiah Shaw, both of Hampton md. 9 July 1792. [TR]
Martha - Capt. Joseph Smith, both of Stratham md. 31 July 1814. [TR][CH]
Molly of Stratham - Joshua Veasy of Deerfield md. 15 Oct. 1777. [CH]
Shadrick - Elisabeth Hill, both of Stratham md. 7 July 1818. [TR][CH]

FILLEY:
Laura Henrietta (19) of Hampton - Leon Stephen Drew Jr. (25) md. 19 Apr.
1941. [AR]

FISHER:
John F. (26) of Boston - Eleanor M. Lang (25) of Portsmouth md. 7 Sep. 1858.
[CH]

FITCH:
Anna - Rev. Nathaniel Gookin md. Jan. 1743. [TR][CH]

FITTS:
Agnes D. (40) of Pittsfield - Chauncey C. Barton (35) md. 7 July 1926. [AR]
Daniel - Abigail Currier md. 4 Dec. 1755. [CH]
Mary - William Clifford of Raymond md. 9 May 1823. [CH]

FLAGG:
George W. of Warwick, R.I. - Abigail Marston of Dover md. 7 May 1835. [CH]

FLANDERS:
Abia - John Welch md. 5 Dec. 1751. [CH]
Ernest R. (34) - Georgie R. Day (29) of Portsmouth md. 6 Nov. 1918 at
   Portsmouth. [AR]
Ezekiel - Sarah Jones md. 15 Jan. 1756. [CH]
Hannah - Samuel Jones md. 25 Aug. 1756. [CH]
Judith - Daniel Jones md. 3 May 1756. [CH]
Nathaniel Jr. - Priscilla Flanders md. 29 ___ 1821. [CH]
Priscilla - Nathaniel Flanders md. 29 ___ 1821. [CH]
Sarah - Caleb Burley (Paisley?) md. 7 Feb. 1752. [CH]
Thomas - Hepsa Chase md. 21 May 1755. [CH]

FLETCHER:
Mary L. (19), d/o Ismail? - Frank N. Garland (20), s/o Moses md. 23 Sep.
   1884. [TR]

FOGG:
Abigail - Samuel Roby md. 21 Apr. 1767. [CH]
Abigail - Levi Marston md. 12 July 1781. [CH]
Addie C. (19) - Edward M. Berry (25) md. 20 June 1882. [TR]
Amy May (20) - Raymond Marshall Allen (22) md. 23 Dec. 1938. [AR]
Carroll W. (42) - Ada E. Moulton (37) md. 22 July 1922. [AR]
Chase of Pittsfield - Comfort Garlon md. 29 May 1786. [TR][CH]
Clara B. - James L. Fowler md. 23 Dec. 1880. [TR]
Clarence L. (30) - Phoebe G. Storer (27) of Bradford, Me. md. 5 Apr. 1917 at
   Bradford. [AR]
David - Elisabeth Marston md. 17 Aug. 1828. [TR][CH]
Dolly - Philip Leavitt md. 12 Nov. 1812. [TR][CH]
Eliza A. (21) - John Moulton (26) md. 10 Dec. 1851. [CH]
Elizabeth C. (18) - Simon B. Dow (26) md. 3 Oct. 1852. [CH]
Emery (21), s/o Simon - Ida L. Norton (18), d/o Joshua md. 15 Nov. 1873. [TR]
Forrest S. (28) - Nellie E. Seymour (20) of Portsmouth md. 19 Jan. 1905 at
   Portsmouth. [AR]

FOGG Cont.

Ida L. (48) - Orrin C. Marston (55) md. 12 Mar. 1904. [AR]

Irena H. of Kensington - Green Perkins of Seabrook md. 22 June 1831. [CH]

Jessie R. (26) - Chester L. Howe (33) of Watertown, MA. md. 19 Aug. 1919 at
     Hampton. [AR]

Dr. John - Sally/Sarah Dearborn md. 24 July 1793. [TR][CH]

John - Ruth Chapman md. 16 Jan. 1796. [CH]

Levi H. (30), s/o David - Mary E. Tarlton (25), d/o Nathaniel md. 27 Nov.
     1875. [TR]

Martha H. (22) - Jeremiah Batchelder Jr. md. 27 Mar. 1854. [CH]

Mary - Thomas Leavitt md. 14 Apr. 1767. [CH]

Mary - Joseph Philbrick md. 14 May 1782. [CH]

Mary - Joshua Taylor md. 7 Aug. 1817. [TR][CH]

Mary A. (26), d/o David & Eliza - Jacob Davis (30), s/o Jacob & Betsy md.
     15 Oct. 1861. [TR][CH]

Mary J. (26) - Jacob Davis (30) md. 15 Oct. 1861. [TR]

Ranson - Deborah U. Page, gd/o Noah md. 22 Oct. 1848. [CH]

Ranson (48), s/o Samuel - Mary M. Checkering (38), d/o Abel Corconan? md. 11
     Oct. 1875. [TR]

Richard (28), s/o Richard - Eliza P. Jenness (18), d/o Amos md. 8 Jan. 1868.
     [TR]

Roy E. (26) - Maud D. Moulton (39) md. 30 Oct. 1920 at Hampton. [AR]

Roy Emery (47) - Muriel Gertrude Morton (36) of Boston md. 22 Aug. 1941 at
     Hampstead, NH. [AR]

Sally - Joseph Stevens md. 5 Aug. 1813. [TR][CH]

Samuel - Rhoda Page md. 22 July 1805. [CH]

Simon - Lavinia Marston md. 22 Jan. 1839. [CH]

Winslow R. (22) of Hampton - Gwendolyn A. Bennett (19) of Orland, Me. md. 27
     June 1936 at Newfields. [AR]

FOLSOM:

Anna of Newmarket - Winthrop Marston Jr. of Brentwood md. July or Aug. 1778.
     [CH]

Elizabeth of Newmarket - Winthrop Hilton Jr. md. blank [CH]

James 3d of Exeter - Olive Wedgwood of Greenland md. 14 Oct. 1810. [TR][CH]

Martha O. - Joseph J. Jenness md. 25 Mar. 1850. [CH]

Nehemiah of Exeter - Elesbeth Taylor md. 13 June or 18 July 1791. [TR]

FOSS:

Clark - Eunise Wells Eaton of Newbury, MA. md. 10 Nov. 1818. [TR]

James of Barrington - Mrs. Betty Cotton of Rye md. Jan. 1787. [CH][TR]

John of Stratham - Ruth Dearborn md. 14 May 1770 .[CH]

Jonathan of Epping - Susannah Jewell of Stratham md. 18 June 1771. [CH]

Olive of Rye - Joseph Shepherd Jr. of Portsmouth md. 14 May 1815. [TR][CH]

FOSTER:
George H. (22), s/o Chas. W. - Carrie A. Drake (17), d/o Morris md. 23 July 1890 at Portsmouth. [TR][AR]

FOWLER:
Evelyn (24) of Brookline, MA. - Harold D. Reed (38) of Boston md. 16 June 1924. [AR]
James L. - Clara B. Fogg md. 23 Dec. 1880. [TR]
William P. (35) - Ruth H. Miller (36) of Medford, MA. md. 8 Dec. 1935. [AR]

FRENCH:
Abby, d/o Rev. Jonathan - Joseph Dow of Pembroke md. 14 Apr. 1835. [CH]
Abigail - Offen French md. 7 Nov. 1751. [CH]
Annie D. (23), d/o John f. - John F. Hobbs (21), s/o John W. md. 12 Aug. 1879. [TR]
Clara E. (28) of Stratham - George W. Jenness (24) md. 17 June 1900 at Greenland. [AR]
David - Clarissa Wiggin, both of Stratham md. 1 Jan. 1809. [TR][CH]
Elizabeth, widow - Thomas Eastman md. 24 Jan. 1751. [CH]
Elizabeth (26), d/o Nathaniel - Charles A. Watson (51) s/o Samuel md. 24 Oct. 1866. [TR]
Elizabeth D., d/o Rev. Jonathan - John W. Farrer of Lincoln, Mass. md. 25 Oct. 1848. [CH]
Ellen L. (27), d/o John - Newell Wells Healey (37), s/o Wells md. 17 Nov. 1871. [TR]
Hannah - Samuel Mudget of Gilmonton md. 9 Mar. 1817. [CH]
Jacob. Lt. - Sally Bartlett md. 30 May 1813. [CH]
John F., s/o Rev. Jona. - Lomira Leavitt md. 8 Nov. 1848. [CH]
Joshua of E.K. - Caroline Gottwood of E. K. md. 12 Dec. 1827. [CH]
Joseph 3d - Judith Dimond md. 12 Dec. 1752. [CH]
Judith - John F. Odlin, both of Exeter md. 11 Aug. 1828. [TR][CH]
Lizzie F. (29) - Charles Watson (51) of Boston md. 24 Oct. 1866. [CH]
Mary H., d/o Rev. Jona. - Jonathan Hobbs 3d md. 16 Apr. 1833. [TR][CH]
Nahum of Northwood - Ann Currier md. 7 __ 1821. [CH]
Offen - Abigail French md. 7 Nov. 1751. [CH]
Oliver J. (24), s/o John F. - Clara B. Drake (21), d/o Nathaniel md. 6 Dec. 1875. [TR]
Otis B. (44), s/o David - Mary L. Marston (31), d/o James md. 1 Jan. 1879. [TR]
Rachel - Henry Pottle, both of Stratham md. 13 Dec. 1814. [TR][CH]
Samuel of So. Hampton - Anna Leavitt of Hampton md. 25 June 1771. [CH]
Samuel F., s/o Rev. Jona. - Ann R. Pickering md. 20 Apr. 1836. [CH]
Sarah d/o Rev. Jona. - Rev. Sereno Timothy Abbott of Hampton Falls md. 15 Aug. 1839. [CH]
Susan B., d/o Reuben - Perley W. Tenney, s/o Perley md. 28 May 1868. [TR][CH]

FRIZZELL:
Anthony W. (24) - Ellen S. Locke (25) md. 25 Dec. 1890. [TR][AR]

FROST:
George E. (22), s/o Pepperol - Maria C. Hall (22), d/o Ephraim md. 13 Nov. 1878. [TR]
George P. (29) - Eva E. Storer (33) of Norridgewock, Me. md. 19 Mar. 1914 at Norridgewock. [AR]
George P. (51) - Evelyn Rice (34) of Claremont, NH md. 16 May 1936 at Calemont. [AR]
John C. (22), s/o Wm H. & Julia A. - Lizzie A. Garland (22), d/o Calvin & Elizabeth md. 10 Aug. 1868. [TR]
Lydia A. (23), d/o Peperill - William J. Breed (25), s/o Otis J. md. 28 Nov. 1871. [TR]
Pepperell (64) - Hannah L. White (63) md. 3 July 1880. [TR]

FULBUTON/FULLONTON:
Joseph of Raymond - Abigail Robinson md. 26 Feb. 1834. [TR][CH]

FULLER:
Jemima C. (18), d/o James G. - Thomas W. Lang (22), s/o Thos. & Elizabeth md. 24 Nov. 1866. [TR]
Mary (24) - Robert Lloyd Henderson (27) of Boston md. 7 Sep. 1940. [AR]

FURBER:
Abigail - James C. Pickering, both of Newington md. 13 Oct. 1808. [TR][CH]

GARDNER:
Christian - Samuel B. Phenney, both of Portsmouth md. 6 June 1825, [TR][CH]

GARLAND:
Anna - Nathan Godfrey md. 3 Nov. 1795. [CH]
Annah A. (20), d/o John C. - Charles N. Knowles (29), s/o John md. 23 Nov. 1868. [TR]
Benjamin 3d - Sally Philbrick of Rye md. 24 July 1870. [TR][CH]
Charles L.A. (24) - Alice Jones (21) of Dover md. 23 Nov. 1898. [AR]
Comfort - Charles Fogg of Pittsfield md. 29 May 1786. [TR][CH]
Elisha C. (28) - Eliza J. Jones (19) md. 6 Feb. 1863. [TR]
Emeline of Rye - Horatio D. Hobbs md. 29 Dec. 1835. [CH]
Flora M. (35) - Marvin F. Mevis (53) md. 12 June 1911. [AR]
Frank N. (20), s/o Moses - Mary L. Fletcher (19), d/o Ismail? md. 23 Sep. 1884. [TR]
George L. (21), s/o Samuel - Isadore Page (20), d/o Simon D. md. 21 Apr. 1874. [TR]
Georgie E. (37) - Sheldon L. Marston (27) md. 12 Jan. 1915 at Hampton. [AR]
Hannah M. - Simon O. Lamprey (25) md. 27 Nov. 1862. [TR][CH]
John of Pittsfield - Mary Lane of Stratham md. 22 Nov. 1809. [TR][CH]

GARLAND Cont.

Laura P. (18), d/o Joseph - William P. Brown (21), s/o Stacy md. 17 Nov. 1869. [TR]

Lizzie A. (22), d/o Calvin & Elizabeth - John C. Frost (22), s/o Wm H. & Julia A. md. 10 Aug. 1868. [TR]

Lydia - Thomas Ward, both of Hampton md. Sep. 1793. [TR]

Mary - William Towle md. 12 Nov. 1795. [CH]

Mary A. (28), d/o M.L. & L. Lock - Warren Brown (28), s/o D.F. & N.C. Perkins md. 24 May 1865. [TR]

Mary O. - Jonah or Josiah Sandborn Jr., both of Hampton md. 24 Sep. 1828. [TR][CH]

Moses C. (28), s/o George & Polly - Eliza J. Downs (19), d/o John b. & Martha O. of Gosport md. 6 July 1863. [TR]

Norma (16), d/o Rufus - Horace L. Brown (22), s/o Joseph md. 10 Nov. 1868. [TR]

Roy (29) - Marjorie Purvis (34) md. 20 Feb. 1913. [AR]

Samuel - Hannah Marston of Hampton md. 24 Oct. 1833. [TR][CH]

Sarah E. (28), d/o Richard - John H. Gilpatrick (38), s/o John T. md. 1 Jan. 1866. [TR]

Simon of Rye - Abigail Norton of Portsmouth md. 20 Apr. 1785. [CH]

Simon - Mary Marston md. 16 Jan. 1793 by Samuel Shepard of Brentwood. [TR]

William H. (28), s/o William - Mary W. Dalton (28), d/o Michael md. 12 Nov. 1867. [TR]

GARRARD:

John P. - Hannah Brown md. 12 July 1829. [TR]

GASSETT:

Charles W. (21), s/o Varum - Cora E. Jenness (23), d/o John md. 9 Feb. 1872. [TR]

GATIS:

Idolla A. (18) of Exeter - Chester A. Deal (24) of Stratham md. 16 Aug. 1927. [AR]

GELLENGER:

John W. (31) - Doris L. Hammond (29) both of Salem, MA. md. 3 Aug. 1930. [AR]

GEORGE:

Adoniram of Hampton Falls - Sally Perkins of Seabrook md. 13 May 1827. [TR][CH]

Eleanor - Bagley Weed md. 11 Feb. 1751. [CH]

Mary - Jacob Hoyt md. 18 Mar. 1736. [CH]

GILMAN:
Clifton (25) - Viola Jones (25) both of Portsmouth md. 14 Apr. 1934. [AR]
Susannah of Exeter - Levi Batchelder of Kensington md. 1 Apr. 1793. [TR][CH]
Tabitha of Exeter - Dr. Samuel Fenny md. 28 Sep. 1786. [TR]
Tabitha of Exeter - Dr. Samuel Tenney md. 23 Sep. 1788. [TR]

GILPATRICK:
John H. (38), s/o John T. - Sarah E. Garland (28), d/o Richard md. 1 Jan.
    1866. [TR]
William M. (25) - Alice Kershaw (25) of Rye md. 3 Oct. 1904 at Rye. [AR]

GIPSON:
John - Dorothy Griffin, widow md. 5 Sep. 1751. [CH]

GLOVER:
Andrew H. (21), s/o Andrew J. - Ida K. Moe (17), d/o Ephraim md. 23 Dec.
    1878. [TR]

GODFREY:
Abby D. (31), d/o Oliver - Alphenus C. Lane (27), s/o William nd. 12 Apr.
    1877. [TR]
Anna - David Coomes of Stratham md. 2 Sep. 1810. [TR][CH]
Dixie G. (24), d/o Albert & Sarah - Charles C. Marston (29), s/o Thos. L. &
    Mary Bailey md. 1 Jan. 1866. [TR]
Eliza A. (21) - Levi M. Jenness (24) md. 24 Oct. 1853. [CH]
Elizabeth - Dearborn Lane, both of Hampton md. 20 Apr. 1814. [TR][CH]
Elizabeth A. (27) - John R. Moulton (26) md. 24 Dec. 1895. [TR]
Grace G. (31) of Hampton - George A. Tourtillott, Jr. (27) md. 9 June 1907 at
    Hampton. [AR]
Hannah - John Philbrick Jr., both of Hampton md. 4 July 1814. [TR][CH]
Hannah M. (19) - John H. Brown (21) md. 7 Aug. 1862. [TR][CH]
Isaac of Hampton - Patience Batchelder md. 21 July 1783. [CH]
James - Sarah Marston of Stratham md. 19 Dec. 1767. [CH]
Jeremiah - Sarah Batchelder md. 1 Oct. 1788. [TR]
Jeremiah - Sally Perkins, both of Hampton Falls md. 15 Nov. 1826. [TR][CH]
Joseph - Sally Dearborn md. 26 Sep. 1808. [CH]
Mary of Hampton - Samuel Page md. 17 Oct. 1819. [TR][CH]
Mary of Hampton - John Palmer md. 27 Oct. 1824. [TR][CH]
Nancy, Mrs. (53), d/o Richard Dow - Eleazer F. Knowles (52), s/o Amos md. 3
    Dec. 1873. [TR]
Nathan - Anna Garland md. 3 Nov. 1795. [CH]
Patience - Levi Dearborn, both of Hampton md. 21 Nov. 1793. [TR]
Patience - Josiah Lane Jr. of Hampton md. 21 Nov. 1810. [TR][CH]
Sarah of Rye - Joseph Moulton Jr. md. 26 Jan. 1773. [CH]
Sarah - David Nudd md. 18 Dec. 1814. [TR][CH]
Simon of Hampton - Ann Lamprey md. 24 Nov. 1831. [CH]

GOLTER:
Edith C. (23) of Portsmouth - Gordon S. Dow (28) md. 1 Nov. 1933 at
Portsmouth. [AR]

GOODHUE:
Frances W. (30) of Concord - C. Russell Chevalier (26) md. 28 Nov. 1935 at
Concord. [AR]

GOODWIN:
Charles W. (29) - Martha L. Bachelder (23) md. 16 June 1896. [TR][AR]
Daniel G. (23) of Saco, Me. - Ruth B. Cousens (22) md. 18 Sep. 1907 at
Hampton. [AR]
Susie E. (21), d/o David L. - Nelson J. Norton (28), s/o Joshua J. md. 22
Jan. 1899. [TR]
Thomas J. - Betsey Merrill md. 8 Dec. 1823. [CH]

GOOKIN:
Daniel - Abigail Dearborn, d/o Dr. Levi md. 14 Nov. or 6 Dec. 1787. [TR][CH]
Eliza - James B. Thornton of Saco md. 20 Jan. 1817. [TR][CH]
Gideon of Portsmouth - Sally Marshall md. 17 Apr. 1796. [CH]
Mary - Lt. Stephen Weeks, both of Greenland md. 21 Jan. 1808. [CH]
Rev. Nathaniel - Ann Fitch md. Jan. 1743. [CH]
Rev. Nathaniel - Love Wingate md. 17 Nov. 1748. [CH]
Sarah - Seth Storer Jr. Esq. of Saco md. 27 Sep. 1812. [TR][CH]

GOSS:
Clarence Albert (16), s/o Richard P. - Mary Mace (20), d/o John A. md. 21
Jan. 1876. [TR]
Harriet D. (22) of Rye - Ernest J. Moulton (24) md. 1 June 1910 at Rye. [AR]
Joseph - Hannah Piper, both of Stratham md. 15 Feb. 1770. [CH]
Joseph - Sarah Seavey, both of Rye md. 6 Mar. 1791. [TR]
Nathan - Sarah Johnson, both of Rye md. 12 May 1768. [CH]
Richard I. (27) - Louise S. Varney (23) of Plymouth, NH. md. 18 Aug. 1928 at
Plymouth. [AR]
Richard I. (31) - Louise Booker (21) md. 14 Feb. 1932. [AR]
William D. of Rye - Date H. Mason of Hampton md. 16 May 1824. [TR][CH]

GOTTWOOD:
Caroline of E.K. - Joshua French of E.K. md. 12 Dec. 1827. [CH]

GOUGH:
Hosea W. (27) of Waltham, MA. - Octavia H. Cousens (27) md. 19 July 1910.
[AR]

GOULD:
Abigail - Major Thomas Pike md. 10 June 1756. [CH]
Christopher - Abigail Shepard md. 11 Oct. 1756. [CH]

GOULD Cont.

Sarah - Henry L(ankester) Jewell md. 11 Jan. 1753. [CH]

Sarah J. (20) - Charles E. Austin (21) md. 24 June 1880. [TR]

GOVE:

Edward - Lydia Locke, both of Seabrook md. 13 June 1798. [CH]

James F. (29), s/o Sheldon & Anne - Eliza A. Page (27), d/o Avi & Lovy, both
   of Raymond md. 7 Aug. 1860. [TR][CH]

GRACE:

Emily (22) - Charles S. Knowles (35) md. 29 Nov. 1882. [TR]

GRANT:

Charles Herbert (50) - Cora Isabella Jackman (49) of Freemont, NH md. 20 Dec.
   1941 at Freemont. [AR]

Fred H. (27) - Sarah A. Leavitt (28) md. 24 Apr. 1887. [TR]

Harold I. (20) - Ethel R. Durant (20) of Hampton md. 6 Oct. 1935 at
   Portsmouth. [AR]

John H. (23), s/o John W. & Alice W. - Mira W. Batchelder (23), d/o Robert
   & Sophia md. 4 June 1865. [TR]

GRATTON:

Alpherena (29) of N. Reading, MA. - Walter E. Taylor (34) md. 21 Oct. 1917 at
   Hampton. [AR]

GRAVELLE:

Fred E. (28) - Emily J. Moulton (26) md. 7 May 1910. [AR]

GREEN:

Abigail of Stratham - Joseph Lowd of Portsmouth md. June 1779. [CH]

Deborah of Stratham - Benjamin Lowell of Portsmouth md. 4 Feb. 1779. [CH]

Ephraim of Newburyport - Mary Smith of Seabrook md. 22 Oct. 1799. [CH]

John - Abigail Nutter, both of Greenland md. 17 June 1807. [CH]

Jonathan of Chichester - Bathsheba Lane of Hampton md. 21 Nov. 1793. [TR]

GREENLEAF:

Richard - Sophia Leavitt, both of Hampton md. 22 Mar. 1821.[TR][CH]

GREENOUGH:

Charles E. (45) - Edmee B. Reisinger (44) of NYC md. 28 Aug. 1920. [AR]

GRETSKY:

Hyman J. (24) of Dorchester, MA. - Blanche Meyerhoff (22) of chelsea, MA. md.
   10 Oct. 1933. [AR]

GRIFFIN:

Dorothy, widow - John Gipson md. 5 Sep. 1751,. [CH]

GROUCARD:
John P. - Hannah L. Brown md. 22 Mar. 1829. [CH]

GROVE:
Benjamin of Exeter - Almira Blake of Hampton md. 13 Mar. 1825. [TR]

HAFFCHE:
Helen R. (35) - Will C. Wood (40) both of Beverly, MA. md. 27 Nov. 1927. [AR]

HAINES/HAYNES:
Comfort - Nathaniel Hains md. 24 Nov. 1773. [CH]
Comfort - John Simpson, both of Greenland md. 29 Mar. 1808. [CH]
Edward H. (24) , s/o Thos. - Gertrude A. Norton (21), d/o Joshua md. 10 Dec.
    1884. [TR]
Ella E. (26), d/o Joseph W. - Elmer E. Drake (32), s/o Joshua md. 14 Feb.
    1894. [TR][AR]
Ella M. (47) - Daniel E. Adams (76) of Wellsley Hills, MA. md. 7 Apr. 1909.
    [AR]
Eunice G. (19), d/o Matthias - Frank B. Ackerman (19), s/o Frank D. md. 8
    Sep. 1860. [TR]
Eunice V. (19) of Greenland - Frank P. Sherman (19) of Portsmouth md. 9 sep.
    1880. [CH]
George F. (21), s/o George - Nellie G. Trefethen (23), d/o Chas. md. 19 July
    1879. [TR]
Lillian F. (30) - Charles J. Ross (40) of Topsfield, MA. md. 30 Nov. 1905.
    [AR]
Nathaniel - Comfort Haines md. 24 Nov. 1773. [CH]
Ruth B. (27) of Kingston, NY - Elias T. Card (48) md. 19 June 1924 at
    Greenland. [AR]
Stephen of Canterbury - Polly Pickering of Greenland md. 31 Jan. 1810. [TR]

HALEY:
Charles Pearson (25) of Keene - Marion Taylor (24) of Portsmouth md. 22 June
    1940 at Portsmouth. [AR]

HALL:
Elizabeth - Samuel Smith, both of Rye md. 17 Mar. 1786. [CH]
Maria c. (22), d/o Ephraim - George E. Frost (22), s/o Pepperol md. 13 Nov.
    1878. [TR]
M. Otis - Rebecca A. Odell, both of Greenland md. 18 may 1847. [CH]

HAM:
George of Portsmouth - Hannah Wormwood of Portsmouth md. 5 June 1814.
    [TR][CH]

HAMILTON:
George F. (21) - Dorothy M. Leary (19) both of Somersville, MA. md. 30 Nov.
    1937. [AR]

HAMMOND:
Doris L. (29) - John W. Gellenger (31) both of Salem, MA. md. 3 Aug. 1930.
[AR]

HANLEY:
Newell Wells (32), s/o Wells - Ellen L. French (27), d/o John md. 17 Nov.
1871. [TR]

HANLON:
Mary Evelyn (38) of Newton, MA. - Ralph Haydon (48) md. 29 Nov. 1928 at
Newton, MA. [AR]

HANSON:
Elizabeth F. (21) of Swampscott, MA. - Harold W. Baker Jr. (23) of Boston md.
29 Jan. 1933. [AR]
Mary - Nathaniel Verrill, both of Rye md. 31 Oct. 1816. [TR][CH]

HARDY:
Charles W. (32) of Leominster, MA. - Pauline E. Wiggin (24) md. 12 Sep. 1937.
[AR]

HARNISH:
William C. (37) of Braintree, MA. - Ethel A. Higgins (25) md. 8 Sep. 1932.
[AR]

HARRINGTON:
Eva V. (36) - Harvey R. Edwards (37) both of Danvers, MA. md. 13 Jan. 1935.
[AR]

HARRIS:
Mary - Jonathan Chase, both of Stratham md. 17 Oct. 1773. [CH]

HART:
Eliza, Mrs. - Michael Whidden, both of Portsmouth md. 8 May 1808. [TR][CH]
Elisabeth Langdon - Hiram Corlis, both of Portsmouth md. 8 Jan. 1823.
[TR][CH]
George - Abigail Pitman, both of Portsmouth md. 5 June 1805. [CH]
Lydia F. (25), d/o Henry - George A. Page (27), s/o David J. md. 5 Jan. 1875.
[TR]

HARFORD:
Joshua - Lucy Mead, both of Newmarket md. 5 Oct. 1794. [TR]

HARVEY:
Maria, Mrs. (63) - Rufus Dalton (68) md. 9 May 1878. [TR]

HAYDON:
Ralph (48) - Mary Evelyn Hanlon (38) of Newton, MA. md. 29 Nov. 1928 at
Newton, MA. [AR]

HAYES:
Gladys (22) of Manchester - Stanley Page Currier (33) md. 19 Nov. 1938 ar
Cambia. [AR]

HAYNES: See Haines.

HAYWOOD:
Ernest (25) of Salem, MA. - Ethel J. Johnston (25) md. 8 May 1915. [AR]

HEALEY:
Wells of Hampton Falls - Elizabeth Pickering md. 2 Mar. 1815. [TR][CH]

HEATH:
George W. (31) - Lily A. Bunn (25) of Phila, PA. md. 8 Oct. 1900. [AR]
Ruth - John Norton, both of Stratham md. 28 Sep. 1823. [TR][CH]

HENDERSON:
Ellen (26) - Stephen W. Wech (36), both of Greenland md. 1 Feb. 1852. [CH]
Robert Lloyd (27) of Boston - Mary Fuller (24) md. 7 Sep. 1940. [AR]

HENDRY:
Carrie M. (17) - George Bourgess (23) of Lynn, MA. md. 3 Dec. 1903 at
Hampton. [AR]

HENNISON:
Joseph of Deerfield - Comfort Bachelder of Hampton md. 12 Aug. 1793. [TR]

HERSEY:
Enoch of Newburyport - Eliza D. Page md. 21 Apr. 1832. [CH]

HIGGINS:
Ethel A. (25) - William C. Harnish (37) of Braintree, MA. md. 8 Sep. 1932.
[AR]

HILL:
Elizabeth - Shadrick Fifield, both of Stratham md. 7 July 1818. [TR][CH]
Florence E. (37) of Melrose Highlands, MA. - William J. Kelly of Chelsea, MA.
md. 8 Feb. 1909. [AR]
George A. (22), d/o James - Annie Batchelder (23), s/o James md. 27 Nov.
1860. [TR]
Gertrude Roberta (19) - Walter T. Houston (21) both of Amesbury, MA. md. 6
Sep. 1930. [AR]
Joshua of Exeter - Lucy Chase of Stratham md. 1 Oct. 1789. [TR]

HILL Cont.

Lizzie B. (21) - Frank A. Philbrick (31) md. 21 Dec. 1881. [TR]

HILLIARD:

Joseph C. - Sally Hodgdon, both of Kensington md. 8 Nov. 1816. [TR][CH]

HILTON:

Eliza of Lee - Joseph Simpson of Portsmouth md. 7 Nov. 1813. [TR][CH]
Winthrop Jr. - Elizabeth Folsom of Newmarket md. - blank -. [CH]

HOAG:

John L. (20), s/o Levi - Mary E. Jewell (23) md. 11 Mar. 1861. [TR]

HOBBS:

Abbie L., Mrs. (45), d/o Reuben Lamprey - John Maynard (59), s/o John md. 9
    June 1877. [TR]
Abby L. - David M. Dow md. 24 Apr. 1845. [TR]
Abigail - William Sanborn md. 20 Mar. 1774. [CH]
Abigail - David Brown Jr. md. 2 Mar. 1813. [TR][CH]
Abigail C. - Jonathan Cotton md. 24 Nov. 1825. [TR][CH]
Ann Jeanette (26), d/o Moses - Jonathan C. Smith, s/o Abram (37) md. 2 Jan.
    1862. [TR][CH]
Annie F. (22) - Joseph O. Brown (28) md. 19 Dec. 1883. [TR]
Beatrice May (22) - James Vernon Cantley (25) both of Beverly, MA. md. 6 Sep.
    1930. [AR]
Bertha of Hampton Jeremiah Kinison of Personfield md. 23 Oct. 1792. [TR]
Betty - Benjamin Page of Rochester md. 17 Feb. 1788. [TR][CH]
Comfort of Hampton - Reuben Dearborn of Effingham md. 7 Apr. 1793. [TR][CH]
Daniel - Sarah Johnson, both of Hampton md. 9 Oct. 1823. [TR][CH]
Data - Reuben Knowles md. 28 Dec. 1842. [TR][CH]
David - Mary Leavitt md. 5 Dec. 1780. [CH]
Elizabeth C. - Christopher Smith md. 5 Dec. 1832. [CH]
Fanny - Thomas Hobbs md. 30 May 1832. [TR]]CH]
Gladys Mina (21) of Beverly - Raymond Morse Chevalier (23) md. 6 Aug. 1927 at
    Exeter. [AR]
Hannah - Eleab Samborn md. 6 Oct. 1789. [TR]
Horatio D. - Emeline Garland of Rye md. 29 Dec. 1835. [CH]
James F. Jr. (30) - Helen Spear (22) md. 10 July 1920 at Hampton. [AR]
John - Hannah Chapman md. 26 Mar. 1792. [TR][CH]
John Jr. - Lucinda Dearborn md. 9 Nov. 1808. [TR][CH]
John 3d - Polly Batchelder md. 19 Jan. 1815. [TR][CH]
John D. - Eliza Turner md. 21 Dec. 1837. [CH]
John F. (21), s/o John W. - Annie D. French (23), d/o John F. md. 12 Aug.
    1879. [TR]
John S. - Josephine Ward md. 23 June 1842. [TR][CH]
John W. (21), s/o John S. - Mira A. Seavey (20), d/o Joseph W. md. 25 Dec.
    1867. [TR]

HOBBS Cont.

John W.F. of Boston - Elizabeth J. Drake md. 17 Nov. 1841. [CH]

John W.F. (57), s/o Jonathan - Olive A. Hobbs (45), d/o Samuel Drake md. 2 Jan. 1873. [TR]

John W.T. of Boston - Elisabeth J. Drake md. 17 Nov. 1841. [TR]

Jonathan Jr. - Elezabeth Ramak of Rye md. 15 July 1791. [TR]

Jonathan Jr. - Data Drake md. 5 Mar. 1792. [TR][CH]

Jonathan Jr. - Fanny Dearborn md. 2 July 1797. [CH]

Jonathan, Lt. - Mary Drake md. 26 Jan. 1808. [CH]

Jonathan 3d - Mary H. French, d/o Rev. Jonathan md. 16 Apr. 1833. [TR]

Joseph B. (30), s/o Moses - Amanda M. Berry (21), d/o Ebenezer md. 9 Sep. 1863. [TR]

Joseph O. (28) - Annie F. Hobbs (22) md. 19 Dec. 1883. [TR]

Joseph O. (50) - Annie W. Hoyt (22) md. 28 feb. 1906. [AR]

Josiah - Molly Wedgwood Marston md. 8 Jan. 1785. [CH]

Josie E. (30), d/o John S. - John W. Mason (35), s/o Joseph md. 5 Dec. 1883. [TR]

Leocenda D. - John Chapman md. 5 Jan. 1831. [TR][CH]

Love - Ebenezer Marden Dalton md. 22 May 1796. [CH]

Luella M. (24) - Gilman H. Moulton (22) md. 17 Oct. 1883. [TR]

Mary - Jeremiah Marston md. 4 July 1814. [TR][CH]

Mary - Benjamin Page or Hobbs md. 30 May 1816. [TR][CH]

Mary - Thomas Cotton Leavitt md. 22 June 1831. [CH]

Mary - Nathaniel Watson, both of Hampton md. 19 Dec. 1856. [CH]

Mary E. (43), d/o Oliver R. - Thomas Philbrick (52), s/o Jonathan md. 30 Dec. 1884. [TR]

Mary Elizabeth (19) - William Edwin Parker (20) of Stratham md. 26 Mar. 1939. [AR]

Mary F. - Joseph Stacy Leavitt of Salem, MA md. 28 Nov. 1822. [TR][CH]

Mary J. (26), d/o Morris & Nancy (Perkins) - Joseph W. Redman (36), s/o John & Betsy (Marston) md. 28 June 1865. [TR]

Mehitable, d/o Benj. & Mary - Benj., s/o Thos. & Deborah md. 26 Jan. 1737/8. [TR]

Molly - Jeremiah Jenness md. 1799. [CH]

Morris - Deborah Leavitt md. 17 Mar. 1768. [CH]

Morris - Nancy Perkins, both of Hampton md. 8 Jan. 1833. [TR][CH]

Moses L., Dr. - Fanny Marston md. 12 Aug. 1829. [TR][CH]

Moses L. (57), s/o Moses L. - Mrs. Nancy J. Marston (53), d/o Thos Felch md. 12 June 1895. [TR][AR]

Nancy B. - Joshua Pickering Jr. md. 9 Oct. 1828. [TR][CH]

Olive A. (45), d/o Samuel Drake - John W.F. Hobbs (57), s/o Jonathan md. 2 Jan. 1873. [TR]

Oliver - Sarah Hobbs md. 24 Nov. 1825. [TR][CH]

Oliver S. (23) - Mary E. Smith (24) md. 24 Dec. 1890. [TR][AR]

Paul W. (24) - Dorothy E. Tarr (22) md. 14 June 1931. [AR]

Raymond A., s/o Oliver L. - ___acy E. ___tts md. 2 Aug. 1894. [TR]

Rebecca A. (20) - James S. Tilton (31) of Stratham md. 16 Apr. 1854. [CH]

HOBBS Cont.

Samuel - Sarah Blake of Kensington md. 25 Jan. 1829. [TR][CH]
Sarah - Oliver Hobbs md. 24 Nov. 1825. [TR][CH]
Sarah (19) - Moses Broadstreet (33) of Rowley, Mass. md. 6 Aug. 1857. [CH]
Sarah L. - John Chapman md. 18 Jan. 1824. [TR]
Simon L. - Martha A.C. Leavitt md. 26 Nov. 1846. [CH]
Thomas - Sarah Sherburne md. 7 Nov. 1771. [CH]
Thomas Jr. - Abigail Leavitt md. 1 May 1799. [CH]
Thomas - Fanny Hobbs md. 30 May 1832. [TR][CH]
Thomas D. (27) - Olive A. Drake (23) md. 2 July 1851. [CH]

HOBSON:

Mildred E. (25) of Concord - Charles W. Barton (36) md. 6 Oct. 1926 at
   Concord. [AR]

HODGDON:

Louisa A. (17) - Thomas W. Rand (23) md. 13 May 1858. [CH]
Sally - Joseph C. Hilliard, both of Kensington md. 8 Nov. 1816. [TR][CH]
Wesley F. (23), s/o George W. - Elizabeth Leonhard (23), d/o Philip md. 1
   Apr. 1892. [TR][AR]

HODGES:

Polly (24), d/o Samuel - Oliver A. Brown (32), s/o Oliver md. 19 Sep. 1876.
   [TR]

HOIT:

Capt. Joseph - Miriam Smith, both of Stratham md. 30 Jan. 1808. [CH]

HOLMAN:

Marshall S. (22) - Dorothy Dean (24) of Mills, MA. md. 23 Apr. 1920. [AR]

HOLMES:

Charles E. (25), s/o Samuel - Lucie E.M. Ranson (18), d/o Margaret L. Chase
   md. 1 July 1866. [TR]

HOLT:

Annie W. (22) - Joseph O. Hobbs (50) md. 28 Feb. 1906. [AR]
Elizabeth M.J. - Nathaniel S. Adams, both of Exeter md. 10 Nov. 1836. [CH]

HOOK:

Humphrey of Salisbury - Mary Brown md. 15 Oct. 1777. [CH]

HORN(S):

Eva M. (18) - Frank P. Brown (28) md. 30 Mar. 1893. [AR]
Mary of Portsmoith - Ezekiel Pierce of Townsend md. Nov. 1777. [CH]

HOUGHTON:
Charles M. (26), s/o George - Annie M. Warner (24), d/o Philip md. 31 Sep.
   1885. [TR]

HOUSTON:
Walter T. (21) - Gertrude Roberta Hill (19) both of Amesbury, MA. md. 6 Sep.
   1930. [AR]

HOWARD:
Thomas P. (49) - Elizabeth H, Knights (39) of Boston md. 26 Apr. 1911 at
   Brookline, MA. [AR]

HOWE:
Chester L. (33) - of Watertown, MA. - Jessie R. Fogg (26) md. 19 Aug. 1919 at
   Hampton. [AR]

HOYT: See Hoit
Annie W. (22) - Joseph O. Hobbs (50) md. 28 Feb. 1906. [AR]
Jacob - Mary George md. 18 Mar. 1756. [CH]
John - Sarah Collins md. 21 Nov. 1751. [CH]
Joseph W. (22) of Portsmouth - Mabel Elizabeth Norton (24) md. 6 Feb. 1943.
   [AR]
Mehitabel - Jonathan Maloon md. 22 Feb. 1753. [CH]
Ruth - Joseph Brown md. 29 Nov. 1756. [CH]

HUGGINS:
Nathaniel - Phebe Ayers of Greenland md. 29 July 1778. [CH]

HULL:
Catherine - Oliver Eaton, both of Seabrook md. 15 Dec. 1851. [CH]

HUNNEWELL:
Marion (19) of Roxbury, MA. - Thomas F. Bavis (22) of Jamaica Plain, MA. md.
   5 Mar. 1937. [AR]

HUNT:
Hannah - John Hunt md. 9 Nov. 1755. [CH]
Harold Ernest (21) of Hingham, MA. - Marvis June Clark (19) of Roslindale,
   MA. md. 23 Aug. 1938. [AR]
John - Hannah Hunt md. 9 Nov. 1755. [CH]

HUSSEY:
Ralph B. (24) - Helen E. Batchelder (18) md. 28 Nov. 1934. [AR]

HUTCHINS:
Russell P. of Wells, Me. - Mary A. Bisbee of N. Livermore, Me. md. 21 Apr.
   1913. [AR]

HUTCHINSON:
 Charles R. (22) of Brighton, MA. - Erna L. Downs (22) of Haverhill, MA. md. 6
   Sep. 1919. [AR]

HYMAN:
 Louise (25) of NYC - Julian A. Pollak (28) of Ohio md. 20 Oct. 1913. [AR]

INGLIS:
 Arlene E. (17) - Richard E. Marston (20) md. 28 Aug. 1943. [AR]

JACKMAN:
 Cora Isabella (49) of Freemnont, NH - Charles Herbert Grant (50) md. 20 Dec.
   1941 at Freemont. [AR]

JACKSON:
 Mary - William Turner, both of Portsmouth md. 9 Sep. 1813. [TR][CH]
 Sylvester H. of No. Berwick, Me. - Mary D. Batchelder md. 30 Nov. 1842. [CH]

JAMES:
 Howard M. (32) - Gladys L. Myrick (20) of Portsmouth md. 12 Aug. 1922. [AR]
 John B. of Deerfield - Esther Dalton md. 15 Sep. 1829. [TR][CH]

JANKOUSKY:
 Stephen Jr. (30) of Exeter - Florence M. Wells (25) of Stratham md. 12 June
   1943. [AR]

JANVRIN:
 David C. of Hampton Falls - Mary P. Towle of Hampton md. 6 Feb. 1820.
   [TR][CH]
 Harriet of Hampton Falls - Samuel White of Pittsfield md. 12 May 1829.
   [TR][CH]

JARRAL:
 Molly Pitts - Stephen Brown md. 13 Jan. 1795. [CH]

JEFTS:
 George W. - Minerva Neal, both of Hampton md. 16 Aug. 1840. [CH]

JENNESS:
 Annie W. (20) - Harlan L. Philbrick (23) md. 20 June 1883. [TR]
 Benjamin of Rye - Dolly Brown md. 27 May 1827. [TR][CH]
 Charles W. (24), s/o Elwin - Eliza A. Davis (21), d/o Jerry md. 3 Jan. 1871.
   [TR]
 Cora E. (23), d/o John - Charles W. Gassett (21), s/o Varum md. 9 Feb. 1872.
   [TR]
 Edwin - Mary Chapman md. Apr. 1842. [TR][CH]
 Eliza P. (18), d/o Amos - Richard Fogg (28), s/o Richard md. 8 Jan. 1868.
   [TR]

JENNESS Cont.

Elizabeth A. (35) - Nathan Brown Jr. (46) md. 20 Mar. 1839. [CH]

Emery C. (29), s/o David - Ellen A. Rand (26), d/o Wm md. 2 Dec. 1871. [TR]

Emma P. (17), d/o J.R. - George C. Dalton (18), s/o J.G. md. 15 Jan. 1879. [TR]

Fannie Wesley (18), d/o Wesley - George Edgar Dow (19), s/o George O. md. 22 Dec. 1873. [TR]

Francis of Rye - Sarah Batchelder md. Sep. 1778. [CH]

Frank W. (27) - Mary S. Berry (32) of Stratham md. 16 June 1899. [AR]

George W. (24) - Clara J. French (28) of Stratham md. 17 June 1900 at Greenland. [AR]

Henry (55) - Almira A. Brown (40) md. 15 Dec. 1881. [TR]

Howard M. (24) - Alberta E. Berry (20) of Hampton md. 16 Nov. 1910. [AR]

James - Lucinda Davis, both of Exeter md. 15 Mar. 1826. [TR][CH]

James (27), s/o Jonathan - Ella M. Weare (22), d/o Joseph md. 8 Sep. 1877. [TR]

Jeremiah - Molly Hobbs md. 1799. [CH]

John of Rye - Lydia Rollins of Stratham md. 17 Nov. 1808. [TR][CH]

Jonathan R. of Rye - Sally E. Marston md. 10 June 1847. [CH]

Joseph B. (42), s/o Benj. - Olive A. Bachelder (42), d/o Mark md. 25 Feb. 1879. [TR]

Joseph B. (55) - Mrs. Mabel S. Kendall (31) md. 17 Sep. 1892. [TR][AR]

Joseph G. (60) - Olivia Marden (38) md. 2 Mar. 1889. [TR]

Joseph J. - Martha O. Folsam, both of Rye md. 26 Mar. 1850. [CH]

Levi of Rye - Sarah Dearborn md. 3 Mar. 1782. [CH]

Levi M. (24) of Roxbury, Mass. - Eliza J. Godfrey (21) md. 26 Oct. 1853. [CH]

Mabel F. (21) - Leslie F. Powhatan (26) md. 21 Nov. 1909. [AR]

Mary of Rye - Jacob Morrill of So. Hampton md. 22 Sep. 1768. [CH]

Mary Ann - Jonathan c. Bachelder md. 21 Nov. 1816. [TR][CH]

Meade (28) - Verina M. Brown (18) md. 24 Dec. 1884. [TR]

Mellisie Hannah (19), d/o Isaac - Frank M. Philbrick (20), s/o Rufus Wm md. 22 Apr. 1872. [TR]

Nancy - Daniel Cait of Northwood md. 27 Nov. 1788. [TR]

Patty (25) - John Blaisabell (28), s/o Albert md. 8 June 1871. [TR]

Peter of Rye - Abigail Drake md. 26 Dec. 1782. [CH]

Polly - John Brown md. 5 June 1798. [CH]

Polly C. - Lt. David Wedgwood, both of Rye md. 24 Dec. 1817. [TR][CH]

S. Alonzo (31), s/o Edwin - Martha Brown (22), d/o Wm md. 5 Jan. 1875. [TR]

Samuel - Mary Jewell md. 29 Oct. 1756. [CH]

Sarah M. (35), d/o Benjamin - William H. Burleigh (37), s/o Henry md. 28 Jan. 1877. [TR]

Sheriden of Rye - Almira Batchelder md. 30 Dec. 1845. [TR][CH]

Woodbury Levi (22), s/o Levi - Mary Davis Poole, d/o John F. md. 16 July 1874. [TR]

JEWELL:

David Jr. (29), s/o David - Hatie Burleigh (20), d/o Henry md. 2 Mar. 1869. [TR]

E. Bloomer (24), s/o DeWitt - Abbie M. Dow (25), d/o George O. md. 10 Sep. 1874. [TR]

Elizabeth - Thomas Wiggin, both of Stratham md. 11 Feb. 1768. [CH]

Elizabeth - Robert Chase md. 13 Feb. 1827. [CH]

Hannah - Daniel Brown md. 17 Jan. 1754. [CH]

Henry L(ankester) - Sarah Gould md. 11 Jan. 1753. [CH]

Joseph - Elizabeth Eastman, widow md. 18 Dec. 1753. [CH]

Judith - David Blaisdell md. 24 Dec. 1755. [CH]

Levi of Stratham - Hannah Marston md. 13 June 1809. [TR][CH]

Levi Esqr. of Stratham - Elizabeth Marston md. 11 Sep. 1834. [TR][CH]

Mary - Samuel Jennis md. 29 Oct. 1756. [CH]

Mary E. (23) - John L. Hoag (26), s/o Levi md. 11 Apr. 1861. [TR][CH]

Sarah of Stratham - Reuben Davis of Poplin md. 3 Dec. 1772. [CH]

Susannah of Stratham - Jonathan Foss of Epping md. 18 June 1771. [CH]

JEWETT:

Aaron - Nancy Smith, both of Stratham md. 14 Nov. 1808. [TR][CH]

Dr. Henry A. of Northboro, Mass. - Sarah A. Lawrence of Hampton md. 31 May 1849. [CH]

JOHNSON:

Benjamin of Epping - Elizabeth Dalton md. 14 Nov. 1786. [TR][CH]

Eliphalet - Ann Ayers, both of Greenland md. Aug. 1794. [CH]

Emma P. (22) , d/o Joseph - Otis G. Brown (26), s/o Simon md. 24 June 1872. [TR]

Hannah - Sewell Brown, both of Hampton md. 24 Dec. 1834. [TR][CH]

J__tha - Dr. Samuel Tenney, both of Exeter md. 23 Sep. 1788. [CH]

James - Betsy Dearborn, both of Hampton md. 31 Mar. 1818. [TR][CH]

Martina L. (19), d/o Rufus S. - Wilson H. Fairbanks (25), s/o Washington md. 1 July 1873. [TR]

Olarvan (21), d/o Mathew - Edwin Burke (25), s/o David md. 21 Apr. 1876. [TR]

Rudolph (28) of Roslindale, MA. - Mae P. Moulton (27) md. 14 Oct. 1914. [AR]

Sarah - Nathan Goss, both of Rye md. 12 May 1768. [CH]

Sarah - Daniel Hobbs, both of Hampton md. 9 Oct. 1823. [TR][CH]

Winthrop of Greenland = Miriam Dearborn md. 30 Jan. 1781. [CH]

JOHNSTON:

Ethel I. (25) - Ernest Hayward (25) of Salem, MA. md. 8 May 1915. [AR]

JONES:

Alice (21) of Dover - Charles L.A. Garland (24) md. 23 Nov. 1898. [AR]

Anna - John Brown md. 3 Apr. 1825. [CH]

Daniel - Judith Flanders md. 3 May 1756. [CH]

Dorothy - Jacob Eliot md. 29 Dec. 1752. [CH]

JONES Cont.
Eliza J. (19) - Elisha C. Garland (28) md. 6 Feb. 1863. [TR]
Jacob - Betsey Ewens md. 23 Apr. 1826. [CH]
Samuel - Hannah Flanders md. 25 Aug. 1756. [CH]
Sarah - Ezekiel Flanders md. 15 Jan. 1756. [CH]
Sarah - Jacob Eastman md. 14 Feb. 1817. [CH]
Viola (25) - Clifton Gilman (25) both of Portsmouth md. 14 Apr. 1934. [AR]

JOYCE:
Mary A. (23) - Roger J. Moore (26) md. 23 Sep. 1917 at Hampton Beach. [AR]

KAHARL:
Alice K. (17) of Exeter - Maurice R. Wright (31) md. 5 Sep. 1916 at Exeter.
[AR]

KAMS:
Irving (26) - Jeannette P. Bardenstein (24) both of Dorchester, MA. md. 27
Feb. 1937. [AR]

KAPISH:
John James Jr. (22) of Worc., MA - Marion Elizabeth Moore (21) of Boylston,
MA md. 19 May 1940. [AR]

KEACH:
Nellie A. (42) - William T. Coates (60) both of Malden, MA. md. 2 Jan. 1943.
[AR]

KEEN/KEENE:
Georgiana H. (18) - Charles N. Downs (21), both of Portsmouth md. 29 June
1851. [CH]
Gladys Belle (29) - Reginald H. Davies (26) of NYC md. 11 Aug. 1928 at Rye
Beach.

KELLEY/KELLY:
Joseph - Molly Thurston, both of Stratham md. 19 Feb. 1795. [CH]
William J. of Chelsea, MA. - Florence E. Hill (37) of Melrose Highlands, MA.
md. 8 Feb. 1908. [AR]

KENDALL:
Mabel S. Mrs. (31) - Joseph B. Jenness (55) md. 17 Sep. 1892. [TR][AR]

KEOUS:
Abigail - David Chapman md. 24 Nov. 1822. [CH]
Deborah - Jacob Brown Jr. md. 19 Mar. 1820. [CH]

KERNS:
Abigail - David Chapman md. 24 Nov. 1822. [TR]

KERSHAW:
Alice (25) of Rye - William M. Gilpatrick (25) md. 3 Oct. 1904 at Rye. [AR]

KIMBALL:
Samuel - Hannah Eliot md. 18 May 1753. [CH]

KINGSBURY:
Joseph - Sally Dearborn md. 26 Feb. 1797. [CH]

KINISON:
Jeremiah of Personfield - Bertha Hobbs of Hampton md. 23 Oct. 1792. [TR]

KNIGHTS:
Elizabeth H. (39) of Boston - Thomas P. Howard (49) md. 26 Apr. 1911 at
    Brookline. [AR]

KNOWLES:
Betsy - Thomas Newman of Portsmouth md. 18 June 1812. [TR][CH]
Brandon Kenneth (24) - Olive Annetta Moore (23) md. 12 Nov. 1941. [AR]
Charles N. (29), s/o John - Annah A. Garland (20), d/o John C. md. 23 Nov.
    1868. [TR]
Charles S. (35) - Emily Grace (22) md. 29 Nov. 1882. [TR]
David - Sarah Ann Leavitt of Stratham md. 16 Nov. 1846. [CH]
David S. - Eleanor J. Leavitt md. 5 Nov. 1839. [CH]
David Webster (38) - Louise Vogl (41) md. 21 June 1925. [AR]
Earle H. (20) - Eleanor E. McFarlane (20) both of Medford, MA. md. 22 Feb.
    1920. [AR]
Eleazer F. (52), s/o Amos - Mrs. Nancy Godfrey (53), d/o Richard Dow md. 3
    Dec. 1873. [TR]
Ezekiel of Deerfield - Rachel Dow md. 12 Oct. 1783. [CH]
Forrest E. (52) - Mildred J. Ewen (32) of Twin Mt., Vt. md. 2 June 1934 at
    Twin Mountain. [AR]
Hannah - Thomas Marston Jr. md. 9 Dec. 1783. [CH]
Hannah B. - James Watson md. 28 Mar. 1850. [CH]
Herbert S. (30) - Edith R. Rand (24) md. 9 Dec. 1896. [TR][AR]
L. Blanche (32) - Charles H. Brown (31) of Salisbury, MA. md. 12 Sep. 1919.
    [AR]
Leon M. (21) - Marion T. Drake (15) md. 30 Jan. 1915. [AR]
Leon Marvin Jr. (22) - Grace A. Paschal (19) of Jefferson, NH md. 4 Dec.
    1938. [AR]
Levi W. - Emma E. Courson md. 7 Aug. 1876 md. at S. Newmarket. [TR]
Louise Barbara (56) - Irving Wilson Marston (68) md. 30 Dec. 1940. [AR]
Lizzie A. (19) - Fred A. Brown (31) md. 3 Oct. 1890. [TR][AR]
Mae C. (18) - Nelson J. Norton (19) md. 22 Aug. 1889. [TR]
Mary - John G. Gurney of Newburyport md. 6 Mar. 1839. [CH]
Nathan - Rachel Smith of Stratham md. 30 Mar. 1808. [TR][CH]
Rachel - Joseph Leavitt Jr. of Salem, MA. md. 22 Nov. 1841. [TR][CH]

KNOWLES Cont.

Reuben - Data Hobbs md. 22 Dec. 1842. [TR][CH]
Ruth M. (19) - James F. Leavitt (23) md. 6 Oct. 1914. [AR]
Samuel - Hannah Lampre(y) of Rye md. 26 Apr. 1793. [TR]
Stanley Joy (39) - Marion Eleanor Smith (21) md. 15 June 1929. [AR]
Thomas J. (40). s/o David - Lamira Philbrick (40), d/o Daniel md. 12 Dec.
    1882. [TR]

KOS:

Bertha (24) of Bondsville, MA. - Wallace B. Wile (25) of Ipswich, MA. md. 9
    Feb. 1936. [AR]

KUPISH:

John James Jr. (22) of Worcester, MA. - Marion Elizabeth Moore (21) of
    Boylston, MA. md. 19 May 1940. [AR]

KUPLEC:

Emilia (19) of Ware, MA. - Frank W. Carey (24) of Palmer, MA. md. 10 Mar.
    1935. [AR]

KYSER:

Harvey J. (25) of Portsmouth - Esther P. Drake (21) md. 4 Nov. 1915 at
    Kittery Point, Me. [AR]

LADD:

Timothy - Mary Lane, both of Hampton md. 25 Dec. 1817. [TR][CH]

LAMPREY:

Abbie M. (19), d/o John - Albert Bachelder (25), s/o James md. 22 June 1869.
    [TR][CH]
Abigail - Jacob Brown Jr. md. 21 Feb. 1797. [CH]
Ann - Simon Godfrey of Hampton md. 24 Nov. 1831. [CH]
Annie - James F. Moulton md. 1878. [TR]
Austin (36) - Josephine M. Drake (32) md. 20 Jan. 1904. [AR]
Benjamin - Comfort Shepard md. 3 Feb. 1772. [CH]
D. Morris (24) - Gertrude Dow (22) md. 1 Dec. 1934. [AR]
David - Mrs. Abigail Marston, both of Hampton md. 20 Dec. 1797. [CH]
Dudley - Miriam Lock of Hampton md. 22 Oct. 1793. [TR]
Eliza J. (26), d/o Jacob Rowe - John J. Leavitt (34), s/o Tappen md. 28 Apr.
    1885. [TR]
Ellen A. (22), d/o ___ & Mary A. - Hiram Brown (26), s/o Jacob & Polly md.
    13 Mar. 1865. [TR]
Fred L. (21), s/o Samuel C. - Emma L. Robinson (17) md. 20 Feb. 1872. [TR]
Hannah of Rye - Samuel Knowles md. 26 Apr. 1793. [TR]
James Sawyer of Rye - Sarah Brown md. 17 Aug. 1793. [TR]
Jane of Hampton - Samuel Woodbury of Newburyport md. 20 Apr. 1834. [TR][CH]
Jennie G. (26), d/o Thos. L. - Oliver D. Moulton (26), s/o David P. md. 1
    Jan. 1878. [TR]

LAMPREY Cont.

John - Molly Marston md. 28 Apr. 1773. [CH]
John, Capt. - Mary S. Robinson md. 16 Nov. 1828. [TR][CH]
John 3d - Lydia Locke of Hampton md. 8 June 1837. [CH]
John L. - Olive Wells, both of Kensington md. 26 Jan. 1829. [TR][CH]
Johnson - Harriet Emery, both of Hampton md. 9 Jan. 1837. [CH]
Jonathan - Mary P. Lamprey md. 1 Jan. 1850. [CH]
Mary - Levi Marston md. 4 Feb. 1837. [CH]
Mary A. (28) - Harry A. Naves (36) md. 21 June 1937. [AR]
Mary P. - Jonathan Lamprey md. 1 Jan. 1850. [CH]
Sally - Jonathan Palmer, both of Hampton md. 20 Mar. 1825. [TR][CH]
Sandra A. (24), d/o Thos. L. - George H. Blake (26), s/o Wm md. 23 May 1878.
    [TR]
Simon - Martha Dow of Rye md. 5 July 1780. [CH]
Simon O. (25) - Hannah M. Garland md. 27 Nov. 1872. [TR][CH]

LANE:

Abijah of Hampton Falls - Hannah Wallace md. 8 Dec. 1795. [CH]
Alpheus C. (27), s/o Wm - Abby D. Godfrey (31), d/o Oliver md. 12 Apr. 1877.
    [TR]
Asa Esqr. of Chichester - Mrs. Sarah Towle md. 12 Oct. 1820. [TR][CH]
Bathsheba of Hampton - Jonathan Green of Chichester md. 21 Nov. 1793.
    [TR][TR]
Charles N. (22), s/o Uri - Lillian S. Chapman (19), d/o DeWitt md. 18 Sep.
    1900. [TR]
David A. (39) of W.Va. - Juanita J. Bobson (36) of Ind. md. 12 Aug. 1935 at
    Rye Beach. [AR]
Dearborn of Hampton - Elizabeth Godfree md. 20 Apr. 1814. [TR][CH]
Eleanor (21) of Hampton - Abbott Brown (22) md. 31 Oct. 1929. [AR]
Elizabeth of Hampton - Ezekiel Rowe of Gilmanton md. 16 Feb. 1794. [TR]
Elizabeth - Samuel Sinclar, both of Stratham md. 28 Sep. 1823. [TR][CH]
George H.P. (32) - M. Isabell Mann (24) md. 7 Apr. 1894. [TR][AR]
Hattie A. (22) - Jonathan Rollins (50) md. 8 Nov. 1884. [TR]
James - Mary Ann Blake, both of Hampton md. 1 Feb. 1836. [CH]
Josiah Jr. of Hampton - Patience Godfree md. 21 Nov. 1810. [TR][CH]
Lewis R.H. (29) - Ida S. Tarlton (29) md. 30 June 1885. [TR]
Louise K. (28) - Leslie L. Lovett (24) md. 20 Dec. 1917. [AR]
Marion (49) - George J. Carter (57) md. 1 June 1937 at Hampton. [AR]
Mary - Samuel Leighton of Exeter md. 17 Feb. 1808. [CH]
Mary of Stratham - John Garland of Pittsfield md. 22 Nov. 1810. [TR][CH]
Mary - Timothy Ladd, both of Hampton md. 25 Dec, 1817. [TR][CH]
Moses of Hampton - Anna Marston md. 27 May 1791. [CH]
Nancy - Jonathan Shaw, both of Hampton md. 26 Apr. 1812. [TR][CH]
Nancy L. of Hampton - Samuel D. Lane Int. 10 Feb. 1853. [NHA]
Ruth of Hampton - Jeremiah Rowe of Gilmanton md. 16 Nov. 1796. [CH]
Samuel Jr. - Olly Rollins, both of Hampton md. 22 Mar. 1795. [CH]
Samuel D. of Hampton - Sarah M. Robinson md. 15 Oct. 1845. [TR][CH]

LANE Cont.
Samuel D. - Miss Nancy L. Lane of Hampton Int. 10 Feb. 1853. [NHA]
Uri A. (21), s/o William - Addie J. Palmer (16), d/o John M. md. 6 Sep. 1877.
   [TR]

LANG:
Dorothy - John Whedden, both of Greenland md. 12 Aug. 1792. [TR]
Edward of Exeter - Deborah Marston md. 8 Apr. 1824. [TR][CH]
Eleanor M. (25) of Portsmouth - John F. Fisher (26) of Boston md. 7 Sep.
   1858. [CH]
Eles - William Scott md. 15 Mar. 1791. [TR]
Hannah - Dows Deane?, both of Rye md. 1789. [TR]
John of Rye - Marey Drake md. 1788. [TR]
Polly - Samuel Philbrick Jr. of Effingham md. 7 Dec. 1815. [TR][CH]
Thomas W. (22), s/o Thomas - Jemima C. Fuller (18), d/o James G. md. 29 Jan.
   1866. [TR]

LAUGHTON:
Grace (31) - Charles S. Page (33) md. 28 Apr. 1900. [AR]

LAUTERBORN:
Jack J. (25) - Jean S. Taylor (21) both of Cambridge, MA. md. 11 July 1943.
   [AR]

LAVOIE:
William G. (33) - Reatha M. Cameron (28) both of Manchester md. 7 Sep. 1930.
   [AR]

LAWD:
Joseph of Portsmouth - Abigail C_____ md. 22 Apr. 1779. [TR]

LAWRENCE:
Dr. Ebenezer of Hampton - Abigail Leavitt md. 31 Jan. 1808. [CH]
Sarah A. of Hampton - Dr. Henry A. Jewett of Northboro, Mass. md. 31 May
   1849. [CH]

LEACOCK:
Arthur G. (43) of Exeter - Anne A. Brown (40) md. 24 Aug. 1911. [AR]

LEAH:
Margaret - Benjamin Mason md. 18 July 1771. [CH]

LEARY:
Dorothy M. (19) - George F. Hamilton (21) both of Somerville, MA. md. 30 Nov.
   1937. [AR]

LEAVITT:

Abbie E. (17), d/o James - Frank H. Seavey (23), s/o Joseph W. md. 5 Sep. 1867. [CH][TR]

Abigail - Thomas Hobbs Jr. md. 1 May 1799. [CH]

Abigail - Dr. Ebenezer Lawrence of Hampton md. 31 Jan. 1808. [CH]

Abigail - Charles Brown md. 16 Mar. 1841. [TR][CH]

Abihar - Simon Marston md. 14 Mar. 1798. [CH]

Abihail - Peter Moore md. 3 Nov. 1805. [CH]

Abraham - Sarah Dearborn md. 4 June 1807. [CH]

Anna of Hampton - Samuel French of So. Hampton md. 23 June 1771. [CH]

Anna - Samuel Fogg Smith md. 10 June 1792. [TR]

Benjamin - Abigail Smith md. 29 Mar. 1786. [CH]

Benjamin of Boston - Abigail Ward of Hampton md. 15 Nov. 1826. [CH]

Benson of Boston - Abigail Ward of Hampton md. 15 Nov. 1826. [TR]

Carr - Lydia Smith md. 9 Oct. 1797. [CH]

Clarissa - Ebenezer Loving of Greenland md. 23 Nov. 1810. [TR][CH]

Deborah - Morris Hobbs md. 17 Mar. 1768. [CH]

Delia (21), d/o Tappan - David J. Wiggin (23) md. 2 Nov. 1867. [TR]

Eleanor J. - David S. Knowles md. 5 Nov. 1839. [CH]

Elizabeth of Stratham - John S. Yeaton of Exeter md. 13 May 1832. [TR][CH]

Fred C. (20) - Fannie L. Moulton (20) md. 23 May 1894. [AR][TR]

Hannah - Jeremiah Upton of Middleton, MA. md. 25 Dec. 1845. [TR][CH]

Hazel M. (24) of Hampton - Byron D. Smith (25) md. 22 Sep. 1919. [AR]

Horace (33), s/o Thos. C. - Mary E. Dow (22) md. 1 Feb. 1871. [TR]

Isabella (20), d/o Simon - Morris A. Smith (26), s/o Christopher md. 24 Nov. 1859. [TR][CH]

James F. (23) - Ruth M. Knowles (19) md. 6 Oct. 1914. [AR]

James R. - Elizabeth Marston md. 4 Sep. 1836. [CH]

John - Meream Dow md. 23 Aug. 1790. [TR]

John Jr. - Betsy Drake md. 21 Oct. 1806. [TR][CH]

John of Hampton - Nancy A. MacClintock md. 18 Feb. 1819. [TR][CH]

John J. (34), s/o Tappen - Eliza J. Lamprey (26), d/o Jacob Rowe md. 28 Apr. 1885. [TR]

Joseph E. (21) - Sarah L. Marston (18) md. 24 Dec. 1889. [TR]

Joseph Stace - Mary Darborn md. 11 Sep. 1792. [TR]

Joseph Stacy of Salem, MA - Mary F. Hobbs md. 28 Nov. 1822. [TR][CH]

Joseph S. Jr. of Salem MA. - Rachel Knowles md. 22 Nov. 1841. [TR][CH]

Julia M. (26) - Joseph L. Philbrook (29) md. 24 Nov. 1856. [CH]

Lemira - John F. French md. 8 Nov. 1842. [CH]

Luther - Miriam Dow md. 17 or 27 June 1819. [TR][CH]

Martha A.C. - Simon L. Hobbs md. 26 Nov. 1846. [CH]

Martha Estelle (29) - Edward M. Smith (36) md. 2 Sep. 1902. [AR]

Mary - David Hobbs md. 5 Feb. 1780. [CH]

Mary - Jonathan Marston md. 24 Sep. 1792. [TR]

Mary - Samuel J. Drake md. 19 Apr. 1842. [TR][CH]

Miriam, Mrs. - Capt. Thomas Lovering md. 16 Nov. 1804. [CH]

Moses - Sarah Towle, both of Hampton md. 7 Dec. 1794. [TR]

LEAVITT Cont.
Oliver - Eunice Batchelder md. 13 Apr. 1814. [TR][CH]
Olivia R. - Andrew S. Warner md. 21 May 1837. [CH]
Orrin B. (40) - Mary B. Drake (29) md. 20 Oct. 1888. [TR]
Peggy - Kittery Tuckerman of Portsmouth md. 29 July 1778. [TR]
Philip - Dolly Fogg md. 12 Nov. 1812. [TR][CH]
Polly/Peggy - Kitterick Tuckerman md. 29 July 1778. [TR][CH]
Rebecca F. - Henry M. Philbrook md. 1 Jan. 1856. [CH]
Reuben - Hannah Moore, both of Stratham md. 13 Dec. 1781. [CH]
Sally - Major John Lovering Jr. of Greenland md. 3 July 1814. [TR][CH]
Samuel - Anne Towel md. 20 June 1792. [TR]
Samuel, Capt. - Sophia W. Neal md. 10 Jan. 1819. [TR]
Samuel Fogg - Nancy Towle md. 30 Sep. 1792. [CH]
Sarah - Josiah Wedgwood md. 10 Dec. 1783. [CH]
Sarah A. (28)- Fred H. Grant (27) md. 24 Apr. 1887. [TR]
Sarah Ann of Stratham - David Knowles md. 16 Nov. 1846. [CH]
Sarah D. (26) - Joshua P. Drake (28) md. 23 Apr. 1851. [CH]
Simon - Sarah Drake md. 25 Dec. 1777. [CH]
Simon - Sally Dearborn md. July 1794. [CH]
Simon - Mrs. Abigail Cotton md. 12 Dec. 1805. [CH]
Simon 3d - Abigail Chapman md. 7 June 1818. [TR][CH]
Simon Jr. Dorothy Robinson md. 7 July 1818. [TR][CH]
Simon 3d - Juliana Chapman md. 18 Jan. 1824. [TR][CH]
Sophia - Richard Greenlief, both of Hampton md. 22 Mar. 1821. [TR][CH]
Thomas - Mary Fogg md. 14 Apr. 1767. [CH]
Thomas Cotton - Mary Hobbs md. 22 June 1831. [CH]

LEE:
Lottie M. (39) - Frank D. Carter (57) both of Amesbury md. 30 June 1926. [AR]

LEFEBVRE:
Roland Lake (40) - Ethelda G. Dunn (34) of Auburn, Me. md. 1 Oct. 1941 at
    Nashua, NH. [AR]

LEIGHTON:
Samuel of Exeter - Mary Lane md. 17 Feb. 1808. [CH]

LEMAN:
Maria L. (34), d/o Jacob B. Johnson - George W. Currier (37), s/o William md.
    15 May 1879. [TR]

LEONHARD:
Elizabeth (23), d/o Philip - Wesley F. Hodgdon (23), s/o Geo. W. md. 1 Apr.
    1892. [TR]

LEWIS:
Anna - John Whitten md. 15 May 1768. [CH]
Annie A. (24) - Herbert Steele (19) md. 17 Nov. 1905. [AR]

LITTLE:

Frank P. (20) of Wakefield, MA. - Lillian A. Page (21) md. 22 Nov. 1902. [AR]

LITTLEFIELD:

Lula M. (29) of Oguaquit, Me. - Willard D. Norton (49) of Brookton, MA. md.
   12 Dec. 1909.

Stephen - Eunice Smith of Seabrook md. 19 June 1836. [CH]

LOCKE:

Aaron R. (23), s/o James - Ona M. Rand, d/o Aaron md. 24 Apr. 1871. [TR]

Albert C. (30), s/o Richard A. - Eliza E. Varrell (25), d/o William md. 24
   June 1868. [TR][CH]

Albert E. (22) - Susie A. Berry (19) md. 4 Apr. 1883. [TR]

Betty - Coffin Page md. 16 Apr. 1783. [CH]

Charles W. (26) - Mary A. Page (18) md. 9 Dec. 1882. [tR]

Coffin H. (64), s/o John - Susan Page (45), d/o John md. 26 Apr. 1865. [TR]

David of Kensington - Elizabeth Sanborn of Hampton Falls md. 1 Sep. 1814.
   [TR][CH]

Deborah - abraham Tilton of Stratham md. 20 Aug. 1795. [CH]

Ellen S. (25) - Anthony W. Frizzell (24) md. 25 Dec. 1890. [TR][AR]

Emma E. (21) - John W. Berry (21), s/o Joseph E. md. 30 Jan. 1889. [TR]

Ethel (21) - George A. Bachelder (20) md. 30 June 1888. [TR]

Hannah - Samuel Rand, both of Portsmouth md. 29 Sep. 1811. [TR][CH]

Jeremiah - Lois Sanborn, both of Seabrook md. 20 Feb. 1800. [CH]

John of Portsmouth - Abigail Dearborn md. Sep. 1800. [CH]

John Wilkes (26), s/o Jesse - Sarah Hannah Randell (24), d/o William md. 23
   Oct. 1872. [TR]

Joseph 4th - Olive Berry, both of Rye md. 4 Aug. 1811. [TR][CH]

Joseph 4th - Sarah W. Wedgwood, both of Rye md. 29 Nov. 1816. [TR][CH]

Locada? - Levi B. Trefethren, both of Rye md. 14 May 1826. [TR][CH]

Lucinda Perkins - Capt. Thomas Chase Jr., both of Seabrook md. 29 Nov. 1830.
   [TR][CH]

Lydia - Edward Gove, both of Seabrook md. 13 June 1798. [CH]

Lydia of Hampton - John Lamprey md. 8 June 1837. [CH]

Mary A. (29) - Bernard C. Small (24) md. 2 July 1921 at Hampton. [AR]

Melvin P. (28) - E. Gertrude Brown (29) of Berwick, ME. md. 29 June 1921 at
   Norwalk, Ct. [AR]

Miriam of Hampton - Dudley Lamprey md. 22 Oct. 1793. [TR]

Patience of Hampton - Perley Bartlett md. 15 Jan. 1818. [TR][CH]

R. Jenness (34) of Rye - Bessie L. Bachelder (23) md. 23 Feb. 1898. [AR]

Samuel - Mary Dearborn md. 3 July 1825. [TR][CH]

LONG:

Paul - Phebe Swain md. 16 July 1784. [CH]

LOVERING:
Anne - William Sanborn of Exeter md. 16 Feb. 1794. [TR]
Ebenezer Jr. - Mehitabel Hardy Marden md. 27 Nov. 1806. [CH]
Ebenezer of Greenland - Clarissa Leavitt md. 23 Nov. 1810. [TR][CH]
Elizabeth of Greenland - Nehemiah Sanborn of Hampton md. 23 July 1837. [CH]
John, Major of Greenland - Sally Leavitt md. 3 July 1814. [TR][CH]
Lydia - Nehemiah Sanborn of Hampton md. 2 Mar. 1797. [CH]
Lydia - Levi Brown md. 17 Nov. 1803. [CH]
Sally of Greenland - John D. Shaw md. 25 July 1810. [TR][CH]
Thomas - Hannah Thurston md. 9 Sep. 1782. [CH]
Thomas, Capt. - Mrs. Miriam Leavitt md. 15 Nov. 1804. [CH]

LOVETT:
Francis S. Jr. (24) - Dorothy L. Eaton (21) of Kingston md. 18 Sep. 1915 at
  Kingston. [AR]
Hazel (21) - John Wm Whenal (25) md. 18 Sep. 1943. [AR]
Leslie L. (24) - Louise K. Lane (28) md. 20 Dec. 1917. [AR]
Roger S. (21) - Lydia M. Davis (17) md. 1 Jan. 1915 at Kensington. [AR]

LOW/LOWE:
John - Betsy Tucker, both of Stratham md. 19 May 1816. [TR][CH]
Virginia (20) - Franklin Smith (23), both of Hampden, Me. md. 6 Dec. 1936.
  [AR]

LOWD:
Joseph of Portsmouth - Abigail Green of Stratham md. June 1779. [CH]

LOWELL:
Benjamin of Portsmouth - Deborah Green of Stratham md. 4 Feb. 1779. [CH]
George G. (23), s/o Oliver C. - Abbie C. Dow (21), d/o Levi md. 30 May 1875.
  [TR]

LOWERY:
William H. (30) of Allston, MA. - Lula E. Moulton (25) md. 15 Apr. 1903. [AR]

LUNN:
Katherine Fowler (35) - Marland Pratt Billing (36) of Roslindale, MA. md. 27
  Apr. 1938. [AR]

LYNCH:
Frances M. (22) - Henry C. Sanborn (26) md. 30 Sep. 1905. [AR]

McCLARY:
Michael of Epson - Sally Dearborn md. Oct. 7 1778. [CH]

McCLURE:
David, Rev. - Hannah Pomery, d/o Rev. Benj. Pomery DD of Hebron, CT. md. 19
  Dec. 1780. [TR]

McDANIEL:
Hattie L. (29), d/o Noah - Charles E. Seavey (34), s/o Joseph md. 21 Nov. 1868. [TR]

McDONALD:
Elizabeth L. (34) of Newport, R.I. - Charles Proschold (50) md. 22 Nov. 1897. [AR]
Lillie (23) - Thomas J. Bachelder (43), s/o Jeremiah md. 19 Oct. 1880. [TR]

McFARLANE:
Eleanor E. (20) - Earle H. Knowles (20) both of Medford, MA. md. 22 Feb. 1920. [AR]

McGRAD:
John H. (25) - Mira B. Batchelder (23) md. 4 June 1865. [TR]

McINTIRE:
Clara L. (28) - William Bridle (33) both of Portsmouth md. 27 July 1899. [AR]

MacKENZIE:
John (27) - Louise A. Tabor (28) md. 3 Nov. 1934. [AR]

MacKINLAY:
Frank L. (35) of Medford, MA. - Edith M. Fenwick (35) md. 1 Dec. 1913. [AR]

McLANE:
William Thos. Jr. (18) of Stratham - Greta Margurite Storm (18) md. 2 June 1938. [AR]

McLAUGHLIN:
Grace (31) - Charles S. Page (33) md. 28 Apr. 1900. [AR]

McLEAN:
John A. (22) - Martha M. Simpson (21) md. 18 Apr. 1915. [AR]

MACE:
Joshua - Sally Qualls, both of Hampton md. 9 Mar. 1795. [CH]
Mary (20), d/o John A. - Clarence Albert Goss (16), s/o Richard P. md. 21 Jan. 1876. [TR]
Nathaniel T. (21) - Hannah J. Robinson (16) of Kingston md. 24 Nov. 1858. [CH]

MACCLINTOCK:
Nancy A. - John Leavitt of Hampton md. 18 Feb. 1819. [TR][CH]

MACK:
George Kennedy (63) - Amy Gertrude Stewart (63) md. 31 May 1939 at Hampton. [AR]

MAHER:
Louise M. (33) of N. Kennebeckport, Me. - Leland L. Blake (32) of Saco, Me. md. 1 June 1937 at Hampton. [AR]

MALENFANT:
Francis (23) of Amesbury - Mary E. Smith (20) of Newburyport md. 1 Feb. 1931. [AR]

MALON(E):
John W. (35), s/o Joseph - Josie E. Hobbs (30), d/o John md. 4 Dec. 1883. [TR]
Morton R. (40) - Mina Crowell (38) both of Everett, MA. md. 12 Aug. 1925. [AR]

MALOON:
Jonathan - Mehitabel Hoyt md. 22 Feb. 1753. [CH]

MANN:
M. Isabell (24) - George H.P. Lane (32) both of Greenland md. 7 Apr. 1894. [TR][AR]
Thelma (23) - Kenneth Gerry Blaney (25) md. 14 June 1941. [AR]

MANSFIELD:
Katie T. (22) - Oliver W. Page (23) md. 30 Oct. 1890. [TR][AR]

MARBLE:
Walter P. (22) of Haverhill - Fannie J. Moore (20) md. 9 Apr. 1902. [AR]

MARCH:
Violet - Cassel Weeks, both of Greenland md. 2 July 1777. [CH]

MARDEN:
Charles F. (38), s/o Richard A. - Eliza E. Varrell (25), d/o William md. 24 June 1868. [TR]
Charles F. (38) - Nellie E. Swan (23) md. 21 Oct. 1868. [TR] (See above?)
Charles T. (24) - Julia L. Brown (25) md. 2 Aug. 1888. [TR]
Isreal of Portsmouth - Sally Tilton of Hampton Falls md. 28 June 1827. [TR][CH]
Mary Jane (30), d/o William - Henry L. Varrill (28), s/o william md. 8 July 1868. [TR][CH]
Mehitabel Hardy - Ebenezer Lovering Jr. md. 27 Nov. 1806. [CH]
Nathaniel - Elizabeth Moulton, both of Rye md. 4 Sep. 1769. [CH]
Olivia (38) - Joseph G. Jenness (60) md. 2 Mar. 1889. [TR]
Polly A. (21), d/o Nathaniel - George G. White (28), s/o Parkman md. 29 Sep. 1869. [TR][CH]

MARSH:
William of Newburyport - Mary H. Brown of Hampton md. 5 Sep. 1831. [CH]

MARSHALL:
Dorothy - Nathaniel Nutter both of Newington md. 8 June 1784. [CH]
John - Mary Perkins, both of Hampton Falls md. 24 Nov. 1825. [TR][CH]
Sally - Gideon Gookin of Portsmouth md. 17 Apr. 1796. [CH]

MARSTON:
Abigail, Mrs. - David Lamprey, both of Hampton md. 20 Dec. 1797. [CH]
Abigail of Hampton - Thomas Sandborn of Exeter md. 17 Aug. 1825. [TR][CH]
Abigail of Dover - George W. Flagg of Warwick, R.I. md. 7 May 1835. [CH]
Abigail - Jacob M. Rowe of Exeter md. 1 Apr. 1838. [CH]
Anna - Moses Lane of Hampton md. 27 May 1791. [CH]
Benjamin, s/o Thos. & Deborah - Mehitable Hobbs, d/o Benj. & Mary md. 26 Jan.
   1737/8. [TR]
Carrie A. (22) - John Whenal (32) md. 20 Nov. 1901. [AR]
Charles C. (29), s/o Thos. L. - Dixie G. Godfrey (24), d/o Albert md. 1 Jan.
   1866. [TR]
Clarence D. (22) - Doris Woodburn (18) of Seabook md. 6 Apr. 1911 at
   Hampton. [AR]
Clarissa - Levi Batchelder md. 24 Oct. 1837. [CH]
Comfort, Mrs. - Cotton W. Marston md. 18 Apr. 1811. [TR][CH]
Cotton W. - Mrs. Comfort Marston md. 18 Apr. 1811. [TR][CH]
Curtis Dearborn (25) - Louise Webb (21) md. 7 Dec. 1939 at N. Berwick, Me.
   [AR]
Daniel, s/o Simon & Hannah - Anne Winget, d/o Joshua & Mary md. 13 Nov. 1733.
   [TR]
Daniel, s/o Simon & Hannah - Sarah Clough, d/o Samuel & Sarah md. 30 Dec.
   1735. [TR]
Daniel - Mary Smith md. 28 May 1789. [TR]
David - Mary Page md. 4 Apr. 1782. [CH]
Dearborn - Sally Batchelder md. 27 Nov. 1805. [CH]
Deborah - Edward Lang of Exeter md. 8 Apr. 1824. [TR][CH]
E. Everett (31) - Effie L. Crowell (27) md. 9 Sep. 1906 at Greenland. [AR]
Easter - William Norton md. 10 Sep. 1788. [TR]
Edward S. (28) - Adeline S. Burleigh (21) md. 27 July 1902. [AR]
Elizabeth - John Pike of Hampton Falls md. Nov. 1797. [CH]
Elisabeth - David Fogg md. 17 Aug. 1828. [TR][CH]
Elisabeth - Levi Jewell Esqr of Stratham md. 11 Sep. 1834. [TR][CH]
Elizabeth - James R. Leavitt md. 4 Sep. 1836, [CH]
Emily A. (23), d/o James - Samuel A. Dow (22), s/o Samuel md. 29 Dec. 1869.
   [TR]
Ephraim - Hannah Roby md. 22 Dec. 1799. [CH]
Fanny - Moses L. Hobbs md. 12 Aug. 1829. [TR][CH]
Grace H. (23) - Jeremiah H. Merrill (27) md. 19 Feb. 1903 at Boston. [AR]
George A. (46) - Carrie A. Drake (38) of Hampton md. 13 Oct. 1897. [AR]

MARSTON Cont.

Hannah - Levi Jewell, of Stratham md. 13 June 1809. [TR][CH]

Hannah of Hampton - Samuel Garland md. 24 Oct. 1833. [TR][CH]

Harry C. (27) - Mabel J. Dearborn (20) of Hampton md. 8 Nov. 1910. [AR]

Hatie F. (26), d/o James - Allan Fenwick (26), s/o E.B. md. 1 Mar. 1878. [TR]

Herman L. (37) - Fannie A. Rollins (36) md. 18 Sep. 1902. [AR]

Irving Wilson (68) - Louise Barbara Knowles (56) md. 30 Dec. 1940 at Hampton. [AR]

Jeremiah - Nabby Marston md. 15 Aug. 1808. [TR][CH]

Jeremiah - Mary Hobbs md. 4 July 1814. [TR][CH]

Jessie H. (39) of Brookline - Orice J. Moulton (36) md. 1 Oct. 1899. [AR]

Jonathan - Mary Leavitt md. 24 Sep. 1792. [TR]

Jonathan - Molly Philbrick of Hampton md. Dec. 1793. [TR]

Lavinia - Simon Fogg md. 22 Jan. 1839. [CH]

Leota (23) of Hampton - Rex C. Perkins (23) md. 23 Dec. 1916 at Hampton. [AR]

Levi - Abigail Fogg md. 12 July 1781. [CH]

Levi - Mary Lamprey md. 4 Feb. 1837. [CH]

Lucinda - Daniel Dow or Downs md. 9 Jan. 1821. [TR][CH]

Lucy E. (23), d/o James Carwell - John N. Sanborn (35), s/o Levi md. 4 Dec. 1878. [TR]

Lula E. (24) - Walter T. Parshley (25) md. 26 May 1910. [AR]

Lydia - Samuel Dearborn Jr. md. 2 Aug. 1818. [TR]

Lydia of Hampton - Joseph Moulton md. 8 May 1837. [CH]

Mary - Simon Garland md. 16 Jan. 1793 by Samuel Shepard of Brentwood. [TR]

Mary A. (24) - John P Elkins of Hampton md. 15 Sep. 1851. [CH]

Mary B. (18) - Frank C. Murrey (23) md. 30 Apr. 1887. [TR]

Mary C. - Reuben L. Moulton md. 4 Nov. 1844. [CH]

Mary L. (31), d/o James - Otis B. French (44), s/o David md. 1 Jan. 1879. [TR]

Merenim - Jonathan Towle of Hampton md. 21 Jan. 1773. [CH]

Minsonni (27) - Charles E. Davis (26) md. 2 Dec. 1860. [TR]

Molly - Nathan Barker of Greenland md. 4 Oct. 1770. [CH]

Molly - John Lamprey md. 28 Apr. 1773. [CH]

Molly Wedgwood - Josiah Hobbs md. 8 Jan. 1786. [CH]

N. Dearborn (30) - Sarah Dodge Curtis (31) md. 31 Jan. 1893. [TR][AR]

Nabby - Jeremiah Marston md. 15 Aug. 1808. [TR][CH]

Nancy - Winthrop Rowe of Kensington md. 28 Feb. 1798. [CH]

Nancy J., Mrs. (53), d/o Thos. Felch - Moses L. Hobbs (57), s/o Moses md. 12 June 1895. [TR][AR]

Norman Edward (19) - Gertrude Mae Durant (18) of Hampton md. 25 June 1938 at Hampton. [AR]

Norman O. (25) - Letitia M. Mason (22) of Amesbury md. 15 Jan. 1931 at Amesbury. [AR]

Orrin C. (55) - Ida L. Fogg (48) md. 12 Mar. 1904. [AR]

Polly - John Cotton, both of Hampton md. 7 July 1818. [TR][CH]

Rebecca P. (20), d/o Levi - John L. Smith (25), s/o Christopher md. 14 Nov. 1860. [TR][CH]

MARSTON Cont.

Reuben - Mary Batchelder md. 28 Mar. 1745. [TR]
Richard E. (20) - Arlene E. Inglis (17) md. 28 Aug. 1943. [AR]
Robay of Stratham - Hannah Drake of Hampton md. 4 Jan. 1788. [CH]
Sally E. - Jonathan R. Jenness of Rye md. 4 Jan. 1788. [CH]
Sarah of Stratham - James Godfrey md. 17 Dec. 1767. [CH]
Sarah - Josiah Page of Eastown md. 29 June 1774. [CH]
Sarah of Hampton - Benjamin Tilton of Hampton Falls md. 9 Mar. 1819. [TR][CH]
Sarah L. (18) - Joseph E. Leavitt (21) md. 24 Dec. 1889. [TR]
Sheldon L. (27) - Georgie E. Garland (37) md. 12 Jan. 1915. [AR]
Sherburne (53), s/o Simon & Charlotte - Olive J. Carston (40), d/o Elisha &
    Elizabeth md. 25 Apr, 1865. [TR]
Simeon - Elizabeth Dearborn md. 13 sep. 1770. [CH]
Simeon - Abihar Leavitt md. 14 Mar. 1798. [CH]
Simon - Charlotte Dalton md. 31 Mar. 1811. [TR]
Sophia E. (25) - George O. Taylor (26) md. 26 Dec. 1885. [TR]
Thomas Jr. - Hannah Knowles md. 9 Dec. 1783. [CH]
Thomas C. (26), s/o Benj. - Margaret A. Dow (26), d/o George md. 4 Jan. 1869.
    [TR]
Thomas Franklin (25) - Elizabeth Abigail Batchelder (23) md. 6 Oct. 1850.
    [CH]
Thomas S. (21), s/o George F. - Emily J. Welsh (19), d/o Samuel md. 6 Oct.
    1880. [TR]
Winthrop Jr. of Brentwood - Anna Folsom of Newmarket md. July/Aug. 1778. [CH]

MASON:

Benjamin - Margaret Leah md. 18 July 1771. [CH]
Date H. of Hampton - William D. Goss of Rye md. 16 May 1824. [TR][CH]
Elizabeth of Hampton - Samuel Moulton md. 17 may 1770. [CH]
John W. (38), s/o Joseph - Josie E. Hobbs (30), d/o John md. 5 Dec. 1883.
    [TR]
Letitia M. (22) of Amesbury, MA. - Norman O. Marston (25) md. 15 Jan. 1931 at
    Amesbury. [AR]
Love, Mrs. - Simon Dow md. 23 Nov. 1788. [CH]
Margaret - Joseph Taylor md. 14 Mar. 1811. [TR][CH]

MASSEY:

Marion (22) of Shrewsbury, MA. - Arthur R. Moore (30) of Boylston, MA. md. 3
    July 1932 at Nashua. [AR]

MATHERS:

Harry A. (42) of Rockland, Me. - Maud E. Barton (28) md. 15 Nov. 1916 at
    Portsmouth. [AR]

MATTHEWS:

Betsy - William Warner md. 24 July 1806. [CH]

MAXIM:
Harry Wallace (20) - Margueritte Rosella Doucet (22) both of Lewiston, Me.
md. 3 July 1928. [AR]

MAY:
Bessie A. (20) - W. Francis Doliber (22) of W. Lebanon, Me. md. 19 May 1917.
[AR]

MAYNARD:
John (59), s/o John - Mrs. Abbie L. Hobbs (45), d/o Reuben Lamprey md. 9 June
1877. [TR]

MEAD:
Lucy - Joshua Harford, both of Newmarket md. 5 Oct. 1794. [TR]

MEADER:
Florence Hazel (40) - Andrew Paulson (62) md. 21 Oct. 1941. [AR]

MERRILL:
Abigail - John Currier Jr. md. 28 Oct. 1756. [CH]
Betsey - Thomas J. Goodwin md. 8 Dec. 1755. [CH]
Jeremiah H. (27) - Grace H. Marston (23) md. 19 Feb. 1903 at Boston. [AR]
Jesse - Betty Pifield, both of Stratham md. 7 Nov. 1781. [CH]
Priscilla Louise (20) - Olton Rader Bennehoff (32) of Ohio md. 15 Dec. 1928.
[AR]

METRICK:
Veronica (14) of Portsmouth - Gilman Morrill Moulton (27) md. 1 Nov. 1940 at
Portsmouth. [AR]

MEVIS:
Martin F. (53) - Flora M. Garland (35) md. 17 June 1911. [AR]

MEYER:
Anna (44) - Alfred Zapff (33) of W. Roxbury md. 13 Mar. 1935. [AR]

MEYERHOFF:
Blanche (22) of Chelsea, MA. - Hyman J. Gretsky (24) of Dorcester md. 10 Oct.
1933. [AR]

MILES:
Obediah of Wheelock, Vt. - Betsy Pease of Newmarket md. 3 Jan. 1805. [CH]

MILLER:
Ruth H. (36) of Medford, MA. - William P. Fowler (35) md. 8 Dec. 1935. [AR]

MILLIKEN:
Octivia L. (20) - George A. Booth (20) md. 30 Oct. 1895. [AR]

MILLS:
Richard of Portsmouth - Hannah Peverly md. 21 Aug. 1773. [CH]

MITCHELL:
Robert L. (29) - Mina E. Rand (21) md. 1 Feb. 1894. [TR]

MOE:
Ida K. (17), d/o Ephraim - Andrew H. (21), s/o Andrew J. md. 23 Dec. 1878.
   [TR]

MOODY:
Margaret H. (33) of L.A., Calif. - Alfred H. Balsley (33) of Reidsville, NC
   md. 11 July 1925. [AR]

MOORE:
Anna - Nathaniel Stevens md. 21 Jan. 1768. [CH]
Arthur R. (30) of Boylston, MA. - Marion Massey (22) of Shrewsbury, MA. md. 3
   July 1932 at Nashua. [AR]
Christopher T. (64) - Abby C. Odiorne (64) md. 28 June 1887. [TR]
Elizabeth - Richard Sinclair md. 26 Aug. 1771. [CH]
Fannie J. (20) - Walter P. Marble (22) of Haverhill md. 9 Apr. 1902. [AR]
Hannah - Reuben Leavitt, both of Stratham md. 13 Dec. 1781. [CH]
John Jr. of Stratham - Sarah Ann Parker md. 30 Dec. 1830. [TR][CH]
Marion Elizabeth (21) of Boylston, MA. - John James Kapish Jr. (22) md. 19
   May 1940. [AR]
Martha of Stratham - Jeremiah Palmer md. 2 Jan. 1784. [TR][CH]
Nancy B., Mrs. - John Chapman md. 3 Jan. 1865. [TR]
Olive Annette (23) - Brandon Kenneth Knowles (24) md. 12 Nov. 1941. [AR]
Peter - Abigail Leavitt md. 3 Nov. 1805. [CH]
Roger J. (26) - Mary A. Joyce (23) md. 23 Sep. 1917. [AR]

MORRILL:
Edmund (49) of Salisbury, Mass. - Mrs. Abigail Brown (38) md. 8 Apr. 1857.
   [CH]
Hannah, widow - Abraham Brown md. 24 Dec. 1755. [CH]
Jacob of So. Hampton - Mary Jenness of Rye md. 22 Sep. 1768. [CH]
Micajah - Hannah Taylor, both of Hampton md. 1 Sep. 1778. [CH]
Moses - Miriam Currier md. 18 Feb. 1755. [CH]
Theophilus - Sarah Barnard md. 25 Dec. 1755. [CH]

MORSE:
Grace L. (18) of Hampton - Lewis A. Chavalier (20) md. 6 Oct. 1902. [AR]
Nancy B. Baker, d/o Joseph - John Chapman (62), s/o Martha md. 3 Jan. 1865.
   [TR]

NORTON:
Muriel Gertrude (23) of Portsmouth - Clinton Breed Norton (38) md. 20 Apr.
    1929 at Portsmouth. [AR]
Muriel Gertrude (36) of Boston - Roy Emery Fogg (47) md. 22 Aug. 1941 at
    Hampstead. [AR]

MOULTON:
Abigail of Raymond - Lt. Daniel Page of (E.K.) md. 25 Apr. 1813. [CH]
Abigail K. - Joseph Young, both of Hampton md. 25 May 1823. [TR[[CH]
Ada E. (37) - Carroll W. Fogg (42) md. 22 July 1922 of Hampton. [AR]
Bethiah - Jonathan Smith of Rye md. 3 Dec. 1772. [CH]
Cora Jane (21), d/o Samuel - George Henry Brown (21), s/o Langdon md. 21 Dec.
    1876. [TR]
Dolly - Moses True both of Seabrook md. 17 Mar. 1755. [CH]
Elizabeth of Rye - Nathaniel Marden of Rye md. 4 Sep. 1769. [CH]
Elisabeth of Stratham - Noah Randlet md. 25 Apr. 1819. [TR][CH]
Elizabeth - Noah Randlet, both of Stratham md. 25 Apr. 1819. [TR]
Emily J. (26) - Fred E. Gravelle (28) md. 3 May 1910. [AR]
Ernest J. (24) - Harriet Goss (22) of Rye md. 1 June 1910 at Rye. [AR]
Erwin B. (25) - Maude A. Dalton (26) md. 5 Feb. 1908. [AR]
Esther - William Norton of Greenland md. 20 Dec, 1788. [CH]
Esther S. (22), d/o David P. - Fred W. Berry (21), s/o John C. md. 5 June
    1876. [TR]
Eunice, Mrs. - Josiah Dow, both of Hampton md. 29 Apr. 1835. [CH]
Fannie P. (20) - Fred C. Leavitt (20) md. 23 May 1894. [AR][TR]
Frank Hamilton (22) - Yvone Rose Alma Butler (18) md. 11 May 1929 at
    Waterville, Me. [AR]
Freeman T. (24), s/o John - Amy A. Brown (20), d/o Adam md. 1 Jan. 1880. [TR]
Gilman H. (22) - Luella M. Brown (24) md. 18 Oct. 1883. [TR]
Gilman M. (20) - Doris P. Spackman (18) of Rye md. 6 May 1934 at Rye. [AR]
Gilman Morrill (27) - Veronia Metrick (14) of Portsmouth md. 1 Nov. 1940 at
    Portsmouth. [AR]
Grace L. (18) of Hampton - Lewis A. Chevalier (20) md. 6 Oct. 1902. [AR]
Horace A. (25), s/o David - Annie M. Feely md 8 June 1882 [TR]
Iola Ellis (24) of Wells River, Vt. - Glenn Warren Blair (30) of Bath, NH md.
    17 May 1941 at Woodsville. [AR]
Jacob - Phebe M. Palmer, both of Hampton md. 3 July 1825. [CH]
James - Phebe Palmer md. 21 Feb. 1787. [TR]
James F. - Annie L. Lamprey md. 1878. [TR]
John (26) - Eliza Fogg (21) md. 10 Dec. 1861. [CH]
John B. (26) - Elizabeth Godfrey (27) md. 24 Dec. 1895. [TR][AR]
John B. (36) - Sarah W. Fairfield (25) of Greenland md. 3 June 1905 at
    Greenland. [AR]
Joseph Jr. - Sarah Godfrey md. 26 Jan. 1773. [CH]
Joseph - Phebe H. Palmer, both of Hampton md. 3 July 1825. [TR]
Joseph - Lydia Marston md. 8 May 1837. [CH]
Josephine E. (19) of Kittery - Cyrus R. Bartlett (23) md. 20 Nov. 1902. [AR[

MOULTON Cont.

Lila C. (24) - Wilbur S. Drew (20) md. 19 Apr. 1919 at Hampton. [AR]

Lula E. (25) - William H. Lowery (30) of Allston, MA. md. 15 Apr. 1903. [AR]

Lydia Frances of Exeter - Abraham R. Warner md. 25 Dec. 1849. [CH]

Mabel W. (19) of York, Me. - Joel H. Perkins (23) of Wells, Me. md. 31 Dec. 1904. [AR]

Mae R. (27) - Rudolph Johnson (28) of Roslindale md. 14 Oct. 1914. [AR]

Maud D. (39) - Roy E. Fogg (26) md. 10 Oct. 1920 at Hampton. [AR]

Nellie E. (21) - Charles C. White (23) of Hampton md. 28 Nov. 1906. [AR]

Nellie F. (18), d/o Curtis - George W. Tarlton (25), s/o Nathaniel md. 22 Dec. 1878, [TR]

Oliver D. (26), s/o David P. - Jennie G. Lamprey (26), d/o Thos. L. md. 1 Jan. 1878. [TR]

Oliver D. (34) - Lizzie H. Sleeper (21) md. 12 Nov. 1885. [TR]

Orice J. (36) - Jessie H. Marston (39) of brookline md. 1 Oct. 1899. [AR]

Prentice F. (22) - Eleanor C. Bachelder (20) md. 3 Nov. 1933. [AR]

Russell D. (20) - Edythe S. Coffin (23) of Hampton md. 4 Jan. 1911 at Hampton. [AR]

Reuben L. - Mary C. Marston md. 4 Nov. 1844. [CH]

Sally - Huntington Porter md. 30 Mar. 1797. [CH]

Samuel - Elizabeth Mason md. 17 May 1770. [CH]

Sarah of Hampton - Ebenezer Tilton of Hampton Falls md. 4 July 1771. [CH]

Sarah M. - William Deming md. 9 Nov. 1878. [TR]

Simeon - Betsy Philbrock md. 18 Feb. 1793. [TR]

Thomas F. (17) - Frances M. Smith (18) of Waterboro, Me. md. 25 Dec. 1917 at Waterboro. [AR]

Warren B. (29) - Elvira B. Briggs (22) md. 3 Sep. 1891. [TR][AR]

William - Molly Page Int. 9 Oct. 1797. [NHA]

Willie E. (21), s/o Daniel G. - Annie C. Remery (19), d/o Albion md. 28 Nov. 1877. [TR]

MUDGET:

Samuel of Gilmonton - Hannah French md. 9 Mar. 1817. [CH]

MURREY:

Elda Carrie (28) - Ernest Wm Riley (42) md. 28 Sep. 1938 at Hampton. [AR]

Frank C. (23) - Mary B. Marston (18) md. 30 Apr. 1887. [TR]

Samuel of Rye - Hannah Dalton md. 4 May 1769. [CH]

Thomas E. (22) - Mildred A. Carpenter (20) md. 3 Mar. 1935 at Hampton. [AR]

MYRICK:

Gladys L. (20) of Portsmouth - Howard M. James (35) md. 12 Aug. 1922. [AR]

NYSEN:

Anna J. (22) of Boston - Jonas T. Downing (21) md. 1 Nov. 1911. [AR]

NAVES:
Harry A. (36) - Mary A. Lamprey (28) md. 21 June 1937 at Hampton. [AR]

NEAL:
Anna - Phineas Dearborn md. 4 May 1771. [CH]
Eliphalet of Merrimack - Mary Peavy md. 9 Aug. 1770. [CH]
Elizabeth - John Clark of Stratham md. 16 Dec. 1773. [CH]
Minerva - George W. Jefts md. 16 Aug. 1840. [CH]
Sophia W. Capt. Samuel Leavitt md. 10 Jan. 1819. [TR][CH]

NELSON:
Augusta J. (29) of Middleton, MA. - Cortlandt R. Crowley (41) of Topsfield,
MA. md. 20 June 1937. [AR]

NESBITT:
Margaret E. (19) of Exeter - Hayden M. Brown (22) md. 27 May 1932 at Exeter.
[AR]
Viva M. (19) of Exeter - Herbert T. Brown (25) of S. Hampton md. 17 Feb. 1931
at Exeter. [AR]

NEWCOMB:
Francis J. of Quincy, Mass. - Abigail C. Roby md. 31 Aug. 1848. [CH]

NEWMAN:
Daniel of Newburyport - Hannah Brown md. 26 Dec. 1811. [TR][CH]
Thomas of Portsmouth - Betsey Knowles md. 18 June 1812. [TR][CH]

NICHOLS:
Ezra Jr. - Waity G. Brown, both of Seabrook md. 4 July 1814. [TR][CH]

NOOD:
Mary - Josiah Robie md. 1787. [TR]

NORRIS:
Samuel - Jean Dennet, both of Portsmouth md. 23 Mar. 1812. [TR] [CH]

NORTON:
Abigail of Portsmouth - Simon Garland of Rye md. 20 Apr. 1783. [CH]
Annie M. (41) of York - William L. Staples (41) of S. Framington, MA. md. 14
Apr. 1909. [AR]
Clinton Breed (38) - Muriel Gertrude Morton (23) of Portsmouth md. 20 Apr.
1929 at Portsmouth. [AR]
Eliza of Portsmouth - Joseph Odiorne of Rye md. 17 Dec. 1818. [TR]
Frank C. (34) - Abbie T. Breed (19) md. 24 dec. 1888. [TR]
Gertrude A. (21), d/o Joshua - Edward H. Haines (24), s/o Thos. md. 10 Dec.
1884. [TR]
Herman L. (23) - Mary E. Young (28) of Deerfield md. 25 Oct. 1916 at Hampton.
[AR]

NORTON Cont.

Ida L. (18), d/o Joshua - Emery Fogg (21), s/o Simon md. 15 Nov. 1873. [TR]

John - Ruth Heath, both of Stratham md. 28 Sep. 1823. [TR][CH]

Jonathan of Chester - Susanna Towle md. 22 Jan. 1788. [CH]

Lizzie E.W. (25), d/o Nathan - Alonzo J. Smith (25), s/o Jonathan md. 16 Apr. 1868. [TR]

Mabel Elizabeth (24) - Joseph W. Hoyt (22) of Portsmouth md. 6 Feb. 1943 at Ypsilanti, Mich. [AR]

Nelson J. (19) - Mae C. Knowles (18) md. 22 Aug. 1889. [TR]

Nelson J. (28), s/o Joshua - Susie E. Goodwin (21), d/o David L. md. 22 Jan. 1899. [TR]

Willard D. (49) of Brockton, MA. - Lulu M. Littlefield (29) of Ogunquit, Me. md. 12 Dec. 1909. [AR]

William of Greenland - Esther Moulton md. 20 Dec. 1786. [CH]

William - Easter Marston md. 10 Sep. 1788. [TR]

NOYES:

Benjamin - Sarah Wing, widow md. 2 June 1756, [CH]

NUDD:

Betty - Simeon Dearborn md. 14 Dec. 1794. [CH]

David - Sarah Smith md. 17 June 1793. [TR]

David - Sarah Godfree md. 18 Dec. 1814. [TR][CH]

Eliza - Sewell Brown of Hampton Falls md. 20 Sep. 1821. [TR][CH]

Lydia - Nathan Dearborn md. 10 Nov. 1813. [TR][CH]

Philip G. - Sarah A. Redman, both of Hampton md. 21 July 1846. [CH]

Ruth - Amos Cilley of Hampton md. 26 Jan. 1809. [TR][CH]

Thomas - Susanna Brown both of Hampton md. 28 Oct. 1793. [CH]

Thomas - Nabby Towle, both of Hampton md. 12 Nov. 1812. [TR][CH]

NUTTER:

Abigail of Greenland - John Green md. 17 June 1807. [CH]

Betsey of Stratham - Jonathan Smith md. 8 Mar. 1820. [TR][CH]

Henry - Elizabeth Whidden md. 28 Feb. 1796. [CH]

Mary - Samuel Davis md. 8 Sep. 1819. [TR][CH]

Nathaniel - Dorothy Marshall, both of Newington md. 8 June 1784. [CH]

ODELL:

Rebecca A. - M. Otis Hall, both of Greenland md. 18 May 1847. [CH]

ODIORNE:

Abby C. (64) - Christopher T. Moore (64) md. 28 June 1887. [TR]

Joseph of Rye - Eliza Norton of Portsmouth md. 17 Dec. 1818. [TR]

ODLIN:

John F. - Judith French, both of Exeter md. 11 Aug. 1828. [TR][CH]

PACHERING: Pickering?
Sarah of Greenland - Berjamin Darborn md. 14 Oct. 1792. [TR]

PAGE:
Benjamin of Rochester - Betty/Betsy Hobbs md. 17 Feb. 1788. [TR][CH]
Benjamin - Mary Hobbs md. 30 May 1816. [TR][CH]
Betty - Noah Page md. 13 Jan. 1806. [CH]
Charles S. (33) - Grace McLaughlin (31) md. 28 Apr. 1900. [AR]
Coffin - Betty Locke md. 16 Apr. 1783. [CH]
Daisy A. (23) - James E.G. Downing (26) of Newcastle md. 11 Nov. 1891.
    [TR][AR]
Daniel, Lt. (of E.K.) - Abigail Moulton (of Raymond) md. 25 Apr. 1815. [CH]
Deborah - John Dow Jr. md. 10 Dec. 1807 by Elias Smith. [TR]
Deborah U. - Ransom Fogg md. 22 Oct. 1848. [CH]
Dudley - Betsy Weeks md. 25 Dec. 1787 or 15 Jan. 1788. [TR][CH]
Eleanor - William Brown Clough md. 24 Sep. 1751. [CH]
Eliza A. (27), d/o Avi - James J. Gove (27), s/o Sheldon, both of Raymond md.
    4 Aug. 1860. [TR][CH]
Eliza D. - Enoch Hersey of Newburyport md. 21 Apr. 1852. [CH]
Ellen Addie (24), d/o Joseph - William Ray Puman? (41), s/o Stephen md. 26
    Feb. 1874. [TR]
Ephraim - Hannah Currier md. 15 Dec. 1753. [CH]
George A. (27), s/o David J. - Lydia F. Hart (25), d/o Henry md. 5 Jan. 1875.
    [TR]
Isadore (20), d/o Simon D. - George L. Garland (21), s/o Samuel md. 21 Apr.
    1874. [TR]
John of Hampton - Betsy Tuck of Brentwood md. 16 Mar. 1817. [TR][CH]
Josiah of Eastown - Sarah Marston md. 29 June 1774. [CH]
Lillian A. (21) - Frank P. Little (20) of Wakefield, MA. md. 22 Nov. 1902.
    [AR]
Martha E. (28) - George G. Carter (24) md. 6 Jan. 1904. [AR]
Mary - Benjamin Brown md. 18 Feb. 1768. [CH]
Mary - Clement Emery of Orford md. 23 Apr. 1771. [CH]
Mary - David Marston md. 4 Apr. 1782. [CH]
Mary A. (18) - Charles W. Locke (26) md. 9 Dec. 1882. [TR]
Molly - Simeon Philbrick of Hampton Falls md. 17 Dec. 1794. [TR][CH]
Molly - William Moulton Int. 9 Oct. 1797. [NHA]
Noah - Betty Page md. 13 Jan. 1806. [CH]
Oliver W. (23) - Katie T. Mansfield (22) md. 30 Oct. 1890. [TR][AR]
Reuben - Phebe Dow, both of Hampton md. 26 Dec. 1811. [TR][CH]
Rhoda - Samuel Fogg md. 22 July 1805. [CH]
Samuel - Mary Godfree of Hampton md. 17 Oct. 1819. [TR][CH]
Stephen - Eliza Dow md. 24 June 1813. [TR][CH]
Stephen - Eliza Wortham md. 28 Aug. 1823. [TR][CH]
Susan (45), d/o John - Coffin H. Tuck (64), s/o John of Brentwood md. 26 Apr.
    1865. [TR]

PAIPER: Piper?

Nathaniel of Stratham - Hannah Smith md. 1787. [TR]

PALMER:

Addie J. (16), d/o John M. - Uri A. Lane (21), s/o William md. 6 Sep. 1877. [TR]

Annie (20), d/o John M. - Emmons L. Brown (24), s/o Abel T. md. 27 Nov. 1787. [TR]

Deborah of Hampton - Joshua Shaw md. 17 Nov. 1771. [CH]

Hannah - John Blak, both of Hampton md. 7 Nov. 1792. [TR]

Jeremiah - Martha Moore of Stratham md. 2 Jan. 1784. [TR][CH]

John - Mary Godfrey of Hampton md. 27 Oct. 1824. [TR][CH]

Jonathan - Sally Lamprey, both of Hampton md. 20 Mar. 1825. [TR][CH]

Mary - Micall Dalton, both of Hampton md. 20 Mar. 1825. [CH]

Phebe - James Molton md. 21 Feb. 1787. [TR]

Phebe M. - Joseph Moulton, both of Hampton md. 3 July 1825. [TR][CH]

Samuel - Mary Ann Williams, both of Hampton Falls md. 17 Oct. 1824. [TR][CH]

Susan (20), d/o John M. - Emmons L. Beacon (24), s/o Abel md. 20 ___ 1878. [TR]

PARKER:

Lucy - Nathaniel Dearborn md. 11 Sep. 1810. [TR][CH]

Sarah Ann - John Moore Jr. of Stratham md. 30 Dec. 1830. [TR][CH]

Susannah - Capt. Enoch G. Parrot, both of Portsmouth md. 29 Jan. 1809. [TR][CH]

Washington of Quincy, Mass. - Mary E.A. Roby md. 22 Mar. 1848. [CH]

William of Portsmouth - Bathsheba Robie md. 28 June 1808. [TR]

William Edwin (20) of Stratham - Mary Elizabeth Hobbs (19) md. 26 Mar. 1939. [AR]

PARKS:

Walter Everett (32) of Gloucester - Dawn Elizabeth Seavey (26) md. 6 Aug. 1927. [AR]

PARROT:

Capt Enoch - Susannah Parker, both of Portsmouth md. 29 Jan. 1809. [TR][CH]

PARSHLEY:

Walter T. (25) - Lulu E. Marston (24) md. 26 May 1910. [AR]

PASCHEL:

Grace Althea (19) of Jefferson, NH - Leon Marvin Knowles Jr. md. 4 Dec. 1938. [AR]

PAUL:

Gladys I. (27) - Edward P. Sadler (43) md. 21 July 1943 at Seabrook. [AR]

PAULSON:
Andrew (62) - Florence Hazel Meader (40) md. 21 Oct. 1941. [AR]

PAYNE:
Seibert A. (35) of Boston - Emma E. Wilson (34) md. 28 June 1914. [AR]

PEARSON:
Albert C. (33) - Alice M. Bellow (33) of Hampton Falls md. 6 Nov. 1932 at
   Exeter. [AR]
George H. of Saugus, Mass. - Lucasta Dearborn md. Apr. 1856. [CH]

PEASE:
Betsy of Newmarket - Obadiah Miles of Wheelock, Vt. md. 3 Jan. 1805. [CH]

PEAVY:
Mary - Eliphalet Neal of Merrimack md. 9 Aug. 1770. [CH]

PELTON:
Edith W. (26) of Winchester, MA. - Evan D. Brown (28) md. 8 June 1931 at
   Cambridge, MA. [AR]

PENMAN:
Ether (27) - Bertha E. Allen (24) md. 22 Sep. 1933. [AR]

PERKINS:
David of Hampton - Asenath H. Batchelder md. 1 Mar. 1825. [TR][CH]
Edgar G. (21), s/o George - Edith G. Bachelder (18), d/o Thos. md. 27 Oct.
   1883. [TR]
Green of Seabrook - Irene H. Fogg of Kensington md. 22 June 1831. [CH]
James of Hampton - Sarah Rand of Rye md. 23 July 1824. [TR][CH]
Joanna M. of Hampton - Capt. George L. Brown of Hampton Falls md. 7 Nov.
   1849. [CH]
Joel H. (23) of Wells, Me. - Mabel W. Moulton (19) of York, Me. md. 31 Dec.
   1904. [AR]
Jonathan - Miriam True md. 11 Dec. 1752. [CH]
Josiah of Rye - Betsy Batchelder md. 13 Sep. 1807. [CH]
Mary - John Marshall, both of Hampton Falls md. 24 Nov. 1825. [TR]]CH]
Nancy - Morris Hobbs, both of Hampton md. 8 Jan. 1833. [TR][CH]
Percy T. (22) - Emma F. Coleman (23) md. 25 Oct. 1913 at Greenland. [AR]
Rex G. (35) of Boston - Leota Marston (23) of Hampton md. 23 Dec. 1916 at
   Hampton. [AR]
Sally - Jeremiah Godfree, both of Hampton Falls md. 15 Nov. 1826. [TR][CH]
Sally of Seabrook - Adoniram George of Hampton md. 13 May 1827. [TR][CH]
Susy G. (19) - Frank E. Berry (26) md 27 June 1904 at Hampton. [AR]

PETERSON:
Wolberg (46) of W. Watertown, MA. - Frank E. Berry (47) md. 21 Oct. 1935 at
   Portsmouth. [AR]

PEVERLY:
Hannah - Richard Mills, both of Portsmouth md. 21 Aug. 1825. [CH]

PHENNEY:
Samuel B. - Christian Gardner, both of Portsmouth md. 6 June 1825. [TR][CH]

PHILBRICK:
Adeline S. - William S. Rand, both of Rye md. 12 July 1846. [CH]
Benjamin - Abigail Brown md. 4 Oct. 1794. [TR]
Betsy B. - John Y. Remick, both of Rye md. 17 Feb. 1825. [TR][CH]
Charles W. (46), s/o David - Sarah E. Taylor (31), d/o J. Jenness md. 20 Nov.
    1895. [TR][AR]
Cornnelius O. (24), s/o Oliver B. - Mary P. Powers (24), d/o George md. 3
    Sep. 1876. [TR]
Eliza J. (20), d/o Joseph - Wilfred J. Chambers (24), s/o Lewis md. 14 Apr.
    1880. [TR]
Eliza P. (37) - James W. Barton (34) md. 9 May 1888. [TR]
Frank A. (31) - Lizzie B. Hill (21) md. 12 Dec. 1881. [TR]
Frank H. (21) - Dora B. Crowell (18) md. 12 Dec. 1900. [AR]
Frank M. (20), s/o Rufus Wm - Mellisie Hannah Jenness (19), d/o Isaac md. 22
    Apr. 1872. [TR]
J. Warren (28) - Janice S. Berry (22) md. 29 Oct. 1883. [TR]
John Jr. - Hannah Godfree, both of Hampton md. 4 July 1814. [TR][CH]
Joseph Jr. of Hampton - Mary Fogg md. 14 May 1782. [CH]
Katie E. (19) - Samuel R. Dalton (24) md. 29 Oct. 1890. [TR][AR]
Lamira (40), d/o Daniel - Thomas J. Knowles (40), s/o David md. 12 Dec. 1882.
    [TR]
Leonard P. (26) - Florence L. Dudley (25) of Wakefield md. 23 Oct. 1920 at
    Union. [AR]
Maria G. (33) of Portsmouth - George L. Seavey (50) md. 2 Oct. 1925 at
    Newton, MA. [AR]
Molly of Hampton - Jonathan Marston md. Dec. 1793. [TR]
Reuben of Rye - Mary Wedgwood md. 22 Dec. 1772. [CH]
Sally - John Cotton md. 22 July 1805. [CH]
Sally - Benjamin Garland 3d, both of Rye md. 24 July 1817. [TR]
Samuel Jr. of Effingham - Polly Lang md. 7 Dec. 1815. [TR][CH]
Shubal - Lucy Haines md. 25 Dec. 1786. [CH]
Simeon - Molly Page of Hampton Falls md. 17 Dec. 1794. [TR][CH]
Thomas of Rye - Clarissa Shaw of Hampton md. 11 Aug. 1822. [TR][CH]
Titus of Rye - Abigail Allen of Greenland md. 22 Oct. 1767. [CH]
Walter S. (27), s/o Rufus - Emma L. Brown (26), d/o Abel L. md. 14 Dec. 1882.
    [TR]
Wilma L. (31) - Fred A. Todd (43) of Detroit md. 26 Oct. 1931 at Hampton.
    [AR]

PHILBROOK:
Betsy - Simeon Molton md. 19 Feb. 1793. [TR]
Harlan L. (23) - Annie W. Jenness (20) md. 20 June 1883. [TR]
Henry M. - Rebecca F. Leavitt md. 1 Jan. 1856. [CH]
Joseph L. (29) - Julia M. Leavitt (25) md. 24 Nov. 1856. [CH]
Lizzie J. (20), d/o Joseph - Wilfred J. (24), s/o Lewis md. 14 Apr. 1880.
    [TR]
Mary A. (21), d/o John - James A. Rand (23), s/o James B. md. 24 Nov. 1864.
    [TR]
Rachel of Hampton - John Brown Jr. of Hampton md. 10 Feb. 1803. [CH]
Ruben of Sanbornton - Elesebeth Brown md. 21 Feb. 1791. [TR]
Thomas (52), s/o Jonathan - Mary E. Hobbs (43), d/o Oliver md. 12 Jan. 1884.
    [TR]
Willard H. (31), s/o Henry - Grace W. Dunham (18), d/o Wm H. md. 31 July
    1888. [TR]
Willard H. (50) - Nora L. Sanborn (47) md. 29 May 1907. [AR]

PICKERING:
Abigail of Newington - James Burnham of Rochester md. 25 Apr. 1783. [CH]
Ann R. - Samuel F. French md. 20 Apr. 1836. [CH
Elizabeth - Wells Healey of Hampton Falls md. 2 Mar. 1815. [TR][CH]
Ephraim (39) of Newington - Margaret Elizabeth Henderson (20) of Greenland
    md. 1 Feb. 1852. [CH]
James C. - Abigail Furber, both of Newington md. 13 Oct. 1808. [TR][CH]
Joshua Jr. - Nancy C. Hobbs md. 9 Oct. 1828. [TR][CH]
Lydia - Isaac Dow, both of Portsmouth md. 25 Feb. 1809. [TR][CH]
Mary O. - Frederick A. Batchelder md. 3 Nov. 1842. [TR][CH]
Mehitabel - Samuel Drake md. 1 Feb. 1818. [TR][CH]
Polly of Greenland - Stephen Haines of Canterbury md. 31 Jan. 1810. [TR][CH]
Rosemond - Nathan Brown of Hampton Falls md. 13 Nov. 1828. [TR][CH]

PIERCE:
Ezekiel of Townsend - Mary Horn of Portsmouth md. Nov. 1777. [CH]

PIKE:
John of Hampton Falls - Elizabeth Marston md. Nov. 1797. [CH]
Robert (55) - Mary E. Carr (45), md. 20 June 1881. [TR]
Thomas, Major - Abigail Gould md. 10 June 1756. [CH]

PIPER:
Abigail of Stratham - Simon Cole of Sanbornton md. 23 Mar. 1789. [TR]
Hannah - Joseph Goss, both of Stratham md. 15 Feb. 1770. [CH]
Tabitha - Thomas Chase, both of Stratham md. 15 Aug. 1790. [CH]

PITMAN:
Abigail - George Hart, both of Portsmouth md. 5 June 1805. [cH]

PLUMMER:
Walter F. (23) of Newbury - Dora C. Bachelder (23) md. 21 Oct. 1903. [AR]

POLLAK:
Julian A. (28) of Ohio - Louise Hyman (25) of NYC md. 20 Oct. 1913. [AR]

POMERY:
Hannah, d/o Rev. Benj. of Hebron, CT - Rev. David McClure md. 10 Dec. 1780.
    [TR]

POOLE:
Mary Davis (21), d/o John F. - Woodbury Levi Jenness (22), s/o Levi md. 16
    July 1874. [TR]

PORTER:
Huntington - Sally Moulton md. 30 Mar. 1797. [CH]

POTTLE:
Henry - Rachel French, both of Stratham md. 13 Dec. 1814. [TR][CH]
William of Stratham - Abigail Thomas md. 21 Nov. 1771. [CH]

POWERS:
Mary P. (24), d/o George - Cornnelius O. Philbrick (24), s/o Oliver B. md. 3
    Sep. 1876. [TR]

POWHATAN:
Leslie F. (26) - Mabel F. Jenness (21) md. 21 Nov. 1908. [AR]

PRESCOTT:
James - Sally Sanborn, both of Hampton Falls md. 26 Sep. 1833. [TR][CH]
Mary - Francis Blake, both of Hampton md. 20 Mar. 1832. [TR][CH]
Weare N. of Kensington - Mary Sandborn of Hampton md. 27 Dec. 1826. [TR][CH]

PROSCHOLD:
Charles (54) - Elizabeth L. McDonald (34) of Newport, R.I. md. 22 Mar. 1897.
    [AR]
Elizabeth (43) - Herbert M. Allen (42) md. 29 Apr. 1908 at Exeter. [AR]

PUMAN?
William Ray (41), s/o Stephen - Ellen Addie Page (24), d/o Joseph md. 26 Feb.
    1874. [TR]

PURINGTON:
Walter F. (21) - Hazel M. Chapman (22) md. 22 Oct. 1932.]AR]

PURVIS:
Marjorie (34) - Ray Garland (29) md. 20 Feb. 1913. [AR]

QUALLS:
Sally - Joshua Mace, both of Hampton md. 9 Mar. 1795. [CH]

RAMERY:
Annie L. (19), d/o Albion - Willie E. Moulton (21), s/o Daniel S. md. 28 Nov.
    1877. [TR]

RAMAK:
Elezabeth of Rye - Jonathan Hobbs md. 15 July 1791. [TR]

RAND:
Bickford L. of Ipswich - Martha Batchelder md. 9 Oct. 1842. [TR][CH]
Edith (24) - Herbert S. Knowles (30) md. 9 Dec. 1896 [AR]
Ellen A. (26), d/o William - Emery C. Jenness (29), s/o David md. 2 Dec.
    1871. [TR]
Frank P. (25), s/o William W. - Nellie S. Gaswell (21), d/o Samuel md.
    21 Sep. 1878. [TR]
Herbert S. Knowles (30) md. 9 Dec. 1896. [TR]
James A. (23), s/o James - Mary A. Philbrook (21), d/o John md. 24 Nov. 1864.
    [TR]
Katherine (22) of Brentwood - Bartlett A. Bachelder (32) md. 1 Jan. 1934 at
    Brentwood. [AR]
Mina E. (21) - Robert L. Mitchell (29) md. 1 Feb. 1894. [TR][AR]
Ona M., d/o Aaron - Aaron R. Locke (23), s/o James md. 24 Apr. 1871. [TR]
Samuel - Hannah Locke, both of Portsmouth md. 29 Sep. 1811. [TR][CH]
Sarah of Rye - James Perkins of Hampton md. 23 July 1824. [TR][CH]
Sarah O. (31) - Albert H. Warner (32) md. 18 Nov. 1877. [TR]
Thomas W. (25) of Rye - Louisa A. Hodgdon (17) of Greenland md. 13 May 1858.
    [CH]
William S. - Adeline S. Philbrick, both of Rye md. 12 July 1846. [CH]

RANDALL:
Mary of Stratham - Reuben Sanborn of Brentwood md. 8 Apr. 1788. [CH]
Sarah Hannah (24), d/o William - John Wilkes Locke (26), s/o Jesse md. 23
    Oct. 1872. [TR]
William of Rye - Rachel Harriss md. 1 Jan. 1770. [CH]

RANDLET:
Mary of Stratham - Ruben Samborn of Brentwood md. 8 Apr. 1788. [TR]
Noah - Elisabeth Moulton of Stratham md. 25 Apr. 1819. [TR][CH]
Simon - Abigail Stockbridge of Stratham md. 1788. [TR]

RANSON:
Lucie G.M. (18), d/o Margaret L. Chase - Charles E. Homes (25), s/o Samuel
    md. 1 July 1866. [TR]

RAWLINS/ROLLINS:
Hannah of Stratham - David Wiggins md. 30 Nov. 1783. [CH]
Polly - John Stackbridge of Stratham md. Sep. 1793. [CH]

REDDEN:
Viola M. (23) of Portsmouth - James L. Bachelder (24) md. 27 Oct. 1909 at
Portsmouth. [AR]

REDMAN:
Hannah - John S. Towle md. 24 Nov. 1825. [TR][CH]
Joseph W. (36), s/o John - Mary J. Hobbs (26), d/o Morris md. 28 June 1865.
[TR]
Lydia - Jeremiah Sanborn, both of Hampton md. 2 Dec. 1814. [TR][CH]
Margaret - Zebulon Wyman md. 31 Dec. 1755. [CH]
Sarah - Philip C. Nudd, both of Hampton md. 21 July 1846. [CH]

REED:
Harold D. (38) of Boston - Evelyn Fowler (24) of Brookline, MA. md. 16 June
1924. [AR]

REISINGER:
Edmee B. (44) - Charles E. Greenough (45) both of NYC md. 28 Aug. 1920. [AR]

REMERY:
Annie C. (19) - Willie E. Moulton (21) md. 28 Nov. 1877. [TR]

REMICK:
John Y. - Betsy B. Philbrick, both of Rye md. 17 Feb. 1827. [TR][CH]

RICE:
Evelyn (34) of Claremont - George P. Frost (51) md. 16 May 1936 at Claremont.
[AR]
William W. (23) - Ari L. Talton (19) md. 3 Mar. 1901. [AR]

RICHARDSON:
Joseph of Moultonboro - Abigail Drake md. 26 Feb. 1784. [CH]

RICKER:
John of So. Berwick - Nancy N. Simpson of Stratham md. 18 Oct. 1835. [CH]

RIDEOUT:
Marion Elizabeth (20) - Richard Alden Batchelder (22) md. 10 Jan. 1941 at
Eliot, Me. [AR]

RILEY:
Dorothy Pearl (23) - Earl Langtry Spear (25) md. 24 Nov. 1928 at Newcastle.
[AR]
Ernest William (42) - Elda Carrie Murrey (28) md. 28 Sep. 1938 at Hampton.
[AR]

RING:
Henry A. (39), s/o John - Addie Bachelder (32), d/o Levi md. 16 Sep. 1877.
[TR]
Susannah - Thomas Eliot Colby md. 29 Mar. 1755. [CH]

ROBERTS:
Eugene H. (24) - Mildred F. Dow (21) md. 28 May 1932 at Exeter. [AR]
Susannah of Seabrook - John Souter of Hampton md. 24 July 1772. [CH]

ROBIE: See Roby
Alice (32) of Stratham - Fred B. Wiggin (33) md. 25 Jan. 1899 at Stratham.
[AR]
Bathsheba - William Parker of Portsmouth md. 28 June 1808. [TR][CH]
Henry of Hampton Falls - Delia B. Drake of Hampton md. 1 Feb. 1821. [TR][CH]
Josiah - Mary Nood md. 1787. [TR]

ROBINSON:
Abigail D. - Joseph Fullenton of Raymond md. 26 Feb. 1835. [TR][CH]
Bertha (23) of Pittsfield - Cedric H. Dustin (25) md. 9 May 1925 at
   Newmarket. [AR]
Dorothy - Simon Leavitt Jr. md. 7 July 1818. [TR][CH]
Emma L. (17) - Fred L. Lamprey (21), s/o Samuel C. md. 20 Feb. 1872. [TR]
Gertrude L. (25) - Fred L. Dow (23), s/o Samuel A. md. 27 Oct. 1896. [TR][AR]
Hannah J. (16) of Kingston - Nathaniel T. Mace)21) md. 24 Nov. 1858. [CH]
Mary S. - Capt. John Lamprey md. 16 Nov. 1828. [TR][CH]
Rachel - Mayhew Clarke md. 21 Dec. 1775. [CH]
Sarah M. - Samuel D. Lane of Hampton md. 15 Oct. 1845. [TR][CH]
William - Abigail Barker, both of Stratham md. 26 Nov. 1807. [CH]

ROBY: See Robie
Abigail C. - Francis J. Newcomb of Quincy, Mass. md. 31 Aug. 1848. [CH]
Hannah - Ephraim Marston md. 22 Dec. 1799. [CH]
Mary E. - Washington Parker of Quincy, Mass. md. 22 Mar. 1848. [CH]
Samuel - Abigail Fogg md. 21 Apr. 1767. [CH]

ROLLINS/RAWLINGS:
Elisha - Abigail Taylor, both of Stratham md. 22 Oct. 1806. [CH]
Fannie A. (36) - Herman L. Marston (37) md. 15 Sep. 1902. [AR]
Jonathan (50) - Hattie A. Lane (22) md. 8 Nov. 1884. [TR]
Rienze Ridge (25), s/o Chas. A. - Emma O. Adams (22), d/o Oliver md. 12 Jan.
   1884. [TR]

ROLLINS Cont.
Lydia of Stratham - John Jenness of Rye md. 17 Nov. 1808. [TR][CH]
Olly - Samuel Lane Jr., both of Hampton md. 22 Mar. 1795. [TR][CH]

ROSS:
Charles J. (40) of Topsfield - Lillian F. Haines (30) md. 30 Nov. 1905. [AR]

ROWE:
Ezekiel of Gilmanton - Elizabeth Lane of Hampton md. 16 Feb. 1794. [TR]
Jacob of Seabrook - Mary Chase of Hampton Falls md. 12 Nov. 1826. [TR][CH]
Jacob M. of Exeter - Abigail Marston md. 1 Apr. 1838. [CH]
Jeremiah of Gilmanton - Ruth Lane of Hampton md. 16 Nov. 1796. [CH]
Winthrop of Kensington - Nancy Marston md. 29 Feb. 1798. [CH]

ROWE:
Ezekiel of Gilmanton - Elizabeth Lane of Hampton md. _____ 1794. [TR]

ROWELL:
John W. - Sarah A. Stevens of Exeter md. 17 May 1835. [CH]

RUMERY:
Albion (39), s/o William - Elizabeth Clough (25), d/o Nathan md. 18 Nov.
    1866. [TR]

RUNDLETT:
Daniel H. - Frances Blake, both of Exeter md. 1 Oct. 1826. [TR][CH]
Jenny of Stratham - John Elsworth of Brentwood md. 9 Dec. 1783. [CH]
John - Sarah Brown, both of Stratham md. 4 July 1812. [TR][CH]
Noah - Elizabeth Moulton, both of Stratham md. 25 Apr. 1819. [TR]

St. CLAIR:
Helen R. (24) of Springfield, MA. - Warren M. Davis (24) md. 10 Mar. 1934 at
    Hampton. [AR]

SABALL:
Gertie W. (24), d/o Joseph - Charles E. Barton (32), s/o Chas. E. md. 20 Nov.
    1889. [TR]

SADLER:
Edward P. (43) - Gladys I. Paul (27) md. 21 July 1943 at Seabrook. [AR]

SAFFORD:
Sophia of Exeter - Josiah Smith Jr. of Stratham md. 19 Nov. 1837. [CH]

SALTER:
Fannie W.P. (33), d/o John C. Philbrick - William E. Carter (28), s/o
    Mitchell md. 29 Jan. 1887. [TR]

SANBORN: See Sanborn

SAMMIS:
Edward A. (36) of Stamford, Ct. - Frances H. Drake (34) md. 12 Aug. 1909 at
   Portsmouth. [AR]

SANBORN/SANDBORN:
Abijah - Mary Sanborn md. 14 Aug. 1768. [CH]
Alfred of Exeter - Nancy J. Towle md. 22 Aug. 1838. [CH]
Benjamin - Anne Cate, both of Sanborn Town md. 9 Nov. 1768. [CH]
Benjamin, Dr. of Sanbornton - Hulda Smith md. 15 Mar. 1781. [CH]
Bertha G. (24) of Hampton Falls - Charles C. Seavey (24) md. 29 Nov. 1904 at
   Hampton Falls. [AR]
Betsy of Hampton Falls - Jeremiah Brown 3d md. 12 Apr. 1837. [CH]
Ebenezer, s/o John & Sarah - Ruth Samborn, d/o John & Ruth md. 1 May 1735.
   [TR]
Ebenezer - Leadey Samborn md. 27 May 1789. [TR]
Eleab - Hannah Hobbs md. 6 Oct. 1789. [TR]
Elizabeth of Hampton Falls - David Locke of Kensington md. 1 Sep. 1814.
   [TR][CH]
Henry C. (26) - Frances M. Lyuch (22) md. 30 Sep. 1905 at Portsmouth. [AR]
James - Sarah Dearborn md. 23 Dec. 1786. [TR][CH]
Jeremiah - Lydia Redman, both of Hampton md. 2 Dec. 1814. [TR][CH]
Jeremiah B. of exeter - Mary E. Swasey of Exeter md. 16 July 1840. [CH]
Jesse of Kensington - Abigail Choate md. 17 Aug. 1790. [TR]
John of Hampton Falls - Elesebeth Batchelder md. 2 Jan. 1792. [TR]
John N. (35), s/o Levi - Lucy E. Marston (23), d/o James Carwell md. 4 Dec.
   1878. [TR]
Jonah or Josiah Jr. - Mary D. Garland, both of Hampton md. 24 Sep. 1828.
   [TR][CH]
Leadey - Ebenezer Sambron of Kensington md. 27 May 1789. [TR]
Lois - Jeremiah Locke, both of Seabrook md. 20 Feb. 1800. [CH]
Lucy - Caleb Tilton, both of Hampton Falls md. 3 July 1827. [TR][CH]
Mary - Abijah Sanborn md. 14 Aug. 1768. [CH]
Mary of Hampton - Weare N. Prescott of Kensington md. 27 Dec. 1826. [TR][CH]
Nehemiah of Hampton - Ldyia Lovering md. 2 Mar. 1797. [CH]
Nehemiah of Hampton - Elizabeth Lovering of Greenland md. 23 July 1837. [CH]
Nora L. (47) of Tilton, NH - Willard H. Philbrook (50) md. 29 May 1907 at
   Sanbornton. [AR]
Reuben of Brentwood - Mary Randall of Stratham md. 8 Apr. 1788. [CH]
Ruben of Brentwood - Mary Randlot of Stratham md. 8 Apr. 1788. [TR]
Ruth, d/o John & Ruth - Ebenezer Samborn, s/o John & Sarah md. 1 May 1735.
   [TR]
Sally - James Prescott, both of Hampton Falls md. 26 Sep. 1833. [TR][CH]
Sewell of Hampton Falls - Betsey Towle md. 15 Apr. 1818. [TR][CH]
Simon - Harriet Dearborn, both of Epsom md. 10 Mar. 1811. [TR][CH]

SANBORN Cont.

Thomas of Exeter - Abigail Marston of Hampton md. 17 Aug. 1825. [TR][CH]
William - Abigail Hobbs md. 20 Mar. 1774. [CH]
William of Exeter - Anne Loverin md. 16 Feb. 1794. [TR]

SANFORD:

Rose (18) - Otto W. Berry (25) md. 1 Mar. 1893. [TR][AR]

SCAMMON:

James Jr. - Sally Smith, both of Stratham md. 4 Apr. 1816. [TR][CH]
Lydia (18), d/o Stephen - Isaac D. Stockbridge (23), s/o James md. 13 Oct. 1866. [TR]
Polly - Edward Burleigh, both of Stratham md. 8 Aug. 1783. [CH]

SCHLOSEK:

Bernice (22) of Ware, MA. - Alfons Anthony Warka (29) of Palmer, MA. md. 29 Mar. 1936. [AR]

SCOTT:

Esther J. (22) - Ralph Bartlett Seavey (22) md. 11 Sep. 1929 at Hampton. [AR]
Katie (21) - John Dinsmore (26) md. 22 May 1861. [TR]
Maggie J. (25) of Boston - Willie F. Simpson (27) md. 29 Nov. 1899 at Rye. [AR]
William - Eles Lang md. 15 Mar. 1791. [TR]

SEABORN: Sanborn?

Margaret - Jonathan Fifield, both of Hampton md. 9 Mar. 1768. [CH]

SEAVEY:

Arthur E. (30), s/o Chas. E. - Hattie M. Tarlton (23), d/o Joseph A. md. 23 Jan. 1894. [TR][AR]
Charles C. (24) - Bertha G. Sanborn (24) of Hampton Falls md. 29 Nov. 1904 at Hampton Falls. [AR]
Charles E. (34), s/o Joseph - Harrie L. McDaniel (29), d/o Noah md. 21 Nov. 1868. [TR]
Dawn Elizabeth (26) - Walter Everett Parks (32) md. 6 Aug. 1927. [AR]
Elizabeth J. (23) of Portsmouth - Jack Fenwick (26) md. 17 Oct. 1906. [AR]
Frank H. (23), s/o Joseph W. - Abbie E. Leavitt (17), d/o James md. 5 Sep. 1867. [TR][CH]
George L. (29) - Mary A. Bartlett (22) of Salisbury, MA. md. 27 Sep. 1904 at Salisbury. [AR]
George L. (50) - Marie G. Philbrick (33) of Portsmouth md. 1 Oct. 1925 at Newton, MA. [AR]
John - Abigail Chapman md. 16 Oct. 1800. [CH]
Mira A. (26), d/o Joseph W. - John W. Hobbs (21), s/o John S. md. 25 Dec. 1867. [TR]
Moses of Deerfield - Mrs. Ruth Tarlton of Greenland md. 22 Dec. 1788. [CH]

SEAVEY Cont.
Ralph Bartlett (22) - Esther J. Scott (22) md. 11 Sep. 1929 at Hampton. [AR]
Sarah - Joseph Goss, both of Rye md. 6 Mar. 1791. [TR]
Thomas of Deerfield - Betsy Tarlton md. 22 Dec. 1788. [TR]

SELLERS:
Chester J. (31) of Bostob - Carrie M. Burgess (27) md. 27 Dec. 1913 at Hampton. [AR]

SEYMOUR:
Nellie E. (20) of Portsmouth - Forrest S. Fogg (28) md. 19 Jan. 1905 at Portsmouth. [AR]

SHAW:
Andrew - Polly Dearborn md. 4 Jan. 1808 by Elias Smith. [TR]
Clarissa of Hampton - Thomas Philbrick of Rye md. 11 Aug. 1822. [TR][CH]
John D. - Sally Lovering of Greenland md. 25 July 1809. [TR][CH]
Jonathan - Nancy Lane, both of Hampton md. 26 Apr. 1812. [TR][CH]
Joshua - Deborah Palmer, both of Hampton md. 17 Nov. 1771. [CH]
Josiah - Lydia Fifield, both of Hampton md. 9 July 1792. [TR]
Samuel - Deborah Clark, both of Hampton md. 11 Feb. 1808. [CH]
Sarah - Jonathan Batchelder of Northwood md. 27 June 1786. [CH]

SHERBURNE:
Sarah - Thomas Hobbs md. 7 Nov. 1771, [CH]

SHERMAN:
Frank P. (19) of Portsmouth - Eunice V. Haines (19) of Greenland md. 9 Sep. 1860. [CH]

SHEPARD:
Abigail - Christopher Gould md. 11 Oct. 1756. [CH]
Comfort - Benjamin Lamprey md. 3 Feb. 1772. [CH]
Joseph Jr. of Portsmouth - Olive Foss of Rye md. 14 May 1815, [TR][CH]

SILVA:
Albert F. (46) - Rita V. Slaney (23) both of Gloucester md. 27 June 1943. [AR]

SILVER:
John - Elizabeth Coker md. 14 Dec. 1755. [CH]

SIMPSON:
Capt. David - Olive Brown, both of Greenland md. 13 June 1813. [TR][CH]
John - Comfort Haines, both of Greenland md. 20 Mar. 1808. [CH]
Joseph of Portsmouth - Eliza Hilton of Lee md. 7 Dec. 1813. [TR][CH]
Margaret - Nutter Brown , both of Greenland md. 12 Mar. 1812. [TR][CH]

SIMPSON Cont.
Martha M. (21) - John A. McLean (22) md. 18 Apr. 1915. [AR]
Nancy of Greenland - Nathaniel Wiggin 3d of Stratham md. 2 May 1809. [TR][CH]
Nancy M. of Stratham - Joseph Ricker of So. Berwick md. 18 Oct. 1835. [CH]
Willie F. (27) - Maggie J. Scott (25) of Boston md. 29 Nov. 1899 at Rye. [AR]

SINCLAR:
Richard - Elizabeth Moore md. 26 Aug. 1771. [CH]
Samuel - Elisabeth Lane, both of Stratham md. 28 Sep. 1823. [TR][CH]

SLANEY:
Rita V. (23) - Albert F. Silva (46) both of Gloucester md. 27 June 1943. [AR]

SLEEPER:
Jennie O. (20), d/o Martin - Alvin C. Brown (23), s/o Abel T. md. 17 Apr.
1876. [TR]
Lizzie H. (31) - Oliver D. Moulton (34) md. 12 Nov. 1885. [TR]
Thomas - Mary Davies, both of Kingston md. 27 Aug. 1771. [CH]

SMALL:
Bernard C. (24) - Mary A. Locke (29) md. 2 July 1921 at Hampton. [AR]

SMITH:
Abigail - Benjamin Leavitt md. 29 Mar. 1786. [CH]
Alonzo J. (25), s/o Jonathan - Lizzie E.W. Norton (25), d/o Nathan md. 16
Apr. 1868. [TR]
Byran D. (25) - Hazel M. Leavitt (24) of Hampton md. 27 Sep. 1919. [AR]
Charles F. (22), s/o Joshua - Lizzie M. Drake (22), d/o Charles A. md. 4 Feb.
1886. [TR]
Christopher - Elizabeth C. Hobbs md. 5 Dec. 1832. [CH]
Debora L. - Reuben Smith Jr., both of Brentwood md. 5 July 1823. [TR][CH]
Edward M. (36) - Martha Estelle Leavitt (29) md. 2 Sep. 1902. [AR]
Eunice of Seabrook - Stephen Littlefield md. 19 June 1836. [CH]
Ezra - Marcy Burley, both of Newmarket md. 17 July 1794. [CH]
Frances M. (18) of Waterboro, Me. - Thomas F. Moulton (17) md. 25 Dec. 1917
at Waterboro. [AR]
Frank Elmer (32) - Grace Beale (31) of Greenville Jnt, Me. md. 9 June 1928.
[AR]
Franklin (23) - Virginia Lowe (20) both of Hampden, Me. md. 6 Dec. 1936. [AR]
Hannah - Joseph Bryant md. 16 May 1771, [CH]
Hannah - Nathaniel Paiper of Stratham md. 1787. [TR]
Huldah - Dr. Benjamin Sanborn of Sanbornton md. 15 Mar. 1781. [CH]
John E. (26), s/o Joshua P. - Ella May Stover (20), d/o Wm R. md. 12 Oct.
1893. [TR][AR]
John L. (25), s/o Christopher - Rebecca P. Marston (20), d/o Levi md. 14 Nov.
1860. [TR][CH]

SMITH Cont.

Jonathan of Rye - Bethiah Moulton md. 3 Dec. 1772. [CH]

Jonathan - Betsey Nutter both of Stratham md. 8 Mar. 1820. [TR][CH]

Jonathan C. (37), s/o Abram - Ann Jeanette Hobbs (26), d/o Moses md. 2 Jan. 1862. [TR][CH]

Joseph - Abigail Clarke, both of Newmarket md. 9 Sep. 1783. [CH]

Capt. Joseph - Martha Fifield, both of Stratham md. 31 July 1814. [TR][CH]

Josiah Jr. of Stratham - Sophia Safford of Exeter md. 19 Nov. 1837. [CH]

Lydia -Carr Leavitt md. 9 Oct. 1797. [CH]

Marcy - Joseph Stockbridge, both of Stratham md. 26 Nov. 1807. [CH]

Marion Eleanor (21) - Stanley Joy Knowles (39) md. 15 June 1929. [AR]

Mary - Daniel Marston md. 28 May 1789. [TR]

Mary of Seabrook - Ephraim Green of Newburyport md. 22 Oct. 1799. [CH]

Mary - Simeon Dearborn md. 27 Nov. 1799. [CH]

Mary E. (24) - Oliver S. Hobbs (23) md. 24 Dec. 1890. [TR][AR]

Mary E. (20) of Newburyport - Francis Malenfant (23) of Amesbury md. 1 Feb. 1931. [AR]

Maurice B. (27) - Ruth B. Alpaugh (21) of Orange, NJ md. 2 Sep. 1933 at Portsmouth. [AR]

Miriam - Capt. Joseph Hoit md. 30 Jan. 1808. [CH]

Morris H. (26), s/o Christopher - Isabella Leavitt (20), d/o Simon md. 24 Nov. 1859. [TR] [CH]

Nancy - Aaron Jewell or Jewett, both of Stratham md. 14 Nov. 1808. [TR][CH]

Orren - Abby Drake md. 24 Apr. 1845. [TR][CH]

Polly of Stratham - John Taylor of Hampton md. 20 Oct. 1794. [CH]

Rachel of Stratham - Nathan Knowles md. 30 Mar. 1808. [TR][CH]

Reuben Jr. - Debora L. Smith, both of Brentwood md. 5 July 1823. [TR][CH]

Sally - James Scammon Jr., both of Stratham md. 4 Apr. 1816. [TR][CH]

Samuel of Stratham - Rachel Brown md. 1 Feb. 1773. [CH]

Samuel - Elizabeth Hall, both of Rye md. 17 Mar. 1786. [CH]

Samuel Fogg - Anna Leavitt md. 10 June 1792. [TR]

Sarah - David Nudd md. 17 June 1793. [TR]

Stephen - Rachel Dearborn md. 22 June 1799. [CH]

Theophilus Jr. - Nancy Chase, both of Stratham md. 4 Dec. 1820. [TR][CH]

Waity C. - Ezra Nichols, both of Seabrook md. 4 July 1814. [CH]

William - Sukey Bryant md. 4 July 1809. [TR]

SOUTER:

John of Hampton - Susannah Roberts of Seabrook md. 24 July 1772. [CH]

SOUTHWORTH:

Robert A. of Boston - Mary J. Bachelder md. 25 Apr. 1916. [AR]

SPACKMAN:

Doris P. (18) of Rye - Gilman M. Moulton (20) md. 6 May 1934 at Rye. [AR]

SPAULDING:
Reuben - Sarah Chandler md. 2 Jan. 1755. [CH]

SPEAR:
Addie E., d/o Samuel - James M. Barton, s/o Chas. md. 17 Feb. 1877. [TR]
Earl Langtry (25) - Dorothy Pearl Riley (22) md. 24 Nov. 1928 at Newcastle.
   [AR]
Helen (22) - James F. Hobbs Jr. (30) md. 10 July 1920 at Hampton. [AR]

STANWOOD:
Robert O. (38) of Portland, Me. - Emily C. Dinsmore (28) of Anson, Me. md. 27
   July 1853. [CH]

STAPLES:
William L. (41) of S. Framingham, MA. - Annie M. Norton (41) of York, Me. md.
   7 Apr. 1909. [AR]

STEELE:
Herbert (19) - Annie A. Lewis (24) md. 17 Nov. 1905. [AR]

STEVENS:
Alonzo M. (23), s/o David - Clara L. Dalton (17), d/o Michael md. 23 Jan.
   1867. [TR]
Nathaniel - Anna Moore md. 21 Jan. 1768. [CH]
Joseph - Phebe Taylor, both of Stratham md. 24 Mar. 1774. [CH]
Joseph - Sally Fogg md. 5 Aug. 1813. [TR][CH]
Sarah A. of Exeter - John A. Rowell md. 17 May 1835. [CH]

STEWART:
Amy Gertrude (63) - George Kennedy Mack (63) md. 31 May 1939 at Hampton. [AR]

STOCKBRIDGE:
Abigail of Stratham - Sinom Randlet md. 1788. [TR]
Isaac (23), s/o James - Lydia Scammon (18), d/o Stephen md. 13 Oct. 1866.
   [TR]
John of Stratham - Polly Rawlings md. Sep. 1793. [CH]
Josiah - Marcy Smith, both of Stratham md. 26 Nov. 1807. [CH]

STORER:
Eva F. (33) of Norridgewerk, Me. - George P. Frost (29) md. 19 Mar. 1914 at
   Norridgewerk. [AR]
Phoebe G. (27) of Bradford, Me. - Clarence L. Fogg (30) md. 5 Apr. 1917 at
   Bradford. [AR]
Seth Jr, of Saco - Sarah Gookin md. 27 Sep. 1812. [CH]

STORM:
Greta Marguarite (18) - William Thomas McLane Jr. (18) of Stratham md. 2 July
   1938. [AR]

STOVER:
Ella May (20), d/o William R. - John E. Smith (26), s/o Joshua P. md. 12 Oct.
1893. [TR][AR]
Seth Jr. Esq. of Saco - Sarah Gookin md. 27 Sep. 1812. [TR]

STRAW:
Moses - Elizabeth Colby md. 17 Oct. 1751. [CH]

STROUT:
Irving Knight (31) - Jessie Dodge Drysdale (22) md. 29 June 1929. [AR]

SWAIN:
Phebe - Paul Long md. 15 July 1784. [CH]

SWAN:
Nellie E. (23) - Charles F. Marden (38) md. 21 Oct. 1868. [TR]

SWASEY:
Joseph - Sarah A. Davis, both of Exeter md. 2 Sep. 1839. [CH]
Mary E. - Jeremiah B. Sanborn, both of Exeter md. 16 July 1840. [CH]

SYMONDS:
Clarence E. (36) - Flora M.L. Durant (31) both of Salem, MA. md. 18 Dec.
1932. [AR]

TABER:
Louise A. (28) - John MacKenzie (27) md. 3 Nov. 1934 at Winthrop, MA. [AR]

TALTON:
Comfort of Rye - Abrahm Dore of Milton md. 22 Apr. 1816. [CH]

TAPPAN:
Sargent - Maria Eaton md. 22 Dec. 1818. [CH]

TARBELL:
George W. (29) - Martha P. Brown (27) md. 3 Sep. 1881. [TR]

TARLTON:
Ada B. (17), d/o Stephen - Willie P. Drew (22), s/o Nathan md. 2 Apr. 1884.
[TR]
Ari L. (19) - William W. Rice (23) md. 2 Mar. 1901. [AR]
Betsy - Thomas Seavey of Deerfield md. 22 Dec. 1788. [TR]
Comfort of Rye - Abraham Dore of Milton md. 22 Apr. 1816. [TR][CH]
Ella M. (18), d/o J. Artwell - Fred A. Drew (22), s/o Nathaniel md. 28 Mar.
or 2 Apr. 1893. [TR][AR]
George W. (25), s/o Nathaniel - Nellie F. Moulton (18), d/o Curtis md. 22
Dec. 1878. [TR]

TARLTON Cont.

Hattie M. (23), d/o Joseph A. - Arthur E. Seavey (30), s/o Charles E. md. 23 Jan. 1894. [TR][AR]

Ida S. (29) - Lewis R.H. Lane (29) md. 30 June 1885. [TR]

Mary E. (25), d/o Nathaniel - Levi H. Fogg (30), s/o David md. 27 Nov. 1875. [TR]

Nathaniel - Sarah A. Taylor md. 22 Nov. 1849. [CH]

Nellie G. (23), d/o Charles - George F. Haynes (21), s/o George md. 19 July 1879. [TR]

Ruthy, Mrs. of Greenland - Moses Seavey of Deerfield md. 22 Dec. 1788. [CH]

Samuel - Abigail Brown md. 26 Jan. 1819. [TR][CH]

TARR:

Dorothy E. (22) - Paul W. Hobbs (24) md. 14 June 1931. [AR]

TAYLOR:

Abigail - Elisha Rollins, both of Stratham md. 22 Oct. 1806. [CH]

Andrew - Eliza Wiggin, both of Stratham md. 25 Apr. 1820. [TR][CH]

Anna, d/o ___ & Elizabeth - Wear Drake, s/o Abraham & Abigail md. 2 Dec. 1760. [TR]

Anna - Increase Batchelder of Nottingham md. 25 Feb. 1770. [CH]

Charles W. (27) - Elizabeth M. Brown (21) md. 24 June 1903. [AR]

Charlotte B. (26) of Eastport, Me. - Harry T. Whenal (33) md. 4 Sep. 1928 at Eastport. [AR]

Edward J. (20), s/o Ira J. - Nellie N. Bachelder (21), d/o B.D. md. 12 July 1876. [TR]

Edward J. (45) - Eva M. Dalton (36) md. 2 Apr. 1902. [AR]

Edward J. (61) - Lillie G. Dyer (51) md. 10 Sep. 1918 at Hampton. [AR]

Elesebeth - Nehemiah/Nathaniel Folsam of Exeter md. 13 June or 18 July 1791. [TR]

Elias S. of Parsonfield - Lydia Wiggin of Stratham md. 7 July 1816. [TR][CH]

Elizabeth - Nathaniel Batchelder, both of Hampton md. 10 Jan. 1783. [CH]

Elizabeth of Hampton - Nehemiah Folsom of Exeter md. 13 June 1791. [TR]

George O. (26) - Sophia E. Marston (25) md. 26 Dec. 1885. [TR]

Hannah - Micajah Morrill, both of Hampton md. 1 Sep. 1778. [TR][CH]

James W. (26) of L.A., Calif. - Ruth I. Bachelder (19) md. 20 June 1932. [AR]

Jean S. (22) - Jack J. Lauterborn (25) both of Cambridge, MA. md. 11 July 1943. [AR]

John of Hampton - Polly Smith of Stratham md. 20 Oct. 1794. [CH]

John - Mary Fogg md. 7 Aug. 1817. [TR][CH]

John J. (28) - Abbie J. Chase (24) md. 22 Dec. 1881. [TR]

Joseph - Margaret Mason md. 14 Nov. 1811. [TR][CH]

Marion (24) of Portsmouth - Charles Pearson Haley (25) of Keene, NH md. 22 June 1940 at Portsmouth. [AR]

Mary Ann - Carr L. Dearborn 4 Apr. 1839. [CH]

Phebe - Joseph Stevens, both of Stratham md. 24 Mar. 1774. [CH]

Roberta (18) - George A. Craig (19) md. 31 Aug. 1935. [AR]

TAYLOR Cont.
Sarah A. - Nathaniel Tarlton md. 22 Nov. 1849. [CH]
Sarah E. (31), d/o J. Jenness - Charles W. Philbrick (46), s/o David md. 20
    Nov. 1895. [TR][AR]
Walter E. (34) - Alpharena M. Gratton (29) of N. Reading md. 21 Oct. 1917 at
    Hampton. [AR]

TENNEY:
Perley W., s/o Perley - Susan B. French, d/o Reuben md. 28 May 1868. [TR][CH]
Samuel, Dr. - J_tha Johnson, both of Exeter md. 23 Sep. 1783. [CH]
Samuel, Dr. - Tabitha Gilman of Exeter md. 23 Sep. 1788. [TR]
Samuel B. - Christian Gardner, both of Portsmouth md. 6 June 1825. [TR]

THAYER:
Joseph (38), s/o Henry - Emma Clara Warner (27), d/o Andrew md. 27 Nov. 1872.
    [TR]

THOMAS:
Abigail - William Pottle of Stratham md. 21 Nov. 1771. [CH]

THORNTON:
James B. of Saco - Eliza Gookin md. 20 Jan. 1817. [TR][CH]

THURSTON:
Hannah - Thomas Loving md. 9 Sep. 1782. [CH]
Molly - Joseph Kelley, both of Stratham md. 19 Feb. 1795. [CH]

TILTON:
Abraham of Stratham - Deborah Locke md. 20 Aug. 1795. [CH]
Benjamin of Hampton Falls - Sarah Marston of Hampton md. 9 Mar. 1819.
    [TR][CH]
Caleb - Lucy Sanborn, both of Hampton Falls md. 3 July 1827. [TR][CH]
Ebenezer of Hampton Falls - Lucy Sanborn md. 4 July 1771. [CH]
Ida B. (23) - Sherman Bissell (35) of Exeter md. 6 Oct. 1935 at Portsmouth.
    [AR]
James S. (31) of Stratham - Rebecca A. Hobbs (20) & d/o Jona. & Mary H. md.
    16 Apr. 1854. [CH]
Sally of Hampton Falls - Isreal Marden of Portsmouth md. 28 June 1827.
    [TR][CH]
Teresa A. (46) - Irving C. Woodrow (55) of Colebrook, NH md. 30 Oct. 1923.
    [AR]

TODD:
Fred A. (43) of Detroit - Wilma L. Philbrick (31) md. 26 Oct. 1931. [AR]

TOUTILLOTT:

Emma A. (19) - Leon M. Berry (20) md. 31 Oct. 1909 at Rye. [AR]
George A., Jr. (27) - Grace E. Godfrey (21) of Hampton md. 9 June 1907 at Hampton. [AR]
Herbert S. (20) - Sadie S. Fife (24) md. 10 Mar. 1907. [AR]

TOWLE:

Abigail of Hampton - Jesse Prescott of Hampton Falls md. 4 June 1794. [TR]
Abraham P. - Eliza Brown, both of Rye md. 14 Nov. 1824. [TR][CH]
Anne - Samuel Leavitt md. 20 June 1792. [TR]
Betsey - Sewell Sanborn of Hampton Falls md. 15 Apr. 1818. [TR][CH]
Betsy of Exeter - George Daniels md. 15 Oct. 1820. [TR][CH]
David - Lydia Towle, both of Hampton md. 13 Apr. 1793. [CH]
Fanny J. (31) of Hampton - Walter J. Drysdale (31) md. 24 Sep. 1932 at Hampton. [AR]
John S. - Hannah Redman md. 24 Nov. 1825. [TR][CH]
Jonathan of Hampton - Meriam Marston md. 21 Jan. 1773. [CH]
Joshua - Jane Drake, both of Hampton md. 31 Oct. 1771. [CH]
Lydia - David Towle, both of Hampton md. 13 Apr. 1793. [CH]
Mary - Simon Blake, both of Hampton md. 29 Mar. 1795. [CH]
Mary Ann - John Dearborn 3d, both of Hampton md. 12 July 1828. [TR][CH]
Mary P. of Hampton - David C. Janvrin of Hampton Falls md. 6 Feb. 1820. [TR][CH]
Molly - Josiah Batchelder md. 8 Mar. 1806. [CH]
Nabby - Thomas Nudd, both of Hampton md. 27 Sep. 1812. [TR][CH]
Nancy - Samuel Fogg Leavitt md. 30 Sep. 1792. [CH]
Nancy J. - Alfred Sanborn of Exeter md. 22 Aug. 1838. [CH]
Samuel of Rye - Rachel Chapman md. 26 Oct. 1769. [CH]
Sarah - Moses Leavitt, both of Hampton md. 7 Dec. 1794. [TR]
Sarah, Mrs. - Asa Lane, Esqr of Chichester md. 13 Oct. 1820. [TR][CH]
Susanna - Jonathan Norton of Chester md. 22 Jan. 1788. [CH]
William - Mary Garland md. 12 Nov. 1795. [CH]

TREDDICK:

Statira, Mrs. - Capt. William Tullock, both of Portsmouth md. 29 Mar. 1808. [TR][CH]

TREFETHRON:

Levi B. - Lucinda or Locada Locke, both of Rye md. 14 May 1826. [TR][CH]
Nellie G. (23), d/o Charles - George F. Haynes (21), s/o George md. 19 July 1879. [TR]

TRUE:

Miriam - Jonathan Perkins md. 11 Dec. 1752. [CH]
Moses - Dolly Moulton, both of Seabrook md. 17 Mar. 1823. [CH]
Sarah - Henry Currier md. 19 Feb. 1755. [CH]

TUCK:
Betsy of Brentwood - John Page of Hampton md. 16 Mar. 1817. [TR][CH]
Saley - Nathaniel (Blank) both of Rye md. 1787. [TR]

TUCKER:
Betsey - John Low, both of Stratham md. 19 May 1816. [TR]

TUCKERMAN:
Kitterick - Polly/Peggy Leavitt md. 29 July 1778. [TR][CH]

TULLOCK:
Capt. William - Mrs. Statira Treddick, both of Portsmouth md. 29 Mar. 1808.
[TR][CH]

TURNER:
Eliza - John D. Hobbs md. 21 Dec. 1837. [CH]
William - Mary Jackson, both of Portsmouth md. 9 Sep. 1813. [TR][CH]

TUTTLE:
Addie F. (23) of Lawrence, MA. - Abram C. Dow (36) md. 22 June 1899 at
Lawrence. [AR]
Mildred C.S. (22) of Watertown, MA. - John I. Brown (25) of Rangeley, Me. md.
4 Sep. 1908. [AR]

TUXBURY:
Moses M. - Mary Barnard md. 25 Sep. 1823. [CH]

UPTON:
Jeremiah of Middleton, MA. - Hannah L. Leavitt md. 25 Dec. 1845. [TR][CH]

VARNEY:
Hazel May (24) of Plymouth - Martin Wade Whenal (23) md. 24 Sep. 1927 at
Plymouth. [AR]
Louise S. (23) of Plymouth, NH - Richard I. Goss (27) md. 18 Aug. 1928 at
Plymouth. [AR]

VEASEY/VEAZEY/VEAZY:
Ann of Stratham - Daniel Dearborn md. 4 Feb. 1770. [CH]
Daniel of Stratham - Polly Dearborn md. 10 Dec. 1807. [CH]
Joshua of Deerfield - Molly Fifield of Stratham md. 15 Oct. 1777. [CH]
Thomas - Lydia Wiggins of Stratham md. 1 Oct. 1778. [CH]

VERRILL/VORRELL:
Edward of Maine - Anna Dearborn of Greenland md. 2 Mar. 1820. [TR][CH]
Eliza E. (25), d/o William - Albert C. Locke (30), s/o Richard A. both of Rye
md. 24 June 1868. [TR][CH]

VERRILL Cont.

Henry L. (28), s/o William - Mary Jane Marden (20), d/o William both of Rye
    md. 8 July 1868. [TR][CH]
Nathaniel - Mary Hanson, both of Rye md. 31 Oct. 1816. [TR][CH]

VOGL:

Louise (41) - David Webster Knowles (38) md. 21 June 1925. [AR]

WALKER:

Nathaniel - Catherine Beck, both of Portsmouth md. 4 July 1810. [TR][CH]
Olly - James Woodhouse md. 26 Jan. 1772. [CH]

WALLACE:

Hannah - Abijah Lane of Hampton Falls md. 8 Dec. 1795. [CH]

WARD:

Abigail of Hampton - Benson Leavitt of Boston md. 15 Nov. 1826. [TR][CH]
Dorothy (30) of Rye - Arthur Carlson (25) md. 30 June 1934. [AR]
Eliza, Mrs. - Nathaniel Batchelder md. 18 Oct. 1822. [TR][CH]
George A. (30) of S. Hamilton, MA. - Helen H. Brown (22) md. 1 June 1935.
    [AR]
Henry L. (33) - Alice C. Birchall (22) md. 21 Mar. 1889. [TR]
Joseph of Hampton - Eliza Brown md. 24 Jan. 1819. [TR][CH]
Josephine - John S. Hobbs md. 23 June 1842. [TR][CH]
Thomas - Lydia Garland, both of Hampton md. Sep. 1793. [TR]

WARKA:

Alfons Anthony (29) of Palmer, MA - Bernice Schlosek (22) of Ware, MA. md.
    29 Mar. 1936. [AR]

WARNER:

Abraham R. - Lydia Frances Moulton, both of Exeter md. 25 Dec. 1849. [CH]
Albert H. (32) - Sarah O. Reed (31) md. 18 Nov. 1877. [TR]
Andrew B. - Olivia R. Leavitt md. 21 May 1837. [CH]
Annie M. (24), d/o Philip - Charles M. Houghton (26), s/o George md. 31 Sep.
    1885. [TR]
Emma Clara (27), d/o Andrew - Joseph Henry Thayer (38), s/o Henry md. 27 Nov.
    1872. [TR]
Philip A. (62) - Augusta N. Carlson (24) of Lexington, MA. md. 17 July 1900
    at Hampton. [AR]
William - Betsy Matthres md. 24 July 1805. [CH]
William S. - Mary Eaton md. 19 July 1838. [CH]

WATERS:

Dwight of Millbury, Mass. - Sarah Ann Dearborn md. 30 Mar. 1836. [CH]

WATSON:

Charles A. (51), s/o Nathaniel of Boston, Mass. - Lizzie F. French (29), d/o Samuel md. 24 Oct. 1866. [CH]
James - Hannah B. Knowles md. 28 Mar. 1830. [CH]
Nathaniel - Mary Hobbs, both of Hampton md. 10 Dec. 1846. [CH]
Perley B. (32), s/o Henry - Mary A. Berry (21), d/o E.H. md. 26 Dec. 1871. [TR]

WEARE:

Ella M. (22), d/o Joseph - James Jenness (27), s/o Jonathan md. 8 Sep. 1877. [TR]
Jennie (21) - Charles E. Dalton (21) md. 4 July 1894. [TR]

WEBB:

Louise (21) - Curtis Dearborn Marston (25) md. 7 Dec. 1939 at N. Berwick, Me. [AR]

WEBSTER:

Abigail - Samuel Brackett Berry, both of Rye md. 7 Feb. 1798. [CH]
Martha - Ozem Doust md. 3 Nov. 1796. [CH]

WEDGWOOD:

Betsy - Jacob Dearborn md. July 1789. [CH]
Betsy - Joseph J. Berry, both of Rye md. 24 Feb. 1813. [TR][CH]
David, s/o Jona. & Mary - Mary Marston, d/o Jonathan & Sarah md. 21 Nov. 1762. [TR]
David, Lt. - Polly C. Jenness, both of Rye md. 24 Dec. 1817. [TR][CH]
James - Olive Dearborn md. 14 July 1768. [CH]
Josiah - Sarah Leavitt md. 10 Dec. 1783. [CH]
Mary - Reuben Philbrick of Rye md. 22 Dec. 1772. [CH]
Nathaniel, Rev. - Anna Filch of Portsmouth md. Jan. 1742/3. [TR]
Nathaniel, Rev. -Mrs. Love Wingate md. 17 Nov. 1748. [TR]
Olive of Greenland - James Folsom 3d of Exeter md. 14 Oct. 1810. [TR][CH]
Sarah W. - Joseph Locke 4th, both of Rye md. 29 Nov. 1816. [TR][CH]

WEED:

Bagley - Eleanor Ccorge md. 11 Feb. 1751. [CH]

WEEKS:

Betsy - Dudley Page md. 25 Dec. 1787 or 15 Jan. 1788. [TR][CH]
Ceaeser - Violet March, both of Greenland md. 2 July 1777. [CH]
Deborah - William Ayers, both of Greenland md. 8 Jan. 1795. [CH]
Hannah of Greenland - Hon. Josiah Bartlett of Stratham md. 5 Apr. 1812. [TR][CH]
John Jr. of Greenland - Deborah Allen of Stratham md. 28 Oct. 1773. [CH]
Josiah - Mercy Colman of Greenland md. 22 June 1809. [TR][CH]

WEEKS Cont.
Stephen, Lt. - Mary Gookin, both of Greenland md. 21 Jan. 1808. [CH]
Stephen W. (36) - Ellen Henderson (26), both of Greenland md. 1 Feb. 1852. [CH]

WELCH:
Emily I. (19), d/o Samuel - Thomas S. Marston (21), s/o George F. md. 6 Oct. 1880. [TR]
John - Abia Flanders md. 5 Dec. 1751. [CH]

WELLS:
Florence M. (25) of Stratham - Stephen Jankowsky Jr. (30) of Exeter md. 12 June 1943. [AR]
Olive - John L. Lamprey, both of Kensington md. 26 Jan. 1829. [TR][CH]

WENTWORTH:
Barbara Rose (18) - Robert Fred Boisvert (21) of Portsmouth md. 1 May 1940 at Kittery. [AR]
Clara N. (42) of Rochester - Irving W. Brown (43) md. 12 Oct. 1912 at Rochester. [AR]

WHENAL:
George E. (20) - Ester L. Blaney (28) of Kittery md. 6 Sep. 1924 at Dover. [AR]
Henry T. (33) - Charlotte B. Taylor (26) of Eastport, Me. md. 4 Sep. 1928 at Eastport. [AR]
John (32) - Carrie A. Marston (22) md. 20 Nov. 1901. [AR]
John William (25) - Hazel Lovett (21) md. 18 Sep. 1943. [AR]
Martin Wade (23) - Hazel May Varney (24) of Plymouth, NH md. 24 Sep. 1927 at Plymouth. [AR]
Thomas B. (22) - Isabel J. White (19) md. 15 Oct. 1894. [TR][AR]
William T. (24) - Katherine R. Christie (22) of Dover md. 6 May 1933 at Dover. [AR]

WHIDDEN/WHEDDEN:
Elizabeth - Henry Nutter md. 28 Feb. 1795. [CH]
John - Dorothy Lang, both of Greenland md. 12 Aug. 1792. [TR]
Michael - Mrs. Eliza Hart both of Portsmouth md. 8 May 1808. [TR][CH]

WHITE:
Alice A. (22) of Hampton - Fred G. Dalton (28) md. 9 June 1932. [AR]
Charles C. (23) of Hampton - Nellie E. Moulton (21) md. 28 Nov. 1906. [AR]
George E. (28), s/o Parkman - Polly A. Marden (21), d/o Nathaniel md. 29 Sep. 1869. [TR][CH]
Hannah (63) - Pepparill Frost (64), s/o William md. 3 July 1880. [TR]
Isabel J. (19) - Thomas B. Whenal (22) md. 15 Oct. 1894. [TR][AR]

WHITE Cont.
Jeanetta R. (28) of Hampton - Raymond W. Clark (31) md. 27 June 1936 at
   Newfields, NH. [AR]
Phillips - Wid. Sarah Dearborn md. 16 June 1798. [CH]
Phillip, Capt. - Sally White, widow md. 10 Feb. 1816. [CH]
Samuel of Pittsfield - Harriet Janvrin of Hampton Falls md. 12 May 1829.
   [TR][CH]
Sally, widow - Capt. Phillip White md. 10 Feb. 1816. [CH]
Willard Chandler (21) - Beatrice Louise Armstrong (29) both of Newton, MA.
   md. 23 Nov. 1929. [AR]

WHITTEN:
John - Anna Lewis md. 15 May 1765. [CH]

WHITTIER:
Sergeant of Stratham - Martha Cotes md. 7 May 1771. [CH]
Sergeant - Anna Clarke, both of Stratham md. 25 Nov. 1773. [CH]

WIGGIN(S):
Clarissa - David French, both of Stratham md. 1 Jan. 1809. [TR][CH]
David - Hannah Rawlins md. 30 Nov. 1783. [CH]
Daivd (23), s/o John - Delia Leavitt (21), d/o Tappan md. 2 Nov. 1867. [TR]
Eliza - Andrew Taylor, both of Stratham md. 25 Apr. 1820. [TR]
Fred B. (33) - Alice Robie (32) of Stratham md. 25 Jan. 1899 at Stratham.
   [AR]
Lydia of Stratham - Thomas Veazy md. 1 Oct. 1778. [CH]
Lydia of Stratham - Elias s. Taylor of Parsonfield md. 7 July 1816. [TR][CH]
Nathaniel 3d of Stratham - Nancy Simpson of Greenland md. 2 May 1809.
   [TR][CH]
Pauline E. (24) - Charles W. Hardy (32) of Leomister, MA. md. 12 Sep. 1937 at
   Manchester. [AR]
Susanna, Mrs. - John Dearborn of Stratham md. 1787. [CH]
Thomas - Elizabeth Jewell, both of Stratham md. 11 Feb. 1768. [CH]

WILE:
Wallace B. (25) of Ipswich - Bertha Kos (24) of Bondsville, MA. md. 9 Feb.
   1936. [AR]

WILLIKEN:
Octavia L. (20) - George A. Bouthby (24) md. 30 Oct. 1895. [TR]

WILLIAMS:
Mary Ann - Samuel Palmer, both of Hampton Falls md. 17 Oct. 1824. [TR][CH]

WILLS:
Simeon of Rye - Sarah Batchelder md. 16 Nov. 1797. [CH]

WILSON:

Anne E. (34) - Seibert A. Payne (35) of Boston md. 28 June 1914. [AR]

Eleanor (21) - Charles Ellery Beaman (21) both of Gloucester, MA. md. 16 June 1938. [AR]

WILTBANK:

William MacPherson (29) of Phila., PA - Josephine A. Bachelder (24) md. 2 Sep. 1897. [AR]

WING:

Alice (26) of Everett, MA. - Harry C. Wood (25) of Portsmouth md. 10 Oct. 1931. [AR]

Sarah, widow - Benjamin Noyes md. 2 June 1755. [CH]

WINGATE:

Love, Mrs. - Rev. Nathaniel Gookin md. 17 Nov. 1748. [TR][CH]

WINGET:

Anne, d/o Joshua & Mary - Daniel Marston, s/o Simon & Hannah md. 13 Nov. 1733. [TR]

WINSOR:

Robert Jr. (35) of Weston, MA. - Susan R. Baker (19) of Boston md. 27 Sep. 1919. [AR]

WITHERALL:

George W. (45) - Margaret A. Collins (37) md. 8 July 1864. [TR]

WOOD:

Harry C. (25) of Portsmouth - Alice Wing (26) of Everett, MA. md. 10 Oct. 1931. [AR]

Will C. (40) - Helen R. Haffche (35) both of Beverly, MA. md. 27 Nov. 1927. [AR]

WOODBURN:

Doris (18) - Clarence D. Marston (22) md. 6 Apr. 1921 at Hampton. [AR]

WOODBURY:

Samuel of Newburyport - Jane Lamprey of Hampton md. 20 Apr. 1834. [TR][CH]

WOODHOUSE:

James - Olly Walker md. 26 Jan. 1772. [CH]

WOODROW:

Irving C. (55) of Colebrook, NH - Teresa A. Talton (45) md. 30 Oct. 1923. [AR]

WOODWARD:
Phebe Alverna (20) of Brockton - Robert Charles Benson (21) of Beverly, MA.
md. 12 June 1938. [AR]

WORMWOOD:
Hannah - George Ham, both of Portsmouth md. 5 June 1814. [TR][CH]

WORTHEN:
Eliza - Stephen Page md. 28 Aug. 1823. [TR][CH]
Jacob - Mary Brown md, 28 Sep. 1756. [CH]

WRIGHT:
Grace I. (27) of Greenland - J. Russell Dow (21) md. 3 Oct. 1907. [AR]
Jennie S. (19) - Enoch J. Berry (26) md. 14 Dec. 1885. [TR]
Maurice R. (31) - Alice L. Kaharl (17) of Exeter md. 5 Sep. 1916 at Exeter.
   [AR]

WYMAN:
Zebulon - Margaret Redman md. 31 Dec. 1755. [CH]

YEATON:
John S. of Exeter - Elizabeth Leavitt of Stratham md. 13 May 1832. [TR][CH]

YOUNG:
Caroline - Benjamin J. Fifield, both of Exeter md. 19 Aug. 1829. [TR][CH]
Joseph - Abigail K. Moulton, both of Hampton md. 25 May 1823. [TR][CH]
Mary E. (28) of Deerfield - Herman L. Norton (23) md. 25 Oct. 1916 at
   Hampton. [AR]

YURAN:
John of Tunbridge, Vt. - Lauranda Chapman md. 15 Nov. 1832. [TR][CH]

ZAPFF:
Alfred (33) of W. Roxbury, MA. - Anna Meyer (44) md. 13 Mar. 1935. [AR]

ZARNOWSKI:
Eleanora My (22) of Exeter - George Wesley Carter (29) md. 31 Dec. 1938. [AR]

APPENDIX

TOWN OFFICERS

TOWN CLERK:

1743 - 1758   John Wedgewood
1758 - 1794   Jonathan Wedgewood
1794 - 1816   Dr. John Fogg
1816 - 1822   Jonathan Marston
1822 - 1833   George Odell
1833 - 1838   Jonathan Marston
1838 - 1841   Samuel F. French
1841 - 1843   Jeremiah S. Rollins
1843 - 1846   Rufus Leavitt
1846 - 1848   Dr. Moses L. Hobbs
1848 - 1849   John S. Hobbs
1849 - 1863   Thomas D. Hobbs
1863 - 1865   Joseph B. Hobbs
1865 - 1903   Jonathan Rollins
1903 - 1917   Roy R. Rollins
1917 - 1930   James F. Leavitt
1930 - 1942   Ruth K. Leavitt

CONSTABLE/COLLECTOR:

1745 Benjamin Marston Jr.	1787 Benjamin Swet
1749 Zachariah Towl	1788 Benjamin Swet
1753 Jonathan Page	1789 Benjamin Swet
1760 Joseph Knowles	1809 Simon Dearborn
1761 Jonathan Palmer	1810 Simon Dearborn
1762 Jonathan Palmer	1811 Samuel Leavitt
1765 Ebenezer Loving	1812 Morris Hobbs
1766 Ebenezer Sanborn	1813 Jacob Brown Jr.
1767 David Marston	1814 Jacob Brown Jr.
1768 Simon Page	1815 Joshua Pickering
1770 Benjamin Hobbs	1816 Jacob Brown Jr.
1772 Benjamin Hobbs	1817 Capt. David Brown
1774 Samuel Page	1818 Samuel Chapman
1775 Benjamin Leavitt	1819 Daniel Dow
1776 Capt. John Dearborn	1821 Jacob Brown
1777 David Page	1822 Joshua Pickering
1778 David Page	1823 Oliver Leavitt
1779 Ebenezer Sanborn	1824 Joshua Pickering
1780 Thomas Leavitt	1825 Samuel Chapman Jr.
1781 James Wedgwood	1826 Daniel Dow
1782 James Wedgwood	1827 Daniel Dow
1783 James Wedgwood	1828 Dea. Nathaniel Ambrose
1784 Thomas Leavitt	1829 Thomas L. Marston
1785 Simon Ward	1830 Joshua Pickering
1786 Daniel Gookin	

SELECTMAN:

1743 Maj. Joshua Wingate, Capt. Benj. Thomas, Jonathan Page, Ebenezer Sanborn, John Hobbs.

1744 Caleb Marston, Ebenezer Sanborn, Benuni Fuller, John Wedgewoo, Samuel Marston.

1745 Daniel Samborn, James Hobbs, Stephen Batchelder, Co. Joshua Wingate, Zachariah Towle.

1746 Timothy Dalton, Joseph Knowles, Thomas Hains, James Hobbs, John Wedgewood.

1747 Francis Page, Jonathan Page, John Chapman, John Wedgewood.

1748 Thomas Robie, David Page, Reuben Gove Dearborn, Abraham Drake, Jeremiah Page.

1749 Daniel Sanborn, Reuben Marston, Caleb Marston, Jonathan Wedgwood, Joshua Brown.

1750 John Batchelder, John Hobbs, Ebenezer Sanborn, Jeremiah Dearborn, John Leavitt.

1751 Simon Dearborn, Abner Fogg, David Marston, Daniel Marston, John Wedgewood.

1752 Edward Shaw, Samuel Hobbs, Samuel Batchelder, John Wedgewood, James Godfrey.

1753 Dr. Levi Dearborn, Thomas Hains, Reuben Dearborn, Ebenezer Sanborn, John Taylor.

1754 Job Chapman, Jeremiah Page, Daniel Sanborn, Benjamin Hobbs, Samuel Fogg.

1755 Joseph Knowles, Pennel Chapman, Timothy Dalton, Obadiah Marston, John Hobbs.

1756 Simeon Dearborn, Abraham Drake, David Marston, David Knowles, Thomas Hains.

1757 Simon Dearborn, Jonathan Wedgewood, Benjamin Hobbs, Jeremiah Dearborn, Thomas Marston.

1758 John Batchelder, Reuben Dearborn, Capt. Leavitt, Zachary Towle, Dr. Levi Dearborn.

1759 Job Chapman, William Moulton Sr., Ebenzer Lovering, Enoch Sanborn, John Hobbs Sr.

1760 Ebenezer Sanborn, Reuben Gove Dearborn, Joseph Hobbs.

1761 Joseph Hobbs, Benjamin Marston Jr., Stephen Batchelder.

1762 Henry Batchelder, Joseph Hobbs, Daniel Sanborn.

1763 Cornet David Marston, Daniel Sanborn Jr., David Page Jr.

1764 Abraham Drake, Daniel Dow, Benjamin Hobbs.

1765 Benjamin Hobbs, Samuel Chapman, Simon Marston.

1766 Ebenezer Sanborn, Reuben Dearborn, Joseph Hobbs.

1767 Jonathan Page, Joseph Hobbs, Zackariah Towle.

1768 Lt. Reuben Gove Dearborn, David Marston, David Wedgewood.

1769 Ebenezer Neal, Joseph Hobbs, David Marston.

1770 John Leavitt Esq., Reubengove Dearborn, James Batchelder.

1771 Samuel Batchelder, Benjamin Hobbs, Zachariah Towle.

1772 Benjamin Hobbs Sr., Zachariah Towle, Samuel Batchelder.

1773 Reubengove Dearborn, Benjamin Hobbs, Christopher Smith.

SELECTMEN Cont.

1774 David Marston, Benjamin Hobbs, Benjamin Leavitt.
1775 David Marston, Benjamin Leavitt, John Lamprey.
1776 Col. Abraham Drake, Christopher Smith, David Marston.
1777 David Marston, Christopher Smith, Col. Abraham Drake.
1778 Morris Hobbs, Ebenezer Neal, Joseph Hobbs.
1779 Morris Hobbs, Ebenezer Neal, Capt. Moses Leavitt.
1780 Ebenezer Neal, Morris Hobbs, Moses Leavitt.
1781 Morris Hobbs, Benjamin Leavitt, Isaac Marston.
1782 Morris Hobbs, Benjamin Leavitt, Isaac Marston.
1783 Benjamin Hobbs, Christopher Smith, William Godfrey.
1784 Morris Hobbs, Benjamin Hobbs, Isaac Marston.
1785 Simon Brown, Benjamin Leavitt, Morris Hobbs.
1786 Tristram Redman, Stephen Page, Thomas Marston.
1787 Stephen Page, Thomas Marston, Tristram Redman.
1788 Jacob Brown, Stephen Page, Thomas Marston.
1789 Stephen Page, Thomas Marston, Jacob Brown.
1790 Thomas Marston, Jacob Brown, Stephen Page.
1791 Morris Hobbs, Capt. Thomas Leavitt, Simeon Fogg.
1792 Stephen Page, Jacob Brown, Thomas Leavitt.
1793 Thomas Leavitt, Abraham Drake, Jacob Brown.
1794 Thomas Leavitt, Abraham Drake, Jacob Brown.
1795 Thomas Leavitt, Jacob Brown, Abraham Drake.
1796 Maj. Thomas Leavitt, Samuel Dearborn, John Lamprey.
1797 Thomas Leavitt, Samuel Dearborn, John Lamprey.
1798 Thomas Marston, Cornet Abraham Drake, John Lamprey.
1799 Thomas Marston, John Lamprey, Simon Ward.
1800 Thomas Marston, John Lamprey, Thomas Lovering.
1801 Thomas Marston, Thomas Lovering, Levi Marston.
1802 Thomas Marston, Levi Marston, Samuel Dearborn.
1803 Thomas Marston, Samuel Dearborn, Levi Marston
1804 Thomas Marston, Levi Marston, Samuel DEarborn.
1805 Daniel Gookin, Cotton Marston, Tristram Dalton.
1806 Cotton Marston, Tristram Dalton, Daniel Gookin.
1807 Cotton Marston, Tristram Dalton, Daniel Gookin.
1808 Daniel Gookin, Cotton Marston, Tristram Dalton.
1809 Danial Gookin, Cotton W. Marston, Tristram Dalton
1810 Danial Gookin, Cotton W. Marston, Tristram Dalton
1811 Thomas Marston, Jonathan Hobbs, Morris Lamprey
1812 Thomas Marston, Morris Lamprey, Jonathan Hobbs
1813 Thomas Marston, Jonathan Hobbs, Morris Lamprey
1814 Thomas Marston, Jonathan Hobbs, David Brown
1815 Thomas Marston, David Brown, Samuel F. Leavitt
1816 David Brown, Benjamin Leavitt, Samuel F. Leavitt
1817 Jacob Brown Jr., Francis Drake, John Dearborn Jr.
1818 Jacob Brown Jr., Francis Drake, John Dearborn Jr.
1819 Morris Lamprey, Abraham Towle, John Dearborn Jr.

SELECTMEN Cont.
1820 Abrahm Towle, Morris Lamprey, John Leavitt.
1821 Jeremiah Brown, Samuel Leavitt, Jonathan Hobbs
1822 Samuel Leavitt, Jeremiah Brown, Jonathan Hobbs
1823 Samuel Leavitt, Jeremiah Brown, Jonathan Hobbs
1824 Lt. Jonathan Hobbs, Nathaniel Batchelder, Abraham Leavitt
1825 Tristram Dalton, Abraham Leavitt, Nathaniel Batchelder
1826 Tristram Dalton, Abraham Leavitt, Nathaniel Batchelder
1827 Tristram Dalton, Morris Hobbs Jr., Samuel Drake
1828 Tristram Dalton, Morris Hobbs Jr., Samuel Drake
1829 Tristram Dalton, Morris Hobbs Jr., Oliver Leavitt
1830 Benning Leavitt, Morris Hobbs Jr., Oliver Leavitt
1831 Cotton W. Marston, Levi Brown, James Batchelder.
1832 Cotton W. Marston, Levi Brown, James Batchelder.
1833 Cotton W. Marston, Nathaniel Batchelder, James Batchelder.
1834 Nathaniel Batchelder, William Hains, Jonathan Lamprey.
1835 William Hains, Jonathan Hobbs, Jonathan Lamprey.
1836 Jonathan Lamprey, Frederic A. Batchelder, John Lamprey Jr.
1837 Jonathan Lamprey, Frederic A. Batchelder, John Lamprey Jr.
1838 Frederic A. Batchelder, David Marston, Dr. Moses I. Hobbs.
1839 Dr. Moses I. Hobbs, David Marston, Jeremiah Rollins.
1840 Jeremiah Rollins, John Leavitt, Daniel Dow.
1841 John Leavitt, Daniel Dow, Rufus Leavitt.
1842 Rufus Leavitt, Simon Brown Jr., Benjamin Crimball.
1843 Simon Brown Jr., Benjamin Crimball, Samuel F. French.
1844 Levi Marston, Jeremiah S. Rollins, Samuel F. French.
1845 Levi Marston, Jeremiah S. Rollins, George O. Dow.
1846 George D. Dow, Jeremiah Batchelder, Rufus Leavitt.
1847 Rufus Leavitt, Jeremiah Batchelder, David M. Dow.
1848 Rufus Leavitt, David M. Dow, Jacob H. Brown.
1849 Rufus Leavitt, David M. Dow, Jacob H. Brown.
1850 Jonathan P. Robinson, Simon Brown Jr., John F. French.
1851 Jonathan P. Robinson, Simon Brown Jr., John F. French.
1852 David M. Dow, John S. Hobbs, Nathaniel B. Marston.
1853 David M. Dow, John S. Hobbs, Nathaniel B. Marston.
1854 David M. Dow, John S. Hobbs, Nathaniel B. Marston.
1855 David M. Dow, John S. Hobbs, John Batchelder Jr.
1856 John Batchelder Jr., John P. Elkins, Benjamin Marston.
1857 John P. Elkins, Benjamin Marston, Hezekiah B. Lamprey.
1858 John P. Elkins, Hezekiah B. Lamprey, Moses Shaw.
1859 Moses Shaw, Hendrick D. Batchelder, David M. Dow.
1860 Hendrick D. Batchelder, Rufus Leavitt, Jonathan P. Robinson.
1861 Samuel Fogg, David M. Dow, Albert A. Brown.
1862 Samuel Fogg, David M. Dow, Albert A. Brown.
1863 John P. Elkins, David P. Moulton, Tappan Leavitt.
1864 John P. Elkins, David P. Moulton, Tappan Leavitt.
1865 David M. Dow, Nathan Brown, Eben L. Dalton.

SELECTMEN Cont.

1866 David M. Dow, John P. Elkins, Eben L. Dalton.
1867 David M. Dow, John P. Elkins, Eben L. Dalton.
1868 John S. Hobbs, Enoch F. Wiggin, Eben L. Dalton.
1869 John S. Hobbs, Enoch F. Wiggin, George D. Brown.
1870 John S. Hobbs, Enoch F. Wiggin, George D. Brown.
1871 John S. Hobbs, Charles A. Watson, John Moulton.
1872 John S. Hobbs, Charles A. Wiggin, John Moulton.
1873 John S. Hobbs, Charles A. Wiggin, John Moulton.
1874 John S. Hobbs, Horace Leavitt, Albert Batchelder.
1875 John S. Hobbs, Thomas F. Batchelder, Thomas E. Marston.
1876 John S. Hobbs, Thomas F. Batchelder, Thomas E. Marston.
1877 John S. Hobbs, Jacob F. Brown, Charles C. Barton.
1878 John S. Hobbs, Jacob F. Brown, Charles C. Barton.
1879 John S. Hobbs, Jacob F. Brown, Charles C. Barton.
1880 John S. Hobbs, Horace D. Brown, Lewis K.H. Lane.
1881 John S. Hobbs, Horace O. Brown, Albert Batchelder.
1882 John S. Hobbs, Albert Bachelder, John W. Berry.
1883 Albert Bachelder, John W. Berry, Morris H. Smith.
1884 Eben L. Dalton, John W. Hobbs, Thomas E. Marston.
1885 Eben L. Dalton, John W. Hobbs, Thomas E. Marston.
1886 Eben L. Dalton, George F. Taylor, Frank C. Norton.
1887 Eben L. Dalton, George F. Taylor, Frank C. Norton.
1888 Eben L. Dalton, Levi W. Fogg, James W. Barton.
1889 Otis S. Brown, George W. Knowles, James W. Barton.
1890 Otis S. Brown, George W. Knowles, Cyrus Fogg.
1891 Otis S. Brown, Cyrus Fogg, Simon O. Lamprey.
1892 Otis S. Brown, Cyrus Fogg, Simon O. Lamprey.
1893 Otis S. Brown, Cyrus Fogg, Simon O. Lamprey.
1894 Otis S. Brown, Cyrus Fogg, Simon O. Lamprey.
1895 Otis S. Brown, Cyrus Fogg, Simon O. Lamprey.
1896 Otis S. Brown, Freemont P. Moulton, Frank A. Marston.
1897 Otis S. Brown, Freemont P. Moulton, Frank a. Marston.
1898 Otis S. Brown, Simon O. Lamprey, Cyrus Fogg.
1899 Otis S. Brown, Simon O. Lamprey, Cyrus Fogg.
1900 Otis S. Brown, Simon O. Lamprey, Cyrus Fogg.
1901 Otis S. Brown, Cyrus Fogg, Fred L. Cotton.
1902 Otis S. Brown, Cyrus Fogg, Fred L. Cotton.
1903 Otis S. Brown, Oliver S. Hobbs, Irving W. Brown.
1904 Otis S. Brown, Oliver S. Hobbs, Irving Brown.
1905 Otis S. Brown, Irving W. Brown, Arthur E. Seavey.
1906 Otis S. Brown, Irving W. Brown, Arthur E. Seavey.
1907 Otis S. Brown, Irving W. Brown, Arthur E. Seavey.
1908 Otis S. Brown, Irving W. Brown, Arthur E. Seavey.
1909 Otis S. Brown, Irving W. Brown, Arthur E. Seavey.
1910 Otis S. Brown, George L. Garland, Gilman H. Moulton.
1911 Otis S. Brown, George L. Garland, Gilman H. Moulton.

SELECTMEN Cont.

1912 Otis S. Brown, George L. Garland, Gilman H. Moulton.
1913 Otis S. Brown, George L. Garland, Gilman H. Moulton.
1914 Albert Bachelder, George G. Carter, J. Russell Dow.
1915 Albert Bachelder, George G. Carter, J. Russell Dow.
1916 Albert Bachelder, George G. Carter, Irving W. Marston.
1917 Fred L. Cotton, George G. Carter, Irving W. Marston.
1918 George G. Carter, Irving W. Marston, Lewis D. Hill.
1919 George G. Carter, Irving W. Marston, Lewis D. Hill.
1920 Irving W. Marston, James F. Hobbs Jr., Leslie L. Lovett.
1921 Irving W. Marston, James F. Hobbs Jr., Herman L. Norton.
1922 Irving W. Marston, James F. Hobbs Jr., Herman L. Norton.
1923 Irving W. Marston, Herman L. Norton, Melvin P. Locke.
1924 Irving W. Marston, Herman L. Norton, Melvin P. Locke.
1925 Irving W. Marston, Herman L. Norton, Melvin P. Locke.
1926 Irving W. Marston, Herman L. Norton, Irving W. Brown.
1927 Irving W. Marston, Herman L. Norton, Irving W. Brown.
1928 Irving W. Marston, Herman L. Norton, Irving W. Brown.
1929 Irving W. Marston, Herman L. Norton, Joshua F. Drake.
1930 Irving W. Marston, Herman L. Norton, Joshua F. Drake.
1931 Irving W. Marston, Herman L. Norton, Joshua F. Drake.
1932 Irving W. Marston, Herman L. Norton, Joshua F. Drake.
1933 Irving W. Marston, Herman L. Norton, Joshua F. Drake.
1934 Irving W. Marston, Joshua F. Drake, Forrest E. Knowles.
1935 Irving W. Marston, Joshua F. Drake, Forrest E. Knowles.
1936 Irving W. Marston, Joshua F. Drake, Forrest E. Knowles.
1937 Irving W. Marston, Joshua F. Drake, Forrest E. Knowles.
1938 Irving W. Marston, Joshua F. Drake, Forrest E. Knowles.
1939 Irving W. Marston, Joshua F. Drake, Forrest E. Knowles.
1940 Irving W. Marston, Joshua F. Drake, Forrest E. Knowles.
1941 Irving W. Marston, Joshua F. Drake, Forrest E. Knowles.
1942 Irving W. Marston, Joshua F. Drake, Forrest E. Knowles.

EARLY HISTORY

The petition for a new parish was as early as
1719. A committee of Mark Hunking, Shadrick
Walton, Nicholas Giman and Joe Gilman Esqr was
named to determine a boundry line between the
old parish in Hampton and the new. They reported
29 May 1719. The project failed at that time
because it was not acted upon by the N.H. House
of Representatives. No further attempts were
made until 1734. It was rejected. A petition to
the legeslature was finally approved by the
governer 17 Nov. 1738.

At the first meeting held 21 Dec. 1738 John
Dearborn was chosen moderator, John Wedgewood,
clerk, Benjamin Hobbs, John Godfrey and Jonathan
Thomas, accessors, Job Chapman, collector, and
Danile Sanborn and Jeremiah Dearborn were chosen
a committee to agree with Mr. Nathaniel Gookin
to preach for three months. He became their
minister 28 July. The parish was called North
Hill. (Prov. Papers 18:359)

The petition to break away from Hampton is
dated 25 Nov. 1742. It was passed and approved
by the governer 30 Nov. 1742. North Hill became
the Town of North Hampton. (Prov. Papers 5:174)

Source: Dow, History of Hampton, pg 195.

[8-116] Petition of Inhabitants for a Divisional
Line: addressed to the Geneal Assembly, 1742.

The Petition of Sundry Persons who live in the Northerly part of Hampton in
Said Province whose names are hereunto annexed most humbly sheweth, That sometime
since the General Court of this Province by an act made and erected a Parish in
the northerly part of Hampton aforesaid by Polling off sundry Persons and their
Estates but not by any metes & bounds. That there are sundry others who live
convenient to attend the publick worship of God at the meeting house in said
Parish, who are desirous so to do. That the old Parish of Hampton is an able and
large parish and can without being burdened Spare sundry persons and their
estates to another Parish - wherefore your Petitioners pray your Excellency and
Honours to take this Petition under Consideration and in your great wisdom and
Goodness to ratify establish and Confirm the said Parish in the Northerly part

of said Hampton by a divisional line between the old Parish of Hampton aforesaid and the said Northerly Parish whereabouts your Excellency and Honours shall see meet and proper or to Cause that the Ministers of the said Two Parishes be paid By one Rate or otherways as may be Judged Just and equall and your Petitioners as in Duty bound shall ever pray &c.
June the 7th 1742.

We the Subsrcibers of the north part of Hampton desire to put in to this Honarable General Cort to see If they will grant us a Line between the parishs in Hampton or order to maintain the two ministers together or any other way by there Consideration

John Derborn	Joshua Winget	Abner Fogg
Samuel derbon	Timothy Dalton	Samel bachelder
Thomas marston	his m	hanrey bachelder
John Wedwood	henrey X Darbon	James Godfree
Job chapman	Benjamin Marston	Jacob liford
Daniel samborn	Sen	William godfree
Jonathan Marston	John Marston	Bugman Hobs
Simon Dearborn	Joshua Brown	John godfree
John leavitt	Jonathan thomas	Stven behalder Jr.
daniel marston	David Jewell	Ebnezer Samborn
Benjamin marston	Jerimiah darbon	Joh phelbreck
winthrop marston	Stephen Batchelder	John godfree.

Source: NH Early Town Papers, V. 9, p. 76-77.

[Action of the Legislature on the foregoing]

In the House of Representatives 9' 24th 1742.

The within Petition & others relating thereto Read & the Parties heard and the House having considered thereof, voted: That there be a line Setled, vizt to beging at a Great Rock in the High way that Leads from Portsmouth to Hampton over North Hill between ye dwelling Houses of Caleb Marston * Joseph Tole Junr and is the first Great Rock in ye High way to the Southward of the Widow Levits dwelling House & from Said Rock to run on a Strait Line to the Sea at the mouth of the Little River where it now Empties ifSelf into the Sea. And then to begin at the Great Rock aforesaid & then to run on a Straight Line to the Corner Bounds Between Stratham & Exeter at Hampton Line And that the Estates in the old parish yt belongs to the Poles in the new parish Shall pay Rates to the north parish & the Estates belonging to ye Poles in the old parish that lies in the north parish Shall pay Rates to ye old parish and whereon the owner of the land Lives there he & his Estate Shall pay Rates, Notwithstanding ye Line Setled. & if any

Strangers purchase land in Either parish, he Shall pay where the Land Lies: & Its always intended that Every person in Each parish pay his Proportion of the Grant to Mrs. Dorothy Gookin as usual:

  and that the Rates for the present yeare be paid as they are already made & that the Petitioners have liberty to Bring in a Bill accordingly

  And yt ye Select men of Each parish Joyn in ye makeing ye Province Taxes, as also yt both parishes Joyn in Choice of Representative until further order -

James Jeffry Cler assr.

Provr N Hampr Nov: 25th 1742

In Council read & Concurrd

Theodr Atkinson Secr

Eodem Die Assented tp

B Wentworth

[8-117] Petition of Inhabitants relative to Church Affairs: addressed to the General Assembly September 14, 1742.

The Himble Petition of us the Subscribers Most Humbly Sheweth that the houses and habitations of your Pititioners are in the northly Part of the town of Hampton and where as SEveral of our Neighbours were Some years ago Poled of from the town to the Support of a gospe;; minister at North hill and now Several others Joining with them they are Pititioning for a line which if granted will Probably take the houses and habitations of your Pititioners in with them and so Contrery to our Inclinations we shall be forced of from the Minestrey the Church and Congregation in the old town and (with out the aid of your Excellency and Honours) Shall be Compelled to Pay to the Support of the minestrey at north hill If your Excellency and Honours Should in your Grate wisdom See meet to Grant them their Pitition and give them a line we Humbly and Earnestly Pray your Excellency and Honours that your Pititioners and their Estates may be Exampted from Paying to the Support of the Minestry at north hill and that we may still remain under and be taxed to the Support of the Monestrey and the other Publick Chargs of the town as we used to be and your Pititioners as in Dutely bound Shall Ever Pray.

John Smith	Joseph knowles	franis Page
william Moulton	Daniel fogg	William Moulton
Simon knowles	Samuel Fogg	Benj: Lampre
Richard taylor	Thomas Robie	Jona Knowles
Abraham Drake	Zachariah towl	Benjn Johnson
moris hobbes	Ruben darben	Jonathan Palmer
Josiah hobbes	Thomas darben	Joseph Page
John Shaw	Samuel darben	Joseph Moulton
Bengman Smith	Bennony fullor	Benj Johnson
William palmer	nathanil moreton	James Thomas
John Smith Jun	Samuel Bachildor Jr.	John taylor

SIGNERS OF THE ASSOCIATION TEST 7 JUNE 1776

Isaac Jenness	Simon Page	James Nudd
Joseph Hobbs	David Page	Reuben Gove Dearborn
Abner Fogg	Eben Lovering	Daniel Samborn
Samuel Wedgwood	James Wedgwood	William Samborn
Jeremiah Page	Ebenr Samborn	Simeon Marston
Tristram Redman	Reuben Dearborn	Hanery Batchelder
Jacob Brown	Benjamin Lamprey	Samuel Batchelder
Benjamin Brown	Ebenezer Neal	Samuel Page
Thomas Cotton	Henry Batchelder	Stephen Page
Levi Dearborn	James Godfrey	Abner Fogg
John Wingate	Timothy Dalton	Joshua Hains
David Marston	Simon Brown	Zechariah Towl Junr
Caleb Marston	Francis Page	Thomas Marston
Samll Mace	David Knowles	Daniel Dow
Josiah Batchelder	Samuel Hardy	Joseph Dearborn
William Godfree	David Page Juner	Ebenr Lovering
Thomas Hobbs	Samuel Fogg	Reuben Gove Dearborn
Samuel Dearborn	Thomas Leavitt	Joseph Palmer
William Weeks	Abraham Taylor	John Weeks
John Lovering	Joseph Moulton Jr.	Josiah Dalton
John Potter	James Batchelder	Enenr Tilton
Josiah Brown Junr	Samuel Batchelder	Abraham Drake Jr.
Samuel Davis	Moris Hobbs	Phinehas Dearborn
Benjamin Palmer	Benjn Mason	Isaac Marston
Nathaniel Hans	Simon D. Lovering	Jonathan Wedgwood
John Chase	Thomas Samborn	John Leavitt
John Brown	Stephen Shaw	Zachr Towle
Benja Hobbs	Samuel Chapman	John Robie
Seth Fogg	Zaceriah X his mark	Benjamin Marston Jr.
Benjamin Philbrick	Batchelder	Benjamin Leavitt
Thomas Cotton	Joseph Garland	Jeremiah Dearborn
Jonathan Knowles	Nathaniel Hobbs	Moses Leavitt
Moris Lamprey	Samuel Robie	Josiah Dearborn
John Lamprey	Samuel Smith	Joseph Taylor
Reuben Dearborn	John Nudd	Nathaniel Batchelder
Abraham Drake	Jona Page	Joseph Moulton
John Dearborn	Joseph Knowles	Benj Hobbs
Christopher Smith	Edward Shaw	John Marston
Simon Lampere	John Taylor	Dnl Dearborn

WARNING OUT ORDERS

The N,H, State Archives at Concord contain several Warning Out Notice. They are found in loose papers for North Hampton. They include the following:

1763 Sep. 15   Samuel Seavey & his wife.

1767 Apr. 4   Elisha Towle & his wife & family.

1770 June 7   A pauper, not named.

1774 Jan. 1   Sarah Rawlings, d/o John of Greenland.

Warning Out Notice for Sarah Rawlings 1 Jan. 1774:

Province of NewhamS.)
Rockinham Co.   )   To Mr. Samuel Pagr
               Constable of North Hampton in the County aforesd. Greeting:

Whereas information hath been made to me the Subscriber One of his majestrys Justices of the Peace for the County aforesd by the Selectman of North Hampton in Sd County that Sarah Rawlings Spinster hath lately Come into Sd North Hampton to dwell therein and to endeavour to Gain a Settlement therein which would likely be Chargeable to Sd Parish that the Sd Sarah hath been duly warned to Depart out of Sd Parish and Return made agreable to the Law of Sd Province in that Case made and Provided; And that the Sd Sarah hath not by any means gained a Legal residence or Settlement in the Sd Parish of North Hampton; Notwithstanding that the Sd Sarah Continues to reside in Sd Parish more than fourteen Days Since Sd warning Given her to depart and further the Sd Selectmen Inform that Greenland in the County aforesd is the Place of the Last Legal Settlement of Sd Sarah - these are therefore in his Majestys name to be given you forthwith to take the body of the Sd Sarah Rawlings and her Safely Convey and deliver to the Constable of Sd Greenland together with a copy of this Sd Recept, the cost of her removall: being three shillings for Drawing this information and Procept together with your own fees to be Paid by the Sd Sarah if She has ability - Thereof Fail not. And make Return of this Precept and of your Doing therein unto my Self Date at North Hampton aforesd This first Day of January Anno Domini 1774 in the fourteen year of his majesty George, etc.

J. L. Justice

Warning Out Warrant for Elisha Towle, 28 Aug. 1767:

Province of ⎫
NewHampshire ⎰ To Simon Page Constable of the Parish of North
Hampton in Said Province Greetings -

You are hereby In his Majestys name required forthwith to warn & Give Notice to Elisha Towle and his wife and Family (who have lately Come into the Said Parish without being legally admitted there) Immediately to Depart out of Said Parish. (as they have heretofore been Warned to do) on the Pain & Penalties of the Laws in that Case made & Provided - And make due return hereof & of Your Doings herein to the Next Court of General Session of the Peace to be holden at Portsmouth in September next For which this is Your WArrant Dated at North Hampton aforesaid the 28th day of August in the 7th year of his Majesty's reign Anno Domini 1767.

Jonathan Paige ⎫
Zachariah Towle ⎰ Selectman of
Joseph Hobbs   ⎰ NorthHampton

1. **AUSTIN**, Reuben: Enl. 20 Mar. 1778 for 3
   years Capt. Richard Weare's Co. (pg 457)
   (v. 1, pg. 641)

2. **AVERY**, James: Named in Town Return Petition
   R3-75.1 Mar. 1786. by Moses Leavitt, (pg.
   513)

3. **BARKER**, Samuel Served for Town of North
   Hampton but was from Hampton Falls.
   (pg. 257)

4. **BATCHELDER**, Henry: Enl. 5 Jan. 1776 Capt.
   Moses Leavitt;s Co.

5. **CLARK**, Stephen: 6 Dec. 1780, age 18 yrs.
   marched to Worcester. (v.3, pg. 64)

6. **COTTON**, William: 2 Apr. 1777 Capt. Richard
   Weare's Co.

7. **DALTON**, Tim: Enl. 5 Jan. 1776 Capt. Moses
   Leavitt's Co.

8. **DAM**, Ezra: Pvt. Co. A., Capt. James Parson
   24 Nov. 1781.

9. **DEARBORN**, John 3d: 4 Mar. 1777, Capt.
   Richard Weare;s Co., Col. Stammel for 3
   years.

10. **DEARBOERN**, Joseph: Enl. 5 Jan. 1776. capt.
    Moses Leavitt's Co.

11. **DEARBORN**, Levi: Sgt. 3rd Reg'y, Capt.
    Leavitt;s Co. 8 Oct. 1777, Col Abraham
    Drake (pg. 339)

12. **DEARBORN**, Samuel: Enl. 5 Jan. 1776, Capt.
    Moses Leavitt's Co. ; 4 Mar. 1777 Capt.
    Richard Weare's Co., Col. Stammal for 3
    years.

13. **DRAKE**, Abraham: Lt. Col. Commanded Troops
    at Saratoga 8 Sep. 1777 after battle of
    Benington.

14. **ENGLISH**, William: 2nd Reg't Capt.
McGregorer's Cp. 15 Jan. 1781. (pg. 228)

15. **GREEN**, Richard: 13 Apr. 1778 Capt. Richard
Weare's Co. (pg. 641_. 8 Dec. 1779 Capt.
Faye's Co., 3rd NH Regt. 15 Jan. 1781, 2nd
Regt McGregorer;s Co. (v. 3, pg 228)

16. **GREEN**, Robert: 1777 Capt. Weare'sCp., col.
Scammal for 3 yrs. 13 Mar. 1778 Capt.
Richard Weare's Co. (pg 641)

17. **FISHLEY**: George: 1778 Capt. Weare's Co.,
Col. Scammal for 3 yrs. 20 Mar. 1778 Capt.
Richard Weare's Co.

18. **FOGG**, Jonathan: 5 Jan. 1776 Capt. Moses
Leavitt's Co. 18 Sep. 1775 Capt. Dearborn
Co., age 19 from Raymond, farmer. Went to
Canada. 1 Aug. 1775 Pvt. Capt. Henry Elkin
Co., entered 27 May. Served 2 mo. 10 days.

19. **GOOKIN**, Daniel: 1777 Capt. Titcomb, Col.
Hale for 3 yrs. Sgt. Capt. Benj. Titcomb
Co. age 21, 19 Feb. 1777 at Dover (pg 567)
17 Feb. 1786 petition.

20. **GOLD**, Christopher: 5 Jan. 1776 Capt. Moses
Leavitt's Co. (v. 1, p. 158)

21. **GOSS**, Jonathan: 5 Jan. 1776 Capt. Moses
Leavitt's Co. 1 Aug. 1775 Capt. Henry Elkin
Co., enl. 29 May served 2 mo. 8 days.(v. 1,
p. 158 & 225)

22. **HARBOR**, John: 2nd Regt. 14 Feb. 1781, 7th
Co. Capt. Enoch Chase. (v.3, p. 231)

23. **HILL**, John: Served for North Hampton. Came
from Wakefield. (p. 513)

24. **KNOWLES**, Simon: 5 Jan. 1776 Capt. Moses
Leavitt's Co. (v.1, p. 158)

25. **LAMPREY**, Levi: 1st Lt. 26 May 1775 Capt.
Henry Elkin;s Co. 4 Mar. 1777 Capt.
Richard Weare's Co. 5 Jan. 1776 Dapt. Moses
Leavitt's Co. (v.1, p. 158)

26. **LEAVITT**, Moses: Capt. Formed Co. from North
Hampton 5 Jan. 1776. Had 28 volunteers.
Capt. 3rd Regt 8 Oct. 1777, Col. Abraham
Drake. (v.1, p. 158)

27. **LEAVITT**, Simon: 4 Mar. 1776 Capt. Moses
Leavitt's Co.

28. **LONG**, Jorge: Named on Petition for wages
due for service in Army. Pet. filed 30 May
1785.

29. **LONG**, Pasoll? 1777 Capt. Weare's Co. for 3
yrs.

30. **LOVERING**, Simon: Pvt. 4 Mar. 1777 Capt.
Weare, Col. Scammal Regt for 3 yrs.

31. **McCLURE**, Benjamin: 1778 3 yr enl. Capt.
Weare's Co.

32. **MARSTON**, Abraham: In Abraham Drake Regt.
Got sick in N.Y. State. Filed pet. R3-69 12
Feb. 1778. Paid.

33. **MARSTON**, David: 5 Jan. 1776 Capt. Moses
Leavitt's Co.

34. **MARSTON**, Jeremiah: 5 Jan. 1776 capt. Moses
Leavitt's Co.

35. **MARSTON**, John: 5 Jan. 1776 Capt. Moses
Leavitt's Co.

36. **MARSTON**, Jonathan: 9 Apr. 1777 Capt.
Richard Weare's Co., Col. Scammal Regt for
3 yrs.

37. **MARSTON**, Levi: 5 Jan. 1776 Capt. Moses
Leavitt's Co.

39. **MARSTON**, Samuel: 5 Jan. 1776 Capt. Moses
Leavitt's Co.

40. **MOULTON**, Redman: Ens. 8 Oct. 1777, 3rd
Regt. Capt. Leavitt's Co. To Rhode Is. 7
July 1779. (p. 656) Pet. filed 6 Feb. 1778.

41. **NEAL**, Ebenezer: 4 Mar. 1777 Capt. Richard
Weare's Co. for 3 yrs. (p. 641) Died in
Army 20 Nov. 1777.

42. **NEAL**, Walter: 5 Jan. 1776 Capt. Moses
Leavitt's Co.

43. **NUDD**, Thomas: age 18, 4 July 1780 to
Worcester. Disc. 6 Dec. 1780.

44. **PAGE**, Benjamin: 4 Mar. 1777 Capt. Richard
Weare's Co., Col. Scammal Regt. for 3 yrs.

45. **PAGE**, Coffin: 5 Jan. 1776 Capt. Moses
Leavitt's Co. for 3 yrs.

46. **PAGE**, John: age 18, to Worcester 4 July
1789. Discharged 4 Dec. 1780.

47. **PAGE**, Simon: 5 Jan. 1776 Capt. Moses
Leavitt's Co. for 3 yrs.

48. **SANBORN**, Ebenezer: 5 Jan. 1776 Capt. Moses
Leavitt's Co.

49. **SANBORN**, Paul: Served for North Hampton.
Came from Wakefield. at West Point for 6
mo. service.

50. **SANBORN**, William: 5 Jan. 1776 Capt. Moses
Leavitt's Co.

51. **SEAGOLD**, Jacob: Pvt. Capt. Isaac Frye's
Co., 1st regt. 13 Feb. 1781.

52. **SEAVEY**, Samuel: 5 Jan. 1776 Capt. Moses
Leavitt's Co.

53. **SMITH**, Christopher: died 7 Dec. 1814. Grave
    has Rev. war marker.

54. **SMITH**, John: 1781 West Point men for 6
    month service. (p. 257) 7 July 1779 Col.
    Moulton Co. to Rhode Is.

55. **TAYLOR**, Joseph: 5 Jan. 1776 Capt. Moses
    Leavitt's Co.

56. **TAYLOR**, Richard: 5 Jan. 1776 Capt. Moses
    Leavitt's Co.

57. **THOMAS**, Elisha: 9 Apr. 1777 Capt. Richard
    Weare's Co., Col. Scammal for 3 yrs. 7 July
    1779 with Col. Moulton to Rhode Is.
    (p. 656)

58. **THOMPSON**, John: 13 May 1778 paid £20 bounty
    Capt. Caleb Robinson Co. (p. 628)

59. **TRICKEY**, Samuel: 1777 served with Moses
    Leavitt. Petition R3-75 1 Mar. 1786.

60. **TOWL**, Zachariah: 5 Jan. 1776 Capt. Moses
    Leavitt's Co.

61. **WEDGWOOD**, James: 1st Lt. 2 Apr. 1777 3rd
    Regt. In service Nov. 1776 till sep. 1778.
    Petition R3-70 9 June 1781.

62. **WEEKS**, John: Sgt. Co. A. Capt. Isaac Parson
    24 Nov. 1781.

63. **WEEKS**, Joshua: 5 Jan. 1776 Capt. Moses
    Leavitt;s Co.

64. **WELLS**, John Sgt. Co. A. Capt. James Parson
    24 Nov. 1781.

65. **YORK**, Samuel: Petiton R3-75 1 Mar. 1786.
    Named by Moses Leavitt as service man.

SOURCES:

1. Mil. Hist. of N.H. 1678-1861, Chandler E.
   Potter, Concord, 1869.
2. Vol. 14-17, Rev. War. V. 1, 1775-7, V. 2
   1777-80, V. 3 1780-89.
3. State Papers N.H. town Papers V. 13, p. 76-
   87.

BIBILIOGRAPHY

1. Dow, Joseph, *History of Hampton, N.H.*, Chap. 1, p. 195 (1893)

2. N.H. Prov. Papers, v. 5, p. 174; V. 9, p. 359.

3. N.H. Town Records Book 1, p. 196, 241 - 254.

4. North Hampton, NH Town Clerk, Town Records 1738 - 1818.

5. Genealogical Abstract of North Hampton, NH Church Records. 103 pages. (1987)

6. Folsam, Mrs. Wendall B., *Gravestone Inscriptions North Hampton, NH*. D.F. & P. of A., p. 173-211. (1936)

7. idid, GRAVESTONE Inscriptions.

8. North Hampton, NH Town Clerk birth, marriage and death records. Originals at Rockingham Co. Court House, Exeter, NH.

9. Hobbs, Stillman & Helen D., *The Way It Was In North Hampton*, 94 pg. Seabrook (1978)

10. French, Jonathan, *Half Century Discourse, North Hampton, NH*, Ports. (1852)

11. Potter, Chandler E., *Military History of NH 1629 - 1861*, 2 pt., Concord (1869)

12. N.H. State Papers, v. 14-17, Rev. War Rolls.

13. Hammond, Isaac, *Documents Relating to Towns in NH*, v. 12, G-N.

14. North Hampton Annual Town Reports 1889 - 1943.

15. Church Record of North Hampton Cong.
    Church, 2 v. 1766 - 1852. Copy at NHHS

A:BIBL

Heritage Books by William Haslet Jones:

CD: *Genealogies, Volume 6: The William Haslet Jones Collection*

Philip Towle, Hampton, New Hampshire: His English Origins and Some American Descendants

The Rowell Family of New England and Their English Origins, 1560–1900: Descendants of Thomas Rowell 1594–1662

Vital Statistics of Chichester, New Hampshire, 1742–1927

Vital Statistics of Epsom, New Hampshire, 1727–1927

Vital Statistics of North Hampton, New Hampshire, 1742–1942

Vital Statistics of Seabrook, New Hampshire, 1768–1903

William Tilton: His English Origins and Some American Descendants

Winkley Family: The English Origin of Captain Samuel Winkley and Some New England Descendants

The Yeaton Family of New England, 1650–1900